The French Education of
HENRY ADAMS

The

FRENCH

Education of

HENRY

ADAMS

COLUMBIA UNIVERSITY PRESS
New York 1957

The
FRENCH
Education of
HENRY
ADAMS

by MAX I. BAYM

COLUMBIA UNIVERSITY PRESS

New York 1951

TO MY WIFE
Loyal and Patient Collaborator

Preface

In these days when there is so much talk of intercultural relations, one need hardly justify a study of the impact of French thought on Henry Adams, especially when his mind, by long family tradition, had been naturally predisposed to the culture of France.

As a denizen in the world of ideas, Henry Adams was cognizant of the best that was said and thought for over half a century—roughly, from his student days at Harvard to the time when he was stricken with paralysis. All those who have read his *History*, who have studied the *Education*, who have reveled in his *Letters*, who have been perplexed by his theory of history, and who have been fascinated by his *Mont-Saint-Michel and Chartres*, know what he contributed to that world. In this contribution he is indebted to the literature, philosophy, and science which developed in France.

The extent of Adams's indebtedness to French thought can only be known and measured by one who has lived for many years among the books he had read and in which he had underscored passages and frequently had made marginal notes. These books are now found, for the most part, at the

Massachusetts Historical Society. In addition to these, the
present author has had the advantage of examining manuscript material at the Clements Library of Americana, in
the Archives of the Library at Harvard, in Special Collec-
tions at the Boston Public Library, at the Boston Athenaeum, and in the Manuscript Room of the New York Public
Library. He has also secured a full list of the books which
Henry Adams bequeathed to Adelbert College Library at
Western Reserve University, and has studied the marginalia
occurring in them. The Library of Congress and the National
Archives have yielded hitherto unpublished material. To all
these institutions the author herewith expresses his gratitude.

The books in Adams's library tell the story of his scholarly
and imaginative quest. His scorings and marginal notes
are eloquent commentaries on that quest, and his letters
give us the chain of events in which his reading and annota-
tions are important links. Since a good part of the present
work is based on the scorings and marginalia, lengthy quotations were unavoidable, lest Adams's meaning be missed.
(Unless otherwise indicated, Adams's sublineations will be
represented by italics.) The fundamental problem of authen-
ticating Adams's underscorings was facilitated by an examination of those instances where his own marginal notes
make cross references to the texts he underlined. Where
the slightest doubt arose, the author received help from
his late friend, Dr. Samuel A. Tannenbaum, known inter-
nationally as a handwriting expert of great scholarly acumen.

Henry Adams's mental career mirrors practically all the
phases of nineteenth-century thought. To follow him closely
through the various stages of his spiritual development is to
be initiated not only into the meaning of his own century, but
of our own as well. What makes the study of Henry Adams
so rewarding is the fact, pointed out by his brother Brooks,
that "he is part of a large intellectual movement"[1] going

back to the Renaissance and forward to the twentieth century. The claim that Klaus Mann makes for André Gide may be made perhaps as fully for Henry Adams: "All human values on which our civilization is based are at stake in his inner dialogue. He echoes our uncertainties; he articulates our dilemmas. His biography mirrors, and in part anticipates, the tremendous crisis we are passing through. His vision and message will prove relevant to future intellectual developments."

In Adams one will find reflected all the "contradictions and polarities" inherent in the history of the past one hundred and fifty years, not only in America but in Europe as well. Through him, cosmopolitan culture at last made its full entry into these United States. When Henry Adams's biography is finally written, whatever will be valuable in it will deal with his mind as it operated in time, and not with his body as it peregrinated in space. In a sense, the biographer will have benefited by never having known Adams in person, for that person, as he was seen by some who still remember him (Dr. Greenslet for example) was a little thing, bearded to cover up a scrofulous face, getting into chairs specially built to fit its diminutive form—never caring, of course, whether anyone else could get into them—and never, apparently, betraying the slightest love for anyone, except possibly himself.

His mind may be studied in the things it fed on, namely, books. To be taken among the stacks at the Massachusetts Historical Society, where most of his books are now deposited, is to be furnished with an index to Adams's thoughts. Open these books, study their texts along with marginal notes and revealing underscorings, and you have the living clue to Adams's mind—his mind as it developed from the days when, as a child, he read the *Vicar of Wakefield*, given him by his grandmother, who had spent part of her early childhood in Nantes, to the time when, as an aged scholar, he made marginal revisions in his privately printed *Mont-Saint-Michel and Chartres*.

A word on the wearisome question of *influence*. By leaning too heavily on the facile formula that certain ideas are of general currency in a given period, one may easily lose sight of the question as to who really made these ideas current, and to what extent those who made them so were inspired by each other. It is in pointing out resemblances and borrowings in the realm of ideas that we not only prove their currency but show their direction. Great ideas, as Gide has indicated, always have more than one source and always require more than one man to make their beauty or cogency current.

No pretense is made here to a complete presentation of facts. I have dealt only with a few salient ideas. Thus, in my treatment of Adams as an historian or as a student of philosophy, I have limited myself to the literary aspect— the one that Adams himself ultimately valued most.

This study represents part of a larger work involving Adams's approach to philosophy and science, as well as historiography. During the eighteen years or more in which I have been engaged (mostly under adverse conditions) on this project, I have been helped to an education in the history of ideas which transcends artificial partitions between fields of knowledge, even when these divisions are set up by academic authorities.

Lack of space forbids the inclusion of all those to whom the author is indebted. Dr. Stewart Mitchell, Director of the Massachusetts Historical Society, was among the first to help in the promotion of the present project. He not only intervened with the Council of the Society in making manuscripts and marginalia available, but published my initial

article on Adams in the *New England Quarterly*. To him and
to Stephen T. Riley, the Society's librarian, I extend my
heartfelt thanks. For answering a number of questions
touching the Adams Collection and for introducing me to
Worthington Chauncey Ford, I am under obligation to
Henry Adams II; and for some informative conversations,
to Drs. Ferris Greenslet and Waldo Leland.

It is a pleasure to acknowledge my debt to the following
professors at Columbia University: Norman Torrey, for
his general interest and for important suggestions; Wilbur
M. Frohock, for painstaking scrutiny of the whole book, in
the attempt to improve its sequence and manner; Jean-
Albert Bédé, for pertinent criticism throughout; Jean Hytier,
for the correction of minutiae; Nathan Edelman for kindly
and judicious suggestions; and Otis Fellows, for the gift of
his friendship and ready help at all times. For her generosity
and patience in carrying through the editorial phase of the
work, Miss Matilda Berg of Columbia University Press has
earned my gratitude.

In addition, I am greatly indebted to Miss Rose Perez of
Boston for her intelligent and untiring labor in the "rounding
up" of marginalia; Mrs. Rose Silverman and Miss Anne Dieli
for typing innumerable versions of parts of the manuscript;
Miss Elizabeth W. Meade and Mr. Roger Thomas, two good
friends in Annapolis, for their critical reading of the entire
manuscript; Dr. Eugene Dorfman for philologic aid and
other acts of kindness.

Among those who are no longer with us, I wish to memo-
rialize my indebtedness to Worthington Chauncey Ford who,
soon after reading my "Henry Adams and William James,"
wrote me in terms of encouragement and interest; Horatio
Smith, who was responsible in linking my project with
Columbia University; Randolph G. Adams, who made my
work at the Clements Library of Americana fun and high

adventure; Samuel A. Tannenbaum, who through many years of warm friendship contributed to my education in more ways than can here be stated.

Grateful acknowledgment is here made to Houghton Mifflin Company for permission to quote from the following works published by them: *A Cycle of Adams Letters*, 1861–1865 (1920); *Letters of Henry Adams*, edited by W. C. Ford (Vol. I, 1930; Vol. II, 1938); *Letters to a Niece and Prayer to the Virgin of Chartres by Henry Adams with a Niece's Memories*, by Mabel LaFarge (1920); *Mont-Saint-Michel and Chartres*, by Henry Adams (1905, 1933); *The Education of Henry Adams* (1918, 1931); to Harper and Brothers for permission to quote from Ludwig Lewisohn's *The Story of American Literature* (1939).

For timely aid towards publication, I am heavily indebted to Mr. and Mrs. George Barnett of New York City. But first and last my profound gratitude goes to the person to whom this work is dedicated.

M.I.B.

New York
March 9, 1951

Contents

The French Education of
HENRY ADAMS

I

Ancestral Background

ALTHOUGH HENRY ADAMS had no French ancestors,[1] and
his attitude towards things French was never completely
stable,[2] France played a central role in both his life and his
works. The two libraries which he inherited on the death
of his grandfather, in 1848, when Henry was ten years old,
were the basis of a continuity of thought in which the usual
differentiation of *new* from *old* is frequently less striking than
a cyclic recurrence of fundamental ideas. His father, whose
part was always that of mediator between past and present,
helped him open some of the books when Henry played in
these libraries as a child. In the *Education* he pictures the
very small boy that he was having to stand on tiptoe in
front of his grandmother's writing desk to see above it,
through small glass doors, the "little eighteenth-century
volumes in old binding."[3] Beyond those books was the
eighteenth century itself. In them survived the spirit of his
great-grandfather, John Adams. They held part of a family
tradition.

As a Harvard undergraduate, John Adams had been
caught in the winds of conflicting doctrine. With the in-

flux of the ideas of Voltaire, Rousseau, Montesquieu, D'Alembert, La Mettrie, Quesnay, and Turgot, the Calvinistic spell had been broken.[4] The occasional distrust and skepticism with which he received such new ideas as Turgot's optimistic notion of progress and perfectibility,[5] seems in part to have been innate in an introspective nature, marked, according to his own confession, by "feebleness and languor."[6] All of the Adamses were given to introspection— and feared it.[7] The hesitant progression from doubt to doubt, the dwelling on fame, the frequent languor, the introspective cast of mind, the fear of ennui—what have we here but the dualistic personality in the midst of an eighteenth-century rationalistic world, another *promeneur solitaire:* "I wander alone and ponder. . . . I muse, I mope, I ruminate. I am often in reveries and brown studies. The objects before me are too grand and multifarious for comprehension."[8] The one fundamental idea which he assimilated from his reading of Condorcet (whom he met in Paris during his diplomatic missions)[9] was that the science of human relationship took its cue from the natural sciences and that universal law extends into the realms of intellect and ethics.[10] In pondering this idea of the unity of knowledge, John Adams prepared the road for the thought of his great-grandson, Henry, just as Condorcet[11] pointed to Comte, whom Henry Adams was to study thoroughly.

A similar duality hampered the political activity or energy of each one of the Adamses in turn by setting up an emotional countercurrent to the very activity they were engaged in. The truth is, they were nauseated with politics even while they sought power in it. John Adams was as disgusted with the money bags that controlled politics as Henry was to be. When Jefferson succeeded to the Presidency in 1801, John Adams was happy to retire from public life, glad to go back, with greater zeal than ever, to his books and to a few friends with whom he eagerly exchanged ideas.

In spite of his respect for the enlightenment and its zeal for the truth, his opinion of the eighteenth century was not consistently favorable. "I am willing you should call this the Age of Frivolity as you do: and would not object if you named it the Age of Folly, Vice, Frenzy, Fury, Brutality, Daemons, Buonaparte, Tom Paine, or the Age of the burning Brand from the bottomless Pitt; or anything but the Age of Reason."[12]

The great thinkers often bored him.

I am weary of philosophers, theologians, politicians and historians. They are immense masses of absurdities, vices and lies. Montesquieu had sense enough to say in jest, that all our knowledge might be comprehended in twelve pages in duodecimo; and I believe him in earnest.[13]

Why should we trust the Philosophers? Have Frederic, Voltaire, Rousseau, Buffon, Diderot, or Condorcet shown themselves capable of governing mankind? Condorcet has let the cat out of the bag. He has made precious confessions. I regret that I have only an English translation of his "Outlines of an Historical View of the Progress of the Human Mind." But in pages 247, 248, and 249, you will find it frankly acknowledged, that the philosophers of the eighteenth century, adopted all the maxims, and practiced all the arts of the Pharisees, the ancient priests of all countries, the Jesuits, the Machiavellians, etc., etc., to overthrow the institutions that such arts had established.[14]

In spite of such strictures, Adams's opinion of the eighteenth century was more favorable than not. During the course of the century "knowledge and virtues were increased and diffused; arts, sciences, useful to men, ameliorating their condition, were improved more than in any former equal period."[15] Yet even at such moments of approval we witness a darker mood steal irresistibly over Adams. "But after all, what is human life? A vapor, a fog, a dew, a cloud, a

blossom, a flower, a rose, a blade of grass, a glass bubble, a
tale told by an idiot, a *boule de savon*, vanity of vanities, an
eternal succession of which would terrify me almost as much
as annihilation."[16]

The stability of the rationalist is here giving way to the
instability of the pessimist: Voltaire has donned the cloak of
Chateaubriand; the smile of the wit has turned into the
grimace of the Prince of Darkness. Thus, the great-grandson's darker mood has its counterpart in the eighteenth
century's growing uncertainty of itself.

John Adams's undertaking, late in life, the reading of the
twelve volumes of Charles François Dupuis' *Origine de
tous les cultes*, is a strong indication of his persistent belief
in the primary importance of reason, and the project naturally aroused the admiration of Jefferson. "I have been
contented," he writes to Adams (October 14, 1816), "with
the humble achievement of reading the analysis of his works
by Destutt Tracy, in 200 pages Octavo. . . . The marrow
of it in Tracy has satisfied my appetite . . . for the object
of that (work) seems to be to smother all history under the
mantle of allegory."[17]

Adams's answer to this letter shows how important he
regarded the introduction of reason into Christianity to be.

Tracy's Analysis I have read once, and wish to read it a second
time. . . . I have read not only the Analysis, but 8 vols, out of 12
of the *"Origine de tous les Cultes."* We have now, it seems, a national Bible Society, to propagate King James' Bible through all
nations. Would it not be better to apply these pious subscriptions
to purify Christendom from the corruptions of Christianity than to
propagate those corruptions in Europe, Asia, Africa, and America?[18] Suppose we should project a society to translate Dupuis
into all languages, and offer a reward in medals of diamonds to
any man or body of men who would produce the best answer to
it.—Enthusiasm, crusades, French revolutions, are epidemical or
endemical distempers, to which mankind is liable. They are not

tertian or quartan agues. Ages and centuries are sometimes required to cure them.—Conclude not from all this that I have re-
nounced the Christian religion, or that I agree with Dupuis in all
his sentiments.[19]

One month later (December 12, 1816), Adams reports
that he has completed the twelve volumes of Dupuis in the
original, besides a thirteenth of plates. "I have been a lover
and a reader of romances all my life," the letter continues,
"from Don Quixote and Gil Blas to the Scottish Chiefs, and
a hundred others. For the last year or two I have devoted
myself to this kind of study, and have read fifteen volumes
of Grimm, seven volumes of Tucker Neddy's Search, twelve
volumes of Dupuis, and Tracy's Analysis, and four volumes
of Jesuitical History. Romances all. . . . They have made
no change in my moral or religious creed, which has, for
fifty or sixty years been contained in four short words, 'Be
just and good'. In this result they all agree with me."[20]

Adams's wide reading tended to confirm his prejudices
against religion, at least those phases of it which were di-
vorced from reason. His friends, he complained, overwhelmed him with books from all quarters,

enough to obfuscate all eyes, and smother and stifle all human understanding—Chateaubriand, Grimm, Tucker, Dupuis, La Harpe,
Sismondi, Eustace, new translations of Herodotus, by Beloe, with
more notes than text. What shall I do with all this lumber? I
make my "woman kind," as the Antiquary expresses it, read to me
all the English; but as they will not read the French, I am obliged
to excruciate my eyes to read it myself. All to what purpose? I
verily believe I was as wise and good seventy years ago as I am
now.[21]

We should expect Adams, with his persistent belief in
reason and his approval of the scientific attitude, to show
an active antagonism toward Rousseau's thesis that the

arts and sciences are connected with the corruption of humanity.

"Are we not in too great a hurry, in our Zeal for the fine Arts?" This is as noble and beautiful a question, as that of the Academy of Dijon in 1750. It is not probable that it will soon be discussed in America with larger Views, with more learning or more perfect Eloquence, than it was by J. J. Rousseau and his Antagonists, more than half a century ago. I am not however of Rousseau's opinion. His notions of the purity of Morals in savage Nations and the earliest Ages of civilized nations are mere Chimeras.—My humble opinion is that Science and Arts have vastly and immensely ameliorated the condition of Man, and even improved his Morals. The progress however has been awfully slow.

Yet, in what follows (in the same letter February 26, 1817) John Adams seems to reverse himself in favor of Jean Jacques' opinion: "Is it possible to enlist the 'Fine Arts', on the side of Truth, of Virtue, of Piety, or even of Honour? From the dawn of History they have been prostituted to the Service of Superstition and Despotism. Read Herodotus, Pausanius, Plutarch, Lucian, and twenty others, not forgetting several of the Christian Fathers and see how the Fine Arts have been employed. Read Eustace's classical Tour in Italy."[22] On another occasion he couples the name of J.J. Rousseau with that of Helvétius. Both "preached to the French Nation *Liberty*, till they made them the most mechanical slaves."[23]

Like the *philosophes*, John Adams had a thirst for scientific knowledge which was not slaked even as late as January 8, 1825. "I have lately been reading the most extraordinary of all books, and at the same time the most demonstrative by numerous and unequivocal facts. It is Flourens's experiments of the functions of the nervous system, in vertebrated animals."[24] This absorption in neurology and psychology is to be recalled by the reader when he comes to read of the great-grandson's interests in the same field.

Because John Adams was interested in underlying problems touching upon such questions as the distinction between
matter and spirit, he insisted that science transcended in-
cision-knives and that "the faculties of our understanding
are not adequate to penetrate the universe."[25] Already we
have the foreshadowing of Henry Adams's eventual declaration as to the inadequacy of the mind to measure anything
except, perhaps, its own decay. The scientific interest, in the
Adamses, was a contributing factor to their pessimism.

As we have seen, deism, rationalism, liberalism, natural
rights, and general scientific curiosity were all reflected in
the mind and thought of John Adams and found expression
in his writings. His reading included Descartes, Hume,
Locke, Berkley, the French encyclopedists and ideologists,[26]
the works of Turgot, Condorcet, and Dupuis. Besides, John
Adams was among the first, if not the first, in America to
mention Rousseau.[27] He also came out boldly, however,
against the Genevan's notion of the "simple and perfect
democracy,"[28] and in doing so he prepared the way for his
great-grandson's Degradation of the Democratic Dogma.

The transition from John to John Quincy Adams is the
shift from the influence of Voltaire to that of Rousseau, from
reason to sensibility. The "man of feeling" begins to pre-
dominate over the man of reason, though the former, to
sustain his own position, still borrows (on occasion) the
manner of the latter. There is a growing suspicion that perhaps the heart has a reason which Reason cannot always
grasp. The mind as synonymous with the heart—the sum
total of all inner compulsions, passions and desires—becomes a more and more compelling and absorbing study.
We watch this interest grow in John and John Quincy Adams,
to be arrested in Charles Francis, whose attention was mainly
devoted to giving permanent form to the thoughts of his
illustrious ancestors, only to reappear all the more strongly

and opulently in Henry Adams, with whom it assumes an almost central position in his spiritual quest.

John Quincy Adams's imagination was haunted by *Hamlet*, a work which fired him with hopeless desire for literary fame. "But," he complained, "the conceptive power of mind was not conferred upon me by my maker." His thinking tended toward lyricism. Hence the peculiar interest which inheres in such a technical essay as his famous *Report on Weights and Measures*. His thought no longer bears the stamp of eighteenth-century symmetry, but rather reflects the tempestuous onrush of nineteenth-century polyphony; he has hobnobbed with a Madame de Staël and caught intimations of a rising cultural cosmopolitanism; he has read Rousseau closely and lived with the ideas of Condillac, Cousin, Diderot, Helvétius, Lalande, Montesquieu, Vattel, as well as Voltaire. He turns eagerly the pages of the *Bibliothèque des philosophes* and the *Transactions* of academies of science. The Calvinistic creed which began to crack in the lifetime of John has split wide open in the mind of John Quincy Adams.

The distinction between mind and matter continued to attract him as much as it did his father; but he brooded even more on the ultimates of existence: life and death. His pessimism—partly a facet of the Adams temperament but in part the result of a drastic break with a creed not entirely outworn and yet not fully replaced by a new energizing spirit—makes him kin to Leopardi and Sénancour. And in the elaboration of a failure-image of himself he belongs to the company of Amiel, Alfred de Musset, Gérard de Nerval, and Alfred de Vigny. This image which we found first in the great-grandfather, now appears in the grandfather; it will achieve full expression in the great-grandson.

With John Quincy Adams, the Adamses entered the European romantic current, which carried men away from an earthly reality which they abhorred to an independent reality of ideas. This stemmed from Kant. Emerson was to be the American expression of the division in the realities. But this division was to find its best representation in the nineteenth-century revival of the French thinkers Descartes and Pascal, both of whom haunted the Adamses from great-grandfather to great-grandson. It is not until Henry became a professor at Harvard, where his grandfather had once taught Rhetoric, that William James was to insist that these two worlds were related and continuous.

The grandfather's reading during his law clerkship points to the reading and thinking done later by the grandson. John Quincy Adams's diary for October 4 to 6, 1786, records that he had a forensic on the question "whether the diversities in national characters arise chiefly from physical causes" and that he supported the affirmative.[29] Here are found an echo of Montesquieu's theories[30] as well as a premonition of Taine's ideas with which the grandson was to be greatly concerned. At this time his reading also included Vattel's *Law of Nature and Nations* (*Le droit des gens*, 1758), and the *Theory of the Earth* of Buffon, with whose style and manner he was exceedingly pleased. "It is concise, nervous, and elegant. The theory I cannot properly judge till I get through the other volume." When he finished the work, he was all the more pleased with its author. Yet he made some critical reservations. "One part of his theory is merely hypothetical, and might perhaps be called extravagant. He supposed the earth and the other planets were originally a part of the sun, and that they were sever'd from it by the shock of a comet." Even so he admitted this part of Buffon's reasoning to be ingenious. The other part of Buffon's theory, based upon facts, he found supported by strong and convincing arguments, and he added: "If the author is sometimes mistaken, he is certainly everywhere philosophical." He also read

Buffon's *Natural History of Man*, which he found even more entertaining than the *Theory of the Earth*.[31]

To natural history he now added history *tout court*, especially Gibbon. He found Gibbon's style elegant but his "partiality against the Christian religion" he thought equally injurious to Gibbon's character as a philosopher and as an historian.[32] Evidently, at this time, John Quincy Adams was no party to the "frantic crew of deists" of which some travelers to America talked.[33] He certainly did not speak kindly of Larévellière-Lépaux, one of the founders of theophilanthropism,—"a theological and political mixture of deism, morality, anti-christianity, and revolution . . . under special protection of the French Directory."[34] At the same time he thought Knox not only too severe in his criticism of Gibbon, but "very reprehensible."[35]

This record of his reading shows that John Quincy Adams belonged more to the nineteenth century than to the eighteenth. Yet, his son, Charles Francis, in editing his father's *Memoirs*,[36] found it natural to compare him with men in the earlier century. "If it were all to be published," says Charles Francis in his preface to the *Memoirs*, "as was that of Voltaire, it would be likely quite to equal in quantity the hundred volumes of that expansive writer." His father's record is "comparable to the elaborate memoirs of St. Simon which fill twenty volumes and those of Diderot and Grimm, which make sixteen more."[37]

As we read the *Memoirs* what strikes us is less its eighteenth-century copiousness than the profusion of interests and appetites which it attests. Here are the names of Cabanis, Chateaubriand, Chénier, La Fontaine, Massillon and Mme de Staël. We learn that Adams went through the *Bibliothèque des philosophes*. References to Voltaire abound everywhere. And at one point, the tone of the Diary[38] is romantic in the French sense. Like his father before him, John Quincy

Adams was elected to the presidency of the American Academy of Arts and Sciences. But the honor did not balance the literary fame he had not earned:

The summit of my ambition would have been by some great work of literature to have done honor to my age and country, and to have lived in the gratitude of future ages. This consummation of Happiness has been denied to me. . . . It would have been a great comfort to me if all or either of my children inherited this propensity. George is not entirely without it. The others have it not, and I have found every effort to stimulate them to it, hitherto, fruitless.[39]

Defeat and frustration here speak out. It remained for Henry Adams to compensate, artistically, his grandfather's failure.

Meanwhile it was the lot of the grandfather to distinguish himself in the so-called field of applied literature through his famous *Report of the Secretary of State upon Weights and Measures, Prepared in Obedience to a Resolution of the Senate of the Third March, 1817*, but not to be printed until February 22, 1821.[40] We have evidence of his commencing to work on such a project in 1812. What first turned his attention to the subject was a passion for the improvement of agriculture,[41] which he resolved to study in books. He soon found that he could understand nothing in treatises on this subject without accurate ideas of weights and measures. Hence he postponed (forever) his agricultural enquiries and produced his metrology. In it he paid tribute to the work of Delambre and Méchain, and reiterated his belief that France deserved high praise for its contributions to the history of metrology.[42] In this essay one finds echoes of the language of the encyclopedists, of Buffon and of Rousseau.[43]

But, to the continued existence of the human species, two persons of different sexes are required. Their union constitutes natural society and their permanent cohabitation, by mutual consent, form the origin of domestic society. In connection with dwelling places, superficial measure is essential. . . . Measures of length, therefore, are the wants of individual man, independent of, and preceding, the existence of society. . . . Measures of surface, of distance, and of capacity, arise immediately from domestic society. They are wants proceeding rather from social, than from individual existence.[44]

Then follows a Rousseauistic paragraph:

The legislator has no power over the properties of matter. He cannot give a new constitution to nature. He cannot repeal her law of universal mutability. He cannot square the circle. He cannot reduce extension and gravity to one common measure. . . . The power of the legislator is limited over the will and actions of his subjects. His conflict with them is desperate, when he counteracts their settled habits, their established usages; their domestic and individual economy, their ignorance, their prejudices, and their wants: all which is inavoidable in the attempt radically to change, or to originate, a totally new system of weights and measures.

To these sources of diversity in the nature of things, must be added all those arising from the nature and history of man.[45]

These diversities in man are still further complicated by the vexing problems of law and language.[46]

The legislator having no distinct idea of the uniformity of which the subject [of weights and measures] is susceptible, not considering how far it should be extended, or where it finds its boundary in the nature of things and of man, enacts laws inadequate to their purpose . . . sometimes stubbornly resisting, at others weakly yielding to inveterate usages or abuses; and finishes by increasing the diversities which it was his intention to abolish, and by loading his statute book only with the impotence of authority, and the uniformity of confusion.[47]

Language itself confounds matters further. "Even things which nature has discriminated so clearly, that they cannot be mistaken, the antipathy of mankind to new words will misrepresent and confound."[48] He is moved to exclaim: "But where is the steam engine of moral power to stem the stubborn tide of prejudice, and the headlong current of inveterate usage?"[49]

After apologizing to Congress for the length, as well as for the numerous imperfections of his report, his final word is on the question of uniformity.

Uniformity of weights and measures, permanent, universal uniformity, adapted to the nature of things, to the physical organization and to the moral improvement of man, would be a blessing of such transcendent magnitude, that, if there existed upon earth a combination of power and will, adequate to accomplish the result by the energy of a single act, the being who should exercise it would be among the greatest of benefactors of the human race. But this stage of human perfectibility is yet far remote. The glory of the first attempt belongs to France.[50]

A subject to which all the power and "All the philosophical and mathematical learning and ingenuity of France and of Great Britain have been incessantly directed," was, to him, "a fearful and oppressive task." Naturally, he was glad to see it finished. His opinion of it was that, "after all the time and pains bestowed upon it," it was "a hurried and imperfect work." This self-deprecatory manner was characteristic of the Adamses as well as of some of their distinguished colleagues, William James, for example. Actually, John Quincy Adams did not think that the report was such a bad piece of work.

I have no reason to expect that I shall ever be able to accomplish any literary labor more important to the ends of human exertion, public utility, or upon which the remembrance of my children may dwell with more satisfaction.[51]

Going more and more into "brown studies," as his father did before him, he exclaimed with the satirist Persius,

O Curas Hominum! O quantum est in rebus inane![52]

As life began to draw towards its close, he sought to square
his philosophical account. His search on the shoreless ocean
of knowledge sharpened his insights. In the vacant time of
one November day in 1827 he opened the pages of the *Lettres
Provinciales*. In Pascal he encountered a kindred spirit, a
spirit in search of light and peace. Pascal had also taken
science as a vehicle on a "voyage au bout de la nuit." What
was a vacuum? What were the laws of chance? These questions preoccupied the man who, when only a child, had been
busy with a book on Conic Sections. Now after a life all too
brief in pleasure, all too long in pain, he found refuge in
"the arms of Port-Royal." In opening the *Provinciales*,
John Quincy Adams discovered (in Pascal's own phrase) the
esprit de géométrie coupled with the *esprit de finesse* in the
very style of the man. The theological controversy involved
did not matter so much either to John Quincy Adams or to
others at a later period, though Adams's mind was attracted
by such theological writings as the sermons of Massillon.
It remained for his grandson (as we shall see later) to wander
into "the vast forests of scholastic science."[53] As for Pascal,
John Quincy Adams's grandson accounted him "one of the
greatest minds between Descartes and Newton."[54]

However, no satirist—not even so great a one as Pascal or
Voltaire—could lure the Adamses from the consideration of
ultimates, of the essential meaning of existence. "Existence
itself, and duration, are incomprehensible things. That they
should be everlasting is not more unintelligible than that it
should be. Matter undergoes perpetual mutation, but is
never destroyed; why not the same of mind"[55]—mind, that
was to preoccupy so much the thought of his grandson. The
Calvinist in John Quincy Adams turned to the Gospels for
proofs of immortality. As ever, he found in Cicero the appropriate text: VITA ENIM MORTUORUM IN MEMORIA VIVORUM

EST POSITA (The life of the dead consists in the memory of the living).[56]

He kept up with the latest articles in the *North American Review*. He was interested in Cousin's "New system of philosophy, which is mystifying the French nation." He read D'Olivet's translations of Sappho, where he found a footnote to the effect that "death was an evil, inasmuch as none of the Gods have ever chosen to die." Old Shakespearean student that he was,[57] he sought, through great deeds, to gain advantage over time. Thus we read in the last line of one of his own sonnets: "By deathless deeds to give Eternity to Time."[58]

One of the entries in John Quincy Adams's diary reads:

I stayed at home . . . and answered a letter from the Rev. Joseph Emerson, dated at New London, Conn., making enquiries about a translation of Voltaire's Philosophical Dictionary, published under the name of John Quincy Adams, and secretly circulating as he says, about the country as my work.[59]

The matter of this imputation is continued in another entry, under date of August 6, 1843:

On my return home from Canada, I found among the newspapers on my table one with the title of Boston Investigator devoted to the protection and development of infidel principles, vol. XIII, No. 13, Wednesday August 2nd, 1843. It had apparently been sent to me for a scurrilous article on the second page, entitled "Another Specimen of Christian Criticism," being a knavish commentary upon the Rev. Joseph Emerson's letter to me, and my answer, respecting the translation of Voltaire's Philosophical Dictionary, imputed to me, because the title-page announces it as printed and published by J. Q. Adams. The article now states that it was published in 1836, at the Investigator Office, and purports to be with additional notes, both critical and argumentative, by Abner Kneelan. This man was an avowed atheist and preacher of atheism, of which his translation of Voltaire's dictionary was one of the gospels. He was shortly after convicted upon an indictment for blasphemy, imprisoned, and soon pardoned. His atheist

church was broken up; but it seems his weekly atheist newspaper
still continues. Two or three days since, I received an octavo
weekly journal, edited by G. Vale, at New York, 5th August,
third series, vol. I, No. 18, The Beacon, seventh year, a coadjutor
of the Boston Investigator in the propagandism of the atheistic
church. In this paper there is an article, headed "Voltaire and
J. Q. Adams," containing my letter of 17th June, 1843, to Mr.
Emerson, with one from him to the editors of the New York Ob-
server, requesting them to publish it. The correspondent of the
Beacon extracts them from the Journal of Commerce, without
noticing the offensive fraud of palming upon me the act of printing and publishing these excrements of Voltaire, but with a malig-
nant imputation of false pretences in my remarks upon the base
and filthy infidelity of Voltaire. These periodical publications,
The Investigator and The Beacon, indicate the pertinacity with
which this little atheistic club pursue their will-of-the wisp over
the low swampy lands of Christendom.[60]

Whether the John Quincy Adams referred to in this story
was himself (*the* John Quincy Adams), or not, one thing is
certain: he protested too much on the score of infidelity.

As partial proof of this, we place here beside the above
story J. Q. Adams's indirect jibe at priestcraft.

A story I once heard Dr. Franklin tell, of a convent of monks, who
had a very inconvenient hill in front of their monastery, and, upon
their faith like a grain of mustard-seed's being sufficient to cast
the mountain into the sea, set up a general onset of prayer to
remove the mountain, which they perseveringly pursued till, tired
of the obstinate adherence of the mountain to its place, one of the
friars gave out that there was a mistake in the translation of the
text, and the true reading should be that with faith like a mountain it is possible to move a mustard-seed.[61]

Here was the tradition which Charles Francis Adams interpreted to his son. While the father was preparing for publication the "Life and Works" of his grandfather, Henry,
now a boy of eleven, was made to read proof, and was thus
initiated early in the history of the Adams heritage.

II

Initiation

HAVING SKETCHED the background of the Adams tradition
to which Henry fell heir we are ready to follow him through
the primary stages of his own development: first at Harvard
and then in England where he served as secretary to his
father.

While Adams was a freshman at Harvard, a certain
Monsieur Émile Arnould, M.D. was instructor in French.[1]
The catalogue for that year indicates that M. Arnould
lived in Boston, where he may have been a practicing phy-
sician. French was not then one of the freshman subjects;
it was taught in the sophomore year. Fasquelle's *New
Method of Learning the French Language* was used. Guizot's
"Washington" was read; so were Molière's Comedies and
Sales' edition of the *Fables de La Fontaine*. In the junior
year, Sismondi's *History of the Roman Empire* was used.
And in the senior year the students read Guizot's *History
of the Origin of Representative Government in Europe*. In the
freshman and sophmore years, all courses were required;
in the junior and senior years all were required except
ancient and modern languages and mathematics.

During Henry's freshman year the university catalogue merely indicated by a dash the incumbent of the Smith Professorship of Languages and Literature and of Belles Lettres, but in his sophomore year James Russell Lowell, A.M., is named as the occupant of this chair. The sophomores read Molière, La Fontaine, and used Fasquelle's Grammar.[2] As a junior Henry attended Professor Lowell's Lectures in Modern Literature. The Charge Books for that year indicate that he withdrew from the college library volumes one to five of Sismondi's *Histoire*. In his senior year, in philosophy, he studied Reid *On the Intellectual Powers;* Bowen's *Ethics and Metaphysics,* and Whatley's *Logic* or Thomson's *Outlines of Thought in Rhetoric;* Guizot's *History of Civilization in Europe;* Mill's *Logic;* and Jouffroy's *Introduction to Ethics.*

The only books Adams took out of the College Library as a freshman were the works of Edgar Allan Poe. It is strange to think that it was this sombre poet who may have planted in the young student and future historian the earliest seed of interest in Comte; for in *Eureka* Poe cites Comte's opinion on Laplace. However, the strangeness diminishes when one realizes that by 1854 Auguste Comte was far from unknown to the literary cognoscenti along the Atlantic seaboard and that interest in him had been promoted by some public preachments against his irreligion. The vulgarization and compact statement of the leading ideas of Comte's otherwise formidable *Cours de philosophie positive* was accomplished in France in 1844-1845 through Emile Littré's *De la philosophie positive,* a work which was later to find its way into Henry Adams's library and which was to appear in translation in this country in 1847.[3]

As an undergraduate young Adams already showed a keen interest in French thought and letters. We find in his contributions to the Harvard Magazine, between 1855 and

1858, a number of references which it becomes interesting
to follow up in his later thinking and writing.

He thought it regrettable, and a matter fit for censure,
that Harvard students had little or no knowledge of the
literatures of foreign countries. "It is a most rare thing to
meet a student who has read any foreign author, unless,
perhaps, we should make an exception in favor of Dumas,
Eugene Sue, George Sand, and Paul de Kock."[4]

Adams's early penchant for flippantly epigrammatic and
episodic humor makes itself felt in the quotations he chooses
from Buffon: "There are not more than five great geniuses of
modern times; Bacon, Leibnitz, Newton, Montesquieu, and
myself."[5] Or he gets in a satiric touch, which was to become
a dominant characteristic in his later writing, by starting
off in storytelling manner: "Once upon a time there lived an
individual named George Scudery. He wrote sixteen heroic
tragedies, the last entitled Arminius, and it was called by
critics, 'the downfall of mediocrity.' "[6]

In the same vein, writing of the vanity of Mr. Thomas
Keightly, he delivers himself of a double salvo in the following:

It is said that when Rousseau, the French philosopher, was at
London, in the year 1766, so great was his fame that the whole
world, including the King and Queen, went to the theatre to stare
at him, while Garrick on the boards was ignored; and so great was
the philosopher's anxiety to show himself, that Mrs. Garrick, in
whose box he sat, had to hold on by the skirts of his coat all the
evening lest he should tumble into the pit. Mr. Thomas Keightly
has rivalled the celebrated Frenchman, but unfortunately seems
to have had no friend to hold him back.

And here he adds in the manner of a *pensée* the genial remark:
"Self-conceit is an amiable weakness."[7] And we add: Adams
should have known . . .

Harvard, in the person of James Russell Lowell, sent him

to Berlin. There Henry soon discovered that "wherever else he might, in the infinities of space and time, seek for education it should not be again in Berlin." Indeed, long before April he was making comparisons of Berlin and Paris, in favor of the latter. He despaired of "ever becoming a German." On June 7, 1859, when he wrote from Dresden that the French had entered Milan, he tried hard to remain neutral, but experienced a strong temptation to open his mouth "and express to assembled Saxony that I, H. B. Adams, consider them a pack of cowardly, stupid idiots."[8]

"Napoleon is playing Villa Franca over again," he wrote to his mother again from Dresden on March 6, 1860.

People say there'll be no war. I think they are crazy. War or revolution, or both, and it's my belief that if Napoleon hopes to turn conservatist now, it'll only make the troubles worse and the success less. . . . To us who stand so far on the extreme left that all European parties and party fights seem matters of the last century, this doubt about the present is irritating to a degree.[9]

Shortly thereafter he left for Paris and was back in Washington the following December.

In May, 1861, he arrived in London to start a new set of experiences, including that of his private secretaryship to his father, who came as Ambassador to England. For Henry, England meant the opportunity to meet Richard Monckton Milnes, Swinburne, and Mill. These men served as important intermediaries in introducing him to French ideas and belles-lettres.

Not so long after his arrival in London, young Henry Adams found himself moving socially in the midst of a glittering elite, largely through the good offices of Richard Monckton Milnes with whom the Adamses stopped at Fryston, in Yorkshire.[10] It was Milnes (or Lord Houghton) who introduced Henry to John Stuart Mill and Algernon Swinburne. This trio, then, became for him professors extraordinary in the fields of belles-lettres, philosophy, and political science. In addition there were men like Henry Reeve, with whom Adams had personal dealings, and Matthew Arnold whose influence was potent even at a distance. Henry Adams entertained Arnold in Washington during the latter's American lecture tour of 1883.[11] All of these men, whose names were to recur in his *Education* and in his *Letters*, had a particular interest in French thought and literature and were to direct the ardor and inquisitiveness of the young American's mind in that direction.

In Milnes, Adams found a man who was to become one of the conspicuous figures in European Society.[12] His friendships included the names of the most eminent men and women of the mid-century: Prince Louis Napoleon, whose confidant he was; King Louis Phillippe; Thiers, an exile in London in 1852; Guizot, Lamartine, Lamennais; Cousin, with whom he had delightful conversation on politics; Victor Hugo, of whom he spoke enthusiastically; the Chevalier Bunsen; Galignani, Montalembert, Count d'Orsay; Tocqueville, who helped him meet leading political celebrities. In 1861, two years after Tocqueville's death, Milnes wrote an enthusiastic account in the *Quarterly Review* of "this most estimable" of Frenchmen. Others that he met and knew were Heine (who spoke of "that good Milnes" in a letter to Lady Duff Gordon), George Sand (whose *Consuelo* he thought first rate), Baron Humboldt—so French in many respects, and who wrote to Milnes: "Moi qui suis le père éternel de tous les voyageurs"—the Duke de Broglie, Louis Blanc, Duvergier, Mme Mohl, the Duke de Nemours, and Rémusat. When Lord Houghton had been asked by the English Government to be one of the jurors at the International Exhibition held in Paris in 1867 under the auspices of the Emperor, the French Government emphasized the compliment by asking him to become president of the

group of Liberal Arts—an invitation which he accepted.
Milnes enjoyed meeting Edmond About, Daudet, Flaubert,
Tourgenieff, Émile Zola—in this *annus mirabilis.*

I went to Madame Mohl's in the evening, and found myself talking
to Renan—as if I had been in Paris a month. Comme la vie est
facile ici! I was with Thiers at the opera last night. I dined yesterday with Madame Mohl—quite a crack intellectual party—I have
seen old Guizot once. M. and Madame Guillaume dined at Madame Mohl's. She seems rather liked at Paris. Montalembert is
worse—Rio is in great force—the Americans swarm—I dined at
Prince Napoleon's—Performance of Misanthrope—We dine today
with M. Thiers, and go to the opera afterwards—I sit with the
Conseil Superieur, making speeches utterly irrespective of tenses
or genders. But, as one of the Chamiers said to me, "You are here
to look after English interest, not French grammar"—The Exhibition is vulgar and speculative—a congeries of incongruous interests, of real industrial usefulness and the lowest form of gratified
curiosity—Disraeli is triumphant, and Christian hero Gladstone
in the dust. Resurgat![13]

As can readily be inferred, Milnes was a great student
of French letters. He had read Rousseau, Voltaire, Molière,
studied Cousin's philosophy; he knew the works of Lalande
and Laplace; he knew French history, especially the period
of the Revolution; he knew particularly well French literature of the nineteenth century.[14] He knew Tocqueville
and his work, and was one of those who were instrumental
in stimulating Henry Adams's interest in his writings, especially in *La Démocratie en Amérique,* as well as in the work
of such men as Guizot.

The impression that Swinburne made upon Adams was
a lasting one. In a letter to Elizabeth Cameron in 1916
he echoed the poet's *Itylus* in one of his phrases: "Swallow
sister! Sweet sister swallow!"[15] Only one year before his
death Adams had a friend read to him Gosse's book on the
poet.

When Henry Adams came to England, interest in Swinburne was in the ascendant. The poet was becoming a force in the diffusion of taste for French literature, particularly poetry, on the other side of the Channel. Henry himself tells of his meeting with the author who spoke of France as "the nursing mother" of his ancestors and as "the well beloved."

The poet of *Atalanta in Calydon* was one year Henry's junior. If Adams found in his great-grandfather's and in his grandfather's libraries innumerable French books to whet his curiosity and to stimulate his mastery of the tongue they were written in, Algernon could have steeped himself in eighteenth-century French literature in which the library of his grandfather, Sir John Edwards, abounded. And if Charles Francis Adams took the trouble to teach French to young Henry, Swinburne's mother taught her son French and Italian to a degree that he could capture the modern language prize at Eton. There one of his tutors, Henry Tarver, had introduced him to the works of Victor Hugo.

During Henry Adams's senior year at Harvard, Swinburne had published the first Canto of *Queen Yseult* in *Undergraduate Papers*, 1858, and had begun work on *Chastelard*. Already he was occupied with thoughts of the Tristan legend.[16] In 1861 he wrote a translation of Villon's "La Belle Heaulmyère," the earliest of the translations from Villon, and "La Fille du Policeman," a skit on French travesties of English life and on English middle-class morality. The following year (1862) he wrote his reviews of Hugo's *Les Misérables* and Baudelaire's *Fleuers du mal*. In 1867, on a premature report of the death of Baudelaire, he wrote "Ave Atque Vale." And in 1870 there appeared his *Ode on the Proclamation of the French Republic*, followed in 1872 by *Le Tombeau de Théophile Gautier*, which he had con-

tributed on the invitation of Heredia. His study of Victor
Hugo did not appear until 1886.[17]

Readers of the *Education* know how Swinburne tested
Henry's taste for French poetry by what to him was "the
surest and quickest of standards," namely, Victor Hugo;
and how Adams reacted with a parade of "an affection for
Alfred de Musset."[18]

Besides that initial meeting with Swinburne at Fryston,
we know of at least one more occasion when the young
American met the poet. On Wednesday, May 2, 1866,
Henry Adams wrote to his friend Charles Milnes Gaskell,
in a seemingly jocund mood, "Where think you that I go
tonight? To swell the noble Houghton's trains. I dine for
the Literary Fund and if you were the man I took you for,
you would go there too."[19]

At this point, Swinburne's note addressed to Lord Houghton in April, 1866,[20] is instructive:

Dear Lord Houghton,
   I got a note yesterday about the dinner, and will say my say as
I can. Of course, I shall blow a small trumpet before Hugo, I
thought something might be said of the new influence on Contemporary French and English Literature, e.g. the French studies
of Arnold and the English of Baudelaire.
                              Yours Affly,

At this dinner Swinburne declared his passion for Hugo
and his admiration for Baudelaire. It was that evening, too,
that Adams heard from Swinburne not only of Anglo-French
mutual literary influences, but his favorite theory of the
triplicity of medieval imagination: Dante, the Italian noble;
Chaucer, the English gentleman; Villon, the French plebian.
Chaucer touches Dante with reluctance, uses him for a
little, drops him. But, when Chaucer comes upon the poetry
of France, he feels instantly at home. He even translates
the intolerable *Roman de la Rose*.[21]

Soon after the Literary Fund dinner, Adams must have read Swinburne's "William Blake,"[22] which opens with this passage from Baudelaire, as a headpiece:

Tous les grands poetës deviennent naturellement, fatalement, critiques. Je plains les poetës que guide le seul instinct; je les crois incomplets. Dans la vie spirituelle des premiers, une crise se fait infailliblement, où ils veulent raisonner leur art, découvrir les lois obscures, en vertu desquelles ils ont produit, et tirer de cette étude une série de préceptes dont le but divin est l'infaillibilité dans la production poétique. Il serait prodigieux qu'un critique devînt poëte, et il est impossible qu'un poëte ne contienne pas un critique.

Baudelaire was "born and baptized into the church of rebels,"[23] and Adams was ready just then to become more and more familiar with rebels of the spirit.[24] His letters of the period all bespeak this fact. Another reference in "Blake" indicates Swinburne's espousal of what Baudelaire called "l'hérésie de l'enseignement." This, too, interested Adams.[25] Years later, in his *Life of George Cabot Lodge* we find Adams mentioning Baudelaire twice. In both instances he is quoting letters of young Lodge to his friend Mitchell. One of these letters speaks of Baudelaire as "really a great poet, one of the torchbearers"; in the other, Baudelaire's sonnets are singled out as among the "first rate ones [which] are terribly few and in diverse forms."[26]

According to Welby:

It is perhaps no exaggeration to say that the sweep of Swinburne's mind over literature makes most other great poets seem dwellers in an intellectual parish. From the Greek dramatists to Baudelaire, from Catullus to Christina Rossetti, from the early French romances and Chroniclers to Stendhal and Dickens, from Villon to Gautier, he ranged unwearyingly and with perfect naturalness.[27]

Contact with a man like Swinburne could well prove electric for an ardent seeker in the field of ideas. From him Adams

caught the meaning of commerce with great writers and the
emotional experience which that entails. Welby speaks of
Swinburne's power of conversation in such matters.[28]

Adams may first have heard of Paul de Saint-Victor from
Swinburne who had in the former, "an elder brother after
his own heart." "Like the studies of [Paul de Saint-Victor]
Swinburne's early monographs are impetuous and inflamed
impressions of literature."[29] And Adams surely did not
overlook the footnote in Swinburne's "Blake" which led
him to a just appreciation of Balzac.[30]

At a dinner given by the Duke of Argyle on February 13,
1863, Henry took particular pains to be introduced to John
Stuart Mill, whom he thought about the ablest man in
England. Henry Adams had started a study of Mill two
years earlier. It was Mill's works, "thoroughly studied,
that led him to the examination of philosophy and the great
French thinkers of our time (i.e. of the 19th century); they
in their turn passed him over to the others."[31] Thirty years
later,[32] Mill was still in his foreconsciousness: "The Paris
of Guizot, Louis Phillipe, and Tocqueville, as well as the
London of John Stuart Mill, Macaulay, and Robert Peel,
were but varieties of the same upper class bourgeoisie that
felt instinctive cousinship with the Boston of Ticknor, and
Motley."[33]

The wide influences that formed Mill's thought also formed,
in many respects, Adams's. An instance of this is found in
the enthusiasm for Tocqueville which Mill communicated
to Henry Adams. In his *Autobiography*, which Adams read
with care, Mill tells of the change which his political ideal
had undergone, thanks to his early reading of Tocqueville's
Democracy in America, where the excellences as well as the
specific dangers of democracy were pointed out. Mill admired (as Adams did after him) the masterly analysis of

popular government with all its virtues and weaknesses, as well as the collateral problem of centralization.

The powerful philosophic analysis which he applied to American and to French experience [says Mill] led him to attach the utmost importance to the performance of as much of the collective business of society, as can safely be so performed, by the people themselves, without any intervention of the executive government, either to supersede their agency, or to dictate the manner of its exercise. He viewed this practical political activity of the individual citizen, not only as one of the most effectual means of training the social feelings and practical intelligence of the people, so important in themselves and so indispensable to good government, but also as the specific counteractive to some of the characteristic infirmities of democracy, and a necessary protection against its degenerating into the only despotism of which, in the modern world, there is real danger—the absolute rule of the head of the executive over a congregation of isolated individuals, all equals but all slaves.[34]

For Adams, Mill's works constituted a school of French thinking; through them he was introduced not only to the ideas of Comte and Tocqueville, but to countless other sources of French thought. Perhaps Avignon acquired a special meaning for Adams because of its association in his mind with the place where Mill's wife died in 1858, and where Mill himself lived to the time of his death in 1873.[35]

The course of events during the period of Adams's stay in England, as private secretary to his father, was such as to stimulate his awareness of the historic process both in its contemporary and past phases. The intermediaries who served to introduce him to ideas current on the other side of the channel helped in great measure to make him cognizant of the necessity of marrying form to content in the expression of historic events.

III

Introduction to History

HENRY ADAMS returned to Washington in 1868, his mind whirring with ideas which he was to spend the rest of his life in developing.[1] It might well be stated at this point that there were two phases of historical awareness in Adams: the factual phase, which was largely operative when he wrote his *History;* and the aesthetic phase (including the scientific) which led him to *Mont-Saint-Michel and Chartres.* Michelet, Renan, and Taine, as we shall see later, played important roles in the development of the second phase. But for the moment Adams was occupied with the writing of articles for the *North American Review*, the *Edinburgh Review*, and the *Nation;* also in reading Gibbon's *Decline and Fall* with notes by Guizot.[2] A trip to Europe in the summer of 1870 permitted but a short stay in Paris, for Henry had to hurry to Bagni di Lucca where his sister was dying of tetanus.

His stay in Washington was also brief; in October, 1870, he moved with his belongings and ideas into his rooms at Harvard. There he found within reach "the liveliest and most agreeable of men—James Russell Lowell, Gurney, John Fiske, William James and a dozen others."[3] All of these men had some concern with French ideas. Fiske, for example, gave a lecture course on Comte's positivism;[4] whereas James was preoccupied with the French School of psychology. Eliot, as the new president of Harvard, authorized Bôcher's University Lectures on the French Language and Literature.[5] In the course entitled "French and German Philosophy" the textbook used was Bouillier's *Histoire de la philosophie cartésienne*.[6] Adams could discuss with Fiske some of the knotty problems of positivism. The William James whom Adams encountered in 1870 was conversant with the work of Charcot and the whole field of abnormal psychology which the latter helped so much to advance.[7]

As editor of the *North American Review*, a post which he had accepted with the assumption of his teaching, he did not necessarily read and retain all that went into the magazine; but he did take particular notice of those articles which appealed to him especially. In this respect he was in a class with *interested* readers. And in matters touching history, science, or philosophy Adams was such a reader. We instance but a few items in these fields which concerned him. In psychology there were: *La Psychologie morbide dans ses rapports avec la philosophie de l'histoire; ou, De l'influence des névropathies sur le dynamisme intellectuel*, by Dr. I. Moreau, of Tours (Paris, 1859);[8] James T. Bixby's review of Taine's *On Intelligence* (translated by T. D. Haye and revised with additions by the author, and published by Holt and Williams in 1872);[9] and Ferrier's *Functions of the Brain*.[10] In philosophy some of the items were: *La Philosophie contemporaine en Italie; Essai de Philosophie Hégélienne* by Raphael Mariano (Paris, 1868);[11] *L'Année philosophique* (1867);[12] *Pierre Bayle* by F. Sheldon;[13] John Fiske's *Outlines of Cosmic Philosophy* (2 vols.), "Based on the Doctrine of Evolution, with Criticisms on the Positive Philosophy" (1875);[14] E. Grysanowski's article on Comtism.[15] In the realm of science there were the following: a notice on Claude Bernard's *Rapport sur le progrès et la marche de la physiologie générale*, 1867;[16] Gravier's *Découverte de l'Amérique*.[17] In the matter of history, Adams was especially attracted to J. H. Stirling's review of Thomas Buckle's *History of Civilization in England and France, Spain and Scotland*.[18] In the January-April Number of the *Review* Adams contributed a discussion of *The Ancient City: a Study on the Religion, Laws, and Institutions of Greece and Rome* by Fustel de Coulanges, translated from the latest French edition by Willard Small (Boston: Leo and Shepard, 1874);[19] also Fustel de Coulanges's *Histoire des institutions politiques de l'ancienne France* (1875).[20]

We add a few literary items: Gauthier's *Histoire du Romantisme*;[21] *La Légende des Siècles* (new series, Paris, 1877) by Victor Hugo and the same author's *L'Art d'être grandpère*,[22] as well as Brillat-Savarin's *Physiologie du goût* (translated by R. E. Anderson, 1877)[23] and a notice of John Morley's *Rousseau*.[24]

One of the former editors and proprietors of the *North American Review* was Francis Bowen, professor of philosophy at Harvard during the years covering Adams's undergraduate days[25] as well as his period of teaching. The first to give a direct presentation of Kant's critical philosophy in America, Bowen also wrote an article on the philosophy of Cousin, whom he regarded as the most able interpreter of Kant. We shall have occasion to give a brief review of Adams's early preoccupation with French philosophy in a subsequent chapter.

The genesis of Henry Adams's active interest in history and the philosophy of history is recorded in a letter addressed to his brother, Charles Francis, Jr., from London on October 23, 1863:

Two years ago [in 1861] I began on history, of our own time. I labored at financial theories, and branched out upon Political Economy and J. S. Mill. Mr. Mill's works, thoroughly studied, led me to the examination of philosophy and the great French thinkers of our own time; they in their turn passed me over to others whose very names are now known only as terms of reproach by the vulgar: the monarchist Hobbes, the atheist Spinoza and so on. Where I shall end, *das weiss der liebe Gott!*[26]

When Adams was pitchforked (to use his own words), as Fiske's (really Gurney's) successor into medieval history of which he said he knew nothing,[27] he began to read seriously, and the Charge Books at the Harvard College Library bear witness to this. Among the books he withdrew (in 1870) were the following:[28]

Thierry   Conquète de l'Angleterre vols. 1 & 2
               Lettres sur l'Histoire de France
Martin   Histoire de France
Palgrave   Normandy
Pardessus   Loi Salique
L'Art de Vérifier les dates Vols. 9, 10, 11
Documents sur l'Histoire de France
Froissart 2 Vols.
Polytique de l'Abbé Irumman
Collection des Mémoires sur l'Histoire de France
Froissart's Chronicles
Cherrier[29]

In the spring term of 1873-74, he withdrew Beaumanoir, vols. I and II, and again, Froissart's *Chronicles*. In 1876-77 he took out *Gil Blas*, Lennep's *Hesiod*, Boiteux's *Quatre Poétiques*, 2 vols. On July 12, he ordered *Voyage dans l'intérieur des États-Unis*, *Voyage en Amérique*, Vols. I and II; *États-Unis*, Liancourt Vols. I-VII. His reading in medieval historical literature took him to the books of Ruskin, Fergusson and Freeman.[30] He was reading Viollet le Duc's *Dictionary of Architecture*. "I wish," he wrote to Gaskell,

"I had a good historical collection of cathedrals in photo-graph." Already we can descry in his mind the seed of *Mont-Saint-Michel and Chartres*.

French thinking, in a sense, was responsible for the fact that Adams was appointed to his Harvard chair. In a letter, Henry announces: "My predecessor was turned out because he was a Comtist!!!"[31] This Comtist (with three exclamation marks) was none other than John Fiske. We have it from Fiske himself that in December, 1869, he went to see Professor Poey, a French geologist and positivist "who has got a list of all the books in existence relating to Posi-tivism."[32] In July, Fiske had been chosen as one of the university lecturers on philosophy for the year 1869-70. The subject on which he had been especially invited to de-liver a course of lectures was positivism. He regarded this as an opportunity to finish a book on the subject with which he had busied himself for four years,[33] although eight years earlier, as an undergraduate, he had been threatened with dismissal from college for talking Comtism to everyone. He considered that his appointment indicated a change of feeling at Harvard. But he was mistaken in thinking that his temporary post would lead to a professorship of history. President Eliot[34] did renominate him (in December) as lecturer on the Positive Philosophy, and upon Professor Gurney's election to the deanship of the faculty Fiske was made acting professor of history for the spring term (Feb-ruary 17 to Commencement). His specific task was the same as Henry Adams's, namely, the interpretation of medieval history to the senior class.[35]

During his teaching period at Harvard, Adams produced no books, though he edited *Documents Relating to New Eng-land Federalism (1800-1815)*, which came out in 1877.[36] It was not until 1879, when his *Life of Albert Gallatin* appeared, that he seriously set to work on his *History*. That same year

he had met, in England, the French archeologist Henry
Waddington, a friend of Renan; and in Paris, Marcel Thé-
venin, the historian who had contributed to the *North American Review*, under the editorship of Adams. He already
knew Professor Monod, the editor of the *Revue historique*.
He undoubtedly spoke to these men of his book on Gallatin
in which he tried to suggest "the inevitable isolation and
disillusionment of a really strong mind—one that combines
force with elevation." And therein he saw the "romance
and tragedy of statesmanship."[37] In the pages of this book
we come upon many names of interest to us: among them,
Voltaire, Rousseau, Chateaubriand, and Mme de Staël.

In the course of his researches Henry Adams was, inevitably, to fall back on some intermediaries who were to
help him either to gain entry to centers of archival material,
or to secure for him copyists to handle thousands and
thousands of manuscripts. One such intermediary was of
especial importance, since he was in a strategic position to
help the historian, and also was a scholar in his own right:
Henry Vignaud. We present here some of the salient facts
about him, especially as they relate to his contacts with
Adams.[38]

Henry Vignaud had served as a Confederate Captain and
was made captive when New Orleans was taken. Escaping
to Paris, he collaborated there as propaganda journalist
with Hotze and Slidell, writing for the Parisian *Mémorial
diplomatique* and the London *Index* in 1864. It was in the
pages of the latter that Adams, secretary to his father in
London, first encountered Vignaud's name.[39] The two
probably met later, at the Geneva Conference, where the
Louisianian turned up as a translator. However this may be,
it is now an established fact that Adams made direct contact with Vignaud shortly before 1880.

In 1879 Adams was forming plans for the writing of his

History. Ready to initiate his researches, and realizing that "diplomacy has its uses," he now appealed to Hitt, then American Chargé d'Affaires in Paris, to help him gain access to the Marine archives. Not only did Hitt bestir himself but he got Vignaud, Second Secretary by this time, to help too. Accordingly, Mr. Hitt addressed the following letter to the Minister of the Marine:[40]

29 Octobre '79

Monsieur le Ministre:

Mon compatriote M. Henry Adams qui s'occupe d'une Histoire de l'administration du Président Jefferson serait très désireux d'être admis à la faveur de consulter les archives de la marine pour la période comprise entre les années 1800 et 1804 en ce qui concerne particulièrement St. Domingue[41] et la Louisiane.

Monsieur Adams appartient à une famille illustre dans notre histoire nationale; c'est un homme d'un grand mérite dont le dernier ouvrage sur "Albert Gallatin" a obtenu un légitime succès. Je vous serais reconnaissant s'il vous était agréable de lui accorder la faveur qu'il sollicite.

Veuillez agréer, Monsieur le Ministre, l'assurance de ma haute considération.

Le Chargé d'affaires des États-Unis

R. R. Hitt

Son Excellence
Monsieur l'Admiral Jauréguiberry
Ministre de la Marine
        etc. etc.

With this entree secured, Henry Adams settled down to such concentrated work at the Archives that he hardly had time to find out what Paris was like. "I see nothing of it except manuscripts and books," he wrote.[42] He hoped to finish the state papers there by the middle of January and go back to London. But with a "mountain of papers and books to digest," it was obvious that he would need a copyist to help him. It was at this point that Vignaud offered help in having materials copied from the Affaires étrangères[43] and to supervise the copyist's work. Adams could now feel free to leave for England.

Upon his arrival in London, "after six weeks of dull and dismal hibernation in Paris,"[44] he wrote to the Second Secretary:[45]

> 22 Queen Anne's Gate
> St. James' Park London
> 5 February 1880

Dear Sir:

Thanks for Sevellon Brown's[46] engagement, or rather wedding-cards.

I understand that Faugère has been decapitated.[47] In any case, if you happen to be at the Foreign Office an inquiry about my papers would do no harm. I expect them to raise difficulties which had best be met in time.

I have a volume[48] for you which I shall send one of these days if the post will take it.

> I am very truly yours,
>
> Henry Adams

Henry Vignaud, Esq.

A letter from Vignaud in the State Department Archives in Washington seems to indicate that between February and July the copyist (apparently under Vignaud's surveillance) had been busy compiling a whole volume of materials for the historian. The following note is Vignaud's report to Adams:[49]

> 10 July '80

Dear Sir:

The copyist has given me a bundle containing the copies made up to date. It is of the size of a 4° volume and represents, he says, about half of the work. How shall I send it to you? By express? It could not be sent by post without having each end open which would not be safe. I have given the copyist 300 francs; enclosed please find his receipt.

> Truly yours,
>
> Henry Vignaud

Henry Adams, Esq.
23 Queen Anne's Gate S. W. London

The receipt reads:

Je, sousigné, reconnais avoir reçu de Monsieur Adams la somme de trois cents francs à-compte sur les copies faites et à faire, d'un travail de recherches aux affaires Étrangères sur les États-Unis d'Amérique.

Sous (?), 13 juillet 1880
Grenoy (?)

The history of the Administrations of Jefferson and Madison was begun and brought to practical completion between 1879 and 1889. By August, 1890, Adams still had some proofreading to do on it, but being entirely absorbed by preparations for his impending trip to the South Seas, he left the details of seeing the work through the press to his friend and companion Theodore F. Dwight,[50] who also knew Vignaud and (as a subsequent letter shows) collaborated with him at least once in helping Adams. During that same decade Vignaud too had made exemplary progress, not only in his diplomatic career but in the fields of journalism, literature, and scholarship. His extensive and varied library at Bagneux reflected his extraordinary growth in these fields.[51] As the corpus of his unpublished materials reveals, he too was then working in American History.

In the early part of January, 1892, after returning from the South Sea Islands and before sailing for England,[52] Adams saw Vignaud. With the *History* and *Historical Essays* behind him, the historian was now contemplating new work. In fact, his South Sea experiences were productive of a manuscript to be published as *Memoirs of Marau Taaroa, Last Queen of Tahiti*; and this now needed additional documentation. Also, further researches had to be made in view of new revisions and editions of his *History*. In all this he again needed Vignaud's help. His own restlessness took him home to Washington and back to Scotland. It was from there that he wrote to Henry Vignaud—again he was concerned about copyists.[53]

Aboyne, Aberdeen
16 Sept. 1892

Dear Mr. Vignaud:

I have heard not a word of that angel copyist since I saw you last in January, and I have since then been home, and come back, and passed the summer here, beyond the reach of copyists. I cannot help occasionally feeling qualms of doubt for fear she should have piled tons of paper on you, and left you not a centime to your back. As I expect to return to America by the Majestic, October 5, and shall not go to Paris on the way, I write to give you time to unload on me any burdens you may have assumed. After the 23rd my address is to Baring Bros. Limited London.

Pray give my regards to the Minister. I am sorry not to be able to pay my respects in person; but as he is probably occupied with the public business[54] at some watering-place at this season, I only regret he is not here.

Yours truly,

Henry Adams

Mr. Vignaud.

About a fortnight later—this time from London—he wrote once more to Vignaud:[55]

London, Oct. 2, '92

My Dear Mr. Vignaud:

I suppose you can get money, even at Paris, on a check, as well as on any other form of draft, so I send you herewith a check for 20, and will settle with Dwight. Thanks for your aid.

Dwight has been City Librarian at Boston since last April. He was in Italy June and July, but I do not know whether he was in Paris. He is now in Boston on duty and I imagine he must have his hands full.

I sail for New York next Wednesday 5th. My address, as usual, will be 1603 H Street, Washington. I wish I were coming to Paris for a few days at least, but it is not convenient; so please remember me to the Minister and believe me

Yours truly,

Henry Adams

Incidentally, the date of the letters just reproduced was the Columbus anniversary year. It was then that Vignaud became interested in the colorful and controversial history of Christopher Columbus. This interest was productive of works which gained for him the rank, subsequently, of one of the world's outstanding Americanists.[56]

How often Adams was in touch with Vignaud after 1892 one cannot at present say; but it is clear that in 1898 Brooks Adams—and probably Henry too—had dealings with him, as the following hitherto unpublished letter indicates:[57]

4 Rue de Verneuil
Jan. 30, 1898

Dear Mr. Vignaud:

My niece Miss Abigail Adams wants to consult some books in costume which I suppose can best be seen in the National Library. If you would be so kind as to send me the regular form for readers issued by the Embassy, so that I can get her a reader's ticket, you would add to the many obligations under which I already stand toward you.

Very truly yours,

Brooks Adams

In a letter to Elizabeth Cameron in 1901 Adams speaks of Vignaud as "dying or dead." Though he puts these words into the mouth of "old Morton,"[58] we can credit them to Adams's familiar penchant for what we may be allowed to call "literary alarmism." As a matter of fact, in 1901, Vignaud—far from being dead or dying—still had an active score of years before him, and he was to survive Adams by four years. At seventy he launched out in the sea of historic scholarship with that stout, steady venturesomeness which characterized the very Columbus he wrote about. He died in 1922.

The historic imagination is fired when one pictures some

of Adams's works looking out from the shelves of Vignaud's library,[59] at Bagneux, upon an ancient garden and grove, once part of the county seat of Cardinal Richelieu.[60] It was as if Adams himself had come to salute the ground of his Norman ancestors from the study windows of Vignaud.

The role of the intermediaries whom Henry Adams called upon to help him gain admission to sources of information, and to expedite the copying of vast amounts of materials in France, is made clear in the instance of Vignaud. The sources used by Adams in the writing of his *History* were to a great extent French. How extensive these were can be gathered from even a casual examination, at the Library of Congress, of Adams's transcripts of the Affaires Étrangères. Below we give a list of the sources now to be found in Western Reserve University as well as at the Massachusetts Historical Society.[61]

Adams starts his *History* with a picture of the European background in 1796 or thereabouts. "In 1796 America was in swaddling clothes. . . . Europe was on the verge of an outburst of genius." Among French names he alludes to Balzac, Cuvier, and Napoleon, who was taking command of the French armies.

If the average human being (Adams reflected) could accustom himself to reason with the logical processes of Descartes and Newton! What then? He goes on to show how for nearly a century Voltaire had carried on, in the face of all odds, a protest against "an intellectual despotism contemptible even to its own supporters," and how Priestley, trying to do in England what Voltaire did in France, was driven to America.[62] But there, cultural conditions even in the state of Massachusetts, were poor. True, some Bostonians could speak French, "but Germany was nearly as unknown as China, until Madame de Staël published her famous work in 1814."[63] However, if deeper studies were rare in America, they were also rare in England and France, Adams reflected. A man like Jefferson

seemed during his entire life to breathe with perfect satisfaction nowhere except in the liberal literary, and scientific air of Paris in 1789. . . . [He] aspired beyond the ambition of a nationality, and embraced in his view the whole future of man.[64]

In view of the period dealt with in the *History*, it is natural that Napoleon's name recur throughout the nine volumes. By gleaning some of the paragraphs that deal particularly with Napoleon, we are helped to a considerable portrait of his personality.

Most picturesque of all figures in modern history, Napoleon Bonaparte, like Milton's Satan on his throne of state, although surrounded by a group of figures little less striking than himself, sat unapproachable on his bad eminence . . . His moral sense regarded truth and falsehood as equally useful modes of expression.[65]

He had two rooted hatreds.

The deeper and fiercer of these was directed against the republic,— the organized democracy, and what he called ideology, which Americans knew in practice as Jeffersonian theories; the second and steadier was his hatred of England as the chief barrier to his military omnipotence. The cession of Louisiana to the United States contradicted both these passions, making the ideologists supreme in the New World.[66]

If one act in Bonaparte's career [says Adams] concentrated more than another the treason and violence of a lifetime, it was the coup d'état of the 18th Brumaire, in 1799, when he drove the Legislature at the point of the bayonet from the hall at St. Cloud, and annihilated French liberty, as he hoped forever.[67]

In drawing a parallel between Napoleon and Canning, Adams remarks:

Canning had several qualities in common with Bonaparte, and one of them was the habit of classifying under the head of fools persons whose opinions he did not fancy,—from the man who believed in a republic to the man who liked dry champagne.[68]

He resumes the parallel somewhat later:

In 1804 Bonaparte—then only First Consul, but about to make himself a bastard Emperor—flung before the feet of Europe the bloody corpse of the Duc d'Enghien, so George Canning in 1807 about to meet Bonaparte on his own field with his own weapons, called the world to gaze at his handiwork in Copenhagen; and the world then contained but a single nation to which the fate of Copenhagen spoke in accents of direct and instant menace. The annihilation of Denmark left America almost the only neutral, as she had long been the only Republican State.[69]

Adams, no mean psychologist, makes the following observation:

In a character so interesting as that of Napoleon, the moments of perplexity were best worth study; and in his career no single moment occurred when he had more reason to call upon his genius for a resource than when he faced at Bordeaux the failure of his greatest scheme.[70]

Perhaps even the humorous aspect of the man is related to his brooding perplexity. This aspect is brought out by Adams in an incident he culls from the *Mémoires* of Mme de Rémusat.

Mme de Rémusat told how Grétry, who as a member of the Institute regularly attended the Imperial audiences, was almost regularly asked by Napoleon, "Who are you?" Tired at last of this rough question, Grétry replied by an answer equally blunt: "Sire, toujours Grétry," and henceforth the Emperor never failed to remember him.[71]

Napoleon is further presented as a term of comparison as well as a source of inspiration.

Jefferson's personality during the eight years [of office] appeared to be the government, and impressed itself, like that of Bonaparte, although by a different process, on the mind of the nation.

Again,

Jefferson resembled all rulers in one peculiarity of mind. Even Bonaparte thought that a respectable minority might be useful to censors; but neither Bonaparte nor Jefferson was willing to agree that any particular minority was respectable.

Aaron Burr, the Vice-President, is spoken of as having been

imbued in the morality of Lord Chesterfield and Napoleon Bonaparte. He pleased himself with saying, after the manner of the First Consul of the French Republic, "Great souls care little for small morals."[72]

The characters of George III, Pitt, Canning, Castlereagh and, of course, Talleyrand are classed with that of Bonaparte. "Talleyrand, most active in directing the coup d'état, was chiefly responsible for the ruin of France." Adams quotes from Chateaubriand as once having said that "When M. Talleyrand is not conspiring he traffics."[73] Yet he goes on to say that although Talleyrand was incarnate conservatism, he was "wider-minded and more elevated in purpose than Napoleon," and that he had no faith in Napoleon's methods and was hostile to his projects against Spain. Finally,

No picture of American history could be complete which did not show in the background the figures of Bonaparte and Godoy, locked in the struggle over Don Carlos IV.[74]

As an offshoot of his *History*, Adams published in the *Revue historique* for April 1884 an article, "Napoléon Ier à Saint-Domingue." There he deals with Napoleon's treatment of Toussaint l'Ouverture.[75]

Obliged to abandon the design of punishing Toussaint according to law for crimes he had not committed the First Consul was still able to inflict equal punishment on him for the crimes for which

he had been pardoned. Toussaint was taken, with every precaution
of secrecy, to the Fortress of Joux in the Jura Mountains. . . .
The severity with which Toussaint was treated in prison, without
pretence of authority in law, resulted from the orders of the First
Consul, given through Decrès to the commandant. These orders
had some historical interest, showing the system under which
prisoners of state were managed during the consulate.

In his humorless cruelty, as in many other respects, Napoleon
was not French, Adams maintains;

else he would never have preached to Toussaint a sermon so grim
in its defiance of absurdity. Between Toussaint, Decrès, Leclerc,
and Bonaparte, critics might perhaps differ in establishing the
correct order in dissimulation and hypocrisy; but the position of
Toussaint at Joux proved decisively that he was the least profi-
cient of the four.[76]

Adams's reading of historical sources went hand-in-hand
with his reading of the French historians,[77] for instance,
Babeau, Guizot, Houssaye and Thiers. But the three whom
he read most studiously, not only for their historic value but
for the literary interest they held for him, were Michelet,
Renan, and Taine. To them we devote the following chapter.

IV

The Literary Use of Three
French Historians

For all Adams's insistence on a plenitude of facts in building up his own *History*, he nevertheless considered imagination "the highest quality of the mind" and regretted that it was "utterly wanting in our American character and of course in the best of our students." It was in Michelet that he found this "highest quality." In Renan he perceived a mixture of science and metaphysics reduced to art; whereas in Taine he discovered the power to generalize on a grand scale.

From the advice that he offered Lodge, it is clear that Adams was in quest of a general philosophy of history from the very beginning of his career.

Unless you can find some basis of faith in general principles, some theory of the progress of civilization which is outside and above all temporary questions of policy, you must infallibly think and act under the control of the man or men whose thought, in the time you deal with, coincides most nearly with your prejudices. This is the fault with almost every English historian. Very few of them have had scientific minds and still fewer have honestly tried to keep themselves clear of personal feeling.[1]

Indeed, Adams discovered that the three French historians just mentioned employed science (that is, history) as a form of aesthetic contemplation; for the recollection of the past is essentially an aesthetic activity. History, in spite of its chronicle aspects (presumably matters of fact), is an aesthetic process.

The collective memory of the race is a great reservoir of aesthetic appeal to the individual, be he writer or reader. That things which are no more should, through the incitement of written history, come to life again in the mind, is itself the greatest proof of the artistic fiat of the historian. And the first to impress Adams with this fact was Michelet.

MICHELET'S *Histoire de France*

The first volume of Michelet's *Histoire de France* (with which we shall be particularly concerned here) appeared in 1833. In August of the following year Michelet went to England, and a few years later, starting in 1841, studies and appreciations of his work began to appear in English magazines. From then on Americans interested in the history of France and its literature were to become more and more acquainted with his work, since translations of his books made their appearance simultaneously in England and in America.[2]

Although neither Morison's history of Harvard University nor the college catalogues for 1854–58, the years of Adams's undergraduate career, show that Michelet was required reading, we know that the French historian must have come within Adams's purview during that period; for, in 1858 he listed Michelet's *History of France* among the books he then possessed.[3] It is this copy that he used and made scorings in when he returned to Harvard as assistant professor of history, to give, among other courses, his History II.[4] We shall subsequently show the manner and the extent of his use of it.

Pursuing the imagination, as Adams said, "into its remotest haunts," he followed (though perhaps unconsciously) the path of Chateaubriand and the whole train of his romantic disciples, for whom history was essentially an imaginative reconstruction of the past. In following this path it was inevitable that Michelet should occupy a place in Adams's foreconsciousness from his initial mention of him in 1858 to his ultimate reference to him in 1905. For, during the half century marked by these two dates, Michelet attracted the attention of many of the personalities whom Adams knew or with whom he had any intellectual commerce. Adams's attention was bound to be drawn repeatedly to the author of the *History of France* in a number of ways: through the English journals which he read earnestly during his secretaryship to his father in London; through John Stuart Mill whose work he studied carefully; through the *Atlantic Monthly* and the *North American Review;* and through his friendship with Gabriel Monod,[5] the editor of the *Revue historique.*

For all of Adams's admiration for German methodology,[6] then, he turned to Michelet in his imaginative reconstruction of the Middle Ages. If the facts had to suffer, so much the worse for the facts, as long as the mind of the reader could be made to grasp the reality of Chartres and the age that gave rise to it. Thus we witness how what originally presented itself as a mere text, became through the long span of half a century, a generative factor in the begetting of a classic like *Mont-Saint-Michel and Chartres.*

How well was Adams acquainted with Michelet's *History* and precisely how did he make use of it during his teaching period at Harvard? We have already said that he underscored many passages in his copy of the *History*.[7] As a matter of fact, his syllabus for the so-called History II which he gave at Harvard shows that he followed fairly closely the text of that book. Since the second volume of Michelet's work has practically no scorings,[8] we shall present the passages scored by Adams in Volume I.[9]

On page 144 Michelet quotes from Augustin Thierry's letters on the history of France. The following are the parts of this quotation which Adams scored:

To the revolution of 888 there corresponds in the exactest manner a movement of another kind, which raises to the throne a man who is an entire stranger to the Carlovingian Family. This King—the first to whom our history can assign the title of King of France, as opposed to that of King of the Franks, is Ode, or according to the Roman pronunciation which then began to prevail, Eudes, son of Robert the Strong, Count of Anjoy.[10]

We note that in the History II Syllabus[11] which Adams used in his teaching at Harvard, Item 225 is "The election of Eudes; his reign." The sentence that follows the passage just quoted mentions Eudes's election.

The next passage (p. 144) is:

It was not through caprice, but policy, that the Barons of the north of Gaul, Franks by origin, but attached to the interests of the country, violated the oath taken by their ancestors to the family of Pepin, and consecrated King at Compiegne a man of Saxon descent.[12]

What follows tells of Charles the Simple or the Foolish not being able to hold out against the power of Eudes and seeking the protection of Arnulph, King of Germany (and again underscored by Adams):

After having offered large presents to Arnulph, (he) was invested by him with the sovereignty whose title he had assumed.[13] Com-

mands were issued to the counts and bishops who dwelt near the
Moselle to lend him every aid,—but all was of no avail.

—Charles the Simple, received as their King (i.e. by the Germans,
after the death of Eudes), *in 898*, reigned at first two-and-twenty
years without any opposition. The first duke was faithful to the
treaty of alliance which he had contracted with Charles the Simple,
and supported him, though feebly enough, against Rodbert, or
Robert, King Eudes' brother, who was elected to the throne in 922.
His son, William I., at first pursued the same policy; and when
the hereditary monarch was dethroned and imprisoned at Laon,
he declared for him against Radulf or *Raoul, Robert's brother-in-law,
who had been elected and crowned King* through hate of the Frank
dynasty; but some years afterwards, changing sides, he forsook
the cause of Charles the Simple, and entered into an alliance with
King Raoul. In 936, expecting greater advantages from a return
to his early track, he lent an energetic assistance to the return of
Charles' son *Louis, surnamed d'Outremer* (*from beyond the sea*).[14]

At this point an examination of the Syllabus will show a close
following of Michelet's text; for Item 226 reads "Charles
the Simple; his relations with the Normans"; Item 227,
"Election of Robert to the throne; his reign; election of
Raoul of Burgundy"; Item 228, "Fate of Charles the
Simple"; and Item 229, "How did Louis d'Outremer obtain
the throne?"

On the page following (145), Adams underscored as
follows: "On the demise of Louis d'Outremer, *in the year 954,
his son Lothaire succeeded* him without any apparent opposition." In the right margin he wrote "Lothaire 954."

The history of Michelet goes on to tell (p. 146—and he is
still quoting from Thierry) of King Lothaire's breaking with
the German powers. But as his power diminished it

passed into the hand of Hugh—the son of Hugh the Great—count
of the isle of France and of Anjou,[15] surnamed in the French of the
time *Capet* or *Chapet*. . . . The German princes were deterred by
the difficulties of every kind which opposed a fourth restoration of

the Carlovingians (A.D. 987), and sent no army to the assistance of Charles, brother of the last king but one.[16]

Charles was finally betrayed and given up by one of his own party.

Hugh Capet confined him in the tower of Orleans, where he died. . . . [What follows here, p. 147, was marked by Adams]: Although the new king was of German stock—his want of relationship with the imperial dynasty, and the very obscurity of his origin, which could not be traced beyond the third generation, pointed him out as a candidate to the native race, whose restoration had been preparing since the dismemberment of the empire. In our national history, the accession of the third race far exceeds in importance that of the second. Strictly speaking, it constitutes *the end of the reign of the Franks, and the substitution of a national* monarch for a government founded on conquest.[17]

Here, too, Items 230 through 235 of the Syllabus parallel the text just given, parts of which Adams scored.[18]

No further markings occur in the text until we reach page 184.[19] There Adams marked this passage:

It was the universal belief of the middle ages, that the thousandth year from Nativity would be the end of the world. In like manner, before Christianity, the Etrusci had fixed ten centuries as the term of their empire; and the prediction had been fulfilled. Christianity, a wayfarer of this earth, a guest, exiled from heaven, readily adopted a similar belief. The world of the middle age was without the external regularity of the ancient city, and the firm and compact order within was not easily discernible.

On the same page he also underscored this:

Then, [i.e. in a world of miracles] might it well have happened that what we call life would have been found to be death; and that the world, in coming to a close, might, like the saint of the legend, begin to live and cease to die; ("et tunc vivere incepit, morique desiit").

Also: "The idea of the end of the world, sad as that world was, was at once the hope and the terror of the middle age." (But suffering continued.) "Some other advent was needed; and men expected that it would arrive." And on page 185, "All longed to be relieved from their suffering, no matter at what cost!" On pages 195, 196,[20] Michelet says: "On the earth there is the pope, and the emperor, who is the reflection of the pope, a mere reflection, a pale shadow—let him recognize who he is." To this statement there is the following footnote which Adams underscored:

Gregorii VII. Epist. Ad reg. Angl. ibid 6. Sicut ad mundi pulchritudinem oculis carneis diversis temporibus disposuit (Deus) luminaria, sic. . . . See, also, Innoc. III. i. epist. 401-Bonifacii VIII. repraesentandam, Solem et Lunam omnibus aliis eminentiora epist. ibid. 197. Fecit Deus duo luminaria magna, scilicet, Solem, id est, ecclesiasticam potestatem, et Lunam, hoc est, temporalem et imperialem. Et sicut Luna nullum lumen habet nisi quod recipit a Sole, sic. . . . The following calculation occurs in the gloss of the Decretals: "Since the earth is seven times greater than the moon, but the sun eight times greater than the earth, therefore the pontifical dignity is fifty-six times greater than the regal." Laurentius goes further . . . "the pope is a thousand seven hundred and four times greater than emperor or Kings." (Gieseler, ii. pt. ii. p. 98.)

Michelet points out (p. 197) that "The historians of the conquest of England and of Sicily, have taken a pleasure in assigning their Normans the mould and colossal height of the heroes of chivalry," and that the enemies of the Normans without denying their valor, "do not attribute such supernatural strength to them." Adams marks what then follows:

The Germans who opposed them in Italy, derided their shortness of stature;[21] and in their war with the Greeks and Venetians, these descendants of Rollow and of Hastings show themselves but poor sailors, and are fearfully alarmed by the tempests of the Adriatic.[22]

The only other passage we found scored by Adams is on page 199,[23] namely, "Duke Robert had had him (i.e. William the Bastard), by chance, by the daughter of a tanner of Falaise. He was not ashamed of his birth, and drew round him his mother's other sons."[24]

In general then, when one compares the items of the Syllabus with Michelet's *History*, it becomes apparent that Adams's outline for History II as given at Harvard, was based in the main on Michelet's work. This does not mean that the Syllabus was based exclusively on that text, although all indications are that this was the chief source.

Now what use did Adams make of the *History* in the writing of his *Mont-Saint-Michel and Chartres*? There is only one direct reference to Michelet in the *Mont-Saint-Michel*, when Adams talks of Pierre de Dreux, who presumably detested Blanche of Castile.[25] On the left of one of the Chartres windows where Saint Anne is portrayed, there is the figure of David, Adams tells us, symbolizing the energy of the state and "tramping on a Saul, suggesting suspicions of a Saul de Dreux." In talking of Pierre's contentious, shrewd, lion-hearted, restless, bold character (which he reconstructs from the chronicler and Joinville), Adams adds: "full of courtesy and 'largesse'; but very hard on the clergy; a good Christian but a bad churchman! Certainly the first man of his time says Michelet!"[26]

But his failure to mention Michelet more often does not mean that Adams has forgotten him. A juxtaposition of the section in the *History* which is entitled "Abelard—His Doctrines (A.D. 1102–1140)"[27] with certain parts of Adams's fascinating chapter on Abelard reveals the points at which the latter got his clue from Michelet.[28] Here follow the respective texts:[29]

Michelet	Adams
[After the first crusade] Paris was the centre to which life flowed. . . . The first sign . . . is the rise of the schools and the voice of Abelard. . . . Two pupils of St. Anselm's of Canterbury, Anselm of Laon and William of Champeaux, presided over the schools of Laon and of Paris. . . . The existence alone of the school of Paris constituted a portentous and dangerous novelty. Ideas . . . began to converge to a common centre. . . . The beginner of this revolution was—a handsome young man of brilliant talents. . . . None wrote love verses, like his, in the vulgar tongue; he sang them, too.	In the year 1100 Jesuit colleges did not exist, and even the great Dominican and Franciscan schools were far from sight in the future; but the school of Notre Dame at Paris existed, and taught the existence of God much as Archbishop Hildebert described it. The most successful lecturer was William of Champeaux, and to any one who ever heard of William at all, the name instantly calls up the figure of Abelard, in flesh and blood, as he sang to Heloise the songs which he says resounded throughout Europe. The twelfth century, with all its sparkle would be dull without Abelard and Heloise.

It is with infinite regret that Adams leaves Héloïse out of the story, "because she was not a philosopher or a poet or an artist, but only a Frenchwoman to the last millimetre of her shadow."[30] According to Michelet, she was "Young, lovely, accomplished"; and in a footnote he supports his description by quoting from the *Liber calamitatum*: "Not the last in beauty, she was first in extent of learning." Her uncle put her (says Michelet) under the tuition of Abelard, who seduced her. This presumed fact Adams metamorphosed to read as follows:

French standards, by which she must be judged in our ignorance, take for granted that she philosophized only for the sake of Abelard, while Abelard taught philosophy to her not so much because he believed in philosophy or in her as because he believed in himself.[31]

In the following passages, both dealing with Abelard's electric charm, one can see how Adams keyed Michelet to his own humorous stylistic pattern:

Michelet	Adams
Abelard's wonderful success is easily explained. All the lore and learning which had been smothered under the	The first crusade seems, in perspective, to have filled the whole field of vision in France at the time; but, in fact,

heavy, dogmatical forms of clerical instructions, and hidden in the rude Latin of the middle age, suddenly appeared arrayed in the simple elegance of antiquity, so that men seemed for the first time to hear and recognize a human voice. The daring youth simplified and explained everything; presenting philosophy in a familiar form, and bringing it home to men's bosoms. He hardly suffered the obscure or supernatural to rest on the hardest mysteries of faith. It seemed as if till then the church had lisped and stammered; while Abelard spoke. All was made smooth and easy. He treated religion courteously and handled her gently, but she melted away in his hands. Nothing embarrassed the fluent speaker; he reduced religion to philosophy, and morality to humanity. . . . The doctrine spread instantaneously, crossing at once, sea and Alps, and penetrating among all classes. . . . The Simple were shaken, the saints staggered, the Church was silent.[32]

France seethed with other emotions, and while the crusaders set out to scale heaven by force at Jerusalem, the monks, who remained at home, undertook to scale heaven by prayer and absorptions of body and soul in God. . . . At the same time—that is about 1098 or 1100—Abelard came up to Paris from Brittany, with as much faith in logic as Bernard had in prayer or Godfrey of Bouillon in arms, and led an equal or even a greater number of combatants to the conquest of heaven by force of our reason. None showed doubt. Hundreds of thousands of young men wandered from their provinces mostly to Palestine, largely to cloisters, but also in great numbers to Paris and the schools, while few ever returned.[33]

At that time, Michelet tells us, the Church was swayed by St. Bernard, the simple Abbot of Clairvaux. In talking of this Saint's influence, Adams's remarks follow rather closely those of the French historian. However, the former's terseness makes him, at times, more charming than Michelet.

Michelet

So overpowering was the effect of his preaching, that mothers kept their sons from hearing him, wives their husbands; or all would have turned monks. As for him when he had breathed the breath of life into the multitude, he would hasten back to Clairvaux, rebuild his hut of boughs and leaves, and soothe in studies of the Song of Songs, the interpretation of which was the occupation of his life, his love-sick soul.[34]

Adams

. . . the Cistercian Order was founded in 1098, and was joined in 1112 by young Bernard, born in 1098 at Fontaines-les-Dijon, drawing with him or after him so many thousands of young men into the self-immolation of the monastery as carried dismay into the hearts of half the women of France.[35]

Adams's adoration of woman as a central power in the
organization of society reflects an attitude which he held in
common with Michelet.[36] Numerous references in the *Mont-
Saint-Michel* to Queen Blanche of Castile have been inspired
by three pages in the *History*.[37]

Without mentioning his source, Adams quotes verbatim,
at least once, from Michelet. In connection with one window
at Chartres which represents Pierre de Dreux and his family
(his wife Alix and their two children Yolande and Jean),
he explains:

Jean was born in 1217. Yolande was affianced in marriage in 1227,
while a child, and given to Queen Blanche to be brought up as the
future wife of her younger son John, then in his eighth year. When
John died, Yolande was contracted to Thibaut of Champagne in
1231

and from this point on Adams copies the words from a
footnote in his unnamed source—

and Blanche is said to have written to Thibaut in consequence:[38]
"Sire Thibauld of Champagne, I have heard that you have cov-
enanted and promised to take to wife the daughter of Count Perron
of Brittany.[39] Wherefore I charge you, if you do not wish to lose
whatever you possess in the Kingdom of France, not to do it. If
you hold dear or love aught in the said Kingdom, do it not."[40]

Both Adams and Michelet followed the *Historia Calamitatum* for significant and critical moments in Abelard's career.
Both drew their respective chapters on *Abelard* to a close on
a wistful one. "Such was the end of the restorer of philosophy in the middle age," said Michelet; and Adams:
"This was the end of Abelard."

There are other instances of indebtedness. The section
in the *History* dealing with the *Legend of St. Francis* and
Mystic Representations[41] was, in my opinion, the germinal
starting point for Adams's chapter on the "Mystics," especially St. Francis. And in his last chapter, "Saint Thomas

Aquinas," we see an elaboration on Michelet's meager section[42] entitled "Saint Thomas." There are telltale instances that illustrate Adams's close reading of his source and his opulent and generous treatment of the material found there. With regard to a scholastic dispute, Michelet simply says "Saint Thomas noted down in his memory the whole discussion, and wrote an account of it."[43] In Adams we find:

Perhaps Thomas's success was partly due to his memory which is said to have been phenomenal; for, in an age when cyclopaedias were unknown, a cyclopaedic memory must have counted for half the battle in these scholastic disputes where authority could be met by authority; but in this case, memory was supported by mind.[44]

"In the schools," Michelet continues, "he [Thomas] was called by his companions the large mute ox of Sicily."[45] And Adams: "Outwardly Thomas was heavy and slow in manner, if it is true that his companions called him 'the big dumb ox of Sicily.' "[46]

Both writers in seeking to communicate to the modern reader the spirit of the poetry and the architecture of the Middle Ages, bemoan in an "O tempora!" manner the imperviousness of our age to underlying meanings and meaningful implications. "Gross-minded men," writes Michelet, "who look upon these stones as stones, and do not feel the sap and life-blood which circulate there!"[47] And Adams, after him: "Our age has lost much of its ear for poetry, as it has its eye for colour and line, and its taste for war and worship, wine and women."[48]

Both writers take, in a similarly personal way, the aesthetic attitude toward religious ritual, so characteristic of the romantic's approach to religious practice. Michelet declares:

Here exists a something great and eternal, whatever be the fate of this or that religion. The future fate of Christianity makes no difference here. Let it henceforward be religion or philosophy, let it pass from mysticism to rationalism, the victory of human morality must ever be adorned in these monuments. Not in vain were Christ's words—"Let these stones become bread." The stone became bread; the bread became God, matter, spirit—the day on which the great sacrifice honored, justified, transfigured, transubstantiated them: incarnation, passion, synonymous words, are explained by a third-transubstantiation. By three different stages, here is the struggle, the hymen, the identification of the two substances: a dramatic and dolorous sacrifice; *the death*, a *voluntary death*.[49]

Adams remarks:

Not one man in a hundred thousand could now feel what the eleventh century felt in these verses of the "Chanson," and there is no reason for trying to do so, but there is a certain use in trying for once to understand not so much the feeling as the meaning. The naïveté of the poetry is that of society. God the Father was the feudal seigneur, who raised Lazarus—his baron or vassal from the grave, and freed Daniel, as an evidence of his power and loyalty; a seigneur who never lied, or was false to his word. God the Father, as feudal seigneur, absorbs the Trinity, and, what is more significant, absorbs or excludes also the Virgin, who is not mentioned in the prayer. To this seigneur, Roland in dying, proffered (puroffrit) his right-hand gauntlet. *Death was an act of homage*.[50]

With characteristic romanticism,[51] both responded aesthetically to the form of church ritual in its verbal and architectural phases.

While there are no passages in the *Mont-Saint-Michel* which are definitely parallel to the section in the *History* entitled "Gothic Ecclesiastical Architecture,"[52] there are references in common to Caumont's works on medieval architecture and to Turpin's Romance of Charlemagne; yet one overhears, generally at least, faint echoes of Michelet in Adams. Sometimes they concur in a common source;

for example, in their treatment of Saint Louis, both writers lean considerably on Joinville.[53]

In their manner and method of recreating the past Michelet and Adams have much in common. Both "Germanized" and had their period of apprenticeship to the German school of historiography; Hegel and some of the other classic German historians served as background for both writers. For both, science was a mode of aesthetic contemplation; for both, the writing of history was intimately bound up with literary and philosophic predilections. In the welter of multiplicity, both sought unity and seemed to find it in the Middle Ages. And just as Michelet wandered in the solitary galleries of the Record Office for twenty years in search of his image of the past, so summer after summer, year after year Adams lingered in the shadow of Chartres in quest of his. Strange how fiction can stimulate and beget a realistic quest and that Walter Scott should have been the source or at least one of the chief sources of that stimulation in both these men who sought to write history, not romance.[54] In both Michelet and Adams, science and imagination are the twin vehicles of creation. Both are motivated by an imperious need for uncovering the facts and for exploring the beautiful and the heroic in the remote past. If with Michelet the *History of the Middle Ages* was merely an introduction to his work on the French Revolution, with Adams his *Mont-Saint-Michel and Chartres* was an introduction to his *Education*.

Long before Adams and Michelet, Sismondi had declared: "L'étude des faits sans philosophie ne seroit pas moins decevante que celle de la philosophie sans fait."[55] Both had an indispensable need for philosophizing. In both, philosophy was tinged with fatalism: in Michelet it expressed itself in the picture of humanity pitted in a struggle against the fatalities of Nature; in Adams it took the form of a runningdown Universe, or entropy.[56]

The romanticism of Michelet has often been discussed— by Michelet himself and by his commentators. Edmund Wilson quotes Michelet as remarking about romanticism that "It is a disease in the air we breathe. He is lucky who has equipped himself early with enough good sense and natural feeling to react against it."[57] And Gabriel Monod, a disciple of Michelet's says: "Ce n'est pas par entraînement romantique que Michelet a écrit l'Histoire du moyen âge; c'est pour exécuter le plan d'histoire philosophique qu'il avait conçu."[58] Michelet himself admits that "we are all more or less romantics." We can best understand his remark in terms of the very laws of romantic irony, which made the members of the renowned movement inveigh frequently against the current of which they were so much a part. This was true of Heine, Musset, and Baudelaire. Michelet may have disapproved of romantic fiction posing as history; but the cast of his imagination—and this goes for Adams— lent the color and movement of fiction to the history he was recreating.[59] The realism of the romantic imagination is, in the last analysis, the most important facet of its untiring effort to transcend the world of illusions. Both Adams and Michelet are parts of the literary movement in which we find the great masters of nineteenth century historiography[60] —Thierry, Barante, Guizot, Mignet, Thiers. Implicit in romanticism is the idea that the recollection of the past, in spite of its chronicle-aspects (presumably, matters of fact), is essentially an aesthetic process. The historian *selects* the facts in reconstructing the past; i.e., he arranges, he composes his materials. His arrangement, his composition is conditioned by the quality of his imagination which, willy-nilly, infuses into the facts the image he has of that which he is reconstructing. That image then colors the facts and creates for us, who read history, the appeal to our own imagination. Through the enticements of the historian, we are led to contemplate the past aesthetically. It is this process which creates our fascination for *Mont-Saint-Michel and Chartres* and links Adams to Michelet, both having started with an appreciation for the exact manipulation of facts according to *la méthode venue d'Allemagne*.

Subsequent to his first visit to France, in the summer of 1860, that country had become Adams's second home— and this in spite of his strictures against France, in and out of temper. Certainly his interest in the Middle Ages reached its maturity there through his close observation of the Norman Churches in 1895. It was then that his vacillations about France ended. The man who some thirty years earlier had "imposed Germany on his scholars with a heavy hand,"[61] now turned, in the making of a work of imaginative as well as historical reconstruction, to a French romantic historian for illumination. "Et pour la première fois," says Le Breton, "en comprenant le moyen âge, Henri Adams comprit la France. Il revint transformé de son excursion en Normandie."[62] But Adams received his first impulse towards that music which was now rising within him (that of *Mont-Saint-Michel*) from his reading of Michelet's *Histoire de France*. In 1900 Adams includes this historian in a nostalgic reference to that "history, as we boys understood it, in the days of Macaulay, Mommsen, Michelet."[63] Only a few years after this he was to write the name of Michelet into his own image of the Middle Ages.

But, when one keeps in mind that Adams tried to orient his thought to the thinking of his time, one must turn to another historian, namely, Renan, whose character he paralleled in many respects.[64]

In the Tracks of Renan

In the spring of 1858, as Adams was nearing graduation from Harvard, he probably read Renan's review of Cousin's *Fragments et souvenirs* in the *Revue des deux mondes*. In the autumn of that year, while in Germany, Adams read— staying up all night to do so—the *Letters* of Alexander von Humboldt,[65] whose *Cosmos*[66] back in 1848, had such a great influence on Renan.[67] Soon (in the 1860s) young Adams was to move in the brilliant circles of London where he overheard a good deal of the buzzing attendant upon Renan and his *Life of Christ*. Henry read Sainte-Beuve's articles on Renan in the *Nouveaux lundis*,[68] which were presently translated.

Not long after Adams had embarked upon his career of teaching medieval history at Harvard, John Fiske took up the cudgels for the French historian, who (in February, 1871) was not only exposed to actual bombardment in Paris, but was equally open to a bombardment of American criticism. Since Fiske was still lecturing at Harvard, Adams surely knew of his ideas at first hand, and may even have discussed with him American reaction to Renan.

At this point, one is tempted to reflect for a moment on the contrast in the lives of the two men with whom we are concerned. While projectiles were falling over Renan's roof, forcing him to flee to Sèvres where he tried to forget the present by turning to the past, Adams was discoursing, "with a regularity which was beautiful to see," on "the true principles of mediaeval history" to some fifty undergraduates.[69] Out of the chaos which Renan knew, and tried to escape, came his *Dialogues philosophiques*. To "shoot order through chaos" was an artistic ideal which Adams realized only twenty years later. For the present, the siege of Paris caused him, as editor of the *North American Review*, to order an article dealing with that event from his friend Gaskell.

When Adams encountered Mommsen in 1872, at Bancroft's house in Berlin, he beheld in him a person whose relationship with Renan had caused a variety of comment bordering in some instances on maliciousness. In protest against certain misstatements made by a Mr. Young, Renan wrote to the editor of the *Journal de Lyon* and spoke of the German historian as le "savant illustre qui s'est voué à l'exploration critique de l'antiquité avec tant de largeur et de desintéressement."[70] Renan has a reference to Mommsen in *Les Apôtres* and Adams could easily have seen it in his 1866 edition of that work. Whether or not Renan and Adams were of one mind on Mommsen, they certainly had a common view of Macaulay, namely, that it was hard for him to understand contraries.[71] Of George Eliot both had a high opinion. But, whereas the Frenchman referred to her "haute philosophie de l'âme qui n'a ni race, ni nationalité,"[72] the American half facetiously remarked that it made him miserable to see "that wicked woman, George Eliot, scratch and claw her poor heroines with a cruelty as fiendish as Mrs. What's-her-name tortured her apprentices with."[73]

The next person who preoccupied the minds of both historians was none other than Gibbon. If, as has been said, the reading of Gibbon might facilitate one's understanding of Renan,[74] it is equally true that such reading would help one to understand Adams. We find references to the author of the *Decline and Fall* in both Adams and Renan. A kind of historic humor inheres in the fact that these three infidels (from the point of view of the church) dealt in varying degrees of passion with the historic and aesthetic reconstruction of the church. A continuity of thinking and feeling is supplied by the autobiographical writings of these three men. They all manage, with great artistic cunning, to weave the yearning ego into the fabric of history, so that historic fact becomes charged with psychologic nuances reflecting the various facets of the modern ego, from 1760 through at least 1860; from the time "when the idea of writing the *Decline and Fall* of the city first started to the mind of Gibbon" [75] to that when the figures of Jesus and Paul were to cast off their dust and ghostliness and rise living again fresh from the mind of Renan; and when another historian-to-be, a young wandering American student, was to seek, at sunset in his weariness, rest "on the steps of the Church of Santa Maria di Ara Coeli." [76] The American student of 1860 who repeated the famous words of Gibbon, "in the close of the evening as I sat musing in the Church of the Zoccolanti or Franciscan Friars, while they were singing Vespers in the Temple of Jupiter, on the ruins of the Capitol," [77] is one in spirit with the French student of 1849-50, who, most likely having the same words in his mind, wrote: "cette curieuse église de l'Ara Coeli est, jusqu'à la dernière pierre, composée des débris du temple de Jupiter Capitolin." [78]

If, as an already famous historian, Adams "never tired of quoting the supreme phrase of his idol Gibbon, before the Gothic Cathedrals: 'I darted a contemptuous look on the stately monuments of superstition,' " [79] he was not the first. From Rome, on February 7, 1850, Renan wrote to Adolphe Garnier: "Rome, Monsieur, exerce sur moi une attraction, toute particulière . . . Je vous avoue qu'à beaucoup d'égards je suis tenté de relever la thèse de Gibbon, la réhabilitation du paganisme, contre la religion qui l'a remplacé." [80]

Naturally, both historians had enough humor with which to meet humor. "Ah! que n'étiez vous hier et aujourd'hui avec moi," Renan writes to Berthelot, "à l'Ara Coeli, à voir cette foule naïve, toute ébahie devant la Madonna et il Bambino!" [81] He too, like Adams, would

have paid largely for a photograph of the fat little historian, on the background of Notre Dame of Amiens, trying to persuade his readers—perhaps himself—that he was darting a contemptuous look on the stately monument for which he felt in fact the respect every man of his vast study and active mind always feels before objects worthy of it.[82]

If Gibbon appealed to Adams as belonging to the line of those rigorous thinkers who saw "thought as one continuous Force without Race, Sex, School, Country, or Church,"[83] he must have appealed to Renan, as well as to other French historians of the nineteenth century, *because* he sought "a scale for the whole," or, as Adams would further have said, "a line of force." That scale becomes in the *Vie de Jésus* the "marche organique" of which its author spoke in a letter to Berthelot;[84] and the recognition of this scale may have provided the first impulse for the subsuming of the Middle Ages in one moving image as we find it for all time in the pages of *Mont-Saint-Michel and Chartres*.

Adams's reading of George Eliot,[85] Meredith, Arnold, and John Addington Symonds, all of whom were imbued with the scientific spirit, helped to center his attention on Renan. Both Eliot and Meredith [86] had the same enthusiastic things to say about *La Vie de Jésus* in the year of its appearance. Like Arnold, Adams had "a deep sense of affinity" with Renan.[87] Indeed, it is not at all impossible that a good deal of Adams's reading in French Literature (Sénancour, Sainte-Beuve, George Sand, the Guérins, Amiel, Rémusat, and Renan) [88] may first have suggested itself to him in the pages of *Essays in Criticism*,[89] or such of Arnold's poems as *Saint Brandon* and *Paladium*.[90] In a number of instances Adams echoes Arnold with those ideas which were inspired by Renan.

In 1848 Arnold was impressed by the "idea-moved masses" of France in contrast to the "insensible masses" of England and the "intolerable LAIDEUR of the well-fed American masses." [91] Later, when the metamorphosis of this idea came to be expressed in *Culture and Anarchy*, he leaned heavily on Renan, who hoped that "general intelligence might spread . . . attention to the reason of things." [92] Thus Arnold hoped to free England from the danger of "intellectual mediocrity." Adams, fretting over the rarity of honest minds in Anglo-German-American thought, considered Arnold's "the most honest" mind he had met.[93] In talking of the majority of society, Adams remarks, "and we know pretty well what intellectual stage that is. . . . We started to straddle an upper-middle-class. Matt Arnold and others told us what that was." [94] Adams definitely places Renan among the "others." [95] Indeed, Renan quotes Amiel [96] as saying: "L'ère de la médiocrité en toute chose commence." Abhorrence of cultural *philistinism*, then, is a theme common to Adams, Arnold, and Renan. That we are all "Eddying at large in blind uncertainty" (Arnold) is a thought expressed in Renan's famous Apostrophe to the "Abîme" in his *Prière sur l'Acropole*, a prose-poem which Adams orchestrated in verse of his own making.

It is interesting, for the sake of the record, to add here the case of John Addington Symonds who, in his intellectual development (towards the end of the third quarter of the nineteenth century), followed in so many respects the path of Henry Adams. Both had countenanced scientific pantheism and stoical morality; both read Seeley's "Ecce Homo"; both were Comtists, and both were attracted by Renan's "seductive portrait of 'le Doux Gallilien.' " Only Symonds recognized in it "a survival of the old religious sentiment denuded of dogma replaced by means of scholarship and romantic emotion upon a treacherous ground of poetical sympathy." While Symonds did not wish to deny "the respectability of such efforts to modulate from the old to the new," he did not feel that he should "be saved by any of these palliatives," that is, by Seeley's religion of humanity, Comte's worship of the "Être-Suprème" and Renan's pure or poetic religion.

Having lost the consolations of faith in redemption through Christ, . . . I had gained in exchange this, that I could
                    Lay myself upon the knees
      of Doom and take mine everlasting ease.[97]

He sought this "ease" in the Alps and in loneliness. Adams sought redemption, too, in quietism and a *Doom* which called for profound understanding,—the law of Entropy. That was his way of laying himself "upon the knees of Doom." Adams, however, partook more of Renan's sense of humor; this helped him to confront humanity's failure as a form of tragedy.

When Adams first began to read Renan's work seriously,[98] a change had taken place in the scholarly world, which accounts perhaps, for his turning from German scholarship to French. Sir Frederick Pollock, who knew Renan and German scholarship, and also knew Adams through the late Justic Holmes, wrote this shortly after Renan's funeral:

He lived to see a great and beneficent change. . . . It is now the young French scholars who are large-minded, full of scientific zeal, versed in foreign tongues, eager for wide induction and comparison. While too many Germans are resting in the generalities of their predecessors, a solid array of Frenchmen, lucid as Frenchmen always have been, patient as Germans used to be,—are building up historical and political science. While the men of steel and explosives at the Canet work-shops are developing unheard-of muzzle velocities, with new quick-firing guns, the men of books are preparing a nobler revenge, and, unless the Germans look shrewdly to themselves, will accomplish it before the century's end: may it be the only one that comes in our time or our children's.[99]

In a letter which he wrote in 1903,[100] the very year when
he completed his manuscript of *Mont-Saint-Michel and
Chartres*,[101] Adams speaks of Morley's portrayal of Gladstone as follows:

As a parallel character [for Gladstone], one should study the *Life of
Renan*. Both men were trying to do the same thing,—orient their
minds to the mind of their time. Both started from the thirteenth
century, and neither got to the twentieth; but, of the two, I very
strongly suspect that Morley has more real sympathy with Renan
and his honest failure. He at least saw something besides himself.
He saw that he could not see.

It is remarkable to what extent Adams's observation, in this
passage, holds true if we substitute his own name for that of
Gladstone.

In 1904 the *Mont-Saint-Michel* came out in its prime
format, and it is there that Renan is first mentioned by
Adams in print. After a prefatory remark to the effect that
Renan "is the highest authority," Adams quotes the follow-
ing passage, which he translates from the 1866 edition of
Averroès et l'Averroïsme: [102]

One of the most singular phenomena of the literary history of the
Middle Ages is the activity of the intellectual commerce and the
rapidity with which books were spread from one end of Europe to
the other. . . . The philosophy of Abélard during his lifetime
(1102–42) had penetrated to the ends of Italy. The French poetry
of the trouvères counted within less than a century translations into
German, Swedish, Norwegian, Icelandic, Flemish, Dutch, Bohe-
mian, Italian, Spanish. . . . Such or such a work, composed in
Morocco or in Cairo, was known at Paris and Cologne in less time
than it would need in our days for a German book of capital importance to pass the Rhine.[103]

Adams adds:

and Renan wrote this in 1852 when German books of capital importance were revolutionizing the literary world. . . . The mer-
cantile exchanges which surprised Renan, and which have puzzled

historians, were in ideas. The twelfth century was as greedy for them in one shape as the nineteenth in another. France paid for them dearly, and repented for centuries: but what creates surprise to the point of incredulity is her hunger for them, the youthful gluttony with which she devoured them, the infallible taste with which she dressed them out.[104]

In his reading of *Averroès et l'Averroïsme* Adams came upon Hauréau whom he used as one of the authorities in his *Mont-Saint-Michel and Chartres*. He found a clue in this sentence: "On verra surtout de quelle utilité m'ont été les belles recherches de M. Hauréau sur la philosophie scolastique." [105] There are only two specific references in the *Mont-Saint-Michel* [106] to Hauréau's *De la philosophie scolastique*.[107] But Adams used this authority generally throughout his book whenever he dealt with scholastic philosophy. In his chapter on Saint Thomas Aquinas [108] and in Renan's discussion of Aristotle and Ibn Roschd (namely, Averroes) [109] the two historians are both following Hauréau, though in one or two instances Adams seems to have an eye on Renan's use of the common source.[110] Renan claims that as philosopher Saint Thomas owes nearly all to Averroes, in adapting the latter's *Commentary* on Aristotle as a form of philosophic expression.[111]

In discussing the scholastic principle of the *individualization of the soul*,[112] one can especially witness how Adams allows himself to be guided by Renan in the use of such sources as Hauréau's *Philosophie scolastique* and Jourdain's *Philosophie de Saint-Thomas*.[113] Adams labors at length the problem of Thomas's doctrine of matter and form and the Saint's vehement opposition to "the idea that intellect was one and the same for all men, differing only with the quantity of matter it accompanied." [114] But all of it is contained in two statements by Renan in which he has recourse to Jourdain and Hauréau: "C'est surtout contre la théorie de l'unité de l'intellect que Saint Thomas déploie toutes les resources de sa dialectique. Pour Averroès, le principe d'individuation est la forme; pour Saint Thomas, c'est la matière." [115]

In the presence of the ideal, logic is helpless; and both Adams and Renan agree that it must not be opposed to the ideal. The Virgin and Saint Francis, Adams maintained, "were human ideals too intensely realized to be resisted merely because they were illogical." [116] And Renan exclaimed, "Qui de nous, pygmées que nous sommes, pourrait faire ce qu'ont fait l'extravagant François d'Assise, l'hystérique Sainte Thérèse?" If such natures pass our ordinary understanding, we had better be humble. "Inclinons-nous devant ces demi-dieux. Ils surent ce que nous ignorons: créer, affirmer, agir." [117] Almost antiphonally, Adams remarked, "Until mankind finally settles to a certainty where it means to go, or whether it means to go anywhere, . . . Saint Francis may still prove to have been its ultimate expression." [118]

On the history of the Church itself and of its two principal figures (next to that of Christ) Adams follows Renan's *Saint Paul.* "L'établissement du Christianisme ne s'expliquerait pas sans les synagogues. . . . Les rapports des synagogues de Rome avec Jérusalem étaient continuels." [119] These two sentences are summed up in Adams's clipped manner: "The synagogue is stronger than the Church, but even the Church is Jew." [120]

L'Idée que Paul était l'apôtre des gentils, et Pierre l'apôtre de la circoncision, était des plus acceptées; conformément à cette idée, Pierre allait évangélisant les juifs dans toute la Syrie.[121]

Describing the central window at Chartres, Adams says:

Saint Peter and Saint Paul are in their proper place as the two great ministers of the throne who represent the two great parties in western religion, the Jewish and the Gentile.[122]

Renan adds: "L'apôtre des juifs et l'apôtre des gentils s'aimaient." [123]

The question of miracles is regarded by both historians in a purely psychologic light; not as something to prove or refute, but merely as something to be recorded. However, Renan feels that some explanation is needed: "La condition du miracle, c'est la crédulité du témoin." [124] Elsewhere he remarks: "Le monde était affolé de miracles." [125] Adams, too, finds that the twelfth and thirteenth centuries "might almost be said to have contracted a miracle habit, as morbid as any other form of artificial stimulant." Like children, they had "an attitude of gaping wonder." [126] It is the business of the historian to communicate this wonder to future generations.

L'historien, lui ne vise qu'à raconter. Des faits matériellement faux [as in poetry, for example], des documents même apocryphes ont pour lui une valeur, car ils peignent l'âme, *et sont souvent plus vrais que la sèche vérité.*[127]

Adams echoes this: "For us the poetry is history, and the facts are false." [128]

Why do we cling to Christianity? Because it is our invention. Renan's expression of this idea apparently appealed to Adams, as his sublineation of it in his copy of *Feuilles détachées* indicates.

Tout ce qu'il y a de meilleur dans le Christianisme, nous l'y avons mis, . . . et voilà pourquoi il ne faut pas le détruire. Le Christianisme, en un sens, est bien notre oeuvre, et, en y cherchant la trace de nos sentiments les plus intimes, Havet[129] *ne cherchait pas une chimère.*[130]

Indeed, the scorings in this work enable us to follow not only Adams's interest in Renan but their common interests:

the origins of Christianity, Pascal's *Pensées*, Amiel's *Diary*, the foundations of religious and philosophic belief.

Renan's answer to Amiel's charge that he (Renan) took religion with a smile or even with irony [131] seemed to please Adams, judging from what he underlined. It was so much in accord with the reply he would have given:

Eh bien! en cela je crois être assez philosophe. Une complète obscurité, providentielle peut être, nous cache les fins morales de l'univers. Sur cette matière, on parie; on tire à la courte paille; en réalité on ne sait rien. *Notre gageure à nous, notre real acierto à la façon espagnole, c'est que l'inspiration intérieure qui nous fait affirmer le devoir est une sorte d'oracle, une voix infaillible, venant du dehors et correspondant à une réalité objective. Nous mettons notre noblesse en cette affirmation obstinée; nous faisons bien: il faut y tenir, même contre l'évidence. Mais il y a presque autant de chances pour que tout le contraire soit vrai. Il se peut que ces voix intérieures proviennent d'illusions honnêtes, entretenues par l'habitude et que le monde ne soit qu'une amusante féérie dont aucun dieu ne se soucie. Il faut donc nous arranger de manière que, dans les deux hypothèses, nous n'ayons pas eu complètement tort. Il faut écouter les voix supérieures mais de façon que dans le cas où la seconde hypothèse serait la vraie, nous n'ayons pas été trop dupes. Si le monde, en effet, n'est pas chose sérieuse ce sont les gens dogmatiques qui auront été frivoles, et les gens du monde, ceux que les théologues traitent d'étourdis, qui auront été les vrais sages.*[132]

In giving Amiel such an answer, both Adams and Renan glimpsed Pascal's *"il faut parier"* [133] as one of the chief characteristics of nineteenth century enlightenment. It was this enlightenment that brought back Pascal's *Pensées* in a new psychologic context: a dualism sprung of the conflict between religion and science expressed in a tonality of literary skepticism, using the comic spirit as the main vehicle of its expression. Both Adams and Renan were great masters of its use, though the former was under some obligation to the latter in the mastery of it, as the scorings indicate.

Renan regarded Amiel as the victim of an aggravated

introspectivism. He contrasted his introverted mind and his subjective skepticism with the extraverted mind of a man like Hugo who, according to Renan, never had time to look at himself.[134] This egoism—"source de nos tristesses"[135] —was also responsible for Amiel's artistic impotence in the face of an impossible perfectionism which he sought.[136]

On n'est pas homme de lettres sans quelque défaut. *L'homme parfait comme le rêve Amiel n'aurait pas de talent: le talent est un léger vice, dont un saint doit avant tout se corriger.*[137]

To both Renan and Adams, Amiel was an example of aggravated introspection, a modern disease that gained dominance in the nineteenth century.[138] Renan refers to it as "ce mal étrange, cette étude inquiète de soi-même."[139] To Adams "no tragedy [is] so heartrending as introspection."[140] Were Adams and Renan free of this *mal du siècle*?

Eagerly Adams followed Renan's *Examen de conscience philosophique*.[141] But here he thought that it was high time to turn the smile of skepticism and literary banter on the Skeptic himself. We must first quote the passage which provokes Adams's argumentative remark. Says Renan:

Il n'est donc pas impossible qu'en dehors de l'univers que nous connaissons (fini ou infini, n'importe) il y ait un infini d'un autre ordre, pour lequel notre univers ne soit qu'un atome. Cet infini, qui pour nous serait Dieu[142] peut ne se révéler qu'à des intervalles selon nous extrêmement longs, insignifiants au sein de l'absolu. A ce point de vue, l'existence d'un Dieu aux volontés particulières, qui n'apparaît pas dans notre univers, peut être tenue pour possible au sein de l'infini, ou du moins il est *aussi téméraire de la nier que de l'affirmer.*[143]

Following this text, in the blank space, is this forensic note by Adams: "By parity of reasoning that God must imply an infinity of infinities (Gods) which returns to the equivalent of no Gods at all."

Likewise does Adams's comic spirit pursue Renan [144] in his affirmation of the relationship between morality in a race and its scientific productivity. He underscores the following:

Nous aimons l'humanité, parce qu'elle produit la Science; nous tenons à la moralité, parce que des races honnêtes peuvent seules être des races scientifiques.[145]

In the left margin opposite this sentence, Adams placed a question mark. This interrogation point carries with it the smile of Voltaire when he asked whether God's goodness revealed itself in the Lisbon earthquake. And we can see in it, too, a terrific judgment of *our* credulity. . . . Yet we cling withal to an ideal of objectivity in history.

To the extent that Adams and Renan strove for historical objectivity, they were direct followers of Ranke; but the moment they yielded to relativism [146]—the idea that each age recreates the past in its own image—they were apt followers of him who framed the now famous relativistic apothegm: "The world is my idea." [147] That Renan had been reading Schopenhauer before 1876 we know from a letter he wrote to Ritter.[148] And in one sentence Adams gives us the history of his own thought which was partly rooted in that of the famous Pessimist:

Throughout all the thought of Germany, France and England,— for there is no thought in America,—runs a growing stream of pessimism which comes in continuous current from Malthus and Karl Marx and Schopenhauer *in our youth* [italics added], and which we taught then, but which is openly preached now on all sides.[149]

Renan parts company with Schopenhauer in the former's belief in human progress and the role that the development of science plays in it. Indeed, the universe itself is not something finite but depends, somehow, for its development on the apocalyptic power of science.[150] In this the Frenchman was more consequent in his logic than the German, as Nordau has shown.[151] Renan tied up the universe with humanity where progress can be observed (since it has its origin in the human mind) and thus obviated the necessity of considering the picture of an eternally fixed world where no progress is possible. Schopenhauer, who began by centering the universe in man's creative mind, forgot his starting point when he argued the falsity of the theory of progress on the ground that the world is eternal and fixed. But what about humanity which (as Nordau says) does not share its eternity? [152] Notwithstanding the vagaries of his temperament, which caused him to side at times with Schopenhauer, Adams agreed with Renan; for, as a follower of Lyell, Buckle and Darwin, he, too, was bound to believe in human progress. Science, Adams hoped—unless "science itself would admit its own failure"— would ultimately bring man, "the most important of all its subjects," within its range.[153] The pessimistic note was a mannerism to which he returned even late in life, as we shall see presently.

Both Renan and Adams regretted their failure to acquire training in science in their youth.[154] Without rejecting metaphysics,[155] they regarded highly the experimental method of science, and both turned to evolution for the light it threw on the development of the Cosmos, the human mind, and language as well as history, which tries to chronicle and clarify these developments in one consistent form. Renan's evolutionism antedates the *Origin of Species;* he defined it for himself as early as 1848, at which time he considered Herder, Cousin, and Michelet as his masters, and Berthelot as his guiding friend in matters scientific. "J'étais évolutionniste décidé en tout ce qui concerne les produits de l'humanité, langues, écritures, littératures, législations, formes sociales." [156] And two years later, in making clear what he meant by history, he definitely linked it with the evolutionary process.[157]

If history, which had gained so much from the inductive sciences, was to advance further, it would be on the basis of a dispassionate penetration of zoologic morphology— "étudié avec plus de philosophie, avec l'oeil pénétrant d'un Geoffroy Saint-Hilaire, d'un Goethe, d'un Cuvier non tourmenté de la manie d'être officiel." [158] Again: "Si les sciences historiques laissaient le public aussi calme que la chimie, elles seraient bien plus avancées." [159] Renan cites the names of Lyell and Darwin and goes on to express the idea that the sciences combined will help to pierce the obscurity that envelops the history of the period during which man came into being on this planet. But what is the planet? The solar system itself is only a point of space. The nebulae are the documents of the history of the sun. Ultimately we have the mechanics of the pure atom, freed from chemical quality. And here the mind loses itself in the "antinomies" of Kant, the mathematics of the infinite, the necessity for supposing a beginning to the universe and the impossibility of admitting it. But mathematics, dealing only with symbols (not implying any reality), would be true even if nothing existed.[160] Now, Renan and Adams look towards the Bergsonian *élan vital*, away from Cartesian mechanism, and thus envision a science that would act as a nexus between physical and spiritual energy. For Renan, Science becomes the methodologic approach to the Apocalypse; for Adams, it is the means of a grand, all-inclusive generalization. It is quite clear that both historians—the one associating with men like Berthelot and Claude Bernard, the other with Gibbs and Raphael Pumpelly, and both at home in the main stream of nineteenth-century scientific thought—"felt that they stood on the brink of a generalization"[161] that would make of history a sort of over-all science." Nothing in the history of philosophy is more distinctly marked than the effort of physics and metaphysics, since 1890, to approach each other." [162] Renan died only two years after these words were written, but already in his letter to Berthelot (cited above) we are made to realize that he was fully aware of this effort. The tone and manner of both writers are strikingly similar at times in spite of the difference in linguistic medium. The passages that follow will illustrate this similarity. We start with a passage in which Renan addresses an English audience:

Quand vous ferez le voyage, asseyez-vous là un peu [i.e. aux eaux Salviennes, *alle tre fontane*] pas trop longtemps (on y prend vite la fièvre), et, pendant que le trappiste vous donnera à boire de l'eau qui jaillit aux trois bonds que fit la tête de Paul, pensez à celui qui vint ici causer avec vous de ces légendes, et que vous voulûtes bien écouter avec tant de courtoisie et de bien-veillante attention. [163]

And now listen to Adams addressing the nieces of the world:

Some future summer, when you are older, and when I have left, like Omar, only the empty glass of my scholasticism for you to turn down, you can amuse yourselves by going on with the story after the death of Saint Louis, Saint Thomas, and William of Lorris, and after the failure of Beauvais. [164]

Both Renan and Adams had a way of dramatizing personal events with conscious art, and the dramatization of the one sometimes echoes that of the other. A case in point is Adams's lament for his beloved sister, who died of tetanus in 1870 at Bagni di Lucca. We catch in it an echo of Renan's lament for his dearly loved sister Henriette who died at Byblos in 1861. In view of the fact that death is a recurrent poetic theme, [165] it is perhaps natural that such an echo should occur. At any rate, here are the two respective expressions of sorrow.

Renan's plaintive note is struck in his dedication of the *Vie de Jésus:*

A l'âme Pure de Ma Soeur Henriette . . . Morte a Byblos, Le
24 Septembre 1861.—Te Souviens-tu du sein de Dieu ou tu re-
poses, de ces longues journées de GHAZIR, où seul avec toi, j'écri-
vais ces pages inspirées par les lieux que nous avons visités ensemble? Silencieuse à côté de moi, tu relisais chaque feuille et
la recopiais sitôt écrite, pendant que la mer, les villages, les ravins,
les montagnes se déroulaient à nos pieds. Quand l'accablante
lumière avait fait place à l'innombrable armée des étoiles, tes
questions fines et délicates, tes doutes discrets, me ramenaient
l'objet sublime de nos communes pensées. . . . Au milieu de ces
douces méditations la mort nous frappa . . . ; je me réveillai seul!
Tu dors maintenant dans la terre d'Adonis, près de la Sainte Byblos
et des eaux sacrées où les femmes des mystères antiques venaient
mêler leurs larmes. Révèle-moi, ô bon génie, à moi que tu aimais,
ces vérités qui dominent la mort, empêchent de la craindre et la
font presque aimer.

Adams did not dedicate any of his books to the sister
whom he considered to be "much brighter than he ever was"
and who "saw no gain in helping her brother to be Germanized, and . . . wanted him much to be civilized." [166]
He wove the memory of her into his *Education:*

The last lesson—the sum and term of education—began then
[when he found his sister dying of lockjaw at Bagni di Lucca]. One
had heard and read a great deal about death. . . . Death took
features altogether new to him, in these rich and sensuous surroundings. Nature enjoyed it, played with it, the horror added to
her charm, she liked the torture, and smothered her victim with
caresses. Never had one seen her so winning. The hot Italian
summer brooded outside, over the market-place and the picturesque peasants, and, in the singular color of the Tuscan atmosphere, the hills and vineyards of the Appenines seemed bursting
with mid-summer blood. The sick-room itself glowed with the
Italian joy of life; friends filled it; no harsh northern light pierced
the soft shadows; even the dying woman shared the sense of the
Italian summer, the soft, velvet air, the humor, the courage, the
sensual fullness of Nature and man. She faced death, as women
mostly do, bravely and even gaily, racked slowly to unconscious-
ness but yielding only to violence, as a soldier sabred in battle.

For many thousands of years, on these hills and plains, Nature had gone on sabring men and women with the same air of sensual pleasure.[167]

Italy, inescapably, meant Rome. And it was the "matchless fading pageant of Rome" which had a common fascination for both writers, a fascination which stemmed from their common reading of Gibbon, who "Sat musing amidst the ruins of the Capitol" where he conceived "the idea of writing the decline and fall" of Rome.[168] Both beheld the *Urbs Beata* through that romantic haze with which literary tradition had adorned it,—"a mysterious physical splendour," a "ville enchanteresse," a "Mediaeval Rome [that] was sorcery." [169]

Both sound as though they had the same guidebook in hand, as they went about Rome,

Cette curieuse église de l'Ara Coeli est, jusqu'à la dernière pierre, composée des debris du temple de Jupiter Capitolin. Ces colonnes sont celles du vieux temple, et ces colonnes, les Romains eux-mêmes les avaient enlevées du temple de Jupiter Olympien. Voilà bien les religions, n'est-ce pas? Bâtir avec des matériaux anciens des combinaisons nouvelles; piler, triturer les vieux éléments pour qu'ils sortent sous une nouvelle forme.[170]

More than once, says Adams, he was led by the famous quotation from Gibbon's *Autobiography* (see above)

to sit at sunset on the steps of the Church of Santa Maria di Ara Coeli, curiously wondering that not an inch had been gained by Gibbon—or all the historians since—towards explaining the Fall. The mystery remained unsolved; the charm remained intact. Two great experiments of Western civilization had left there the chief monuments of their failure, and nothing proved that the city might not still survive to express the failure of a third.[171]

To Adams Rome was "Like one's glass of absinthe before dinner in the Palais Royal,"; and for Renan it was an "envirement artistique." [172]

The pilgrimage led them (ten years apart) to Naples.
Italy was in a state of turmoil, the revolutionary aspect of
which was personified by Garibaldi whom Renan and Adams
had met. Each recorded his impression of the man. Renan
speaks of him with admiration as a radical in politics; the
other gives us an image of him "in the Senate House towards
sunset, at supper with his picturesque and piratic staff, in
the full noise and color of the Palermo revolution." [173] In
finding expression for their Italian journey, both were aware
of the literary tradition which stemmed from Byron's *Childe
Harold*. It is in this poem that we find the apostrophe,
"Italia! tu Italia," and in which the poet invokes the names
of Voltaire and Gibbon— "The one . . . fire and fickleness
. . . Historian, bard, philosopher, combined. . . . The
other, deep and slow, exhausting thought. . . . The lord
of irony." [174]

"There is something really weird and uncanny," says
William James, "in the contrast between the abstract pre-
tensions of rationalism and what rationalistic methods
concretely can do." [175] It was certainly weird when it became clear to both Renan and Adams—though some forty
years intervened between the respective records of that
awareness—that this contrast existed and called for resolution in their own lives.

For both, reason turned out to be a vastness like a desert
crying for rain; in that endless stretch "the mind itself [be-
came] a dissolving unit."

Le cerveau brûlé par le raisonnement a soif de simplicité, comme
le desert a soif d'eau pure. Quand la réflexion nous a mené au
dernier terme du doute, ce qu'il y a d'affirmation spontanée du
bien et du beau dans la conscience féminine nous enchante et
tranche pour nous la question. . . . La femme nous remet en
communication avec l'éternelle source où Dieu se mire. [176]

Renan spoke well here not only for himself but for his American reader, Henry Adams, who most likely read the "Prière sur l'Acropole" in the same book where the above-cited words appear.[177] Both turned in their spiritual dilemma, to woman,—or, better still, to Woman, as a symbol of the resolution of inner conflict—the true ALMA MATER. They prostrated themselves before her and prayed. We have two prayers and we can ponder them at our ease.

Renan's prayer purports to be addressed to Athena, Goddess of Reason, but actually we discover the face of the Virgin shining through, so that we are not at all surprised at the striking points of resemblance that have been pointed out between this Prière and Chateaubriand's *Itinéraire de Paris à Jérusalem*.[178] Though Renan uses a Greek symbol, the experience which he wishes it to express is nontheless closely associated with a Christian background. We have his own testimony for this: "Quand je vis l'Acropole, j'eus la révélation du divin, comme je l'avais eue, la première fois que je sentis vivre l'Évangile en apercevant la vallée du Jourdain." [179]

Renan's prayer begins with a single exordium of adulation and adoration in which the reference to the passage of time lends point to the fervor of the one prostrate before the Lady. This should be kept in mind when we encounter the same note in Adams's prayer.

O noblesse! o beauté simple et vraie! déesse dont le culte signifie raison et sagesse, . . . j'arrive tard au seuil de tes mystères. . . . Pour te trouver, il m'a fallu des recherches infinies. . . .
Je suis né, déesse aux yeux bleus, de parents barbares, chez les Cimmériens. . . . On y connaît à peine le soleil. . . .
Des prêtres d'un culte étranger, venu des Syriens de Palestine, prirent soin de m'élever. Ces prêtres étaient sages et saints. . . . Leurs temples . . . ne sont pas solides. . . . Mais ces temples me plaisent; . . . j'y trouvais Dieu. . . . On y chantait des cantiques dont je me souviens encore. . . . 'Rose mystique. . . . Étoile du matin'. . . . Tiens, déesse, quand je me rappelle ces

chants,—je deviens presque apostat . . . tu ne peux te figurer
. . . combien il m'en coûte de suivre la raison toute nue. . . .
  Et puis si tu savais combien il est devenu difficile de te servir!
Toute noblesse a disparu. Les Scythes ont conquis le monde. Il
n'y a plus de république d'hommes libres. . . . Une pambéotie
redoutable, une ligue de toutes les sottises, étend sur le monde un
couvercle de plomb, sous lequel on étouffe. . . .
  Toi seule es jeune, ô Cora; toi seule es pure, ô Vierge. . . .
Démocratie, toi dont le dogme fondamental est que tout bien vient
du peuple, et que partout où il n'y a pas de peuple pour nourrir et
inspirer le génie, il n'y a rien, apprends-nous à extraire le diamant
des foules impures. . . . Énergie de Zeus, étincelle qui allumes et
entretiens le feu chez les héros et les hommes de génie, fais de nous
des spiritualistes accomplis. . . .
  Le monde ne sera sauvé qu'en revenant à toi, en répudiant ses
attaches barbares. . . .
  Tu souris de ma naïveté. Oui, l'ennui—Nous sommes corompus:
qu'y faire? J'irai plus loin, déesse orthodoxe, je te dirai la dépravation intime de mon coeur. Raison et bon sens ne suffisent pas. Il y
a de la poésie dans le Strymon glacé et dans l'ivresse du Thrace.
Il viendra des siècles où tes disciples passeront pour les disciples de
l'ennui. Le monde est plus grand que tu ne crois. . . .
  Un immense fleuve d'oubli nous entraîne dans un gouffre sans
nom. O abîme, tu es le Dieu unique. Les larmes de tous les peuples
sont de vraies larmes; les rêves de tous les sages renferment une
part de vérité. Tout n'est ici bas que symbole et que songe. Les
dieux passent comme les hommes, et il ne serait pas bon qu'ils
fussent éternels. La foi qu'on a eue ne doit jamais être une chaîne.
On est quitte envers elle quand on l'a soigneusement roulée dans
la linceul de pourpre où dorment les dieux morts.[180]

  A simple analysis of the salient parts of this prayer reveals the following:
  1. Reason, the Goddess who is addressed, is not adored
fullheartedly. The world, says the worshiper, will be saved
by returning to reason; yet—"Raison et bon sens ne suffisent
pas. Il y a de la poésie dans le Strymon glacé et dans l'ivresse
de Thrace."
  2. A considerable part (in actual number of words) is

devoted to the praise of non-classic virtues, opposed to those symbolized by Athena. "Le monde est plus grand que tu ne crois. . . . Un immense fleuve d'oubli nous entraîne dans un gouffre sans nom. O abîme tu es le Dieu unique."

3. There is more than a hint of the worshiper's deep attachment to a creed opposed to the one built around the goddess to whom this prayer is directed. Even as he prays to Athena he is ready to become an Apostate when he recalls certain hymns of childhood: "Salut, étoile de la mer . . . 'Rose mystique' . . . Tiens, déesse quand je me rappelle ces chants, mon coeur se fond, je deviens presque apostat."

Adams's prayer is addressed directly to the Virgin at Chartres. But it, too, starts with a reference to time.

> Simple as when I asked your aid before;
> Humble as when I prayed for grace in vain
> Seven hundred years ago; weak, weary, sore
> In heart and hope, I ask your help again.

It goes on to tell the Gracious Lady, even as the Prayer to Athena does, of the worshiper's origin and early background:

> You, who remember all, remember me;
> An English scholar of a Norman name,
> I was a thousand who then crossed the sea
> To wrangle in the Paris Schools for fame.[181]

> When your Byzantine portal was still young
> I prayed there with my master Abailard;
> When Ave Maris Stella was first sung,
> I helped to sing it here with Saint Bernard.[182]

Defection set in and apology is in order:

> If then I left you, it was not my crime,
> Or if a crime, it was not mine alone.
> All children wander with the truant Time.
> Pardon me too! You pardoned once your Son![183]

The worshiper then tells how he abandoned the Mother to find the Father, and how, foiled in his search, he defiled and broke the "image on its throne" and then "dethroned the father too."

> And now we are the Father, with our brood,
>   Ruling the Infinite, not Three, but One;
> We made our world and saw that it was good;
>   Ourselves we worship, and we have no Son.
>
> Yet we have Gods, for even our strong nerve
>   Falters before the Energy we own,—
> Which shall be master? Which of us shall serve?
>   Which wears the fetters? Which shall bear the crown?
>
> Brave though we be, we dread to face the Sphinx,
>   Or answer the old riddle she still asks.
> Strong as we are, our reckless courage shrinks
>   To look beyond the piece-work of our tasks.
>
> But when we must, we pray, as in the past
>   Before the Cross on which your Son was nailed.
> Listen, dear Lady! You shall hear the last
>   Of the strange prayers Humanity has wailed.

Follows a prayer within a prayer—

Prayer to the Dynamo

> Mysterious Power! Gentle Friend!
>   Despotic Master! Tireless Force!
> You and We are near the End.
>   Either You or We must bend
> To bear the martyrs' Cross.

This apostrophe to the Dynamo, as it develops, is really an elaboration of the earlier lines:

> Yet we have Gods, for even our strong nerve
>   Falters before the Energy we own.

It is Energy that now challenges our Knowledge and our understanding:

> You come in silence, Primal Force,
>   We know not whence, or when, or why. . . .
>
> We know not whether you are kind,
>   Or cruel in your fiercer mood;
> But be you Matter, be you Mind,
> We think we know that you are blind,
>   And we alone are good.
>
> We know that prayer is thrown away,
>   For you are only force and light,
> A shifting current; night and day;
> We know this well, and yet we pray,
>   For prayer is infinite,
>
> Like you! Within the finite sphere
>   That bounds the impotence of thought,
> We search an outlet everywhere
> But only find that we are here
>   And that you are—are not!
>
> What are we then? The lords of space?
>   The master-mind whose tasks you do?
> Jockey who rides you in the race?
> Or are we atoms whirled apace,
>   Shaped and controlled by you? . . .
>
>   Answer you shall—or die!
>
> We are no beggars! What care we
>   For hopes or terrors, love or hate?
>   . . . We see
> Only our certain destiny . . .
>
> Seize, then, the Atom! rack his joints! . . .
> Grind him to nothing!—though he points
> To us, and his life-blood anoints
>   Me—the dead Atom-King! . . .

A curious prayer, dear Lady! is it not?
    Strangely unlike the prayers I prayed to you!
Stranger because you find me at this spot,
    Here, at your feet, asking your help anew.

Strangest of all, that I have ceased to strive,
    Ceased even care what new coin fate shall strike.
In truth it does not matter. Fate will give
    Some answer; and all answers are alike.

So, while we slowly rack and torture death
    And wait for what the final void will show,
Waiting I feel the energy of faith
    Not in the future science, but in you!

The man who solves the Infinite. . . .

He will forget my thought, my acts, my fame,
    As we forget the shadows of the dusk,
Or catalogue the echo of a name
    As we the scratches on the mammoth's tusk.

But when, like me, he too has trod the track
    Which leads him up to power above control,
He too will have no choice but wander back
    And sink in helpless hopelessness of soul,

Before your majesty of grace and love,
    The purity, the beauty and the faith;
The depth of tenderness beneath; above,
    The glory of the life and of the death. . . .

Help me to see! not with my mimic sight—
    With yours! which carried radiance, like the sun,
Giving the rays you saw with—light in light—
    Tying all suns and stars and worlds in one.

Help me to know! not with my mocking art—
    With you, who knew yourself unbound by laws;
Gave God your strength, your life, your sight, your heart,
    And took from him the Thought that Is—the Cause.

Help me to feel! not with my insect sense,—
   With yours that felt all life alive in you;
Infinite heart beating at your expense;
   Infinite passion breathing the breath you drew!

Help me to bear! not my own baby load,
   But yours; who bore the failure of the light,
The strength, the Knowledge and the thought of God,—
   The futile folly of the Infinite![184]

In a résumé of Adams's prayer we find:

1. The Gracious Lady must share the adoration of the worshiper with another Goddess even as is the case with Renan's Goddess (Athena).

2. The Finite is opposed to the Infinite—"The futile folly of the Infinite." This finds its counterpart in Renan's concern with the "gouffre sans nom"—"Un immense fleuve d'oubli nous entraîne dans un gouffre sans nom." Though, we must add here Renan's exclamation, in a spirit of despair: "O abîme tu es le Dieu unique."

3. The Dynamo, symbol of reason, law and energy, leaves the worshiper unsatisfied and contrite as he turns to Her, with "insect sense" and begs Her to help him "feel" and "bear," "not my own baby load, But yours." Renan, too, turns from his symbol of reason, law and energy (Athena) to cry out imploringly: "Salut, étoile de la mer . . . Rose mystique."

We have talked of two prayers. But are they actually prayers? There is nothing in the lines of either Renan or Adams to indicate a radical conversion such as gave rise in the case of Pascal to his prayer. In both instances we have rather a poetic resolution of an inner intellectual conflict which many sensitive thinkers (or thinkers who could not effect a complete divorce between their *ratio* and their *sensus,* of the advancing nineteenth century) had to contend with and which has become generalized in the history of thought as the *conflict between religion and science*.

This inner conflict called for poetic resolution as a relief from that contemporary loneliness which gripped men like Renan and Adams, who saw (and felt) the transcendent values of sensibility threatened by the immediacy of an onslaught of mechanism, and with it the general leveling process of mediocrity. The ironic image of *Homunculus* in Goethe's *Faust* is perhaps the first modern poetic protest against this growing shadow of the commonplace, cast, strangely enough, by science and the laboratory. "Was uns alle bändigt,— das Gemeine" is what Goethe cried out against; and men like Renan, Matthew Arnold, and Henry Adams echoed these words. "Our century is tending neither towards the good nor the bad; it is tending towards mediocrity. Whatever succeeds in one day is mediocre," wrote Renan in his essay on the *Paris Exhibit*.[185] "Faith in machinery is, I said, one besetting danger." [186]

The two "prayers" then are poems symbolizing resolution of a conflict inherent in the spirit of the time. Both strike the same fundamental note, prostration and contrition before a power that should have attracted each of the penitents earlier in life. In one instance this power was the Goddess Reason behind whom lurked the image of the Virgin; in the other, it was the Virgin behind whom is the presence of Reason in the form of the Dynamo. And just as in Renan's prayer to Reason there is a note of reservation to the effect that reason alone will not suffice, so in Adams's prayer to the Symbol of Love and Intuitive Power there is an intermezzo to the Symbol of Science—the Dynamo—product of the human reason. The world, says Renan, is larger than Reason; the search for the Infinite is folly, says Adams. Renan, even in the presence of Reason, turns to the "Mystic Rose"; Adams turns from the Dynamo to the Virgin. Here, they are at one; just as, in manner, when you place the two poems side by side, they appear to be one. Both might borrow Matthew Arnold's words in the end:

> Ye who from childhood up have calm'd me,
> Calm me, ah, compose me to the end!

About both there arose the legend of dying in the fold of the Catholic Church. When one compares the so-called prayers of Renan and Adams with Pascal's *Mystère de Jésus*, one comes to the realization that their prayers, compared with that of Pascal whom both read and admired, are purely aesthetic constructs. Neither was the consequence of an experience which would express itself in a Mémorial. In spirit they are closest perhaps, as prayers, to Voltaire's *Prière à Dieu*.

THE APPROACH TO TAINE

Though Adams's first written reference to Taine does not occur before 1879 [187] there is evidence to show that he knew of Taine's work possibly during his senior year at Harvard in 1858, and certainly not later than 1861.

We know that in his senior year he read Guizot's *History of Civilization in Europe*, Jouffroy's *Introduction to Ethics*, and Mill's *Logic*.[188] Later these works led him to the study of Taine, in spite of the fact that Lowell, Adams's teacher, scoffed at this critic. On April 29, 1859, Taine's *Les Philosophes français du dix-neuvième siècle* (Paris, 1857) was made available at Harvard College Library.[189] If Adams was not then familiar with that copy, he was to learn of the work two years later. In 1861 Henry Harrisse reviewed it together with Taine's *Essais de critique et d'histoire* and his *La Fontaine et ses fables* in the *North American Review*.[190]

In July, 1861, Adams could read in the *Westminster Review* the article by W. Fraser Rae which introduced Taine

to the English public. In the same magazine, some three
or four years later [191] Adams had the opportunity to read
Rae's reviews of the *Histoire de la littérature anglaise*, which
had just appeared.[192] Another magazine which Adams read,
the *Edinburgh Review*, offered at the same time an unsympa-
thetic opinion of this work.

In 1861, a year of grand resolves and great beginnings for
young Adams, he had begun the serious study of history and
of the works of Mill, who led him to examine French philosophers of the nineteenth century. They, in their turn,
passed him over to Hobbes and Spinoza. Indeed, the three
volumes of the *Oeuvres de Spinoza*, translated by Saisset,
in the Adams Collection, bear the date of 1861.

In the history of the intricate interaction of ideas, it is a
remarkable fact that Mill, to whom Taine was indebted for
the development of his own thought, should have led Henry
Adams to the domain of "the great French thinkers of our
time,"—Taine among them.[193] One must also keep in mind
the possible role of Francis T. Palgrave as an intermediary
in calling Henry's attention to Taine.[194]

In 1862 Adams was already fully in the grip of positivism,
the current of ideas having its egress from Comte and finding
its tributary expression in Littré, Taine, Mill, Lewes, *et al.*
In one of his letters for that year Henry wrote, not without
a note of prophetic and historic misgiving:

Man has mounted science, and is now run away with. I firmly
believe that before many centuries more, science will be the master
of man. The engines he will have invented will be beyond his
strength to control. Some day science may have the existence of
mankind in its power, and the human race commit suicide by
blowing up the world.[195]

At the same time, as a young blade in London, Adams had
been introduced to Swinburne whose twin gods were Shakespeare and Victor Hugo. When Taine's *Histoire de la littéra-*

ture anglaise appeared, the poet of *Atalanta in Calydon* reacted very strongly to the comparison there of Tennyson
and Musset. Although Swinburne's vitriolic essay on this
subject did not appear until much later, Adams must have
heard a good deal about it at the time.

In London, on May 16, 1866, Henry Adams met Marian
(Clover) Hooper at one of Minister Adams's dinners. A
voracious reader, with an appetite for precise knowledge in
literature and art, she (like Esther in Henry's novel by that
name) may very well have fought with him that evening
"after dinner . . . a prodigious battle over the influence of
the Aryan races on philosophy of art." [196] We have, however,
more than mere conjecture and fiction to go by. In Adams's
library we do find two works on art by Taine, *Philosophie de
l'art* and *De l'idéal dans l'art*, the one dated 1865, the other
1867; and both have inscribed on the fly leaf, in her own
hand, "Clover Hooper, 1868." Of course he read these
works which he may quite possibly have bought for her, but
was too diffident at the time to inscribe. Indeed, ten years
later (1878) when he was completing his novel *Democracy*,
he may have had Marian in mind, when he remarked of
Mrs. Lightfoot (one of the characters) that she read philosophy to save herself from ennui and that "Ruskin and
Taine had danced merrily through her mind, hand in hand
with Darwin and Stuart Mill, Gustave Droz and Algernon
Swinburne." [197]

In general, then, throughout the period that Adams was
in London as private secretary to his father, Taine's name
was so generally known in England that the eager young
student of French thought could hardly escape knowledge
of him and his work. In fact, at a dinner in 1866, when Swinburne was invited to propose a toast, the poet spoke of the
great French impress upon English letters and pointed especially to the manifestation of that influence in Matthew

Arnold, who knew and corresponded with Taine. Through
Mill, Francis Palgrave, Swinburne, and Arnold (whom he
followed rather closely) Adams was led to know the work of
Taine. Besides, from 1866 to the year when Adams assumed
his teaching post at Harvard (1870), the *Atlantic Monthly*
and the *North American Review* carried increasingly more
and more items on Taine. These, we know, he read as-
siduously.[198]

In 1870 Taine's *De l'intelligence* came out and immediately
reached interested students both in England and America.
Before that year psychology was to Henry Adams "a new
study, and a dark corner of education."[199] But the wide
use of *De l'intelligence* would indicate that Adams turned to
it himself to relieve his own darkness. He started to teach
at Harvard in 1870 and the following year his former teacher
and present colleague, Professor Bowen, used Taine's book
in his psychology courses. In 1873, the *North American
Review*, which Adams was then editing, contained a review
of the work.[200] About thirty years later, Adams was to recall:

Ever since 1870 friends by scores had fallen victim to it [to psychologic introspection] . . . Harvard College was a focus of the
study; France supported hospitals for it. . . . Nothing was easier
than to take one's mind in one's hand, and ask one's psychological
friends what they made of it.[201]

As it happened, in 1872 William James started to teach
anatomy and physiology at Harvard, and he was the psychologic friend to whom Adams turned to ask what he "made
of it." Though James was not yet teaching psychology, he
had been deeply absorbed in it ever since 1867–68 when, as
a medical student in Germany, he picked up a copy of Lotze's
Medizinische Psychologie. Adams's search for "the direction
of thought" also went back to that year. In England, at
the same time, John Stuart Mill and Herbert Spencer were
approaching the summit of their influence. With the works

of these two men, as well as with those of Maudsley, Bain, and Taine, both James and Adams were thoroughly familiar. James was therefore a likely man with whom Adams could exchange ideas and opinions on *De l'intelligence.* In 1880 James based a whole course on this work.[202] Two years earlier James had begun to write his *Principles of Psychology,* while Adams had started plans for his history and was about to complete *Democracy,* in which appears his first recorded reference to Taine.

John Fiske, Adams's erstwhile colleague, was another man from whom he might have derived a good deal of enthusiasm and interest for Taine. In February, 1870, Fiske had written an essay, "The Christ of Dogma," in which he declared (as, in fact, Renan had done before him) that the dogma of Christ's resurrection was due originally to the excited imagination of Mary Magdalene. This opinion he based on what he found in *De l'intelligence.*[203] Also, in 1872 he published his condensation of Taine's *History of English Literature,* using Van Laun's translation. In his editorial Preface Fiske speaks of the author's "brilliant speculations and lively criticisms" but goes on to criticize him for his "unnecessary lavishness in the use of words and in the citation of illustrative facts." [204] In the light of this criticism it will be interesting to see Adams's remark, written as a marginal note over one of the chapters in his copy of Taine's *Origines de la France contemporaine.* To men like Fiske and Adams, groping for a philosophy of history, Taine's concern with the relationship between philosophy and science was a source of stimulation and enlightenment.

After the fevers and chills of the French Revolution, with its makeshift philosophy of sensualism, which was really less a mode of thought than of action, came the French variety of the Scottish commonsense school,[205] through the agency of Royer-Collard. This school of individualistic reason, which furnished the dominant ideas during the first half of the nineteenth century both in England and America, was given by Royer-Collard a Kantian and therefore transcendental orientation, with its emphasis on the universality of the mind.

One of the assumptions in French philosophy which grew out of this idealism, was, as Mead has indicated, that the philosophical method is essentially a psychological method. The study of self, of the mind, is, then, a study of the world and of nature.[206] Closely linked with this was a preoccupation with history.

The question of the relationship between philosophy and science was steadily coming to the fore at this time. The drive towards unity, towards the conception of the world as a whole, brought with it the concern with *organic* relationships among the sciences; and likewise between the sciences and the over-all picture of them which we may call philosophy. At the heart of all this was the problem of scientific method. This, in turn, brought about a shift from *things* to *events* as objects of observation. The great gain from positivism was the procedure of stating problems in terms of scientific method rather than in terms of results. But the chief contribution of Comte was the recognition that society is an organism which can be made the object of scientific study, and that we must advance to the study of the individual through society rather than vice versa. Now since French philosophy was dominantly psychological, with the emphasis on the individual, it was necessary for Comte, in the interest of his own viewpoint, to reduce psychology to biology and even to deny the possibility of a science of psychology.

With Taine, too, the history of philosophy was soon to become the philosophy of history, and the method of natural history was to be applied to the history of thought. The

philosophy of Hegel attracted him because it identified being
with thought; but this linkage or "enchaînement universel"
he had already encountered before at the age of nineteen,
in Descartes's "les chaînes de la raison." [207] According to
both Fouillée [208] and Boutroux, [209] Taine properly belongs
to the history of the idealistic movement, at least in the new
orientation he gave to positivism.

In their respective attempts to link the moral and physical
sciences, both Adams and Taine appear to have been almost
obstinate followers of Spinoza, whatever part their Hegel-
ianism had in this effort. In our opinion, Giraud shows great
acuity when he remarks that the Spinozistic notion of the
material universe as a double and translation of the moral
world appealed to Taine not only as an explanation of the
universe but also as an explanation of his own nature—of
the little world within him. [210] The *Education of Henry
Adams* is ample proof that this idea exercised an equally
compelling force upon the American, and for like reason.

Here then, we have two modern figures who, in setting
out to explore the universe, really did so in order to discover
their own nature. In this we have their great likeness. Those
who criticize Taine and Adams for confusing literature with
science fail to see what impulse drove them to seek a coales-
cence of the humanistic and the scientific fields of knowledge.
Following in Spinoza's tracks, they sought a world view
which only the unity of knowledge could yield. In this
search they were in the vanguard. The progressive rapprochement of the physical and biological sciences itself
indicated an historic tendency in the direction of proposing
man's nature as a central problem in the universe. Here
again we see Taine and Adams driven instinctively in the
direction of that impulse.

With the onsweep of this current the separation between
imagination and science fades. [211] The historian of belles-

lettres is now a scientist like Taine who tries to grasp the
meaning of imaginative expression as a force and to communicate that meaning to his fellow beings so that they may
the better understand—and perhaps order—their own
imaginings. Or, like Henry Adams, he is the historian of
political, economic, and cultural movements, who ceases
to be a glorified purveyor of old wives' tales and becomes
an analyst of forces which can be fully understood only in
the context where the *esprit de finesse* and the *esprit de
géométrie* converge.

The so-called second phase of the vogue of French philosophy in America [212] was dominated, especially in the
colleges, by Cousin's eclecticism. It was this phase to which
Adams was exposed as a student at Harvard and which
Taine was at the time combating in France. The third
phase was Comte's positivism by which Taine was so much
influenced, and which, even while the doctrines of Cousin
were still being taught, was fast insinuating itself into American minds, particularly through Harriet Martineau's con-
densed translation of the *Cours*—and this in spite of the
"dragon of bigotry" which Miss Martineau found to reign
supreme in America.[213] Indeed, as early as 1848, Poe had
cited in his *Eureka*, Comte's opinion of Laplace. One of the
first books Adams withdrew from the Harvard library in
1854 was Poe's *Tales*.

In 1879–80, when Henry Adams seriously began to write
his *History*, the concern with a philosophy of history was
still relatively new. Thirty years before, Taine, as a young
normalien who was led by his interest in the history of
philosophy to a consideration of the philosophy of history,
wrote in one of his notebooks: "Tout est à faire dans l'histoire de la philosophie comme dans l'histoire." [214] After
the appearance of his *Histoire de la littérature anglaise*, the
link between psychology and history became an inescapable

condition for any philosophy or science of history. And we
find the awareness of that condition in all of Adams's reflection on the nature of the historic process, even before
he wrote directly on this subject. "Philosophers agreed,"
Adams was to say in his *Education*, ". . . that the universe
could be known only as motion of mind, and therefore as
unity. One could know it only as one's self; it was psychology." [215]

Adams's preoccupation with psychology was induced by
his lifelong attempt to formulate a *science* of history. In
reaching out for what ultimately became his "Theory of
Phase in History," he explored the full length of the history
of science, including psychology. There is where he encountered Taine. For Adams, thought was a form of measurable
energy subject to the laws of phase in physics. The *Education* is replete with psychological animadversions on
character [216] and on thought processes in general.

From 1879, when his biography of Albert Gallatin made
its appearance, there is in Adams a growing tendency to
psychologic analysis. This tendency was strengthened by
his reading of Taine and other psychologists like Maudsley.
Thus, he finds Gallatin's scientific interests and preoccupa-
tions too simple because of the latter's failure to appreciate
the non-simplicity of the psychological atmosphere in which
science itself operates and develops. "Mr. Gallatin habitually made too little allowance for the force and complexity
of the human passions and instincts." [217]

In his next biographical work, *John Randolph* (1882), we
overhear the tone of the clinical psychologist very much in
the manner of Taine, when, in treating of Randolph's
approaching end, the author speaks of "the irrational wanderings of a brain never too steady in its progress." [218]
In the 1880s Dr. Weir Mitchell of Philadelphia would drop
in, while at Washington, for tea and literary, psychological,

and medical conversation. Such talk was not of casual interest to Adams, for in 1884 when the first volume of the
History appeared, he was deep in what would now be called
psychosomatic problems.[219]

The *History* abounds in statements and thoughts which
reflect his study of Taine, Buckle, and others. What, for
example, defines the character of a nation?

> The growth of character, social and national,—in the formation of
> men's minds,—more interesting than any territorial or industrial
> growth, defied the test of censuses and surveys. No people could
> be expected least of all when in infancy to understand the in-
> tricacies of its own character. . . . Of all historical problems the
> nature of a national character is the most difficult and the most
> important.

History is also often inadequate in its ability to penetrate
the private lives of famous men. Adams recognized that
"Motives were enigmas too obscure for search." [220]

He was looking for a nexus between mind and physical
energy. He

> wished to be shown that changes in form caused evolution in force;
> that chemical or mechanical energy had by natural selection and
> minute changes, under uniform conditions, converted itself into
> thought.

While he did not undertake to dispute or discuss the principles of any science, he was ready to assert that "the history of the mind concerned the historian alone." [221] In this
he was certainly at one with Taine.

The problem of psychologic determinism, where Will (for
Taine) is nothing but the triumph of a tendency or several
tendencies in the same direction, interested Adams greatly.
He was to follow this problem in his reading of Maudsley's
Body and Will, as well as in William James. From all of
these—Maudsley, James, and Taine—Adams, as an his-

torian, learned to appreciate and to evaluate properly
"the force and complexity of the human passions and instincts." [222]

Among the works Adams read in the French while preparing to write his *History* was Taine's *Les Origines de la France
contemporaine.* Adams's copy [223] contains many of his
scorings plus some critical remarks. In a blank space on
page 179, of volume 2, over the caption, "Chapitre II
(L'Assemblée constituante et son oeuvre)" Adams wrote:
"Surely this chapter consists chiefly of repetitions and ver-
biage. Like several others in this volume, it might to advantage be compressed one half." We have already alluded
earlier to a parallel criticism by Fiske of Taine's lavishness
in the use of words.

The scorings occur in Chapters I, II, and III, entitled
respectively: "*L'Anarchie spontanée*" and "*L'Assemblée
constituante et son oeuvre*" (Chapters II and III). Under the
heading of "L'Anarchie spontanée" where Taine says that
hunger is one of the chief provocatives of social convulsion
and revolution, Adams underlined,

*Sous cette angoisse, l'instinct animal se révolte, et l'obéissance générale,
qui fait la paix publique,* dépend d'un degré ajouté ou ôté au sec
ou à l'humide, au froid ou au chaud. En 1788, année très sèche, la
récolte avait été mauvaise. [224]

At a certain point in Chapter II Taine is discussing the
proper use a democracy can make of its upper class and
shows that by training and birthright the aristocrats are
eminently fitted to be "hommes d'État." Then he goes on
to say, and here Adams follows him, not without some
criticism:

Mais pour qu'ils se préparent et s'entraînent, il faut qu'on leur
montre la carrière ouverte et qu'on ne les oblige pas à passer par
des chemins trop répugnants. Si le rang, la fortune ancienne, la

dignité du caractère et des façons, sont des causes de défaveur auprès du peuple, si, pour gagner son suffrage, il faut vivre de pair à compagnon avec des courtiers électoraux de trop sale espèce, si le charlatanisme impudent, la déclamation vulgaire et la flatterie servile sont les seuls moyens d'obtenir les voix, [Adams underlined as follows] *alors, comme aujourd'hui dans les États-Unis et jadis dans Athènes, l'aristocratie se retire dans la vie privée et bientôt tombe dans la vie oisive.*

Henry Adams registered his critical reaction to this line by putting a question mark in the right-hand margin. "Car un homme bien élevé et né avec cent mille livres de rente n'est pas tenté de se faire industriel, avocat et médecin." [225] This question mark gains in meaning when considered in the historic perspective of his great-grandfather's reflections.

On societal disequilibrium caused by class persecution, in which a democracy may be just as much a party to intolerance as an aristocracy, Adams found this to underscore:

Cent Mille Français chassés à la fin du dix-septième siècle, cent mille Français chassés à la find du dix-huitieme siècle, voilà, comment la démocratie intolérante achève l'oeuvre de la monarchie intolérante. L'aristocratie morale a été fauchée au nom de l'uniformité. L'aristocratie sociale est fauchée au nom de l'égalité.[226]

In Chapter III, Henry Adams notes certain functional aspects of the Constituent Assembly, by writing in the margin the word "American" as follows:

Nulle prise au roi sur le Corps législatif: l'exécutif est un bras qui ne doit qu'obéir, et il serait ridicule que le bras pût en quelque façon contraindre ou conduire la tête (American)—ce n'est pas le monarque qui convoque l'Assemblée ni les électeurs de l'Assemblée; il n'a rien à dire ni à voir dans les opérations qui la forment (American): les électeurs se réunissent et votent sans qu'il les appelle ou les surveille. Une fois l'Assemblée élue, il ne peut ni l'ajourner ni la dissoudre. Il ne peut pas même lui proposer une loi, il lui est seulement permis "de l'inviter à prendre un objet en considération." (American) On le confine dans son emploi exécutif; bien mieux, on bâtit une sorte de muraille entre lui et l'Assemblée, et l'on bouche soigneusement la fissure par laquelle elle et lui pourraient se donner la main.—Défense aux députés de devenir ministres pendant toute la durée de leur mandat et deux ans après son terme: au contact de la cour on craint qu'ils se laissent corrompre et, de plus, quelque soient les ministres, on ne veut pas subir leur ascendant (American). Si l'un d'eux est introduit dans l'Assemblée ce ne sera pas pour y donner des conseils, mais seulement pour fournir des renseignements, pour répondre à des interrogatoires, pour protester de son zèle, en termes humbles et en posture douteuse.[227]

When Adams's *History* was finished and in circulation, Harvard wished to honor itself by bestowing upon the historian a doctorate. Accordingly, in June, 1892, President Charles William Eliot exchanged a few notes on the matter with Adams. The following letter, from the latter to Eliot, is instructive since it reveals the high esteem Adams had of Taine as a standard of achievement among scholars:

Your very kind letter of the 14th leaves little opening for a reply; yet the list you sent is eloquent. Three degrees in thirty years! Palfrey was seventy-three; Parkman was sixty-six; to find a precedent for your proposed honor, you must go back to Motley in 1860 before the University fairly had a standard of scholarship.

Imagine me as a critic commenting on your action. "On any proper standard," I would say, "Henry Adams has no claim to such distinction, either as instructor or author; on any French or German standard—compared for instance with Taine or von Sybel in his own branch—he holds no position in literature and still less in pedagogy; indeed in his own cool judgment he would himself go further still, and say that he had never done any work that he would have acknowledged as his own, if he could have helped it, so imperfect and inconclusive does he know it to be."[228]

In 1901 Giraud's study on Taine [229] was published. Adams saw it reviewed the following year in *The American Historical Review*.[230] Indeed, in the same volume of the *Review* we find frequent references to another student of Taine, namely, A. Aulard, whom Adams read with considerable interest and mentioned in his letter. That year Aulard's *La Société des Jacobins, études et leçons, première série*, was reviewed. In 1905–7 this French scholar who, as a youth, had followed Taine's lectures at the École des Beaux Arts with admiration, gave a public course at the Sorbonne, which resulted in his book, *Taine, historien de la révolution française* (Paris, 1907).

That Adams's remarks about Aulard, in a letter to Gaskell, may gain in point, it is necessary here to tell briefly what the scope of Aulard's book is and what stand it takes. By 1905 when the latter had begun a public course on the historian of the French Revolution, Taine's situation in the public esteem was a paradoxical one. Catholics hailed him as the true historian of the Revolution, and Socialists as well accounted him a great historian, whereas his reputation at the Sorbonne and in some American universities was waning (though in Italy and Germany he was highly admired); yet in France, too, men like Seignobos, Boutmy, Monod, and Sorel, in spite of some qualifications, held him up as a master, both in the use he made of archival materials, his realistic treatment of that which had been formerly encrusted in legend and mysticism, and for his overwhelming erudition.[231]

Placing himself among the dissenting critics, Aulard claims that whereas Colani, who questioned Taine's erudition, had verified only two or three of Taine's sources, he (Aulard) attempted a verification of all of them. But since no one would publish a critical edition of the *Origines de la France contemporaine*, he had to resort to *significant* examples in his analysis. Aulard indicates that Taine exaggerated Herder's ideas which he derived from reading Edgar Quinet's translation of *Ideen zur Philosophie der Geschichte der Menscheit.*[232] These ideas concerned "Ort,"

"Zeit," and "innern Charaktere" by which nations are supposedly modified. Taine does not explain the Revolution by Race, since his thesis is, on the contrary, that the Revolution abnegates tradition and runs counter to race. He does talk of *milieu* and *moment*, but in a general sense (independent of race). In other words, he does *not* apply his famous formula to the Revolution. He invents the *Jacobin*. Taine is guilty of the very thing he charged Royer-Collard with: he either invents or omits the facts.[233] Incidentally, with regard to the so-called *three moments* in Taine's theory, there is a great likelihood that Adams's reading was corrected in this regard by Sainte-Beuve, even as Emerson's was.[234] In his conclusion Aulard says that he wished less to criticize Taine's philosophico-historical theories than his erudition. On this score he finds that his (Taine's) method was bad; that he was tendentious and was embroiled in political passions; that his transcription was often faulty and that his references were inexact; that there are too many lacunae and that his sweeping generalizations lead to mutilation of reality. Yet Aulard grants that if Taine was mistaken, he did not deliberately seek to mislead. Perhaps the fault was that he loved literary glory above all else; so that his so-called scientific conception of history is, in reality, a literary conception.[235] He lacked the patience to go through a manuscript calmly. He could see only that which he was looking for.[236] Aulard's final pronouncement (p. 330) is this: "Son livre, tout compte fait, et en ses résultats généraux, me semble presque inutile à l'histoire. Il n'est vraiment utile qu'à la biographie intellectuelle de Taine lui-même ou à celle de quelques contemporains, ses disciples."

It is in the light of the above résumé of Aulard's book, that we should read what Adams wrote from Paris in June 18, 1908 to his friend Gaskell:

I wonder whether you would care to read the *éreintement* [italics Adams's] of a historian? I think I will send you Aulard's little book on Taine. It is a piece of evisceration, but it makes me cold to think of what would be the result of the same process applied to me. No man's mind and memory are comprehensive enough to carry the relations of a long story. I cannot even rewrite a chapter without greatly changing it, and I think I never have written a chapter less than five times over, unless it were from sheer collapse. If I went on forever, I should always do it differently, and of course each version is a correction. Such a scorching as Aulard gives would skin anyone. He admits it, and tries to deprecate attacks on mere blunders.[237]

Adams's apology for Taine reveals a certain sensitiveness in his own behalf. Perhaps he had recalled the onslaught on himself by "Housatonic." [238]

Taine and Adams both had a great thirst for generalization; with one it found expression in his monumental *Histoire de la littérature anglaise;* with the other, in a seductively beautiful cento of medieval studies, *Mont-Saint-Michel and Chartres.* Both historians were charged at various times with being unscientific. In Taine, the work singled out for stricture was his *Origines de la France contemporaine,* particularly the French Revolution; in Adams, his *Mont-Saint-Michel and Chartres.* (Though "Housatonic" laid him open to the same blame even for his *History,* commonly regarded as a sound work.)

Both had a curiosity which took them far beyond the boundaries of a particular specialty. Both were more than incidentally interested in art; and both sought unity not only as a means of putting the world into scientific order, but also as a means of putting an end to the small storm of dissension in the little room called the mind.[239]

To bring the particular within the general, to find the relation between the apparently isolated fact and a great variety of facts, is to follow an impulse which is at once aesthetic and scientific. Indeed, that impulse lends to science the nature of aesthetic contemplation and to art the solidity of systematic exploration. Science and art obeying the same impulse become two aspects of one process: the exploration of the place of the particular and unique fact in a universal order and the logical guarantee of the Unity of that order. With respect to this process, Adams and Taine were two kindred explorers.

Though a very serious concern with philosophy came rather late in Adams's development, he himself would nevertheless have us understand that even before he was out of Harvard College, he was already dimly aware of the possible advent of a philosophy or science of history, and that this awareness was brought about by his reading of Buckle's first volume when it appeared in 1857 and of Darwin's *Origin of Species* two years later. If that be so, then we may trace his hunger for "a great generalization that would reduce all history under a law as clear as the laws which govern the material world" to the time when he was but a junior in college and in this hunger he would resemble young Taine who likewise wished to "transform these odds and ends of philosophy into one self-evident, harmonious and complete system." [240]

When Adams came to read Taine, therefore, he came as a student already eager to rediscover for himself the highway of modern thought, but glad to find, and to follow, the footsteps of one who had preceded him by some ten years on that highway.

In view of the intricate web-work of the Spirit, one is not surprised to find a familial relation between figures as diverse as Spinoza, Hegel, Emerson, Baudelaire, Taine and Adams. This relation is found in the master idea of Spinoza, of the material universe as a double and translation of the moral world. Emerson in his essay, *The Poet*,[241] expressed

it thus: "The universe is the externization of the soul."
And Baudelaire, in his "Correspondances,"

> La Nature est un temple où de vivants piliers
> Laissent parfois sortir de confuses paroles:
> L'homme y passe à travers des forêts de symboles
> Qui l'observent avec des regards familiers.

This idea, essentially a poetic one, was readily embraced by
Taine (as Giraud points out) because it served to explain to
him not only the universe but the small world he carried
within himself. Because Adams equated energy with
thought, we are justified in relating him to the Spinozistic
circle. His prayer to the Dynamo would bear this out. It is
curious to find a similar note struck in a posthumously published poem of Taine, "Le Poète," [242] of which the last line,
"Et mon coeur tout entier a frémi dans mes vers," has a
Musset echo.

Substituting for the name of Haeckel that of Henry
Adams, we may, in any ultimate evaluation of Taine and
Adams, quote an American critic, who at one time man-
ifested a taste for French literature:

Taine's theory of literary history and [Adams's] monism are two
examples [of] . . . a type of mind that jumped to conclusions
suiting its inner climate and then sought to impose its special inter-
pretations, its somber subjective poetry, upon the world as truth
and fact. . . . Both men strove to rebuild the universe in the
image of their minds. Whatever enduring values their work has
is due to its creative power. It is poetry; it represents the reality
of their souls. With a solution of eternal problems it has little to
do.[243]

In a general way, this amounts to Monod's statement:
"La conception que les penseurs se font de l'Univers n'est
que l'image agrandie de leur propre personalité intellectuelle." [244]

In conclusion, one can see that Taine's practice—the

search for universal principles and their formulation—was Adams's dream. Like Taine, Henry Adams has these two appetites: for generalities and for concrete ideas. In the case of Adams the latter appetite played itself out in his *History*, monographs, and biographies; and the former in *Mont-Saint-Michel* and the *Education*. His letters combined both. In Adams and Taine we find an early tendency to synthesize the three phases of recurrent development in the human spirit: physics, psychology, and metaphysics, dealing successively with appearance and data of sensation, self-knowledge, and the problem of Unity (that is, of the self with all things) or the Absolute. And whereas with Taine the study of the history of philosophy very soon became the philosophy of history, with Adams the pursuit of history and the history of thought led, ultimately, to the same goal.[245] But Adams was much slower in getting there, because his philosophy came as a thirst developed during a long period of writing plain history; while Taine's practice of history was conditioned by his early philosophy. Thus, we are not surprised to find Adams as the pupil and admirer of Taine.

Adams's style, where it runs into aphorism or paradox, represents his attempt (even where he appears as a *poseur*) to communicate his sensations. In this too, he resembles Taine, who, in defending the descriptive passage in his *Voyage aux Pyrénées*, said: "Je demande pardon pour ces métaphores; on a l'air d'arranger des phrases et *l'on ne fait que raconter ses sensations*." [246] Next to music, the best vehicle for imparting sensations, as everyone knows, is literature. And it is to Adams's interest in French Literature that our attention is now called.

V

Belles Lettres

HENRY ADAMS'S INTERESTS in French literature extended to all the genres: poetry, prose, and drama. The extent of those interests can be measured from an examination of the books which constitute his collection (now at the Massachusetts Historical Society), from the references to French literature in his own works, and from the use he makes of his reading.

He used Gaston Paris's *La littérature française au moyen âge* (XIᵉ-XIVᵉ siècles) as well as the same author's *Histoire poétique de Charlemagne* and *La Poésie du moyen âge*[1] to orient himself in the earliest poetry of France. In fact, since he considered Paris the greatest academic authority in the world, it is reasonable to suppose that it was the bibliography in *La littérature française au moyen âge* which was his chief guide. These books were supplemented by innumerable monographs which attacked the minutiae of the subject along philological lines.[2] Naturally, he did not neglect to look into the studies of Bédier.[3] As might be expected the particular subject which occupied him in the early period was the *Chanson de Roland*,[4] for "probably there was never a day, certainly never a week, during several centuries, when portions of the 'Chanson' were not sung, or recited, at the Mount."[5]

As materials for his *Mont-Saint-Michel*, Adams also needed the delicacy of "this little thirteenth-century gem"[6]— *Aucassin et Nicolette*[7]—and its pendant, "Li Gieus de Robin et de Marion",[8] together with the lush richness of the *Roman de la Rose*, and especially *Les Miracles de Nostre Dame*.[9]

Adams includes, in the orbit of his interests in medieval French poetry,[10] many other poets and poems besides those already mentioned. Thus, he deals with Adam de Saint-Victor, "whose hymns are equally famous"; catches the wistfulness of Coeur-de-Lion's prison song—

> Mes campaignons cui j'amoie et cui j'aim

and the reflective lyricism of Thibaut—

> Nus hom ne peut ami recomforter
> Se cele non ou il a son cuer mis

and especially of Thibaut's address to the Queen of Heaven:

> De grant travail et de petit emploit
> Voi ce siegle cargie et encombre
> Que tant somes plain de maleurte
> Ke nus ne pens a faire ce qu'il doit,
> Ains avons si le Deauble trouve
> Qu'a lui servir chascuns paine et essaie.

Here we have the ironic incisiveness of the Mystery of Adam:

> La femme que tu me donas
> Ele fist prime icest trepas
> Donat le mei e jo mangai
> Mal cuple en fist li Criatur.
> Tu es trop tendre e il trop dur.

He is fully aware of Marie de Champagne's role in the creation of the literature of courtly love, and Marie de France's theories on the same, but more especially is he aware of Christian of Troyes—whose "world is sky-blue and

rose, with only enough red to give it warmth, and so flooded
with light that even its mysteries count only by the clearness
with which they are shown."[11] Naturally, he, the professor
who has tried his hand at poetry, is struck by Abélard, "the
poet-professor—the hero of a Latin Quarter, [who] had sung
to Héloïse those songs which resounded through Europe."[12]
Nor does he neglect William of Saint-Pair[13] and Wace of
Normandy; nor the Chanson of Willame. He retells the
charming story, "as reported by Gaultier de Coincy," of the
worthless monk of Cologne, who led a scandalous life and in
behalf of whose soul (after the demise of the monk) Saint
Peter intervened first with the Trinity, then with the arch-
angel, the Apostles, and even the Saints, but was at last
forced to "place himself and his dignity in the hands of the
Virgin, who instantly responded":

> Pierre, Pierre. . . .
> En moult grand poine et por ceste ame
> De mon douz filz me fierai
> Tant que pour toi l'en prierai[14]

Here is the neat and swift manner in which Adams effects
the nexus between the spirit of the *Roman de la Rose* and
that of Villon. "The note of sadness," he says, "has begun,
which the poets were to find so much more to their taste
than the note of gladness. From the 'Roman de la Rose'
to the 'Ballade des Dames du Temps Jadis' was a short step
for the Middle-Age giant Time,—a poor two hundred years.
Then Villon woke up to ask what had become of the Roses:

> Ou est la tres sage Heloïs
>
> Et Jehanne la bonne Lorraine"

This note of sadness seems to be linked in Adams's mind
with "Satire [which] took the place of worship." This, according to him, "William of Lorris was first to see—, and
say it, with more sadness and less bitterness than Villon

showed." The loss of the Rose brought about "the deepest expression of social feeling [which] ended with the word: Despair."[15]

To our way of thinking, Adams has here (perhaps more intuitively than rationally) tapped the real source of modern lyricism, which can best be understood against a background of social history; the kind we get in the transition from the first part of the *Roman de la Rose* to the second, and from that to Villon.

Though Adams's acquaintance with early French prose may first have come through his study of Guizot's *History of Civilization in Europe* during his senior year at Harvard,[16] it is certain that he read the "chroniqueurs" in connection with his teaching of history at his Alma Mater.[17] Among them, he was interested especially in Joinville, who, according to Adams, was "the earliest prose writer in the French language, who gave a picture of actual French life."[18] Adams takes great relish in the candor of this intimate friend of Saint Louis, whose "memories went back to the France of Blanche's regency." He would "rather commit thirty mortal sins than be a leper." And as to Joinville's thoughts of the Virgin, Adams helps himself to a passage which is at once touched with lyricism as it is with humor and frankness.[19]

Another chroniqueur, whom he does not mention but whose *Chronicles* found a place in his library, was John Froissart.[20] This work must certainly have served Professor Adams very well indeed in conveying to his students the struggle between France and England which shook all Europe. We also find two volumes by Enguerran de Monstrelet, who continued, in his *Chronique*, the work of Froissart.[21]

As we shall see later, Adams had the natural penchant of an historian for *Mémoires*. He read, among others, Philippe de Commines—perhaps (thinks Lanson) the first example

of the pure intellectual. Though "two hundred long and
dismal years" divide Joinville and Commines, as well as the
two kings they wrote about—Saint Louis and Louis XI—
Adams sees "no difference between him and Saint Louis, nor
much between Philippe de Commines and Joinville." But
there is, of course, a marked difference between the two
writers. Whereas the latter has a vivid imagination which
brings the first Crusade alive in all its color, but also has
a defective sense of the meaning of events recorded, the
former, lacking in art, is a keen psychological analyst. Of
this surely Adams was aware. The particular point of likeness that for him brings the two together is the power of
Mariolatry over both. Precisely, Adams's statement is this:
"Saint Louis died in 1270. Two hundred long and dismal
years followed, in the midst of wars, decline of faith, dis-
olution of the old ties and interests, until, toward 1470,
Louis XI succeeded in restoring some semblance of solidity
to the State; and Louis XI divided his time and his money
impartially between the Virgin of Chartres and the Virgin
of Paris. In that respect, one can see no difference between
him and Saint Louis, nor much between Philippe de Commines and Joinville."[22]

Adams was naturally concerned, also, with the medieval
theatre. He read the *Théâtre français au moyen âge* (Paris
1839) by Monmerqué and Michel.[23] In addition he gathered
information from Gaston Paris's *La Littérature française
au moyen âge*,[24] *Les Annales du théâtre et de la musique*, and
Sylvain Lévi's *Le Théâtre indien*.[25] He needed this material
for his *Mont-Saint-Michel*.[26]

Whereas the *Mont-Saint-Michel* conveys clearly Adams's
deep concern with the Middle Ages, we have no work from
his pen which would indicate a similar interest in sixteenth
and seventeenth century French poetry. However, his
reading of Sainte-Beuve should guarantee at least a fair

acquaintance with the poets of those centuries.[27] He was
definitely interested in Ronsard although the only references
to him occur in the *Life of George Cabot Lodge*.[28] The Adams
library contains a copy of J. J. Jusserand's *Ronsard*.[29] The
collection also contains a six-volume edition of the *Fables*
of La Fontaine (1765). The volumes containing the *Contes*,
with plates by Charles Joseph Eisen (1720-1778) were lost
in the course of Adams's peregrinations.[30] In a letter of
thanks to Charles Milnes Gaskell who presented him with
this copy of the *Contes*, which contained Lord Sheffield's
bookplate, Adams praises the lord for delighting in La
Fontaine and adds: "A man who loves La Fontaine must
be a good and virtuous citizen."[31] Certainly all of Adams's
grandsires had been such citizens, for they too had delighted
in the fabulist.[32] Adams's reading of Taine must have
further sharpened his awareness of La Fontaine as a literary figure, for, in the chapter in the *Education* entitled
"Darwinism," he gives point to an observation on evolution,
as applicable to the mind, with a reference to one of the
Fables: "Evolution of mind was altogether another matter
and belonged to another science, but whether one traced
descent from the shark or the wolf was immaterial even in
morals. This matter had been discussed for ages without
scientific result. La Fountaine and other fabulists maintained that the wolf, even in morals, stood higher than
man."[33]

Where morals are not the arbitrary imposition of societal
convention on the will of the individual, they are the full
measure of man assuming responsibility for the universe of
his own mind in loneliness. The first of the "moderns" to
articulate this idea was Michel de Montaigne who was des-
tined to be doubly great: once in his own right, through his
works, especially his *Essays*; and again through the great-
ness of his readers. For in France, the eager minds of Des-

cartes and Pascal sought that light in the pages of Mon-
aigne; in England, Shakespeare wrote his name in proud
ownership of the *Essays*; and in America, Emerson, Henry's
friend, included Michel among his *Representative Men*.

Some time after 1862 Adams acquired the four-volume
Louandre edition of the *Essais*. The passages he marked are
instructive.

Le plus fort estat qui paroisse pour le présent au monde est celuy
des Turcs.[34]

Quand les vignes gelent en mon village, mon presbtre en argumente
l'ire de Dieu sur la race humaine, et iuge ge la pepie en tier ne desia
les Cannibales. A veoir nos guerres civiles, qui ne crie que cette
machine se boulverse, et que le iour du iugement nous prend au
collet? Sans s'adviser que plusieurs pires choses se sont veues,
et que les dix mille parts du monde ne laissent pas de galler le bon
temps ce pendant.[35]

Nous sommes insensiblement touts en cette erreur: erreur de
grande suitte et preiudice. Mais qui se presente comme dans un
tableau cette grande image de nostre mere nature en son entiere
maiesté; qui lit en son visage une si generale et constante varieté;
qui se remarque là dedans, et non soy, mais tout un royaume, comme
un traict d'une poincte tres delicate, celuy là seul estime les choses
selon leur iuste grandeur.[36]

Notre vie, disoit Pythagoras, retire à la grande et populeuse
assemblee des ieux olympiques: les uns s'y exercent le corps, pour
en acquerir la gloire des ieux; d'aultres y portent des marchandises
à vendre, pour le gaing:[37] il en est, et qui ne sont pas les pires,
lesquels n'y cherchent aultre fruict que de regarder comment et
pourquoy chasque chose se fait, et estre spectateurs de la vie des
aultres hommes, pour en iuger, et regler la leur.[38]

Ie cognois des hommes assez qui ont diverses parties belles, qui
l'esprit qui le coeur, qui l'adresse, qui la conscience, qui le langage,
qui une science, qui un 'aultre; mais de grand homme en general,
et ayant tant de belles pieces ensemble, ou une en tel degré d'ex-

cellence qu'on le doibve admirer ou le comparer à ceulx que nous
honorons du temps passé, ma fortune ne m'en a faict veoir nul: et le
plus grand que j'aie cogneu au vif, ie dis des parties naturelles de
l'ami, et le mieulx nay, c'estoit Estienne de la Boëtie.[39]

Les plus notables hommes que i'aye iugé par les apparences ex-
ternes (car, pour les iuger à ma mode, il les fauldroit esclairer de
plus prez), ce ont esté, pour le faict de la guerre et suffisance militaire, le duc de Guyse, qui mourut à Orleans, et le feu mareschal
Strozzi; pour gents suffisants et de vertu non commune, Olivier,
et l'Hospital, Chanceliers de France.[40]

Or, les loix se maintiennent en credit, non parce qu'elles sont iustes,
mais parce qu'elles sont loix: c'est le fondement mystiques de leur
auctorité, elles n'en ont point d'aultre; qui bien leur sert. Elles
sont souvent faictes par des sots; plus souvent par des gents qui,
en haine d'egualité, ont faulte d'equité; mais tousiours par des
hommes, aucteurs vains et irrésolus. Il n'est rien si lourdement et
largement faultier, que les loix; ny si ordinairement. Quiconque
leur obeït parce qu'elles sont iustes, ne leur obeït pas iustement
par où il doibt. Les nostres françoises prestent aulcunement la
main, par leur desreglement et deformité, au desordre et corruption qui se veoid en leur dispensation et exécution.[41]

Il fault apprendre qu'on n'est qu'un sot; instruction bien plus
ample et importante.[42]

For Adams the problem of conduct was one which involved
not only relations between the individual and society, but
also an examination of one's self. He first gave his full effort
to a study of American society and its norm of conduct; he
then turned to a study of Henry Adams. The first effort
resulted in a nine-volume history; the second, in the *Education*. Montaigne appears several times in this latter work;[43]
soon after its private appearance he referred to the writer
of the *Essais* in a letter to his friend Gaskell.[44] He had
studied the *Essais*, as we see, in great detail and found there
a spirit congenial to his own. What Pierre Villey says of

Montaigne is equally applicable to Adams: "L'indépendance
jalouse de sa nature l'écartera de la vie pratique et le pous-
sera vers sa méditation solitaire."[45] This sort of "meditative
egotism" which has its rise in classical antiquity and in
successive waves reaches the nineteenth century, when it
was accentuated by the ascendancy of industrialism and
democracy, finds one of its best expressions in the *Education*.
Thus a straight line of filiation exists between the *Moralia*
of Plutarch, Amyot (the translator of Plutarch), Montaigne
(who owed so much to the translation of his favorite author),
Jean Jaques Rousseau (who furnishes Adams with the first
sentence of the preface to the *Education*) and Henry Adams.[46]
Of the three—Montaigne, Rousseau, Adams—the one who
pretends the least as to the ultimate value for others in the
portrayal of himself, is the first. "Ainsi, lecteur, je suis moi-
même la matière de mon livre: ce n'est pas raison que tu
emploies ton loisir en un sujet si frivole et si vaine; adieu
donc." The second insists directly and proudly on the value
of his self-portraiture for others:

Voici le seul portrait d'homme, peint exactement, d'après nature
et *dans toute sa vérité, qui existe et qui probablement existera
jamais*. Qui que vous soyez, que ma destinée ou ma confiance ont
fait l'arbitre de ce cahier, je vous conjure par mes malheurs, par
vos entrailles, et au nom de toute espèce humaine, de pas anéantir
un ouvrage utile et unique, lequel peut servir de première pièce de
comparaison pour l'étude des hommes qui certainement est encore
à commencer, et de ne pas ôter à l'honneur de ma mémoire le seul
monument sûr de mon caractère qui n'ait pas été défiguré par mes
enemis.[47]

There is a bit of Rousseau's pride in Adams's declaration in
the Preface to his book: "Except in the abandoned sphere
of the dead languages, no one has discussed what part of
education has, in his personal experience, turned out to be
useful, and what not. This volume attempts to discuss it."[48]

In addition we have the striking fact that he conceived of his self-portrayal as "The Education of Henry Adams: a Study of Twentieth-Century Multiplicity."[49] What unites the three is, to use Villey's phrase, "la peinture du moi." In a sense, the *Education* is a collection of essays, entitled variously: "Failure," "The Abyss of Ignorance," "Chaos," and so on. The stuff of sentiment which is most marked in the *Confessions* is relatively absent from the *Essais* and occasionally makes itself felt in the *Education*. What is only implicit in the *Essais* and in the *Confessions* is stated powerfully in the *Education*: "everyone must bear his own universe,"[50] "the sense of pain would be the first to educate,"[51] "simplicity is the most deceitful mistress that ever betrayed man";[52] "the only absolute truth was the subconscious chaos below."[53] Throughout the *Education* man and thought are spoken of as *energy* or force. As an historian, Adams felt himself driven back to thought as one continuous force.[54]

Time and time sequence for Montaigne were secure and definite means for measuring the progress of the mind. Thought and its sequences were solid bases for Rousseau's unfolding of feeling and sentiment. So, both Montaigne and Rousseau knew—and were sure they knew—what they meant. But "Adams, for one, had toiled in vain to find out what he meant." By his time, the units of measure and the sequences had changed. As a contemporary of Bergson, he knew that "the mere sequence of time was artificial"; and that "the sequence of thought was chaos." Thus—again as a contemporary of the Poincarés and a rising school of modern physicists—"he turned at last to the sequence of force."[55] But then there was still the question of mind, "itself the subtlest of all known forces," and the dilemma associated with it, namely, that "as the mind of man enlarged its range, it enlarged the field of complexity."[56]

But Adams was essentially an artist, whose "artistic standard was the illusion of his own mind"[57]—and he knew it!
It is the contemplative "I" that interested him, even when
he went afield to find intimations of its nature in other I's.
Well could Adams join Montaigne in saying: "Je m'estudie
plus qu'autre subject. C'est ma métaphysique, c'est ma
phisique."[58] And, indeed, he does say so—in his own manner:
"Among indefinite possible orbits, one sought the orbit
which would best satisfy the observed movement of the
runaway star Groombridge, 1838, commonly called Henry
Adams." It wasn't after all, the Cathedral glass that "had
gone back to the Roman Empire and forward to the American continent" and that "betrayed sympathy with Montaigne and Shakespeare,"[59] but Adams himself, who when
seeking detailed information on life and art under the
Valois[60] opened the pages of Brantôme, "the most gifted
chronicler of his epoch."

But the critical confrontation of Man and his Ego needed
a corrective and balance which history itself furnished in the
laughter of Rabelais. Indeed, in the chapter entitled "The
Grammar of Science," Adams associated the name of
Rabelais with that of Montaigne.[61] In Adams's novel,
Esther, the heroine echoes Rabelais' "Rire est le propre de
l'homme" (a quote from Aristotle), when she says, "Poor
Papa's last words to me were: 'Laugh and you're safe.' "[62]

In 1895, already with thoughts of a book later to be called
"Mont-Saint-Michel and Chartres" in his mind, Adams was
traveling through the Touraine country. In a carping mood,
he wrote to Elizabeth Cameron:

After Mont Saint Michel and the churches of the north, nothing
here seems much worth while. . . . Not a single character or
association seems to lend dignity or character to all this country.
Rabelais, Balzac, civil wars, massacres, assassinations and royal
mistresses are pretty much all it can show. . . . We went yester-

day to Chinon, a superb old military ruin, of a type like Windsor, but without architecture other than the usual military construction. It is not a Mont Saint Michel, but the dirty little town is very Gustave Doré, Rabelais and Balzac.[63]

But how variable Adams's moods were we can see when, upon another occasion (two years after) he ended a letter to Sir Robert Cunliffe: "Adieu, my dear old squire and best beloved of baronets! Touraine was charming. I have never enjoyed it so much. I felt *Rabelaisian*."[64]

From one allusion, we know that Adams had read at least the Gargantua (Book I) and had been impressed—as who hasn't?—with the Giant's stealing of the bells of Notre Dame. Indeed, his reference is woven into an early passage of the *Education*, which is really a succinct statement of the whole theme of the book.

As it happened, he never got to the point of playing the game [that is, of life] at all; he lost himself in the study of it, watching the errors of the players; but this is the only interest in the story, which otherwise has no moral and little incident. A story of education—seventy years of it—the practical value remains to the end in doubt, like other values about which men have disputed since the birth of Cain and Abel; but the practical value of the universe has never been stated in dollars. Although everyone cannot be a Gargantua—Napoleon—Bismarck and walk off with the great bells of Notre Dame, everyone must bear his own universe, and most persons are moderately interested in learning how their neighbors have managed to carry theirs.[65]

A good many of Adams's pronouncements on pedantry give the student an intimation on how great must have been his glee in reading the Master Rabelais' coruscating satire on it. As a professor at Cambridge, he would gladly have seen transferred the inscription over the great gate of Thélème, inveighing against bigots and hypocrites, to a place over the main gate of Harvard Yard.

Adams's reading in the seventeenth century included

Charles Perrault, La Bruyère, La Rochefoucauld, Madame
de Sévigné,[66] and in particular Pascal and Descartes. But
the treatment of the last two is reserved for a later chapter.

Adams, who was careful to report, with seeming pride,
that "there still exists somewhere a little volume of critically
edited Nursery Rhymes with a boy's name in full, written
in the President's [J. Q. Adams] trembling hand on the flyleaf,"[67] would naturally read with delight (when young or
old) Charles Perrault's *Contes de ma mère l'oye.*

The next item we deal with here is recorded in the *1858
Catalogue* and thus represents part of Adams's early readings:
the *Maximes* by La Rochefoucauld.[68] Following are the
numbered maxims scored or underlined by Adams (italics
represent his markings):

Il n'y a point d'accidents si malhereux dont les habiles gens ne
tirent quelque avantage, *ni de si heureux que les imprudents ne
puissent tourner à leur préjudice.* (LIX)

La sincérité est une ouverture de coeur. On la trouve en fort peu
de gens et *celle que l'on voit d'ordinaire n'est qu'une fine dissimulation pour attirer la confiance des autres.* (LXII)

Il n'y a point de déguisement qui puisse longtemps cacher l'amour
où il est, *ni le feindre où il n'est pas.* (LXX)

*L'amour, aussi bien que le feu, ne peut subsister dans un mouvement
continuel et il cesse de vivre dès qu'il cesse d'espérer ou de craindre.*
(LXXV)

*Les hommes ne vivroient pas longtemps en société s'ils n'étoient les
dupes les uns des autres.* (LXXXVII)

Chacun dit du bien de son coeur, et personne n'en ose dire de son esprit.
(XCVIII)

*La plus subtile de toutes les finesses est de savoir bien feindre de tomber
dans les pièges qu'on nous tend et l'on n'est jamais si aisément trompé
que quand on songe à tromper les autres.* (CXVII)

Le vrai moyen d'être trompé c'est de se croire plus fin que les autres.
(CXXVII)

Une des choses qui fait que l'on trouve si peu de gens qui paroissent raisonnables et agréables dans la conversation, c'est qu'il n'y a presque personne qui ne pense plutôt à ce qu'il veut dire qu'à répondre précisément à ce qu'on lui dit. (CXXXIX)
Ce qui nous fait aimer les nouvelles connoissances n'est pas tant la lassitude que nous avons des vieilles, ou le plaisir de changer, *que le dégoût de n'être pas assez admirés de ceux qui nous connoissent trop et l'espérance de l'être davantage de ceux qui ne nous connoissent pas tant.* (CLXXVIII)

En vieillissant, on devient plus fou ou plus sage. (CCX)

Quand on aime, on doute souvent de ce que l'on croit le plus. (CCCXLV-III)

Quelque défiance que nous ayons de la sincérité de ceux qui nous parlent, nous croyons toujours qu'ils nous disent plus vrai qu'aux autres. (CCCLXVI)

Les violences qu'on se fait pour s'empêcher d'aimer sont souvent plus cruelles que les rigueurs de ce qu'on aime. (CCCLXIX)
Si la vanité ne renverse pas entièrement les vertus du moins elle les ébranle toutes. (CCCLXXXVIII)

En amour, celui qui est guéri le premier est toujours le mieux guéri. (CCCCXVII)

Nos ennemis approchent plus de la vérité dans les jugements qu'ils font de nous que nous n'en approchons nous-mêmes. (CCCCLVIII)

De toutes les passions violentes, celle qui sied le moins mal aux femmes, c'est l'amour. (CCCCLXVI)

Dans les premières passions, les femmes aiment l'amant, et dans les autres, elles aiment l'amour. (CCCCLXXI)

Quand on a le coeur encore agité par les restes d'une passion, on est plus près d'en prendre une nouvelle que quand on est entièrement guéri. (CCCCLXXXIV)

Les querelles ne dureroient pas longtemps si le tort n'étoit que d'un côté. (CCCCXCVI)

L'amour, tout agréable qu'il est, plaît encore plus par les manières dont il se montre que par lui-même. (DI)

In the first supplement, the following two *maximes* have been underlined by Adams.

La plupart des femmes se rendent plutôt par foiblesse que par passion. *De là vient que, pour l'ordinaire, les hommes entreprenants réussissent mieux que les autres, quoiqu'ils ne soient pas plus aimables.* (1665, No. 301; LVIII)

N'aimer guère en amour est un moyen assuré pour être aimé. (1665, No. 302; LIX)

De la Conversation

Il ne faut jamais rien dire avec un air d'autorité ni montrer aucune supériorité d'esprit. Fuyons les expressions trop recherchées, les termes durs ou forcés et ne nous servons point de paroles plus grandes que les choses. (p. 109, 2d par.)

While no one of the "Maximes" may be safely adduced as the direct source for any of Adams's own condensation of thought, their spirit inheres in statements like these that appear in the *Education*:

. . . the sense of pain would be first to educate (p. 5).

. . . [to love] the pleasure of hating—one's self if no better victim offered (p. 7).

Chaos often breeds life, when order breeds habit (p. 249).

. . . only on the edge of the grave can man conclude anything (p. 90).

. . . the affectation of readiness for death is a stage role (p. 395)

Nature has educated herself to a singular sympathy for death (p. 501).

Was La Bruyère casting his historic shadow when, at the beginning of his *Education*, Adams wrote of life that "he never got to the point of playing the game at all" because "he lost himself in the study of it, watching the errors of the players"? If so, it was to good purpose, not only in examining "whether life was an honest game of chance, or whether the cards were marked and forced,"[69] but in his thrusts at "goldbugs" and *nouveaux riches* and in his critical approach to progress. In reading La Bruyère's *Caractères* early in his career, Adams was preparing, unknowingly perhaps, for his study of Pascal's *Pensées*. He also found more than a hint there for his subsequent study of La Fontaine and Ronsard, Rabelais and Montaigne, Molière and Racine.

If Adams was interested in La Bruyère's psychological portraits, he was equally absorbed in Mme de Sévigné's picture of the seventeenth century, as it appears in her correspondence. We learn that in 1895 he was reading her night and day.[70] That year, on the way back from Mont Saint Michel to Chartres, he stopped a few miles from the old town of Vitré to examine the Chateau of Mme de Sévigné, "untouched, and for all the world exactly like our Scotch Castles."[71] The stage properties of space, when taken in an historic setting, had a great appeal for Adams who sought diversion in drama and dramatic literature.

His interest in the theatre ranged from antiquity to the latest play of his own day. A book on the drama which he enjoyed and read with care, as some lineations in it indicate, was *Les Deux Masques—Tragédie-Comédie* by Paul de Saint-Victor.[72] In Volume III of this work he could read the history of French drama from its origins through Beaumarchais, with special treatment of Racine's *Andromaque, Britannicus, Mithridate, Esther* and Molière's *L'Étourdi, École des femmes, Don Juan, Misanthrope, Les Femmes savantes, Le Mariage forcé* (Rabelais et Molière), *Amphitrion, M. de Pourceaugnac, Le bourgeois gentilhomme, Le Malade imaginaire,* as well as Diderot.

In print, Henry's first reference to French drama occurs in an article he wrote for the *Harvard Magazine* in his junior year. Adopting the tone of the satiric fable, he writes as follows about one of Corneille's rivals: "Once upon a time there lived an individual named George Scudéry. He wrote sixteen heroic tragedies, the last entitled Arminius, and it was called by critics 'the downfall of mediocrity.' "[73]

Though he had, most likely, read some of the plays of Corneille and Racine, we can find no references to the former and but one to the latter.[74] But he does mention Molière several times.[75] In his *History* Adams refers to the "Lies of Scapin"[76] in talking of the maneuvers of Bonaparte. In *Democracy,* Adams contrives an incident in which the leering, Voltairian Baron Jacobi triumphs over Ratcliffe who is ignorant of the common facts of literature.

The climax of his triumph came one evening when Ratcliffe, tempted by some allusion to Molière which he thought he understood, made reference to the unfortunate influence of that great man on the religious opinions of his time. Jacobi, by a flash of inspiration, divined that he had confused Molière with Voltaire, and assuming a manner of extreme suavity, he put his victim on the rack, and tortured him with affected explanations and interrogations.[77]

The one reference to Molière in the *Mont-Saint-Michel*

occurs in the chapter entitled "La Chanson de Roland":
"Twelfth-century art was not precise; still less 'précieuse,'
like Molière's famous seventeenth-century prudes."[78] Finally, in the *Life of George Cabot Lodge*, Adams names directly two plays that the young poet read, the *École des
femmes* and the *Malade imaginaire*.[79]

In eighteenth-century literature we find only one book
dealing with poetry which attracted Adams's attention,
although it is not mentioned by him in any of his writings.
The Harvard Charge Books for 1876,[80] however, show that
he withdrew the *Quatre Poétiques* by l'Abbé Charles Batteux.[81] Of the four whose doctrines on poetry Batteux
brings together in his work, Boileau is not alluded to anywhere by Adams, neither is Vida nor Horace, but Aristotle
is referred to by him as having attracted the French mind.[82]
Batteux may have been brought to his attention through
his reading of Diderot.[83]

As we have seen earlier, familiarity with the French prose
masters of the eighteenth century was a matter of course
in the Adams family, as far back as Henry's great-grandfather.[84] Thus, both John and John Quincy Adams had
read Voltaire, and John had spoken of his "epigrammatic
wit."[85]

As is indicated in the *1858 Catalogue*, Henry possessed a
copy of Voltaire's *Romans*,[86] which he had read carefully.
His scorings entail the following seven stories:

1. *Zadig ou La Destinée*, Histoire orientale;
2. *Le Monde comme il va*, Vision de Babouc Écrite Par Lui-
   Même;
3. *L'Ingénu*, Histoire véritable tirée des manuscrits du Père
   Quesnel;
4. *L'Homme aux quarante écus;*
5. *Histoire de Jenni; ou, l' Athée et le sage;*
6. *Les Oreilles du Comte de Chesterfield et le chapelain Goudman;*

7. *Le Taureau blanc* traduit du Syriaque Par M. Mamaki, Interprète du roi d'Angleterre pour les langues orientales.

Apparently Adams was impressed with the ability of Zadig to resist affectation and haughtiness in spite of youth and riches. "[Il] *ne voulait point toujours avoir raison et savait respecter la faiblesse des hommes.*" [87] He underscored the fact that Zadig was intellectually curious and always ready to seek out the company of the learned, including the gentle dig at metaphysics. "[Il] n'ignorait pas les principes phy- siques de la nature, tels qu'on les connaissait alors, et *savait de la métaphysique ce qu'on en a su dans tous les âges, c'est- à-dire fort peu de chose.*" Voltaire helped the young student to a vicarious gibe at false authority, when he provided him with the following bit of ironic casuistry which Henry promptly underscored.

[Il] *s'éleva une grande dispute sur une loi de Zoroastre, qui défendait de manger du griffon. Comment défendre le griffon, disaient les uns, si cet animal n'existe pas? Il faut bien qu'il existe disaient les autres, puisque Zoroastre ne veut pas qu'on en mange.* Zadig voulut les accorder, en leur disant: S'il y a des griffons, n'en mangeons point; s'il n'y en a point nous en mangerons encore moins; et par là nous obéirons tous à Zoroastre.[88]

In the next *roman*, the use of devastating paradox im- pressed Adams, whose work was to bear traces of it. In *Le Monde comme il va*, Voltaire relates how Babouc found him- self in a superb temple where an assemblage of men and women were being addressed by a wise man of the East.

Un mage parut dans une machine élevée, qui parla longtemps du vice et de la vertu. Ce mage divisa en plusieurs parties ce qui n'avait pas besoin d'être divisé; il prouva méthodiquement tout ce qui était clair; il enseigna tout ce qu'on savait; il se passionna froidement, et sortit suant et hors d'haleine; toute l'assemblée alors se réveilla, et crut avoir assité à une instruction. Babouc dit: Voilà un homme qui a fait de son mieux pour ennuyer deux ou trois cents de ses concitoyens;

mais son intention était bonne, il n'y a pas là de quoi détruire Persépolis.[89]

This salvo at the deadly profession of teaching is echoed later in the *Education* in such remarks as:

. . . a schoolmaster—that is, a man employed to tell lies to little boys (p. 9).

The dislike of school was so strong as to be a positive gain. The passionate hatred of school methods was almost a method in itself. . . . He thought his mind a good enough machine, if it were given time to act, but it acted wrong if hurried. Schoolmasters never gave time (p. 37).

Most school experience was bad (p. 38).

The chief wonder of education is that it does not ruin everybody concerned in it, teachers and taught (p. 55).
Any large body of students stifles the student (p. 302).

Nothing is more tiresome than a superannuated pedagogue (p. 353).

Yet, the "sage lettré" had one worthwhile thing to communicate to Babouc:

Vous avez lu des choses bien méprisables . . . ; mais dans tous les temps, dans tous les genres, le mauvais fourmille, et le bon est rare. Vous avez reçu chez-vous le rebut de la pédanterie, parce que, dans toutes les professions, ce qu'il y a de plus indigne de paraître est toujours ce qui se présente avec le plus d'impudence.[90]

Well, Persépolis was not destroyed and Babouc was satisfied, unlike Jonas—and Adams underlines the concluding sentence—

qui se fâcha de ce qu'on ne détruisait pas Ninive. Mais quand on a été trois jours dans le corps d'une baleine, on n'est pas de si bonne humeur que quand on a été à l'opéra, à la comédie et qu'on a soupé en bonne compagnie.[91]

Though, for an ironist, Adams took himself too seriously,

yet implicit in all his work is the question, why do human beings take themselves so seriously? Voltaire struck this ironic note early in Adams when as a callow youth he read *L'Ingénu-Histoire véritable tirée des manuscrits du Père Quesnel.* There the question of the right to commit suicide is raised: *"Comme s'il importait à l'Être des êtres que l'assemblage de quelques parties de matière fût dans un lieu ou dans un autre!"*[92] A half century after underlining this passage, Adams wrote:

after sixty or seventy years of growing astonishment, the mind wakes to find itself looking blankly into the void of death. That it should profess itself pleased by this performance was all that the highest rules of good breeding could ask; but that it should actually be satisfied would prove that it existed only as idiocy.[93]

Didn't Voltaire himself behave rather hesitantly as the end approached? One could always trust Adams to state an inescapable dilemma straightforwardly.

Voltaire, whose approach to science was serious, was bound, by the condition of his genius, to be critical of it. In this Adams was to imitate him—consciously or not. In *L'Homme aux quarante écus*, Henry underlined the following passage:

Si la mer avait déposé tant de lits de coquilles en Touraine, pourquoi aurait-elle négligé la Bretagne, La Normandie, La Picardie, et toutes les autres côtes? J'ai bien peur que ce falun tant vanté ne vienne pas plus de la mer que les hommes.[94]

Mais, Monsieur l'incrédule, que répondrez-vous aux huîtres pétrifiées qu'on a trouvées sur le sommet des Alpes?—Je répondrai, monsieur le créateur, que je n'ai pas vu plus d'huîtres pétrifiées que d'ancres de vaisseau sur le haut du mont Cenis; je répondrai ce qu'on a déjà dit, *qu'on a trouvé des écailles d'huître (qui se pétrifient aisément) à de très grandes distances de la mer, comme on a déterré des médailles romains à cent lieues de Rome; et j'aime mieux croire que des pèlerins de Saint-Jacques ont laissé quelques coquilles vers Saint-Maurice, que d'imaginer que la mer a formé le mont Saint-Bernard.*[95]

As we shall see, much of the spirit of the above-quoted passage (and many similar ones) which young Adams read in Voltaire will insinuate itself in his later writings. One may take, for example, the following paragraph written in Fiji in 1891:

Besides the novelty of finding at last an unknown country where the simple savage is truly simple, and would gladly eat you if such were the Christian commandment, we have at last reached a region where science has got another tough job to settle with its conscience. For the last two days we have tramped between vast walls of conglomerate and breccia, the wreck of older mountains long ago broken into small bits and carried down probably below the sea to be compressed solid under heavy weights of wash or lava, and then lifted up again at least seven hundred feet. The torrent has cut deep through these beds, and the natives make use of them for burial places. What interests me more is that we have reached a spot where coral rock is said to lie on or in the mountainside. To-morrow Sir John [Thurston] is to go for that coral, and will take me with him. If we find it, I shall not have the first gleam of an idiotic suspicion when or how it got there, or what it wanted there anyhow, but it will be rather fun. I have been hunting everywhere for a raised coral bank, not because a raised coral bank has the smallest personal interest to me; but because it is a kind of coralline conundrum which, as a serious Darwinian, I am morally bound to defy and repudiate. Darwin says that the coral islands have miraculous powers of sinking, while all the coral islands I have seen are perfectly stupid evidences of rising. Till now I have never seen or heard of a clear case of rise more than perhaps two or three hundred feet. Here they claim a thousand or more feet of it. If we can settle this, I give you all the advantages. The next time you meet a geologist you can hit him on the head with my specimens, like Abner Dean of Angels.[96]

To which Adams, rereading the same *roman* of Voltaire's at the time he wrote this bit on corals, could find the appropriate remark: "Monsieur, monsieur, si on n'a pas découvert de coquilles sur les montagnes d'Amérique, on en découvrira."[97]

The next passage (in the same story) which Adams scored, deals with an entirely different subject. For, as Voltaire says:

C'est le sort de toutes les conversations de passer d'un sujet à un autre. *Tous ces objets de curiosité de science et de goût, disparurent bientôt devant le grand spectacle que l'impératrice de Russie et le roi de Pologne donnaient au monde; ils venaient de relever l'humanité écrasée, et d'établir la liberté de conscience dans une partie de la terre beaucoup plus vaste que ne fut jamais l'empire romain: ce service rendu au genre humain, cet exemple donné à tant de cours qui se croient politiques, fut célébré comme il devait l'être: on but à la santé de l'impératrice, du roi philosophe, et du primat philosophe, et on leur souhaita beaucoup d'imitateurs; le docteur de Sorbonne même les admira;* car il y a quelques gens de bon sens dans ce corps, comme il y eut autrefois des gens d'esprit chez les Béotiens.[98]

Voltaire would get in, before closing his tale, that gibe at *aula academica*, and Adams would be the first to enjoy it; pedagogues were his favorite scapegoats.

In the *Histoire de Jenni; ou, L'Athée et le sage*, Adams encountered three geographic references which had great meaning for him throughout his life: Maryland, Pennsylvania, and Newport. Chapter VII of this *histoire* is entitled: "Ce qui arriva en Amérique."

[Dieu] punit en Amérique des crimes commis en Europe, et . . . la scélérate Clive-Hart est morte comme elle devait mourir. Peut-être le souverain fabricateur de tant de mondes aura-t-il arrangé *les choses de façon que les grands forfaits commis dans un globe sont expiés quelquefois dans ce globe même: je n'ose le croire, mais je le souhaite; et je le croirais, si cette idée n'était pas contre toutes les règles de la bonne métaphysique.*[99]

One might simply remark here that neither Voltaire nor his

reader, Adams, could escape the ultimate confrontation of metaphysical problems, ridicule them as they might.

The opening sentence of *Les Oreilles du Comte de Chesterfield et le chapelain Goudman* was to be echoed a number of times by writers in the nineteenth century; on both sides of the Channel—especially by Matthew Arnold. "Ah! la fatalité gouverne irrémissiblement toutes les choses de ce monde!" Adams, an avid reader of Arnold, had his own penchant for the music of fatalism. What is Nature? What is the Soul? How much Adams was to cogitate these questions later in life! But right now he had before him, as a young man, Voltaire's delicious treatment of these knotty matters through the medium of fiction. It appears—so the fable runs—that Chaplain Goudman had been deprived of his benefice and his mistress because Lord Chesterfield was deaf and mistook the minister of the gospel to have complained of some disease when in reality he was complaining of poverty. Chesterfield said his surgeon, Sidrac, would cure him. For consolation Goudman starts to study nature under Dr. Sidrac. After much observation and experiment Goudman comes to the conclusion that

Il n'y a point de nature, tout est art; c'est par un art admirable que toutes les planètes dansent régulièrement autour du soleil, tandis que le soleil fait la roue sur lui-même; il faut assurément que quelqu'un d'aussi savant que la Société royale de Londres ait arrangé les choses de manière que le carré des révolutions de chaque planète soit toujours proportionnel à la racine du cube de leur distance à leur centre, et il faut être sorcier pour le deviner.[100]

It is this sort of banter that Adams echoed, many years later, when, in reading *La Conservation de l'énergie* (by Balfour Stewart) with which is coupled the *Étude sur la nature de la force* by P. de Saint-Robert, he broke out in this bit of verse in the margin of page 209 of that book:

> Dear me!
> What can matter be?
> Dear me!
> What can motion be?
> Playing all alone
> By their selves?
> First motion dances
> Then matter advances
> Then both prances
> All by their selves
> Dear me!

Well, Dr. Goudman comes to the conclusion: "Certainement il n'y a que de l'art, et la nature est une chimère."[101] Naturally, Dr. Goudman and the anatomist Sidrac were bound to embark on a discussion about the soul. Is there a *soul*? Or is there simply a *thinking faculty*?[102] Adams was to ponder these questions at great length while reading Taine, William James, Henry Maudsley, and William H. Thomson on *Brain and Personality*.[103]

The three thinkers—Sidrac, Goudman, and a Monsieur Grou, the world's greatest metaphysician (!)—decided to dine that they might have converse on sundry matters. (And Adams's pencil indicates his particular attention at this point.)

et comme ils devenaient un peu plus gais sur la fin du repas, selon la coutume des philosophes qui dînent, on se divertit à parler de toutes les misères, de toutes les sottises, de toutes les horreurs qui affligent le genre animal, depuis les terres australes jusqu'auprès du pôle arctique, et depuis Lima jusqu'a Méaco: cette diversité d'abominations ne laisse pas d'être fort amusante; c'est un plaisir que n'ont point les bourgeois casaniers et les vicaires de paroisse, qui ne connaissent que leur clocher, et qui croient que tout le reste de l'univers est fait comme Ex-change-alley à Londres, ou comme la rue de Huchette à Paris.[104]

But poetic irony is at its richest in the final story in which Adams made scorings—*Le Taureau blanc*, traduit du Syriaque Par M. Mamaki, Interprète du roi d'Angleterre pour les langues orientales. The Princess Amaside is not only beautiful but learned as well. How can she be amused with mere stories—she who read *On Human Understanding* "du philosophe égyptien [*sic*!] nommé Locke." "Je veux qu'un conte soit fondé sur la vraisemblance . . . mais surtout, quand ces fadaises sont écrites d'un style ampoulé et inintelligible, cela me dégoûte horriblement."[105] Having lost her lover, Amaside needs to be beguiled. She is told, in a conversation with a serpent, of a handsome young king who was suddently metamorphosed into a bull. "Ah! c'est mon cher Nabu . . . Elle ne put achever." This animal, as it happened, had approached Amaside and kissed her feet. She was very fond of it. The old lady in charge of the bull is told by the eunuch Mambrès, who accompanies Amaside, that she (Amaside) is infatuated with the bull. Vaguely, Mambrès feels that he had seen this old lady somewhere before.

[Il] regarda la vieille au manteau gris avec plus d'attention. Respectable dame, lui dit-il, ou je me trompe, ou je vous ai vue, autrefois. Je ne me trompe pas, répondit la vieille, je vous ai vu, seigneur, il y a sept cents ans, dans un voyage que je fis de Syrie en Égypte, quelques mois après la destruction de Troie, lorsqu'Hiram régnait à Tyr, et Nephel Kerès sur l'antique Égypte.[106]

They were going to sacrifice the bull and exorcise the princess. The poor beast, who understood everything but could say nothing, lay at the feet of Amaside and seemed to implore:

Venez me voir quelquefois sur l'herbe. Le serpent prit alors la parole, et lui dit: Princesse, je vous conseille de faire aveuglément tout ce que mademoiselle d'Endor vient de vous dire. *L'ânesse dit aussi son mot, et fut de l'avis du serpent. Amaside était affligée que ce serpent et cette ânesse parlassent si bien, et qu'un beau taureau qui avait les sentiments si nobles et si tendres ne pût les exprimer. Hélas!*

rien n'est plus commun à la cour, disait-elle tout bas; on y voit tous les jours de beaux seigneurs qui n'ont point de conversation, et de malotrus qui parlent avec assurance.[107]

The King of Tanis, the princess' father, arrives. There is a procession with Amasis, the king, at the head. A herald cries out that the bull should be tied and thrown into the Nile to avenge Amasis for the bewitching of his daughter.

Le bon vieillard Mambrès fit plus de réflexions que jamais: il vit bien que le malin corbeau était allé tout dire au roi, et que la princesse courait grand risque d'avoir le cou coupé; il dit au serpent: Mon cher ami, allez vite consoler la belle Amaside, ma nourrissonne; dites-lui qu'elle *ne craigne rien, quelque chose qui arrive; et faites-lui des contes pour charmer son inquiétude; car les contes amusent toujours les filles, et ce n'est que par des contes qu'on réussit dans le monde.*[108]

As we have seen, the princess has standards for the art of story-telling. *"Vous sentez qu'une fille qui craint de voir avaler son amant par un gros poisson, et d'avoir elle-même le cou coupé par son propre père, a besoin d'être amusée; mais tâchez de m'amuser selon mon goût."*[109]

There are a few direct references to Voltaire in Adams's works. No mention is made of him in his letters before 1897. He ends a letter written to Gaskell in January of that year:

I hope you like growling, for this letter will otherwise not cause your amusement. I have resorted to Voltaire's letters as a solid job. He had his little enemies too, but diverted them by libelling all mankind. I hardly think mankind worth the trouble here, but I am not Voltaire.[110]

Outside of recording his possession of the *Romans* of Voltaire, in his 1858 Catalogue, Adams's earliest reference to this writer comes in 1880 in his *Life of Albert Gallatin*. There Adams quotes a letter from Voltaire[111] to Count d'Argental, in which the former testifies to the fact that there were few battlefields in Europe where some of the Gallatins had not fought.[112] Voltaire was a near neighbor of the Gallatins at Ferney and dozens of little *billets* to them, in his hand, are still preserved.

Some are written on the back of playing-cards. The deuce of Clubs says: Nous sommes aux ordres de Mme Galatin. Nous tâcherons d'employer ferblantier. Parlement Paris refuse tout édit et veut que le roi demande pardon à Parlement Bezançon. Anglais ont vulu rebombarder Hâvre. N'ont réussi. Carosse à une heure ½. Respects.[113]

In Voltaire's works one may find a copy of verses written at the behest of Mme Gallatin, addressed to the Landgrave of Hesse-Cassel, who in 1776 had sent Madame his portrait. Adams further quotes a letter from Voltaire to the Landgrave: "15 septembre, 1772. Monseigneur—Mme Gallatin m'a fait voir la lettre où votre Altesse Sérénissime montre toute sa sagesse, sa bonté et son goût en parlant d'un jeune homme dont la raison est un peu égarée."[114]

There are some further references to Voltaire in *Democracy*, which came out in 1880 with the Gallatin book. The incident in which Baron Jacobi made sport of Ratcliffe, who confused Voltaire with Molière has been given earlier in this chapter.[115]

Adams's biography of *John Randolph* (1884) which came out while he was in the process of writing his *History*, simply tells us that "He [Randolph] read Voltaire, Rousseau, Hume, Gibbon, and was as deistical in his opinions as any of them."[116]

In the nine volumes of the *History* Voltaire's name is mentioned twice and both times in the first volume: once in connection with Timothy Dwight, who published, in 1797, an orthodox "Triumph of Infidelity" introduced by a dedication to Voltaire (a rebuke to mild theology and French deism)[117] and again in discussing man's bitter struggle against intellectual tyranny.

During nearly a century Voltaire himself—the friend of Kings, the wit and poet, historian and philosopher of his age—had carried on, in daily terror, in exile and excommunication, a protest against an intellectual despotism contemptible even to its own supporters. Hardly was Voltaire dead, when Priestley, as great a man if not so great a wit, trying to do for England what Voltaire tried to do for France, was mobbed by the people of Birmingham and driven to America. Where Voltaire and Priestley failed, common men could not struggle.[118]

During his honeymoon year in Europe, Henry Adams took his bride on a pilgrimage to Ferney. She wrote home about it, as follows:

We drove to Voltaire's house at Ferney one afternoon—and such a view of Mont Blanc and the whole range from the garden! They showed his salon and bedroom exactly as he lived in it. On one side of the parlour his heart is buried in a curious gilded monument, and opposite a stove, blue and gold, sent him by Frederick the Great, which I should like to send Father for Beverly. By the house, a simple little chapel with an inscription on the façade, "Deo erexit Voltaire"![119]

One is not disappointed in looking for the name of Voltaire in *Mont-Saint-Michel and Chartres* and *The Education of Henry Adams*. In the first work the name figures in the chapters entitled "La Chanson de Roland" (II), "Roses and Apses" (VII), "The Mystics" (XV), "Saint Thomas Aquinas" (XVI). These are rather strange titles to be associated with the name of Voltaire. Let us look at the passages in *Mont-Saint-Michel:*

These verses [of *La Chanson de Roland*] begin the "Roman du Mont-Saint-Michel," and if the spelling is corrected, they still read almost as easily as Voltaire; more easily than Verlaine (p. 14).

The period of eighteenth-century scepticism about such matters [i.e. regarding the Virgin and her Symbolism] and the bourgeois taste of Voltaire and Diderot have long since passed, with the advent of a scientific taste still more miraculous (p. 107).

Bernard of Clairvaux and Thomas of Aquino were both artists,—
very great artists, if the Church pleases,—and one need not decide
which was the greater; but between them is a region of pure emotion—of poetry and art—which is more interesting than either.
In every age man has been apt to dream uneasily, rolling from
side to side, beating against imaginary bars, unless, tired out, he
has sunk into indifference or scepticism. Religious minds prefer
scepticism. The true saint is a profound sceptic; a total disbeliever
in human reason, who has more than once joined hands on this
ground with some who were at best sinners. Bernard was a total
disbeliever in scholasticism; so was Voltaire. Bernard brought the
society of his time to share his scepticism, but could give the society
no other intellectual amusement to relieve its restlessness. His
crusade failed; his ascetic enthusiasm faded; God came no nearer
(p. 322).

This philosophical apse [Saint Thomas's assertion that God before
creation could choose whatever scheme of creation He pleased and
that, therefore, He did possess free will] would have closed the
lines and finished the plan of his church-choir had the universe not
shown some divergencies or discords needing to be explained. The
student of the Latin Quarter was then harder to convince than
now that God was Infinite Love and His World a perfect harmony,
when perfect love and harmony showed them, even in the Latin
Quarter, and still more in revealed truth, a picture of suffering,
sorrow and death; plague, pestilence, and famine; inundations,
droughts, and frosts; catastrophes world-wide and accidents in
corners; cruelty, perversity, stupidity, uncertainty, insanity; virtue
begetting vice; vice working for good; happiness without sense,
selfishness without gain, misery without cause, and horrors un-
defined. The students in public dared not ask, as Voltaire did,
"avec son hideux sourire," whether the Lisbon earthquake was the
final proof of God's infinite goodness, but in private they used the
argumentum ad personam divinam freely enough, and when the
Church told them that evil did not exist, the ribalds laughed
(pp. 369–370).

   In the *Education*—in Chapter IX entitled "Foes or
Friends" (1862)—Adams describes a dinner party of five in
the country at Monckton Milnes's home with Algernon

Swinburne as one of the guests. When the host drew the poet out into open conversation,

Then, at last, if never before, Adams acquired education. . . . For the rest of the evening Swinburne figured alone. . . . In a long experience, before or after, no one ever approached [Swinburne's talk]; yet one had heard accounts of talkers in all time, among the rest, of Voltaire, who seemed to approach nearest the pattern (p. 140).

Again, in the chapter, "Twilight" (1901) there is a reference to Voltaire;[120] also, in the Chapter entitled "A Dynamic Theory of History" (1904), where he speaks of the fact that each century violently resisted progress in new thought. "Its [Society's] contortions in the eighteenth century are best studied in the wit of Voltaire."[121]

To the last, "the high literary potential of . . . Voltaire"[122] was an invigorating force in Adams's mental life. From Washington, on January 30, 1910, Henry wrote to his brother, Brooks:

I have known you for sixty odd years, and since you were a baby I've never known you when you weren't making yourself miserable over the feelings of the universe. It has been your amusement, and a very good one. I always say that no one can afford to pose as an optimist, short of an income of a hundred thousand a year. Up to fifty thousand, the pose of pessimism is the only dignified one, just as it is after sixty years old. Both are equally good roles. Voltaire settled all that in *Candide*.[123]

We think of Adams seeking consolation in old age, as did Zadig, in philosophy and friendship. His famous breakfasts in Washington and his reading attest to that fact. His house, too, was a repository of art and a meeting place for the learned and the witty. Indeed, he confessed: "I want to look like a sort of American Voltaire."[124]

. . . De quoi te mêles-tu? dit le Derviche, est-ce-là ton affaire? Mais, mon Révérend Père, dit Candide, il y a horriblement de mal sur la Terre.—Qu'importe, dit le Derviche, qu'il y ait du mal ou du bien? Quand sa Hautesse envoye un vaisseau en Egypte, s'embarrasse-t-elle si les souris qui sont dans le vaisseau sont à leur aise ou non?—Que faut-il donc faire? dit Pangloss.—Te taire, dit le Derviche.[125]

Adams's whole education aimed at this as the highest form of wisdom—Silence!

Gathered between the covers of the book containing the *Maximes* of La Rochefoucauld, Adams also found memorable sayings by Montesquieu, the "capsular wisdom" and the pessimistic reflections of the aphorist Vauvenargues, friends of Voltaire. Indeed, here were three *sensibilitists* (to borrow Frost's word) who might be taken as the source of modern aesthetic sensibility, which is a compound of individuation, intellectual analysis, and pessimism. The common denominator of the three is pessimism and serves—on the positive side—as the basis for the creation of beauty. In Adams's novel, *Esther*, Wharton says to Catherine:

Do me a favor when you are there; go to Avignon and Vaucluse; when you come to Petrarch's house, think of me, for there I passed the most hopeless hours of my life . . . *Sadness is made only for poetry or painting.*

This Pateresque doctrine (for he did read Pater) Adams absorbed, *ab initio*, from the wise and sombre sayings which he took the trouble to underline, in the writings of La Rochefoucauld, Montesquieu, and Vauvenargues. Besides, as a New Englander, he was predisposed, through familiarity with the Bible, to *wise sayings*. The three served him early with an education in clarity through brevity and point. They also furnished him with the earliest phase of his sophistication. Of direct references there are but two: once, to La Rochefoucauld when he is quoted by John Randolph;[126] and again to Montesquieu's *Spirit of Laws* which (says Henry) J. Q. Adams read.[127]

Following are some of the *Pensées diverses* of Montesquieu, which Adams noted with his pencil:

Dans les conversations et à table, j'ai toujours été ravi de trouver un homme qui voulût prendre la peine de briller: un homme de cette espèce présente toujours le flanc, et tous les autres sont sous le bouclier.

Quoique mon nom ne soit ni bon, ni mauvais, n'ayant guère que trois cent cinquante ans de noblesse prouvée, cependant j'y suis très attaché, et je serois homme à faire des substitutions.

Ce qui m'a toujours donné assez mauvaise opinion de moi, c'est qu'il y a peu d'états dans la République auxquels j'eusse été véritablement propre. J'ai la maladie de faire des livres et d'en être honteux quand je les ai faits.

On ne sauroit croire jusques où a été, dans ce dernier siècle, la décadence de l'admiration.

Apparently, Adams was in agreement with Montesquieu's declaration that La Rochefoucauld's maxims "sont les proverbes des gens d'esprit."

There is only one saying of Vauvenargue's that Adams underlined: "Le vice fomente la guerre: la vertu combat. S'il n'y avait aucune vertu nous aurions pour toujours la paix" (CCXXV).

Adams's first reference to the author of *Émile* and the *Confessions* is to be found in one of his undergraduate articles in the *Harvard Magazine* for December, 1857.[128]

The next printed reference to Rousseau comes in his book on Gallatin.

Young Gallatin was affiliated with a knot of young men who, if not quite followers of Rousseau, were still essentially visionaries. They were dissatisfied with the order of things in Geneva. They believed in human nature, and believed that human nature when free from social trammels would display nobler qualities and achieve vaster results, not merely in the physical but also in the moral world.[129]

Adams speaks of Gallatin's preference for

a wilderness in his youth, and, as will be seen, continued in theory to prefer it in his age. It was the instinct of his time and his associations; the atmosphere of Rousseau and Jefferson; pure theory, combined with pride.[130]

We have already quoted Adams to the effect that John Randolph[131] read Rousseau[132] and that this reading is reflected, for example, in a passage such as this: "Often do I exclaim, would that you and I were cast on some desert island, there to live out the remainder of our days unpolluted by the communication with man."[133]

The copy of Rousseau's *Confessions* which Adams read and scored in a few instances is in the edition of 1886. Following are the passages he underlined:

Oh! si les âmes dégagées de leurs terrestres entraves voient encore du sein de l'éternelle lumière ce qui se passe chez les mortels, pardonnez, ombre chère et respectable, si je ne fais pas plus de grâce à vos fautes qu'aux miennes, si je dévoile également les unes et les autres aux yeux des lecteurs. Je dois, je veux être vrai pour vous comme pour moi-même: vous y perdrez toujours beaucoup moins que moi. Eh! combien votre aimable et doux caractère, votre inépuisable bonté de coeur, votre franchise et toutes vos excellentes vertus ne rachètent-elles pas de faiblesses, si l'on peut appeler ainsi les torts de votre seule raison! Vous eûtes des erreurs et non pas des vices: votre conduite fut répréhensible, mais votre coeur fut toujours pur.[134]

This passage is, of course, occasioned by the fact that after returning to Mme de Warens from a trip he finds a rival well established, as he thinks, in his place. Rousseau says at this point:

On a dû connaître mon coeur, ses sentiments les plus constants— Quel prompt et plein bouleversement dans tout mon être! Qu'on

142

Belles Lettres

se mette à ma place pour en juger. En un moment je vis évanouir pour jamais tout l'avenir de félicité que je m'étais peint. Toutes les douces idées que je caressais si affectueusement disparurent, et moi qui, depuis mon enfance, ne savais voir mon existence qu'avec la sienne, je me vis seul pour la première fois.[135]

Adams marked that critical moment:

Ce moment fut affreux: ceux qui le suivirent furent toujours sombres. J'étais jeune encore, mais ce doux sentiment de jouissance et d'espérance qui vivifie la jeunesse me quitta pour jamais. Dès lors, l'être sensible fut mort à demi. Je ne vis plus devant moi que les tristes restes d'une vie insipide.[136]

Adams followed, with a great deal of glee, Jean Jacques's eternal scrapes with his distinguished contemporaries—scrapes often carried on in the midst of amatory intrigues at Madame d'Epinay's Hermitage. In the case of his strident differences with Diderot, Mme d'Houdetot intervened with the argument that just then Diderot was very unhappy.

Outre l'orage excité contre l'*Encyclopédie*, il [Diderot] en essuyait alors un très violent au sujet de sa pièce, que, malgré la petite histoire qu'*il avait mise à la tête, on l'accusait d'avoir prise en entier de Goldoni. Diderot, plus sensible encore aux critiques que Voltaire, en était alors accablé.*[137]

Rousseau yielded, and a reconciliation took place.

He specialized in falling into one social difficulty after another. Adams loved to note, with his pencil, some of the pointed instances: such, for example, as Rousseau experienced with the Duc de Villeroy's young nephew, the Marquis de Villeroy, who died on the scaffold in 1794.

Il [the marquis] fit même un soir à table, une incartade dont je me tirai mal, parce que je suis bête, sans aucune présence d'esprit, et que la colère, au lieu d'aiguiser le peu que j'en ai, me l'ôte.[138]

It was this fact with regard to his temperament (or temper)

that made his relationship with Mme du Deffand untenable. Apropos of this, Adams marked the following passage:

J'avais d'abord commencé par m'intéresser fort à madame du Deffand, que la perte de ses yeux faisait aux miens un objet de commisération; mais sa manière de vivre, si contraire à la mienne, que l'heure du lever de l'un était presque celle du coucher de l'autre; sa passion sans bornes pour le petit bel esprit, l'importance qu'elle donnait, soit en bien, soit en mal, aux moindres torche-culs qui paraissaient; le despotisme et l'emportement de ses oracles, son engouement outré pour ou contre toutes choses, qui ne lui permettait de parler de rien qu'avec des convulsions; ses préjugés incroyables, son invincible obstination, l'enthousiasme de déraison où la portait l'opiniâtreté de ses jugements passionnés; tout cela me rebuta bientôt des soins que je voulais lui rendre; je la négligeai; elle s'en aperçut; c'en fut assez pour la mettre en fureur, et quoique je sentisse assez combien une femme de ce caractère pouvait être à craindre, j'aimai mieux encore m'exposer au fléau de sa haine qu'à celui de son amitié.[139]

Whereas in the *History*, Rousseau's name is merely mentioned *en passant*,[140] in *The Tendency of History*[141] Adams speaks of "the astonishing influence exerted by a mere theorist like Rousseau" and adds, "we know what followed Rousseau."[142] (He is, of course, referring to the French Revolution.)

In 1890 an exotic book was burgeoning in Adams's mind as a result of his experiences in the South Seas.[143] In its first form, the *Memoirs of Marau Taaroa, Last Queen of Tahiti*, appeared in 1893; an expanded edition was printed in Paris in 1901. The references to Rousseau are identical in both forms.[144]

Referring first to the report of Bougainville, who touched the eastern side of Tahiti in April, 1768, Adams goes on to say that one of his friends had pointed out to him "another French book, printed in 1779, an 'Essai sur l'isle d'Otahiti,' which offers a pleasant jumble of Montesquieu, Rousseau, and Hawkesworth." And he quotes as follows:

Il est doux de penser que la philanthropie semble naturelle à tous les hommes, et que les idées sauvages de défiance et de haine ne sont que la suite de la dépravation de moeurs, qui ne peut exister chez un peuple qui n'en a pas même l'idée.[145]

On Tahitian primitive goodness and innocence of civilized conventions, Adams writes:

The natural goodness of the human heart and the moral blessings of a state of nature were the themes of all Rousseau's followers, and at that time all Europe was following Rousseau. The discovery of Tahiti, as Wallis and Commerson painted it, was the strongest proof that Rousseau was right. The society of Tahiti showed that European society had no real support in reason or experience, but should be abolished, with its absurd conventions, contrary to the rights and dignity of man.[146]

Three decades after the arrival of Captain Wallis, the glory and the charm had gone out of Tahiti: "In these thirty years Europe had also passed through the experience of centuries; there, too, the dreams of Rousseau and the ideals of nature were already as far away as the Kingdom of Heaven."[147] Diseases and missionaries had infested the South Seas.

The Preface to the *Education* opens with a quotation from the *Confessions:* "I have shown myself as I was . . . I have unveiled. . . ." In a letter written in 1908, Adams asked William James: "Did you ever read the *Confessions of St. Augustine,* or of Cardinal de Retz, or of Rousseau, or of Benvenuto Cellini, or even of dear Gibbon?"[148] Three years later he paid Richard Wagner's *My Life* the compliment of calling it "a wonderful stripping-naked of a great man, which rivals Rousseau's *Confessions.*"[149]

Finally, even in his thinking on the nature of thought,

Adams turned to Jean Jacques for a pointed remark, to this effect:

"The man who thinks is a depraved animal," and in this [Adams adds] he expressed an exact view of psychology. As far as he is animal, the thinker is a bad animal; eating badly; digesting badly; often dying without posterity. In him the degradation of vital energy is flagrant (La dépravation de la nature physique est visible chez lui).[150]

Jean Jacques Rousseau was transported by ecstasy into thought; Henry Adams's path usually led from thought to feeling. Whereas in Rousseau we have a "chain of feelings"[151] reaching out to thought for logical continuity, in Adams we have a chain of thoughts given ultimate form through feelings precipitated by them. In both, the desire for artistic expression or presentation is dominant. America, captured by the noise of the steam engine and the grime of coal, might well symbolize for Rousseau the lost innocence of humanity and its happiness in a primitive state. Adams, the historian of America in its transition from Colonialism to steel, oil, and iron, joined Rousseau's "chain of feelings" in his reaction against the national picture developing before him, an "America where passion and poetry were eccentricities."[152]

Among eighteenth-century playwrights and novelists Adams was acquainted with the works of Diderot[153] (largely through Saint-Victor), Voltaire, Regnard,[154] Beaumarchais,[155] Lesage. To the last named, we find a reference in the *History* apropos the state of medical practice in Philadelphia at the end of the eighteenth century, which (says Adams) was "not much better than when it had been satirized by Le Sage some eighty years before."[156] Adams appreciated Beaumarchais' lighter touch as well as his satire. He refers to this when he compares the character of Thomas Jefferson with that of his own great-grandfather.

Thomas Jefferson—between ourselves, is a character of comedy;
John Adams is a droll figure, and good for Sheridan's school; but
Thomas Jefferson is a case for Beaumarchais; he needs the lightest
of touches, and my hand is as heavy as his own sprightliness.[157]

While Adams worked hard to initiate himself into those
studies which would help him to feel at home in the medieval
world and its poetry, the poets of the nineteenth century
spoke to him with the intimacy of contemporaries who are
addressing one of their own—an "enfant du siècle."

Among the nineteenth-century poets who seemed to occupy Adams's mind from his early college days through his
mature years, was Alfred de Musset. In a posthumous work,
which later received notice in the *North American Review*[158]
Gautier had said, "Alfred de Musset est le poète de la vingt-
jème année."[159] Henry was well nigh that age when, as a
iunior at Harvard, he first became acquainted with Musset's
poems and plays.[160] By the time he met Swinburne, he
could *parade*, as he said, "an affection for Alfred de Musset."[161] He had filled his copies of Musset's poems and
plays with scorings and had written in the margins some
pertinent remarks from Sainte-Beuve. For instance, on
the first page of the *Poésies nouvelles*, right over the title
"Rolla," he wrote this:

Plus d'un sait encore ce splendide début de Rolla, cette apostrophe
au Christ, cette autre apostrophe à Voltaire, surtout ce ravissant
sommeil de la fille de quinze ans.—Sainte-Beuve.

And above and below the large-capped title LA NUIT DE
MAI (p. 44) he copied these words from the same critic:

Les quatre pièces que M. de Musset a intitulées *Nuits* sont de
petits poèmes composés et médités, qui marquent la plus haute
élévation de son talent lyrique. La Nuit de Mai et celle d'Octobre
sont les premières pour le jet et intarissable veine de la poésie, pour
l'expression de la passion âpre et nue. Mais les deux Nuits de

Décembre et d'*Août* sont délicieuses encore, cette dernière par le mouvement et le sentiment, l'autre par la grâce et la souplesse du tour.

Further on in the book (p. 96) he scores with a double line these somewhat Arnoldian verses:

> Je souffre, il est trop tard; le monde s'est fait vieux.
> Une immense espérance a traversé la terre;
> Malgré nous, vers le ciel il faut lever les yeux!

This sentiment was echoed by Matthew Arnold whom Adams valued greatly.[162] And on page 97 he once more uses double scoring, for these lines:

> Descartes m'abandonne au sein des tourbillons,
> Montaigne s'examine, et ne peut se connaître,
> Pascal fait en tremblant ses propres visions.

In singling out these verses, Adams seemed to have provided himself with a program for future thinking and literary creation.

It is curious to see how often and how much Adams deliberately apes in life his literary sources. Back in Washington, towards the end of 1869, he was acting very much the tired Byron who—and the words are his when referring to himself—wished "to wash out the dirty creases which life [was] making in the corners of his soul's eyes."[163] In 1870 he writes to Charles Milnes Gaskell from Washington, of the attentions he is supposed to be paying to one of eight bridesmaids whom he had met at a recent wedding:

just on the threshold of twenty, and in fact not without fine eyes and no figure. Perhaps in your vulgar mercenary eyes her chief attraction would be £200,000. In mine her only attraction is that I can flirt with the poor girl in safety, as I firmly believe she is in a deep consumption and will die of it. I like peculiar amusements of all sorts, *and there is certainly a delicious thrill of horror*,[164] much in the manner of Alfred de Musset, in thus pushing one's amusements into the future world. *Is not this delightfully morbid? I have marked it for a point in my novel which is to appear in 1880.*[165]

Between 1868, when Adams returned to America, and 1886, when he went to Japan, the name of Alfred de Musset had appeared at frequent intervals in magazines and books which he saw or at least heard about. For instance, there were the translations from Musset by Emma Lazarus,[166] the articles of Thomas Sergeant Perry, Eugene Benson, and Henry James, which appeared in the *Galaxy* and *The Atlantic Monthly*, and dealt entirely, or in part, with the poet; the reviews of Lindau's "Alfred de Musset" and of Harriet W. Preston's translation of *The Biography of Alfred de Musset* by Paul de Musset. In one instance there is a stricture on Swinburne's uncritical manner of calling Alfred de Musset names. The reference is to Swinburne's *Essays and Studies.*[167] Throughout this period, Musset's star in the poetical heavens of France was seen alongside those of Victor Hugo and Lamartine, poets with whose work Adams was quite familiar.

From Yokohama in July, 1886, Adams wrote to John Hay, who was one of the friends who had commissioned him to buy certain articles, "I am trying to spend your money."[168] While doing this shopping (largely for works of art), he kept a small expense-account book.[169] It is on page 112 of this little book that Adams wrote from memory the first eight lines of a French poem, which turn out to be part of a sonnet which occurs in Musset's story, "Le Fils du Titien." That Adams wrote from memory is evident from the fact that several mistakes appear in his copy.[170] Why he should have committed these lines to paper while in Japan remains a matter for conjecture, except that one may venture the guess that Adams did so to while away an idle moment. (Or was it prompted by a mood which dictated, in a letter from Japan, the phrase "my melancholy little Esther?")[171] It is not impossible that Adams recalled the sonnet in Musset's story because he now found something in it pertinent to his own life.[172] On the other hand, Swinburne may have furnished an extra stimulus for an interest in a subject which had preoccupied him throughout his life, namely Titian.[173] In 1883 as well as in 1884[174] Adams had Swinburne in mind and spoke of his genius in high eulogism. And he must have read his essay on "Tennyson and Musset" either in *The Fortnightly Review* where it first appeared in February, 1881, or in his *Miscellanies* published in 1886.[175] Scurrilous in tone as this essay is, it nevertheless singles out the sonnets in Musset's "Le Fils du Titien" as "the masterpieces of a poet who had paid to one of [young Titian's masterpieces] the most costly tribute of carven verse, in lines of chiselled ivory with rhymes of ringing gold."[176] It is clear that Swinburne is referring to the sonnets dealing with the portrait of Beatrice Donato by Orazio, the son of Titian. It was one of these which haunted Adams's memory in Japan:

> Béatrix Donato fut le doux nom de celle
> Dont la forme terrestre eut ce divin contour.
> Dans sa blanche poitrine était un coeur fidèle,
> Et dans son corps sans tâche un esprit sans détour.
> Le fils du Titien, pour la rendre immortelle,
> Fit ce portrait témoin d'un mutuel amour;
> Puis il cessa de peindre à compter de ce jour,
> Ne voulant de sa main illustrer d'autre qu'elle.
> Passant, qui que tu sois, si ton coeur sait aimer,
> Regarde ma maîtresse avant de me blâmer,
> Et dis si, par hasard, la tienne est aussi belle.
> Vois donc combien c'est peu que la gloire ici-bas,
> Puisque, tout beau qu'il est, ce portrait ne vaut pas
> (Crois-moi sur ma parole) un baiser du modèle.[177]

The eternal problem of art versus nature, expressed so well by Goethe[178] in his "Kunst und Natur" was here introduced again, and intrigued Adams's attention. Which is greater—

life or art—art which is only an expression of the former?
Adams was enough in the romantic tradition to consider this
problem seriously.[179] If "Esther" was a symbol of life, and
his *History* a symbol of art, then the answer as given by himself is clear:

I care more for one chapter, or any dozen pages of *Esther* than for
the whole history, including maps and indexes; so much more, indeed, that I would not let anyone read the story for fear the reader
should profane it.[180]

The trouble is we can never be absolutely sure of the symbols.
. . . For, as a matter of fact, he was still busy with history[181]
—and suffering (especially when in Quincy) from spells of
"ghastly solitude." During one such spell in 1888 he recalled Musset again.

Under more favorable conditions I could have taken, like my
friend whose name I have forgotten, in Musset's *Caprices de
Marianne*, to a bottle of wine, and tobacco, till stupefaction should
bring back content.[182]

Perhaps one of his nieces spoke truly when she said that
"The Uncle was emotional himself" and that "He was
passionately fond of poetry" and that his restlessness always
sent him "off again on his travels, in search of his 'Princesse
Lointaine,' wherever or whoever she might be."[183] Yes,
he was himself a good deal like the poet to whom he felt
drawn: of a nervous sensibility, a dandy given to melancholy.
In Musset he found a modern variation of the Shakesperean
and Byronic identification of the creative ego with Time and
Love—all raillery to the contrary.

As was stated earlier, Adams paraded his enthusiasm for
Musset when he met Swinburne at Lord Houghton's in
1861[184]; Swinburne, however, estimated that this poet could
not sustain himself "on the wing" and proceeded to introduce
the American to the work of Victor Hugo. Their host,

Richard Monckton Milnes, with his "intelligence ouverte et traversée,"[185] had already spoken, thirty years earlier (the year of *Notre Dame*) with enthusiasm of Victor Hugo,[186] the poet of *Les Orientales*. In July, 1858, Milnes had seen Victor Hugo "là-bas, dans l'île," at Guernsey where he was in resigned exile in "a pretty house."[187] The year of the Fryston party saw, of course, the appearance of *Les Misérables*, which caused a good deal of buzzing both in England and America. In 1864, when the world was celebrating the tercentenary of the birth of Shakespeare, Hugo brought out his symphonic apostrophe to poetry, entitled, "Shakespeare."[188] To Swinburne, Adams's inspiring guide in French poetry, Hugo and Shakespeare were twin names. Indeed, he opens his book on the great Elizabethan with the name of Hugo, and his work on the Satanist with a reference to Shakespeare.[189] The sea forms a sublime unifying theme running through the work of the great and the near-great. Shakespeare's *Tempest* —"the never-surfeited sea"—cast a spell on Hugo, whose Giliat is swallowed by the billows, as it did on Swinburne and Adams. All were sensitively cognizant of the "tragic aspect of water", to use Swinburne's phrase; of "l'océan grandeur", Hugo's phrase;[190] of "the tremor of the immense ocean— *immensi tremor oceani*," the phrase Adams used.[191] Swinburne quotes from *Les voix intérieures:*

> Les pauvres gens de la côte
> L'hiver, quand la mer est haute
>   Et qu'il fait nuit,
> Viennent où finit la terre
> Voir les flots pleins de mystère
>   Et pleins de bruit.
> Ils sondent la mer sans bornes.[192]

Swinburne himself—so he tells us in his autobiographic poem, "Thalassius"—

> . . . set his eyes to seaward, nor gave ear
> If sound from landward hailed him, dire or dear;
> And passing forth of all those fair fierce ranks
> Back to the grey sea-banks,
> Against a sea rock lying, aslant the steep,
> Fell after many sleepless dreams on sleep.[193]

Adams, in all his wanderings in realms terrestrial as well as purely imaginary, finally fixed his mind's eye on the heights where Saint Michael held sway, "on his Mount in Peril of the Sea"[194]—*in periculo maris;* on the summit of a granite rock, whence "the eye plunges down, two hundred and thirty-five feet, to the wide sands or the wider ocean, as the tides recede or advance, under an infinite sky, over a restless sea."[195] The powerful fascination that the sea held for the three—Hugo, Swinburne, Adams—made them realize alike that

> . . . the sea mocks
> Our frustrate search on land.[196]

In any event, we have in Adams's library proof of his having read Hugo's poetry.[197] And, in at least one of his scorings we see that Adams did not confuse the poet's artistic power over him with the picture of Hugo as a collection of human foibles. On page 360 of Renan's *Feuilles Détachées,*[198] which Adams read, Renan discusses the character of Henri-Frédéric Amiel and contrasts his introversion and subjective skepticism with the overtness of a man like Hugo whose thirst for reality pulled his attention away from himself. Then Renan makes this conclusive remark: "C'est ainsi qu'un génie comme Victor Hugo n'a jamais eu le loisir de se regarder lui-même." This sentence Adams scored, and he indicated his dissent from Renan's opinion by putting an interrogation point in the margin.

Now, it is undoubtedly true that Hugo's appetite for action often made him oblivious of self; but poseur that he was, it is equally true that egoism was a constant factor in his personality. It is this second truth that justifies Adams's critical question mark. This also illuminates for us the meaning of the following reference that Adams made to Hugo in one of his letters to John Hay:

King says we ought to publish our joint works under the title of "The Impasse Series," because th y all ask questions which have no answers; but nothing has any real answer, and when one walks deliberately into these blind alleys where Impasse is stuck up at every step, one cannot, without a certain ridicule, knock one's head very violently against the brick wall at the end. Victor Hugo did this, to the delight of Frenchmen; but, for our timider natures, let us go on as before, and, when we see the brick wall, take off our hats to it with the good manners we most affect, and say in our choicest English: *Monseigneur, j'attendrai.*[199]

From a critical point of view, it is perhaps well to indicate that it is very doubtful whether Adams, leaning so much in the direction of the art-for-art's sake proponents, would have shared Hugo's sentiment expressed in *Les Châtiments*, in the poem, "L'Art et le peuple."

> L'art, c'est la pensée humaine
> Qui va brisant toute chaîne!
> L'art, c'est le doux conquérant!
> A lui le Rhin et le Tibre!
> Peuple esclave, il te fait libre;
> Peuple libre, il te fait grand!

On the other hand, Adams, as we know, was in perfect accord with such ideas in *La Légende des siècles* as,

> Un Poëte est un Monde enfermé dans un homme

> Les Shakespeares féconds et les vastes Homères.

For Adams, struggling with the cosmic problems of unity and multiplicity, the words of the *Infinite* (*L'Infini*, in

"Vingtième Siècle") had their rich fateful meaning: "L'être multiple vit dans mon unité sombre." And how well the following words of God (Dieu) expressed his own tragic view of a universe naturally given to degradation:

Je n'aurais qu'à souffler, et tout serait de l'ombre.

But in the end Hugo always invited a humorous note. This the Fryston host, "who felt the splendors of Hugo," supplied to his young guest some ten years after the famous visit, when they met again in Geneva. In the *Education*, Adams recalls that Milnes was then

fresh from Paris, bubbling with delight at a call he had made on Hugo: "I was shown into a large room," he said, "with women and men seated in chairs against the walls, and Hugo at one end throned. No one spoke. At last Hugo raised his voice solemnly, and uttered the words: 'Quant à moi, je crois en Dieu!'—Silence followed. Then a woman responded as if in deep meditation: 'Chose Sublime! un Dieu qui croit en Dieu!'"[200]

From Bagni Di Lucca, on Wednesday the 13th of July, 1870, Adams wrote to his good friend, Charles Milnes Gaskell: "It is all over. My poor sister died this morning."[201] From the manuscript in one of the books now in his collection, we know that three days later he was in Florence. The book he had turned to in his grief was by a poet whose relationship to *his* sister was pretty much what Renan's and Adams's were to their respective sisters.[202] The work was entitled *Journal, lettres et poèmes*, and the author was Maurice de Guérin.[203]

Perhaps the mood Adams was in, when he picked up this volume, led him to score with his pencil the following passage:

Le silence m'enveloppe, tout aspire au repos, excepté ma plume qui trouble peut-être le sommeil de quelque atome vivant, endormi dans les plis de mon cahier, car elle fait son petit bruit en écrivant ces vaines pensées. Et alors, qu'elle cesse: car ce que j'écris, ce que j'ai écrit et ce que j'écrirai ne vaudra jamais le sommeil d'un atome.[204]

With misgivings about his own talents, Adams must have felt that these words, somehow, also spoke for him. He also underlined:

Mon Dieu, fermez mes yeux, gardez-moi de voir toute cette multitude dont la vue soulève en moi des pensées si amères, si décourageantes. Faites qu'en la traversant je sois sourd au bruit, inaccessible à ces impressions qui m'accablent quand je passe parmi la foule; et pour cela mettez devant mes yeux une image, une vision des choses que j'aime, un champ, un vallon, une lande, le Cayla, le Val, quelque chose de la nature. Je marcherai le regard attaché sur ces douces formes, et je passerai sans ressentir aucun froissement.

And this, too: "et il arrive si rarement que je puisse contempler face à face une de mes pensées sans avoir à baisser les yeux."[205]

Adams's interest in Guérin, whose life span was so pathetically short,[206] was strong enough to lead him to read what Sainte-Beuve had to say about this sensitive poet. Thus, we find in his copy of the *Causeries du Lundi* several scored passages which deal with the poet. In his "Lundi" of September 24, 1860, Sainte-Beuve alludes to an article by George Sand in the *Revue des deux mondes* for the 15th of May, 1840, on Maurice de Guérin, "un jeune poëte dont le nom était parfaitement ignoré jusque-là." The poet had died the preceding year (July 19, 1839), at the age of twenty-nine. The occasion for this article was his "magnifique et singulière composition, *le Centaure*."[207] He had been nicknamed by a friend the André Chénier of pantheism. In a previous tome of the *Causeries*,[208] Sainte-Beuve had discussed the *Reliquae* of the poet's talented sister, Eugénie.[209]

The critic quotes a number of passages from the work of

Guérin; for instance, verses dated at La Roche d'Ovelle
(in the Midi) and referring to the autumn of 1832:

> Les siècles ont creusé dans la roche vieillie
> Des creux où vont dormir des gouttes d'eau de pluie,
> Et l'oiseau voyageur, qui s'y pose le soir,
> Plonge son bec avide en ce pur réservoir.
> Ici je viens pleurer sur la roche d'Ovelle
> De mon premier amour l'illusion cruelle;
> Ici mon coeur souffrant en pleurs vient s'épancher . . .
> Mes pleurs vont s'amasser dans le creux du rocher.
> Si vous passez ici, Colombes passagères,
> Gardez-vous de ces eaux: les larmes sont amères.[210]

There was a good deal in the tone of these verses to remind
Henry Adams of Alfred de Vigny.

Maurice de Guérin had read Lamennais's *Paroles d'un
croyant* and Bernardin de Saint-Pierre's *Études de la nature.*
Of the latter, which Adams had read, the young poet said:

C'est un de ces livres . . . dont on voudrait qu'ils ne finissent pas.
Il y a peu à gagner pour la science, mais beaucoup pour la poésie,
pour l'élévation de l'âme et la contemplation de la nature.[211]

Then come those passages from his diary which Adams scored:

Le 19 (mars)—Promenade dans la forêt de Coëtqueu.—Un grand
vent du nord roulait sur la forêt et lui faisait pousser de profonds
mugissements. Les arbres se débattaient sous les bouffées de vent
comme des furieux. Nous voyions à travers les branches les nuages
qui volaient rapidement par masses noires et bizarres, et semblaient
effleurer la cime des arbres.

(le 5 avril) . . . En m'asseyant au soleil pour me pénétrer jusqu'à
la moelle du divin printemps, j'ai ressenti quelques unes de mes
impressions d'enfance: un moment j'ai considéré le ciel avec ses
nuages, la terre avec ses bois, ses chants, ses bourdonnements,
comme je faisais alors. Ce renouvellement du premier aspect des
choses, de la physionomie qu'on leur a trouvée avec les premiers
regards, est, à mon avis, une des plus douces réactions de l'enfance
sur le courant de la vie.

(3 mai) . . . Jour réjouissant . . . La verdure gagne à vue d'oeil; elle s'est élancée du jardin dans les bosquets, elle domine tout le long de l'étang; elle saute, pour ainsi dire, d'arbre, de hallier en hallier, dans les champs et sur les coteaux, et je la vois qui a déjà atteint la forêt et commence à s'épancher sur son large dos. Bientôt elle aura débordé aussi loin que l'oeil peut aller.

(22 mai) . . . Il n'y a plus de fleurs aux arbres . . . Les forêts futures se balancent imperceptibles aux forêts vivantes. La nature est tout entière aux soins de son immense maternité.[212]

The following passage, also underlined by Adams, is Sainte-Beuve's observation:

Dans ses excursions par le pays et quand il traverse les landes, c'est bien alors que la nature lui apparaît maigre et triste, en habit de mendiante et de pauvresse; mais pour cela il ne la dédaigne: il a fait sur ce thème des vers bien pénétrants.[213]

It is instructive to note that in reading Sainte-Beuve's excerpts from Guérin, Adams underlined (at least in one case) what he had already scored previously in reading the poet for himself; for instance, the passage beginning with "Le silence m'enveloppe" and ending, ". . . ce que j'écrirai ne vaudra jamais le sommeil d'un atome."[214]

With the picture of the horrible death of his sister still luridly before him, one can readily understand the affinity in thought and feeling Adams found in reading the following —a letter from Maurice to Eugénie de Guérin:

En vain l'homme étale sa grandeur factice et tâche de cacher son néant sous un pompeux appareil; en vain la gloire et le plaisir prodiguent leurs séductions, son oeil percera le voile et ne verra dessous qu'un *roseau pensant,* jouet de tous les vents qui soufflent sur ce monde: . . . Non. La voix de la mort et de nos misères crie plus fort que toutes les voix des hommes et que les bruyants éclats d'une joie souvent fausse.[215]

Much of the spirit of this letter is paralleled in the por-

tion of the *Education* which speaks of the aftermath in Bagni
di Lucca.

The last lesson—the sum and term of education—began then. . . .
He had never seen Nature—only her surface—the sugar-coat-
ing that she shows to youth. Flung suddenly in his face, with the
harsh brutality of chance, the terror of the blow stayed by him
thenceforth for life. . . . One had heard and read a great deal
about death, and even seen a little of it, and knew by heart the
thousand commonplaces of religion and poetry which seemed to
deaden one's senses and veil the horror. . . . Death took features
altogether new to him, in these rich and sensuous surroundings.
Nature enjoyed it, played with it, the horror added to her charm,
she liked the torture, and smothered her victim with caresses. . . .
Impressions like these are not reasoned or catalogued in the mind;
they are felt as part of violent emotion; and the mind that feels
them is a different one from that which reasons; it is thought of a
different power and a different person. The first serious consciousness of Nature's gesture—her attitude towards life—took form then
as a phantasm, a nightmare, an insanity of force. *For the first time,
the stage-scenery of the senses collapsed; the human mind felt itself
stripped naked, vibrating in a void of shapeless energies.* . . . Society
became fantastic, a vision of pantomime with a mechanical motion. . . . The usual anodynes of social medicine became evident
artifice.[216]

By contrast to this mournful parallel one turns to another
on education and its failure to educate. "J'ai consumé dix
ans dans les collèges, et j'en suis sorti emportant, avec quelques bribes de latin et de grec, une masse énorme d'ennui."[217]

School was what in after life he commonly heard his friends de-
nounce as an intolerable bore. . . . In effect, the school created a
type but not a will. Four years of Harvard College, if successful,
resulted in an autobiographical blank, a mind on which only a
water-mark had been stamped.[218]

Already in 1870 the young professor of history was eager
to meet the intellectual challenge—to find relationship in
knowledge rather than atomism—involved in this question
posed by Guérin apropos a classical education:

Leur a-t-on jamais développé les rapports de ces magnifiques littératures avec la nature, avec les dogmes religieux, les systèmes philosophiques, les beaux-arts, la civilisation des peuples anciens? *A-t-on jamais mené leur intelligence par ce bel enchaînement* qui lie toutes les pièces de la civilisation d'un peuple, et en fait un superbe ensemble dont tous les détails se touchent, se reflètent, s'expliquent mutuellement?[219]

It was this *bel enchaînement* that resulted in the final link called *Mont-Saint-Michel*. Perhaps it was also then, that in reading the poet's journal the problem of dualism was stated for him by one of the entries:

Savez-vous, nous disait M. Féili—(M. de Lamennais) dans la soirée d'avant—hier, pourquoi l'homme est la plus souffrante des créatures? C'est qu'il a un pied dans le fini et l'autre dans l'infini, et qu'il est écartelé, non pas à quatre chevaux, comme dans des temps terribles, mais à deux mondes.[220]

This problem, too, was to find expression in his *Mont-Saint-Michel* and in his *Education*. Like Alfred de Musset, Guérin lingered long in Adams's mind; for, towards the end of the Chapter "Free Fight," dated 1869–70—the year in which Adams bought the poet's *Journal*—he associates Guérin's name with rebirth in nature.

When spring came, he took to the woods, which were best of all, for after the first of April, what Maurice de Guérin called "the vast maternity" of nature showed charms more voluptuous than the vast paternity of the United States Senate.[221]

Certainly, after all the years that had elapsed between 1870 and the time he set himself to write the *Education* (sometime during 1905) he could not remember the phrase quoted, without turning to the passage containing it and underscored by him: "Les forêts futures se balancent imperceptibles aux forêts vivantes. La nature est tout entière aux soins de son immense maternité."[222]

Besides Baudelaire, Musset, Hugo and Guérin, Adams was

acquainted with the work of at least eight other French
poets in the nineteenth century.

In Nodier, Adams found a poet who was not only admired
by Hugo, Musset, and Sainte-Beuve, but one whose romanticism corresponded to his own growing tastes in nature
studies and in philology as well as to his tendency to "Wer-
therean melancholy." He had also read the *Oeuvres* of
Béranger, which, together with works by Béranger's friends,
Chateaubriand and Lamartine, we find in the Adams Collection.[223] While there are some references to Chateaubriand
in the *History*[224] and in the *Life of Gallatin*,[225] there are none
to Lamartine in any of Adams's writings. Lamartine had a
double interest for Adams; his verse and his *Histoire des
Girondins*. In spite of the alleged inaccuracies in that history, Adams found in it, as he had found in Michelet, glow and
color.

Émile Faguet's *Dix-neuviéme siècle* served Adams as one
of his guides through French poetry of the nineteenth century.[226] In his copy of this work we find the famous line of
Vigny's—"*Seul le silence est grand, tout le reste est faiblesse*"
—underlined, the line which found its way into the *Education*. These words from *La Mort du loup* were to be reechoed
by Adams in numerous references to silence[227]—"Shakespearean Silence," since Shakespeare was one of Vigny's great
sources of inspiration. The idea of silence is closely associated
with that of loneliness. Now the idea of the heroic aloneness
of the creative genius as we find it in Vigny comported
harmoniously with the personality image Adams had of
himself.[228] Vigny's conception of the loneliness of genius and
of the poet as an isolated martyr are well known through
his "Moïse" and "Chatterton." This notion spread among
writers throughout Europe and America, particularly with
the advent of industrialism in the nineteenth century.[229]
Adams's friend, Henry James, gave definite expression to

this, and before him it was both implicitly and explicitly expressed by Emerson.[230] Another poet, much later in the century, whom Adams read and in whom solitude is one of the predominant motifs, is Sully Prudhomme.[231] Adams read his translation of Lucretius' *De rerum natura*.[232] This poet had a threefold appeal for Adams: 1) his interest in the confrontation of the creative artist with an acquisitive society; 2) his concern with science and skepticism as a central fact in the modern mind; 3) and his sensibility and melancholy. Adams's interest in Pascal, and in free will as a psychologic problem, may have been derived to some extent from his reading of Prudhomme.[233]

Another poet for whom science had a great fascination, and who, as one of the founders of *Parnasse* belonged to *Les Impassibles*, was Leconte de Lisle. Adams had read and possessed his *Poèmes antiques* (1852). There are many threads of filiation between Adams and Leconte de Lisle: an interest in scientific history, an opposition to the crudity and rapacity of industrialism, a reaching out for cosmic values; metaphysical pessimism linked with Eastern illusionism, and a penchant for exoticism. Adams's "Buddha and Brahma" is in some respects a pendant to Leconte de Lisle's *La Vision de Brahma*. In both, there is a "vision of the great All"; in both the problem of evil is confronted with the solvent of illusionism:

> O Brahma! toute chose est le rêve d'un rêve.

Adams almost seems to elaborate this line of Leconte de Lisle's in contrapuntal fashion when, in his poem, he says:

> For Brahma is Beginning, Middle, End;
> Matter and Mind, Time, Space, Form, Life and Death.

And one may relate these lines:

> Mais rien n'a de substance et de réalité,
> Rien n'est vrai que l'inique et morne Éternité

with:

> The universal has no limit; Thought
> Travelling in constant circles round and round,
> Must ever pass through endless contradictions,
> Returning on itself at last, till lost
> In Silence.
>
> Toute vertu se fond dans ma béatitude—
>   .   .   .
> For he who cannot or who dares not grasp
> And follow this necessity of Brahma,
> Is but a fool and weakling, and must perish.

We might add here another Parnassian to the list of
Adams's poets: Catulle Mendès whose *La Grive des vignes*
is in the Adams library.

Having run the full gamut of nineteenth-century French
poetry, it is hardly to be expected that Adams would neglect
the Symbolists and so-called decadents, as well as their more
strident critics.

René Taupin has already shown that it was the English
who first made the Symbolists known in America. Magazines like the *Dial*, the *Critic*, the *North American Review*,
echoed what was said about symbolism and decadence in
the *Fortnightly Review*, the *Nineteenth Century*, and the
Athenaeum. On these subjects Americans listened with
respect to what Englishmen such as Gosse, Saintsbury, and
Symons had to say. It was not until after 1890 or thereabouts, that men like Peck, Hovey, and Huneker sought
their information directly in Paris.

Meanwhile, following in the track of the English, there
sprang up in America numerous "little mags" in which the
Symbolists were treated and spoken of critically. In one of
these, the *Bachelor of Arts*, for May, 1895, Adams's friend,
the poet J. Trumbull Stickney—one of the first Americans,
incidentally, to receive the doctorate at the Sorbonne—pub-

lished an article on Verlaine.[234] Adams had apparently acquired the *Choix de poésies* sometime in 1891 or soon thereafter.[235] But he first mentions this poet in a letter addressed to Gaskell from Hamburg, August 24, 1896. There he talks of "Verlaine's expiring gnashings of rotten teeth," and adds: "or any of the other refuse of a literary art which has now nothing left to study but the subjective reflection of its own decay."[236] Adams here obviously reflects some of the prevailing, and for a while, fashionable critical reactions to the school of poets with which Verlaine was associated. We are referring, of course, to Max Nordau's *Degeneration* which had appeared in 1893, and which Adams read in the month of June, 1895. Yet Adams spoke of this work as follows:

The other day I thought I saw myself, but run mad and howling. I took up a book without noticing its title particularly and read a few pages. Then vertigo seized me, for I thought I must be inventing a book in a dream. It was Nordau's *Degeneracy*.[237]

For all of Adams's seeming alignment with the doctor-critics[238] against the so-called decadents, Verlaine is mentioned in the *Mont-Saint-Michel*, if only to say that the verses which begin the *Roman du Mont-Saint-Michel* "still read more easily than Verlaine."[239] Naturally, in his biography of George Cabot Lodge, Verlaine is referred to more than once.[240]

In the 1890s, while America's contribution to the art of poetry was still largely in the form of such productions as "Flowers for Mother's Grave," Adams was surely *avant garde* by the very fact that he was concerned with poets like Verlaine, Mallarmé, and the Symbolists generally. Though Mallarmé is mentioned but once in his letters—in fact, in the same letter in which he names Verlaine—we often feel the *parenté* of Adams's sentiments with those expressed in the well known lines:

La chair est triste, hélas! et j'ai lu tous les livres.
Fuir! là-bas fuir! Je sens que des oiseaux sont ivres
D'être parmi l'écume inconnue et les cieux!

Je partirai! Steamer ballançant ta mâture,
Lève l'ancre pour une exotique nature!
Un Ennui, désolé par les cruels espoirs . . .

Mais, ô mon coeur, entends le chant des matelots![241]

"My disease is ennui . . . Probably it will rapidly dis-
appear with travel." [242]

I want to go to the Fiji Islands next summer. . . . The object of
such long expeditions about the Pacific is to tire myself out till
home becomes rest. . . . You have no idea of the insanity of restlessness. Reason is helpless to control it.[243]

My ship is in the bay, all ready at the quay. . . .[244]

Maybe John La Farge, Adams's friend, was not joking
after all when he told a young reporter at Omaha that their
purpose in going to Japan was to find Nirvana. Later, the
artist wrote: "If only we had found Nirvana—but he was
right who warned us that we were late in this season of the
world."[245]

All of the above quotations come from letters which predate
his reading of Mallarmé. But they indicate a temperament
that would readily be predisposed to the fare offered by the
symbolist poets.[246]

That Adams thought of himself as a decadent we know
from an open reference to himself as such in a letter he wrote
while in Paris, in the fall of 1895.[247] In it he is inveighing
ironically against that over-self-consciousness of the tribe
which led to complete inanition. "Why," he asks, "can we
decadents never take the comfort and satisfaction of our
decadence . . . I prefer Rodin's decadent sensualities, but

I must not have them, and though rotten with decadence, I have not enough vitality left to be sensual."[248] That he was aware of the struggle waged between the proponents of decadent art, so-called, and its bitter enemies, we also know, especially from his reference to the famous pronunciamento against the dogma of general decadence, namely, Max Nordau's *Degeneration*.[249] It appears also that his reading in decadent literature was considerable, and that he delved into decadent art as well. His letters, if not his works, bristle with allusions to writers like Mallarmé, Verlaine, Baudelaire, as well as Flaubert, Huysmans, Maupassant, Zola, and a host of others. His talk of art includes the Japanese, the Javenese, Goya and Michelangelo, Gothic architecture and Whistler. He speaks of Wagner and Beethoven. His catholicity and inclusiveness are marked with the decadent stamp of the period. From the diaries which he caused to be destroyed, if we are to gather any intimations from his letters, one might have drawn many points of correspondence between himself and those master searchers for the remote, the exotic, and the recherché—the Goncourt brothers; and his penchant for Buddhism associates him with another decadent who prized highly every *frisson esthétique*, namely, Lafcadio Hearn. In his love of paradox Adams is not unrelated to Oscar Wilde: "One needs only to be old enough in order to be as young as one will."[250] This love of paradox, his friends La Farge and John Hay shared with him.

In the course of his Taylorian lecture on *La Musique et Les Lettres*, given in 1893, Mallarmé referred to Nordau's *Dégénérescence*.[251] Four years later (1897) Bourget, whose *Poésies* Adams read, and to whose *Essais de psychologie contemporaine* he alluded,[252] gave his Taylorian lecture on Gustave Flaubert.[253] In 1893, Bourget had lectured at Harvard; but Adams was then in Washington or South Carolina. However, his young friend George Cabot Lodge, then a student at Harvard, heard Bourget and recorded the unsettling effect that French literature of the moment had upon him.[254] In his lecture Bourget had occasion to mention all those writers who interested Adams: Ronsard, Rabelais, Diderot, Musset, Gautier (l'art pour l'art, l'impassibilité), Hugo, Balzac, Sand, Daudet, Zola.

Just as Adams was guided in his reading of French poetry by certain critics, so he was in prose. Besides Sainte-Beuve, he read Faguet's *Dix-neuvième siècle*, Jules Lemaître's *Les Contemporains*, Villemain's *Choix d'études sur la littérature contemporaine*, Émile Zola's *Documents littéraries*. In addition, he consulted such reference works as: the *Nouvelle biographie générale* in 46 volumes, G. Vaperau's two-volume *Dictionnaire universel des contemporains*, and A. Jal's *Dictionnaire Critique*.[255]

Chateaubriand happens to be the subject with which all three—Faguet, Villemain and Zola[256]—start their respective books. Because of his interest in travel literature, Adams was particularly concerned with Chateaubriand's *Voyages en Amérique, en Italie, au Mont-Blanc*.[257] He had occasion to refer to this author in both his *History* and the *Life of Gallatin*. Apropos of Talleyrand (about whom he read in Sainte-Beuve),[258] Adams quotes Chateaubriand as having once said: "When M. Talleyrand is not conspiring, he traffics."[259] In 1823, Chateaubriand, who was then minister of foreign affairs, was largely responsible for the conflict between France and Spain. Writing of that year, Henry Adams says:

The immediate object of sending a minister to France was to press for a settlement of American claims . . . M. de Chateaubriand, in 1823, ceased to pay his notes any attention at all, and contented himself with replying that they did not alter his view of the subject. This exhausted Mr. Gallatin's patience, and he roundly told M. de Chateaubriand that if France meant to remain friends with America, her conduct must be changed.[260]

Adams must have been sufficiently impressed with the *Mémoires d'outre-tombe* to use the title as a catch phrase in one of his *Galgenhumor* sentences in 1913, after he had suffered a paralytic stroke.

> The day before, Ogden Codman and young Barney took Elsie and Looly Hooper to Amiens to see the Cathedral and inspect the automobile circuit, while Miss Tone and I went shopping to Beauvais, and looked over the Cathedral, which I was astonished to see again, supposing I was dead long ago. It is a very curious sensation, this automobiling *d'outre tombe* like Chateaubriand.[261]

But long before 1913, Adams's imagination had been set afire by the definite but often subtle influence Chateaubriand had exercised in the literature of exoticism. I am referring to the *Memoirs of Marau Taaroa*. But with this matter we shall deal separately.

In his writings on Jefferson and on Gallatin, it was inevitable that the historian should make use of the correspondence and memoirs[262] of Madame de Staël, who admired the president and exchanged many letters with that fellow Genevan who became United States Secretary of the Treasury.

One of the victims of the French Revolution, Mme de Staël joined the army of *émigrés* and fled to an estate called Coppet, outside of Geneva. It is from there, in 1814, that she addressed to Gallatin one of her letters which Adams reproduces in his book:

> Vous m'avez permis de vous demander si nous avons quelque succès heureux à espérer de votre mission. Mandez-moi à cet égad, my dear sir, tout ce qu'il vous est permis de me dire. Je suis inquiète d'un mot de Lord Castlereagh sur la durée de la guerre, et je ne m'explique pas pourquoi il a dit qu'il était de l'intérêt de l'Angleterre que le congrès de Vienne s'ouvrît plus tard. C'est vous Amérique qui m'intéressez avant tout maintenant, à part de mes affaires pécuniaires. Je vous trouve à présent les opprimés du parti de la liberté et je vois en vous la cause qui m'at-

.....

.., ...

tachait à l'Angleterre il y a un an. On souhaite beaucoup de vous voir à Genève et vous y trouverez la république telle que vous l'avez laissée, seulement elle est moins libérale, car la mode est ainsi maintenant en Suisse. Aussi les vieux aristocrates se relèvent et se remettent à combattre, en oubliant, comme les géants de l'Arioste, qu'ils sont déjà morts. J'espère que la raison triomphera, et quand on vous connaît, on trouve cette raison si spirituelle qu'elle semble la plus forte. Soyez pacifique cependant et sacrifiez aux circonstances. Vous devez vous ennuyer à Gand, et je voudrais profiter pour causer avec vous de tout le temps que vous y perdez. Avez-vous quelques commissions à faire à Genève et voulez-vous me donner le plaisir de vous y être utile en quelque chose?

Mille compliments empressés.

Vous savez que M. Sismondi vous a loué dans son discours à St. Pierre.[263]

Mme de Staël, who was "then a power in diplomacy,"[264] again wrote to Gallatin, during one of her intermittent returns to Paris. Her own fortune was at stake and her anxiety is more than apparent:

Ce 30 septembre.
Paris, Rue de Grennelle St. Germain,
No. 105

Je vous ai écrit de Coppet, my dear sir, et je n'ai point eu de réponse de vous. . . . [She expresses anxiety as to the safety of her funds in America.] Je suis si inquiète que l'idée me venait d'envoyer mon fils en Amérique pour tirer ma fortune de là. Songez qu'elle y est presque toute entière, c'est à dire que j'y ai quinze cent mille francs, soit en terres, soit en fonds publics, soit chez les banquiers. Soyez aussi assez bon pour me dire si vous restez à Gand. Mon fils en allant en Angleterre pourrait passer par chez vous et vous donner des nouvelles de Paris. Enfin je vous prie de m'accorder quelques lignes sur tout ce qui m'intéresse. Vous pouvez compter sur ma discrétion et sur ma reconnaissance— et je mérite peut-être quelque bienveillance par mes efforts pour vous servir. Lord Wellington prétend que je ne le vois jamais sans le prêcher sur l'Amérique. Vous savez de quelle haute considération je suis pénétrée pour votre esprit et votre caractère.

Mille compliments.[265]

In the letter that follows, Gallatin reassures Mme de Staël—especially on the soundness of her American investments:

Ce n'est que hier [he writes on October 4, 1814], my dear madam, que j'ai reçu votre lettre du 23 septembre; .... Mais il me semble que vendre vos fonds à 15 ou 20 pour cent de perte serait un sacrifice inutile . . . nous sommes très-riches; nous étions huit millions d'âmes au commencement de la guerre, et la population augmente de deux cent cinquante mille âmes par an. Si je n'ai pas entièrement méconnu l'Amérique, ses ressources et la moralité de sa politique, je ne me trompe pas en croyant ses fonds publics plus solides que ceux de toutes les puissances européennes. . . . Avant de vous connaître je respectais en vous Madame de Staël et la fille de Madame Necker, aux écrits et à l'exemple de qui j'ai plus d'obligation que je ne puis exprimer. Mais je vous avouerai que j'avais grand peur de vous; une femme très élégante et aimable et le premier génie de son sexe; l'on tremblerait à moins; vous eûtes à peine ouvert les lèvres que je fus rassuré, et en moins de cinq minutes je me sentis auprès de vous comme avec une amie de vingt ans. Je n'aurais fait que vous admirer, mais votre bonté égale vos talents et c'est pour cela que je vous aime. Agréez-en, je vous prie, l'assurance et soyez sûre du plaisir que me procurerait l'occasion de pouvoir vous être bon à quelque chose.[266]

Adams points out that Mme de Staël

had established relations with Mr. Gallatin on his first visit to Paris before the negotiations at Ghent. She had been very useful in bringing the Emperor Alexander in contact with American influences. She was herself by birth and residence a Genevan, and a distant relative of the Gallatins. Her daughter was married to the Duke de Broglie in February, 1816, and as a consequence Mr. Gallatin found a new intimacy ready to his hand. American readers of the *Memoirs* of George Ticknor will remember how much the Spanish historian owed to that intimacy with the Broglies, which he obtained through Mr. Gallatin's introduction, among others, to Mme de Staël.[267]

Finally, Adams quotes from a letter written by Gallatin to Jefferson, soon after Mme de Staël's death:

The growing prosperity of the United States is an object of admiration for all the friends of liberty in Europe, a reproach on almost
all the European governments. . . . We have lately lost Mme de
Staël, and she is a public loss. Her mind improved with her years
without any diminution of her fine and brilliant genius. She was a
power by herself, and had more influence on public opinion, and
even on the acts of government, than any other person not in the
ministry. I may add that she was one of your most sincere ad-
mirers.[268]

Henry Adams was familiar with the work of the three fore-
most literary French women writing in prose. Madame de
Sévigné, Mme de Staël and Mme Dudevant (Sand). While
the Staël collection in the Adams library is poor, there is a
comparatively large number of books by Sand, including
three of the works mentioned in the *1850 Catalogue:*[239]
Consuelo (3 vols., 1856), *La Mare au diable* (1856), *François
le champi* (1856), and in addition, *Les Maîtres sonneurs*
(1865), *L'Homme de Neige* (3 vols., 1863-64); *La Dernière
Aldini* (1857), *Contes d'une Grand'mère* (1876), *Lucrezia
Floriani* (1857), *Le Secrétaire intime* (1863), *Mlle la Quin-
tinie* (1864), *Teverino* (1854), *Correspondance 1812-1876*
(6 vols., 1882-84).

As we have seen, his youthful enthusiasm for Alfred de
Musset naturally led him to an interest in George Sand.
From the point of view of social history, her name was to
be associated in his mind with the humanitarian movement
of which, besides herself, some of the leading figures were
Proudhon, Pierre Leroux, and Fourier.

It was through the writing of Sainte-Beuve that Adams
was first initiated into the works of George Sand. In addition, he had later read Faguet's and Zola's critical essays on
her.

In America, the reactions to George Sand and her work
differed with various writers; just as in England, even in the
case of such a couple as the Brownings, the wife differed

radically from the husband: Robert decidedly stayed away
and grumbled, while Elizabeth Barrett, full of enthusiasm,
went to see Mme Sand. Before Thomas Sergeant Perry's
full article on Sand,[270] there appeared Eugene Benson's two
interesting and informative articles in *The Galaxy* for 1867.[271]
The first of these two articles brought down upon the writer's
head some critically vituperative remarks which reflected
the American atmosphere in which the works of George Sand
were received. It was probably Richard Grant White[272]
who thus attacked Benson in the anonymous department
called "Nebulae." White calls Benson's first article "A
Eulogy, not a criticism." He argues that since Sand's novels
are essentially autobiographical, they are "the mere reflex of
her moods of mind at various stages of her checkered and
exceptional life. They are thus not imaginative in the
highest sense." Moreover, they are full of French sentiment,
"that is to say, it is artificial and corrupt." To this White
adds a general stricture on the French people. "The French
are in their daily lives the most prosaic and material of all
peoples." He admits that in philosophy and science they
are the most logical. "But to make up for all this, upon *la
gloire* for the nation and *le sentiment* for the individual, they
run stark, staring mad."[273] White continues:

Even in her soberest book, "Consuelo" George Sand is not free
from this *sentiment*. . . . She has uttered herself superbly; but
her self is not the self of a simple, natural woman, but the self of a
French woman, artificial yet rebelling against conventions, and
bearing upon her soul and transferring to her books the impress of a
life so exceptional, that if it were to become common, civilized
society would not endure for one generation.[274]

To this, Eugene Benson's second article on George Sand
was an answer. After asserting that she was "a great personal force in literature and society," he lunged at "those
vulgar people who characterize a thing as 'Frenchy' when

they wish to berate it or stigmatize it for being immoral and sentimental." He cites the critics of the English *Saturday Review* as speaking with fervor of the genius of George Sand. He also instances Edmond About who has called her "the noblest mind of our epoch." Benson points to her genius for form; and in speaking of her strong maternal element, he says that she "has spoken to Europe from the sacred and inviolable rights of that triple bond of honor; woman, wife, mother." As a literary artist, Benson claims, she has no equal among English writers.[275] "She literally *seduces* the mind with her words and [quoting Heine] *'makes you dream of immense deeps.'* " In his *eulogium*, Benson includes the praises bestowed upon her by Thackeray and George H. Lewes. He ends by drawing an analogy between the inaccessible beauty of the Venus de Milo and that of Sand's writings. "The large, luminous and serious beauty, the majestic sadness and brooding stillness, the dignity and calm of the heroic statue, are traits that have their counterpart in her writings and genius." [276]

Long before these articles were written, Adams, as a student of Alfred de Musset, read "Lélia" in which Sténio equals the poet of the *Nuits*. And a decade after Benson's encomium, Henry Adams, together with his wife, Marian, read with great absorption—partly because of their interest in art—George Sand's *Histoire de ma vie*, in which, Benson had said, "The finest pages of criticism . . . are to be found."[277] Interested in people like Louis Auguste Doré, Alexandre Gabriel Decamps—the one an extraordinary draughtsman, the other a painter of Oriental life—and Eugène Fromentin (attractive both as painter and writer),[278] the Adamses enjoyed what Sand had to say, for instance, on Eugène Delacroix.

It is from Marian Adams that we get a reaction to Sand's long autobiography. "I'm glad," she writes in one of her letters, "you're reading *Histoire de ma vie.* I'm in the 15th volume and think the interest increases." And again: "How are you getting on with George Sand? To me it grows more and more interesting; volume 18 is charming and I'm sorry it ends with volume 20." She thinks the account of the actress, Marie Dorval, "a marvelous bit of character painting."[279]

It appears that a Dr. Bessels, a friend of the Adamses, told them "more or less" about George Sand. He knew her through his brother, who was married to a relative of Alfred de Musset. In a letter Marian tells us further about this:

> He dined with George Sand and Dumas the younger in Paris in 1867 and then passed two days at her château at Nohant—the only other guests, two of her nieces; says it is a charming country, the dining room opened with folding doors on to a terrace, where Chopin dragged his piano and played to the stars; the Chopin piano still stood there. Dr. Bessels says Mme Sand looked like a sheep, had no conversation, scarcely talked at all, but watched others.[280]

However it may be with Adams's view of George Sand as a person, it is comprehensible why he, as a great letter writer himself, and as a reader of the letters of Mme de Sévigné, should have possessed himself of the six volumes of George Sand's *Correspondances.* For there she is revealed—and she was so to Adams, undoubtedly—as one who "sees with the eye of an artist and with the emotion of a poet."[281]

Among other nineteenth-century French novelists, the following are the ones Adams read, at least the ones whose works may now be found in his Collection: Stendhal,[282] Balzac, Mérimée, Gautier, Flaubert, the Goncourts, Alexandre Dumas fils, Ferdinand Fabre, Pierre Loti, Zola, Huysmans, and Anatole France.

Stendhal, the poet of energetic will (or "le poëte de l'énergie") would have great appeal for Adams the student of psychology, as well as for Adams the student of history. We know how much he was concerned with the nature of human will from his studies in psychology.[283] The interest then that drew him to read *La Chartreuse de Parme*—the only work of fiction by Stendhal in the Adams Collection— was a double one: psychologic and historical. Anything that portrayed vividly moments in the Napoleonic era was bound to attract him for obvious reasons. Perhaps Adams read *La Chartreuse de Parme* in the same spirit that he read Thackeray's *Vanity Fair*. Waterloo and the armies of Napoleon are in both of them and though Adams was writing a history based on facts and nothing but the facts, the color of an historical moment projected by the imagination of a Thackeray or a Stendhal could not escape him.

Did Adams think of himself, perhaps, as belonging "to the happy few" to whom *La Chartreuse de Parme* is dedicated in the end—those who are free in the exercise of their intelligence and their passions, at any price? Stendhal was a romantic with a difference. To the extent that he regarded life as Lanson puts it, "comme un champ d'expériences pour la culture de son moi,"[284] he was at one with the romantics. But he differed from them in bringing into play a critical and positive intelligence in whatever he examined. Adams's affinity for Beylisme made of him, too, a romantic with a difference.[285]

Where Stendhal had a poetic sense of the comedy of mind or spirit, Balzac had a feeling for the comedy of things or matter. Adams is, therefore, instinctively correct in coupling Balzac's name with that of Rabelais,[286] the great prose-poet of the material. Though Adams refers in his letters only to the *Contes drolatiques*,[287] he possessed a set of 44 volumes by Balzac.[288] In his *Historical Essays*, Adams writes of the speculations of Jay Gould, James Fisk, and Lane, and of the circumstances that led in 1869 to an investigation by the

Committee on Banking and Currency of the House of Representatives of "the causes that led to the unusual and extraordinary fluctuations of Gold in the City of New York, from the 21st to the 27th of September, 1869."

An intrigue equally successful and disreputable brought these two men [Gould and Fisk] into the Erie board of directors . . . Fisk, Gould, and Lane, became . . . the absolute, irresponsible owners of the Erie Railway . . . an empire within a republic. . . . The vicissitudes of a troubled time placed two men in irresponsible authority; and both these men belonged to a low moral and social type. Such an elevation has been rarely seen in modern history. The most dramatic of modern authors, Balzac himself, who loved to deal with similar violent alternations of fortune . . . with all his extravagance of imagination, never reached a conception bolder or more melodramatic.[289]

Flaubert's ideal of form, imposed on his realistic studies and exotic visions, appealed to Henry Adams the historian and literary artist. It flattered him to think that in his *History* he combined objectivity of fact with the expression of it by *le mot juste*, as did Flaubert. At the same time, we find him referring to this author when he (Adams) is preoccupied with the revision of an exotic work of his own.

I have amused myself [he writes in 1894] by printing (ultrissimo-privately) a small volume of South Seas Memoirs for "my sister Marau, the Queen of Tahiti," and it has amused me much more, and is much better reading, than my dreary American history, which is to me what Emma Bovary was to Gustave Flaubert. But the *Memoirs of Marau* belong to her, and have gone to Tahiti for correction and enlargement.[290]

A decade later Adams linked his literary experience of Flaubert (of Norman origin) with his experience of Norman architecture.

Here we must take leave of Normandy; a small place, but one which, like Attica or Tuscany, has said a great deal to the world, and even goes on saying things—not often in the famous *genre ennuyeux*—to this day; for Gustave Flaubert's style is singularly like that of the Tour Saint-Romain and the Abbaye-aux-Hommes. Going up the Seine one might read a few pages of his letters,[291] or of "Madame de Bovary,"[292] to see how an old art transmutes itself into a new one, without changing its methods. Some critics have thought that at times Flaubert was mesquin like the Norman tower, but these are, as the French say, *the defects of his qualities.*[293] We can pass over them, and let our eyes rest on the simplicity of the Norman flèche which pierces the line of our horizon.[294]

It would be interesting to know whether Adams, who was in London in 1897, went to hear the Taylorian lecture on Flaubert given that year by Paul Bourget. Adams had read a discussion of Bourget in the 1896 volume of Jules Lemaître's *Les Contemporains*,[295] and shortly before this had acquired this author's two-volume work on America.[296] At any rate, the essential ideas Bourget had already expressed in his *Essais de psychologie contemporaine*, with which Adams was familiar. He may even have acquired his copy of *Par les champs et par les grèves* immediately after reading *Appendice D*, dated 1886, in the *Essais*. (This *Appendice* is entitled: "Théories d'Art—A Propos de *Par les champs et par les grèves.*")

With his usual penetration, Bourget quotes from the *Éducation Sentimentale* on the question of the artist's impersonality: "parlant d'un travail d'histoire que fait un de ses héros: 'Il se plongea dans la personalité des autres, ce qui est la seule façon de ne pas souffrir de la sienne.' "[297] We find these words remarkably applicable to the man who sought refuge from his "dreary . . . History" in Tahiti.

To judge from the presence of thirteen volumes by Maupassant in the Adams Collection,[298] Henry devoted a considerable amount of time to the distinguished disciple of Flaubert. He read Maupassant in the early part of 1891 in Paris, upon his return from a journey of eighteen months

round the world "among the remote and melancholy islands."
Speaking in seriocomic fashion, he says that he swallows
"a volume of Maupassant with [his] roast" and then wonders
that he feels "unwell afterwards." Then he gives us a critical
addendum which reflects the literary controversies of the
period regarding realism and naturalism.

I . . . should hesitate to believe that human nature, except in the
Solomon Islands, could be quite so mean and monkey-like in its
intellectual cruelty as the naturalists and realists describe their
fellow-countrymen to be.[299]

And further:

Talk about our American nerves! They are normal and healthy
compared with the nerves of the French, which are more diseased
than anything on earth except the Simple Norwegian blondes of
Mr. Ibsen. In all Paris—literature, theatre, art, people and
cuisine—I have not yet seen one healthy new thing. Nothing
simple, or simply felt, or healthy; all forced even in its effort to be
simple—like Maupassant, the flower of young France—all tor-
mented, and all self-conscious.[300]

Along with Maupassant, Adams was "skimming a volume
of Goncourt."[301] He was reading the *Journals* and made a
hurried and inaccurate reference to them in a letter to
Elizabeth Cameron:

I elope with Sister Anne alone, when she is tired, and take her to
dine in the Bois among hair-curdling society, or in the astounding
Hôtel of Madame de Païva, described by Goncourt in his Diary,
and now a restaurant such as is not in the world outside.[302]

Adams, the historian, found the *Journals* rewarding because
they gave him more "inside" (as he put it) than he could
"get anywhere else."[303]

Adams's interest in Taine may have led him to buy
Prosper Mérimée's *Lettres à une inconnue*, prefaced by a
study on Mérimée by Taine.[304] In 1890, Walter Pater

(whose *Marius the Epicurean* Adams read) delivered his
Taylorian address on *Mérimée*. There, the latter is contrasted with Feuillet. Pater maintained that "Mérimée
loved surprises in human nature, but it is not often that he
surprises us by tenderness or generosity of character, as
another master of French fiction, M. Octave Feuillet, is apt
to do."[305] Whether Adams was acquainted with Pater's
lecture remains questionable; but two things are certain:
1) that in turning to the *Lettres à une inconnue* Adams did
discover the more tender, "romantic" side of Mérimée's
nature; 2) that earlier in his life, Adams had read Feuillet
and had expressed himself as follows in a letter to Gaskell,
written in 1863:

Apropos to Octave Feuillet! You say you have read him through.
Have you done so with his last work, *Sybille?*[306] I have read it
since starting. As one can't quite think that everything depends
on belief in the efficacy of prayer, I am sorry to say that Octave
looks very like a dependent of the Faubourg, writing what he
knows to be decayed matter (*Vulgo*, rot) for an earthly reward
at its hands.[307]

Yet, it is hard to believe that Adams, the professor of the
ideality of woman as a predominant force in society, held
this view of Feuillet.

Adams enjoyed Alexandre Dumas's "extravagances of
imagination."[308] He also read the works of Ferdinand
Fabre,[309] Théophile Gautier's *Le Capitaine Fracasse*,[310]
as well as Alphonse Daudet's *L'Évangéliste* (which we find
in his library). Of Adams's reading of Loti we speak in our
chapter on Exoticism.

As might be expected, Adams read Huysmans's *La Cathédrale*. But, rather oddly, the copy found in his collection
is in Clare Bell's translation.[311] The other book by this
author that he possessed was *La Bièvre et Saint-Séverin*.[312]

His mention of Huysmans in a letter written in 1896[313]

seems to suggest that he was guided in his reading at this time by Jules Lemaître's *Les Contemporains*. In the *Mont-Saint-Michel* there are several citations from Huysmans. Discussing the figures which line the three doorways of Notre Dame at Chartres, Adams says:

if you want to know what an enthusiast thinks of them, listen to M. Huysmans's "Cathedral." "Beyond a doubt, the most beautiful sculpture in the world is in this place." He can hardly find words to express his admiration for the queens, and particularly for the one on the right of the central doorway. "Never in any period has a more expressive figure been thus wrought by the genius of man; it is the chef-d'oeuvre of infantile grace and holy candour. . . . She is the elder sister of the Prodigal Son, the one of whom Saint Luke does not speak, but who, if she existed, would have pleaded the cause of the absent, and insisted, with the father, that he should kill the fatted calf at his son's return."[314]

We now turn to Adams's reading of "the amiable Zola."[315] While he may have read Zola long before 1894,[316] it is in a letter addressed from Washington that year that we find his first reference to the fact. He says that he has taken to reading history again, the history of the Roman Empire. "How much Petronius could give Zola, and yet need no odds!"[317] Two years later, he reflects the contemporary attitude on the part of some critics adverse to the naturalistic school, when he writes: "the only word I catch, indefinitely repeated, is *pourriture*! In English, we call it *rot*. . . . Zola's *Rome* is a very curious study of pathology, as Zola's books always are."[318] In addition to *Rome*, Adams also read *Lourdes*[319] and *Paris*[320] as they came out.

In 1898, Zola's name would inevitably be linked in Adams's letters with that of Dreyfus. His remarks on the Dreyfus affair are not very consistent, nor particularly enlightening.[321] But he does report that "Since Louis Seize was sent to the scaffold, France has done nothing that made the hair rise on end like the sending of Zola to jail."[322] In speculating on future literary taste, in 1903, he asked, rather gruffly, "What will please the palate of the pig to be?" and answered, "Apparently Zola hit it. He was big and coarse enough to suit. Our Chicago school rather feebly follow him." He had in mind particularly Frank Norris's *The Pit* which he was reading at the time.[323]

Besides the series, *Les Trois Villes*, Adams had read *Au bonheur des dames*, *Son excellence Eugène Rougon* and (we have already indicated) *Documents littéraires*.[324] Adams's reading of French prose included only one book by Anatole France, namely, *Le Jardin d'Épicure*. In a letter to Sir Robert Cunliffe, however, whom he asks, "Do you read Anatole France?" he does refer to *L'Orme du Mail* and *Le Mannequin d'Osier* as works which give "a picture of intellectual French anarchy."[325]

Among nineteenth-century playwrights, Adams knew the work of Édouard Ourliac,[326] the *Comédies et proverbes* of Alfred de Musset;[327] he possessed the *Oeuvres choisies* of Scribe,[328] whom he had read early, as an undergraduate,[329] as well as the plays of Joseph Méry.[330] We also find in his library the plays of Charles Bataille,[331] the *Mariana* of Jules Sandeau,[332] plays by Edmond About,[333] ten volumes of the *Théâtre complet* of Eugène Labiche,[334] the *Théâtre complet* in six volumes of Émile Augier (including *Les Effrontés*),[335] the *Théâtre* (in 2 volumes) of Octave Feuillet.[336] Adams's Collection contains, besides, Pailleron's *La Souris*[337] and eight volumes of Ernest Legouvé.[338]

On October 9, 1899, Adams wrote: "Rostand is to try and cap Cyrano. Old Sardou is at work."[339] The following year he addressed himself to Elizabeth Cameron thus: "Some people can even go to the theatres still, and see *Aiglon* and *Sans Gêne* and *Cyrano* and all the old old shows."[340] In 1910 he again referred to "the gigantic force and genius" of Sardou[341] and Rostand.[342] In May of that year, he went to see the latter's *Chantecler* at the Porte Saint Martin.[343]

Henry Adams had seen some of the outstanding French actors of his day, among them Julia Bartet, Réjane, Coquelin, and Sarah Bernhardt. To the last-named, the Adamses did not react favorably, and one is led to feel, especially in Mrs. Adams's pronouncements, that their criticism was not rooted in purely aesthetic criteria.

We went to see *Femme à Papa*. . . . As for Sarah Bernhardt, we detest her—voice, posing, looks, and all. Coquelin, of the same company, who you may remember, a most charming actor, hates her, too, and says openly, "Elle n'est pas sérieuse, ni comme femme ni comme artiste," but she is chic and the rage.[344]

When the noted actress toured America in 1880, Mrs. Adams wrote to her *pater:* "It's so nice that the Bernhardt is being socially tabooed on this side, our English cousins made such asses of themselves. See to it that Boston snubs her off the stage anyway."[345] Croce would hardly recognize this sort of talk as worthy of a critical mind—and Henry seemed to concur with Marian! Finally, the Adamses saw Sarah in *Camille*, performed in Washington. "We went to the Bernhardt matinée . . .; were not impressed and had no reason to reconsider our Paris convictions that to us at least 'she says nothing,' to borrow one of her own idioms."[346] In 1900, in Paris, Adams had seen Réjane again [347] in *Robe rouge* by Eugène Brieux and Jeanne Garnier in Marivaux's *Éducation de prince*.[348] He had seen Bartet give a good performance in Lavenden's *Duel*, though he had found "Bartet's rôle was just a little comical to an American." Indeed, all *pièces à thèse* made him smile at their obvious theatrical conventionality.[349] In May, 1905, he had undertaken (in great secrecy!) to translate for Auguste Émile Bergerat,

Vidocq, a play which Coquelin was to produce the following winter. For a while Adams found amusement and "repose in M. Bergerat whose infantile devices to amuse a tired world make me doubt whether the world is really tired. . . . I have done rather more than half of the MS and find it quite fit for the nursery. . . . It is rot, but it has taught me some French."[350] Nothing came, however, of the whole project; for it never reached the stage.

VI

Philosophic Excursion:
Descartes and Pascal

As has been stated earlier, Adams's reading in French literature included Descartes and Pascal. These, belonging as much to *belles-lettres* as to philosophy, had a double interest for Adams. The struggle within him of the rationalistic and romantic tendencies reflects two historically classic trends in French philosophy, namely, the *rationalism* of Descartes and the *anti-rationalism* of Pascal. In studying Adams's nineteenth-century orientation to old problems, it is well to keep in mind that modern materialism was furnished its outline and direction by the Encyclopaedists' extension of the Cartesian method to include the familiar psychological, social, ethical, and religious concerns of the nineteenth century, and that a noticeable filiation connects the romantic movement, through Rousseau, with the Pascalian tradition.

In his reading of Descartes and Pascal, Adams is tossed between the schools that argued "from unity to multiplicity,

or from multiplicity to unity." We follow him in his effort
to effect a linking of the two.

As between Descartes and Pascal, Adams puts the matter
succinctly before us:

Descartes had proclaimed his famous conceptual proof of God:
"I am conscious of myself, and must exist; I am conscious of God
and He must exist." Pascal wearily replied that it was not God he
doubted, but logic. He was tortured by the impossibility of rejecting man's reason by reason.[1]

It remained for the twentieth century to exert one great
effort in that direction, through the person of Henri Bergson.[2]

When the history of the treatment of Descartes in America
is told in full, Henry Adams will occupy an important place.
Descartes was in the family tradition—as we have seen; it
merely remained for Henry to give the French philosopher
the most serious attention. Aside from the fact that Adams
had very early encountered the name in reading the works
of John and John Quincy Adams, his quest for a scientific
theory of history soon led him to a preoccupation with the
method of science itself. This concern early focused his
attention on Descartes.[3] The *Education* and *Mont-Saint-
Michel* are crowded with references to Cartesian ideas, while
the books which he read in preparation for the writing of
his works are full of scorings. To these scorings we shall
devote a part of the present chapter.

The knotty problem of Realism and Nominalism which
comes up in all Cartesian discussions engaged his attention,
possibly as early as his junior year at Harvard, when he read
Lewes's *A Biographical History of Philosophy* (London,
1852).[4] In Volume II, page 61, of this work, Adams underscored a text whose ideas were to tantalize him forty years
later when he turned in the fullness of his maturity to the
study of Aquinas, Descartes, and Pascal. The text follows:

We are here led to the origin of the world-famous dispute of Realism and Nominalism. . . . The Realists maintain that every General Term (or abstract idea) such as Man, Virtue, etc., has a real and independent existence (apart from concrete instances). The Nominalists, on the contrary, maintain that all General Terms are but the creations of human ingenuity . . . merely used as marks of aggregate conceptions. . . . Plato was the first Realist; M. Pierre Leroux is, we believe, the last.[5]

This passage as well as the following (also underlined by him) served as prologue to his study of Descartes and Pascal.

Light, colour, sound, pain, taste, smell are all states of consciousness, and nothing more. Light with its myriad forms and colours . . . sound with its thousand-fold life . . . make Nature what Nature appears to us; but they are only the investitures of the mind. Nature is an eternal Darkness . . . an eternal Silence.

While the last sentence is perfect Pascal, the following sentences sound very much like the marginal arguments used later by Adams in his study of Descartes: "The finite *cannot* comprehend the infinite; such is the axiom. How *can* the finite comprehend the infinite? Such is the problem. The finite must *become* the infinite; such is the solution!"[6]

As the *1858 Catalogue* of Adams's own library indicates, he must have been reading that year either in course, or on the side, his seven-volume edition of Francis Bacon's works.[7] In Volume IV (1858) we find those scorings which indicate how the younger contemporary of Descartes led Adams to reflect on those problems which engaged the attention of the celebrated French philosopher: the relationship of the mind to the things it contemplates; the development of the sciences; the question of Order.[8]

During Adams's teaching period at Harvard, no less than five new courses in philosophy were introduced. One of these, "French and German Philosophy," made use of Bouillier's *Histoire de la philosophie cartésienne*. We know that he was preoccupied with Descartes sometime before 1884, when both his novel, *Esther*, and the first volume of his privately printed *History* appeared. In the latter, Descartes figures in the contrast drawn between Europe and America at the dawn of the nineteenth century. "In 1796, America was in swaddling-clothes. . . . Europe was on the verge of an outburst of genius" and Adams goes on to reflect, "If the average human being could accustom himself to reason with the logical processes of Descartes and Newton!—what then?"[9]

Esther contains many interesting ruminations on science, philosophy, and religion. Thus, Hazard's sermon includes a reference to the *metaphysics of Descartes* and a discussion of *science and religion*. The Church is no longer afraid of science, says Hazard.

The Church now knows with the certainty of science what she once knew only by the certainty of faith, that you will find enthroned behind all thought and matter only one central idea—that idea which the church has never ceased to embody;—*I am!*—Science like religion kneels before this mystery; it can carry itself back only to this simple consciousness of existence. *I Am* is the starting point and goal of metaphysics and logic, but the church alone has pointed out from the beginning that this starting point is not human but divine. The philosopher says, I am, and the church scouts his philosophy. She answers:—No! You are NOT, you have no existence of your own. You—are only a part of the supreme I Am, of which the church is the emblem.

This passage clearly reflects Adams's preoccupation with the Cartesian *cogito* and scholasticism and the many books he read, pencil in hand, on these subjects, with an eye, no doubt, on *Mont-Saint-Michel*. Adams's humorous reflection on Hazard's sermon is worth adding:

The flock would have been puzzled to explain what was meant by Descarte's *Cogito ergo Sum*. They would have preferred to put the fact of their existence on almost any other experience in life, as that "I have five millions," or "I am the best-dressed woman in the church—therefore I am somebody."[10]

But a full understanding of his concern with the philosopher can best be gained by examining Adams's copy of Jules Simon's edition of Descartes, which is replete with lineations and marginal remarks.[11] Part of a marginal note we find there[12] gives us a clue as to the connection in his mind between Cartesianism and Scholasticism: "The spirit of Cartesianism seems to be essentially realistic and scholastic."[13]

Adams's interest in a Catholic's view of the Cartesian influence in modern philosophy is shown in his underscoring of the following passage in the Abbé Carbonel's *Histoire de la Philosophie*.

Elle [Descartes's Philosophy] produisit d'abord le panthéisme de Spinoza, le monadisme de Leibnitz, le scepticisme de David Hume, et l'Idéalisme de Berkeley avec le psychologisme de Reid; puis le criticisme de Kant, et par lui le subjectivisme de Fichte et de Schelling, ainsi que l'absolu devenir de Hégel. Elle a pénétré, même dans les théories qui lui sont logiquement opposées, quoique en sens inverse, l'ontologisme et le traditionalisme; elle a infecté les oeuvres les plus pures de nos écrivains Catholiques jusqu'à ces dernières anées. Mais son résultat le plus sensible a été d'abord le rationalisme, qui rejette le surnaturel, puis le positivisme, qui rejette la notion même de la substance pour n'être pas obligé de constater l'âme de Dieu.[14]

But more directly, Adams's real introduction to Scholasticism came in his careful reading of Simon's edition of Descartes. There he followed, most intently, the *Objections Faites* par M. Catérus, Savant théologien (pp. 129–137). It is in the course of his argument that Catérus quotes from, and refers to, Saint Thomas, Saint Damascene, and Aristotle. Again, Adams's attention was called to the scholastic point of view in the "Deuxièmes Objections Recueillies par le R.

P. Mersenne de la bouche de divers théologiens et philosophes contre les II°, III°, IV°, V°, VI° Méditations," (pp. 154–160).

His interest in Descartes, therefore, goes hand in glove with his interest in scholasticism. Accordingly, we find that he has made many scorings and marginal notes in his copy of *S. Thomas D'Aquin et la Philosophie Cartésienne.*[15] His library also contains the two-volume treatise of Barthélemy Hauréau, *De la philosophie scolastique* (Paris, 1850).[16] Between pages 282 and 283 of volume one, the present writer found inserted a manuscript page, consisting of a translation by Adams of a passage on page 283. This translation Adams follows up with a series of syllogistic statements (really arguments) on the thoughts advanced in the passage. Following is a transcript of the manuscript:

This is the great point. Intellectual abstraction does not give the composite but the isolated form of matter [and also necessarily of mind.] Now, according to Abélard, and according to the majority of nominalists, it is determined matter which is the principle of individuation [of mind]. If then we leave out the matter, individuality [of mind] disappears; only universality persists, abides; but, with the individual matter [and mind], reality [both of matter and mind] vanishes, and there remains with the universal form [of matter and mind] nothing more than the opposite of reality, namely the abstract concept.[17]

In the blank space that followed this text, Adams wrote:

This seems to be pure Spinoza.
What is an abstract concept?
Concepts exist, quâ mind, or not. What exists, quâ mind, is real quâ mind.
An abstract concept is either real quâ mind, or does not exist.
If it is real, quâ mind, how can it be, as Hauréau says, the opposite of reality?
A triangle is an abstract concept?
A triangle exists, quâ mind, or not?
If it exists, quâ mind, it is real quâ mind, not the opposite of reality.

If it does not exist and is not real, quâ mind, how can it remain
with the universal form? Or does he mean that, after abstracting
the individual from the universal mind, nothing remains but the
abstract concept by the universal mind of its own universality?

Is not this the doctrine of Spinoza?

What then, can produce individuation either in mind or matter
except a third force? and so ad infinitum?

In addition to the use which Adams made of Descartes in
Esther, there are the references to Cartesian philosophy in his
Mont-Saint-Michel, the *Education* and his *Letter to American
Teachers of History*.

As would be expected from what has preceded, Adams, of
necessity, brings together Descartes and the Church Fathers
throughout the *Mont-Saint-Michel*. And we find his marginal
notes now woven into the text of his own book.

The twelfth century had already reached the point where the
seventeenth century stood when Descartes renewed the attempt
to give a solid, philosophical basis for deism by his celebrated
"Cogito, ergo sum." Although that ultimate fact seemed new to
Europe when Descartes revived it as the starting-point of his
demonstration, it was as old and familiar as Saint Augustine to the
twelfth century, and as little conclusive as any other assumption
of the Ego or the Non-Ego.[18]

Adams indicates where the deism of Descartes is opposed
to the theology of Thomas. "God must be a concrete thing,
not a human thought. God must be proved by the senses
like any other concrete thing."[19] Incidentally, Adams makes
no pretense of understanding the great Doctor: "The twenty-
eight volumes [of Saint Thomas] must be closed books for us.
None but Dominicans have a right to interpret them. No
Franciscan—or even Jesuit—understands Saint Thomas
exactly or explains him with authority."[20] Together with
Maumus, Adams is dazzled by St. Thomas's erudition—
"Cette lumineuse clarté."[21] He would agree with Gilson

that all of modern metaphysics is but the shadow of medieval philosophy and that Thomas is at its head.

Saint Thomas is still alive and overshadows as many schools as he ever did; at all events, as many as the Church maintains. He has outlived Descartes and Leibnitz and a dozen other schools of philosophy more or less serious in their day. He has mostly outlived Hume, Voltaire, and the militant sceptics.[22]

In the seventeenth century, the followers of Descartes deserted Saint Thomas and "started afresh with the idea of God as a concept." They found themselves at once "charged with a deity that contained the universe," whereas

the Church required a God who caused the universe. The two deities destroyed each other. One was passive; the other active. Thomas warned Descartes of a logical quicksand which must necessarily swallow up any Church, and which Spinoza explored to the bottom.

It was a question, according to Thomas, of proving cause as cause, "not merely as a sequence." On the point of *proving* God as a true cause, he satisfied neither Descartes nor Pascal.[23]

In the *Education*, Descartes's name is mentioned incidentally and in association with the names of Galileo, Kepler, Leibnitz, Newton, and Karl Pearson.[24] In the *Degradation of the Democratic Dogma*, Adams refers to Descartes as one of the great teachers of the intellect, teaching it "a habit of doubt";[25] also as arbitrator in the long-waged struggle between materialism and idealism.

Man began by usurping the rank of lord of creation. Galileo and Newton succeded in deposing him, much against his will—as the Church very candidly confessed—but he has never despaired of reinstating himself by means of his Reason. . . . Descartes offered a compromise, and in that respect differed from Kelvin. Descartes proposed to free man from material bondage, provided he might mechanize all other vital energies.[26]

We are still faced (Adams avers) with "the same old dilemma of Saint Augustine and Descartes—the deadlock of free-will."[27] In "The Rule of Phase Applied to History," Adams accounts Descartes as one of those who have been instrumental in changing the direction of human thought.[28] Yet in all of Adams's printed letters there is but one incidental reference to Descartes.[29]

Pascal, whom Henry Adams was to pronounce "one of the greatest men between Descartes and Newton,"[30] is, in a sense, a product of the nineteenth century.[31] For, it was not until 1842 that Cousin discovered the full text of the *Pensées*, and called the attention of the French Academy to the necessity of publishing a new edition of this work. Ten years later, Ernest Havet brought out his "Étude" on the *Pensées*, so much admired by both Renan and Taine. It is from then on that the historian of ideas can discern a continuous line of Pascal studies reaching through Léon Brunschvicg's masterly edition of the *Pensées*.

In the nature of the situation, Henry's grandfather, John Quincy Adams, could not very well have possessed an authentic copy of the *Pensées*;[32] but he had in his library, *Les Provinciales; ou, Lettres écrites par Louis de Montalte* (4 vols. Cologne, 1739), with the possessor's inscription in Volume I: "John Q. Adams, Oct. 7, 1795." In 1847, one year before the death of John Quincy Adams, the *North American Review* discussed the characteristics of the genius of Pascal.[33]

The copy of the *Pensées*[34] that the present writer found in the Collection at the Massachusetts Historical Society, with Adams's scorings and his signature on the fly leaf, is fully titled thus: *Pensées de PASCAL sur la religion et sur quelques autres sujets, nouvelle édition, conforme au véritable texte de l'auteur et contenant les additions de Port Royal indiquées par des crochets.*

There are 500 pages. Albert Maire's *Essai Bibliographique Des "Pensées" De Pascal*,[35] dates it 1866. There is nothing to indicate when this book was acquired by its owner, except the fact that the letters constituting Adams's signature would point to some decade after 1880. During this period, he was slowly emerging from the technical phase of history writing and approaching the creative phase, the full expression of which—*Mont-Saint-Michel and Chartres*—is vibrant with the name of Pascal.

As we examine Adams's scorings, we find that only twice does he question Pascal with an interrogation mark in the margin. Once, when he puts it next to the words, "Qu'ont-ils à dire contre la résurrection et contre l'enfantement de la Vierge?"[36] Here, his reading of Renan's *La Vie de Jésus* and the arguments (or explanation) against miracles given in it, dictated his question mark. Now, when Pascal further states that "Les bêtes ne s'admirent point,"[37] Adams as a student of Darwin, was bound to question this, too.

A good many of the passages which Adams scored naturally deal with the problem of the existence of God and fit into the web he was already spinning in his mind. His letters reveal the strands which he was to weave into the completed work. While he was reading metaphysics and studying St. Thomas, he referred,[38] apropos of the existence of God, to "Pascal's famous avowal of it in the simile of the wager."

Disons: Dieu est, ou il n'est pas. Mais de quel côté pencherons nous? La raison n'y peut rien déterminer. . . . Il se joue un jeu. . . . Que gagerez-vous? . . . Mais il faut parier. . . . Gagez donc qu'il est, sans hésiter. . . . Oui, il faut gager; mais je gage peut-être trop.[39]

"All this," he says, "is a sideplay to my interest in twelfth century spires and Chartres Cathedral." In the same letter[40] he declared that he liked Saint Thomas's ideas better than those of Descartes; he did so because, precisely at this time, he was under the spell of Pascal. He fancied himself at the moment "a twelfth century monk in a nineteenth century attic in Paris, looking down upon all of Europe as 'a menagerie' making a 'queer struggle for reality.' " He turned away from the forbidding scene to plod on, as he said in his *Mont-Saint-Michel*, "laboriously proving God,"[41] although Pascal informed him that God was incapable of proof. The passages in the *Pensées* bearing on this have been underlined by Adams. Some of them follow.

First as to skepticism in general:

Je ne puis avoir que de la compassion pour ceux qui gémissent sincèrement dans ce doute (p. 59).

The blasphemy of the impious is simply due to their ignorance of the Christian religion.

Ils s'imaginent qu'elle consiste simplement en l'adoration d'un Dieu considéré comme grand et puissant et éternel: ce qui est proprement le déisme, presque aussi éloigné de la religion chrétienne que l'athéisme, qui y est tout à fait contraire (p. 78).

Man's ignorance of God is closely linked with ignorance of himself.

Il sait si peu ce que c'est que Dieu, qu'il ne sait pas ce qu'il est lui-même (p. 89).

Pascal's axiomatic statement on the excesses in the use of reason was noted by Adams's lineation:

Il n'y a rien de si conforme à la raison que le désaveu de la raison [dans les choses qui sont de foi; et rien de si contraire à la raison que le désaveu de la raison dans les choses qui ne sont pas de foi]. Deux excès: exclure la raison, n'admettre que la raison (p. 91).

On the preceding page in the text Adams had underlined the statement related in thought to the above:

Si on soumet tout à la raison, notre religion n'aura rien de mys-
térieux et de surnaturel. Si on choque les principes de la raison,
notre religion sera absurde et ridicule (p. 90).

Adams follows Pascal's amazement at the boldness with
which some evangelists undertake to speak of God to the
impious; and he underlines what follows:

car il est certain [que ceux] qui ont la foi vive dans le coeur voient
incontinent que tout ce qui est n'est autre chose que l'ouvrage du
Dieu qu'ils adorent. Mais pour ceux en qui cette lumière est
éteinte, et dans lesquels on a dessein de la faire revivre, ces per-
sonnes destituées de foi et de grâce, qui, recherchant de toute leur
lumière tout ce qu'ils voient dans la nature qui les peut mener à
cette connoissance, ne trouvent qu'obscurité et ténèbres, dire à
ceux-là qu'ils n'ont qu'à voir la moindre des choses qui les environ-
nent et qu'ils y verront Dieu à découvert, et leur donner, pour
toute preuve de ce grand et important sujet, le cours de la lune, ou
des planètes, et prétendre avoir achevé sa preuve avec un tel
discours [and the clause that follows Adams underlines doubly],
c'est leur donner sujet de croire que les preuves de notre religion
sont bien foibles; et je vois par raison et par expérience que rien
n'est plus propre à leur en faire naître le mépris (pp. 154-155).

And here is where Pascal comes to the point at issue
(again noted by Adams):

Et c'est pourquoi je n'entreprendrai pas ici de prouver par des
raisons naturelles, ou l'existence de Dieu, ou la Trinité, ou l'immortalité de l'âme . . . cette connoissance, sans Jésus-Christ,
est inutile et stérile. Quand un homme seroit persuadé que les
proportions des nombres sont des vérités immatérielles, éternelles,
et dépendantes d'une première vérité en qui elles subsistent et
qu'on appelle *Dieu*, je ne le trouverois pas beaucoup avancé pour
son salut (p. 156).

The American Historian who was in the midst of the fray
between religion and science must have smiled as he underscored the lines in which the Jansenist threw down the
gauntlet to the opponents of faith:

Les hommes ont mépris pour la religion; ils en ont haine et peur qu'elle soit vraie. Pour guérir cela, il faut commencer par montrer que la religion n'est point contraire à la raison [this clause is italicised by Adams], ensuite qu'elle est vénérable, en donner respect: la rendre ensuite aimable; faire souhaiter aux bons qu'elle fût vraie, et puis montrer qu'elle est vraie; vénérable, parce qu'elle a bien connu l'homme; aimable, parce qu'elle promet le vrai bien (p. 188).

What about the metaphysical attempt to prove God? Adams's curiosity in this respect was answered in a passage underscored by him:

Les preuves de Dieu métaphysiques sont si éloignées du raisonnement des hommes, et si impliquées, qu'elles frappent peu; et quand cela serviroit à quelques-uns, ce ne seroit que pendant l'instant qu'ils voient cette démonstration; mais, une heure après, ils craignent de s'être trompés. Quod curiositate cognoverint superbia amiserunt (p. 156).

Reason is helpless—and irrelevant—in the search for God. Adams finds many passages to this effect in the *Pensées* and he underlines them:

on dit qu'il le faut croire par telle et telle raison, qui sont de faibles arguments, la raison étant flexible à tout (p. 178).

ce n'est pas par les agitations de notre raison, mais par la simple soumission de la raison, que nous pouvons véritablement nous connoître (p. 184).

On n'entend rien aux ouvrages de Dieu, si on ne prend pour principe qu'il a voulu aveugler les uns et éclairer les autres (p. 156).

Ainsi, tous ceux qui cherchent Dieu hors de Jésus-Christ et qui s'arrêtent dans la nature, ou ils ne trouvent aucune lumière qui les satisfasse, ou ils arrivent à se former un moyen de connoître Dieu et de servir sans méditateur, et par là ils tombent dans l'athéisme, ou dans le déisme, qui sont deux choses que la religion chrétienne abhorre presque également (p. 158).

Adams's style, which so often runs into terse statement

touched with irony and tipped with nuanced wistful re-
flectiveness, derived a good part of its pattern from the
literary form of those writers who inspired him to read with
pencil in hand. With this in mind, we are in a position to
understand the full meaning of his underscorings in the case
of the following statements of Pascal which carry with them
the fillip of epigram.

La force est la reine du monde, et non pas l'opinion; mais l'opinion
est celle qui use de la force (p. 209).

Tous les hommes se haïssent naturellement l'un autre (p. 207).

La grandeur de l'homme est grande en ce qu'il se connoît mis-
érable (p. 227).

. . . le présent d'ordinaire nous blesse. Nous le cachons à notre
vue, parce qu'il nous afflige (p. 246).

Qui ne voit pas la vanité du monde est bien vain lui même. Aussi
qui ne la voit, excepté de jeunes gens qui sont tous dans le bruit,
dans le divertissement et dans la pensée de l'avenir? (p. 258).

Si l'homme étoit heureux, il le seroit d'autant plus qu'il seroit moins
diverti, comme les saints et Dieu (p. 258).

L'empire fondé sur l'opinion et l'imagination règne quelque temps,
et cet empire est doux et volontaire; celui de la force règne toujours. Ainsi l'opinion est comme la reine du monde, mais la force
en est le tyran (p. 272).

Diseur de bons mots, mauvais caractère (p. 290).

La vraie éloquence se moque de l'éloquence: la vraie morale se
moque de la morale (p. 384).

As a reader of Montaigne, Adams was both instructed and
entertained by Pascal's reflections on doubt as expressed by
the author of the *Essais:*

Il met toutes choses dans un doute universel et si général, que ce doute s'emporte soi-même, c'est-à-dire s'il doute, et doutant même de cette derniére proposition, son incertitude roule sur elle même dans un cercle perpétuel et sans repos [Adams underscored especially "et doutant . . . repos"]; s'opposent également à ceux qui assurent que tout est incertain et à ceux qui assurent que tout n'est pas, parce qu'il ne veut rien assurer (p. 41).

On the pride of the scientifically minded—"ceux qui [sont] hors de foi"—Pascal found Montaigne incomparable in his power to confound and humble them:

pour désabuser ceux qui s'attachent à leurs opinions, et qui croient trouver dans les sciences des vérités inébranlables; et pour convaincre si bien la raison de son peu de lumière et de ses égarements, qu'il est difficile, quand on fait un bon usage de ses principes, d'être tenté [and Adams underscores what follows] de trouver des répugnances dans les mystères; car, l'esprit en est si battu, qu'il est bien éloigné de vouloir juger si l'Incarnation ou le mystère de L'Eucharistie sont possibles; ce que les hommes du commun n'agitent que trop souvent (p. 54).

The antinomic character of Pascal's statements, especially with regard to the uses of reason and faith, found echoes in Adams's style. He underscored the following:

Jamais on ne fait le mal si pleinement et si gaiement que quand on le fait par [un faux principe] de conscience (p. 194).

La raison agit avec lenteur, et avec tant de vues et sur tant de principes, lesquels il faut qu'ils soient toujours présents, qu'à toute heure elle s'assoupit et s'égare manque d'avoir tous ces principes présents. Le sentiment n'agit pas ainsi: il agit en un instant, et toujours est prêt à agir. Il faut donc mettre notre foi dans les sentiments du coeur; autrement elle sera toujours vacillante (p. 196).

Tout ce monde visible n'est qu'un trait imperceptible dans l'ample sein de la nature. Nulle idée n'en approche . . . [The following is underlined] C'est une sphère infinie dont le centre est partout, la circonférence nulle part (p. 214).

Toutes ces misères-là même prouvent sa grandeur. Ce sont misères
de grand seigneur, misères d'un roi dépossédé (p. 227).

L'homme n'est qu'un roseau. . . . . Une vapeur, une goutte d'eau,
suffit pour le tuer. Mais quand l'univers l'écraseroit, l'homme seroit
encore plus noble que ce qui le tue, parce qu'il sait qu'il meurt; et
l'avantage que l'univers a sur lui, l'univers n'en sait rien (p. 229).

Les sciences ont deux extrémités qui se touchent: la première est
la pure ignorance naturelle où se trouvent tous les hommes en
naissant; l'autre extrémité est celle où arrivent les grandes âmes,
qui, ayant parcouru tout ce que les hommes peuvent savoir, trouvent qu'ils ne savent rien, et se rencontrent en cette même ignorance d'où ils étoient partis. Mais c'est une ignorance savante qui
se connoît (p. 249).

Modern intuitionism, with which Adams was familiar
through Bergson, finds one of its early statements in Pascal
and we find it underlined by our reader:

Nous connoissons la vérité, non-seulement par la raison, mais
encore par le coeur; c'est de cette dernière sorte que nous connoissons les premiers principes, et c'est en vain que le raisonnement,
qui n'y a point de part, essaye de les combattre . . . cette im-
puissance ne conclut autre chose que la foiblesse de notre raison
(p. 265).

Plût à Dieu que nous n'en eussions au contraire jamais besoin,
que nous connussions toutes choses par instinct et par sentiment.
Mais la nature nous a refusé ce bien, et elle ne nous a au contraire
donné que très-peu de connoissances de cette sorte; toutes les
autres ne peuvent être acquises que par le raisonnement (p. 266).

Like Leopardi before him, Adams noted the somber
definitive statements on man's fatal estate: his pathetic
quest for so-called happiness, his desire for majority votes,
his gregariousness and his final act.

Nous sommes incapables de ne pas souhaiter la vérité et le bonheur, et nous sommes incapables et de certitude et de bonheur. Ce

désir nous est laissé, tant pour nous punir que pour nous faire sentir d'où nous sommes tombés (p. 269).

Pourquoi suit-on la pluralité? Est-ce à cause qu'ils ont plus de raison? non, mais, plus de force. Pourquoi suit-on les anciennes opinions? Est-ce qu'elles sont les plus saines? non; mais elles sont uniques, et nous ôtent *la racine de la diversité* [Adams's italics] (p. 272).

Nous sommes plaisants de nous reposer dans la société de nos semblables. Misérables comme nous, impuissants comme nous, ils ne nous aideront pas: on mourra seul. Il faut donc faire comme si on étoit seul, et alors bâtiroit-on de maisons superbes. . . . On chercheroit la vérité sans hésiter; et si on le refuse, on témoigne estimer plus l'estime des hommes que la recherche de la vérité (p. 297).

Le dernier acte est sanglant, quelque belle que soit la comédie en tout le reste. On jette enfin de la terre sur la tête, et en voilà pour jamais (p. 198).

In discussing the accomplishment of the twelfth century in the matter of solving the problem of Unity vs. Multiplicity, Adams compares that century with the seventeenth, and says this, in substance: In the struggle that took place in the twelfth-century schools of thought, where they argued back and forth from unity to multiplicity in an attempt to connect the two, it was found that realism led to pantheism, nominalism to materialism, and that finally a compromise was reached in conceptualism which begged the whole question. Now in the seventeenth century, "the same violent struggle broke out again, and wrung from Pascal the famous outcry of despair in which the French language rose, perhaps for the last time, to the grand style of the twelfth century."[42] Adams is here referring to Pascal's despair over the contradictory uses of reason, some of which we have referred to earlier in this chapter.

Whereas Descartes doubted God and had to recreate him

ab initio in a self-conscious logical process, Pascal wearily replied, as has already been said, "that it was not God he doubted, but logic."[43] At this point Adams quotes (this time in his own translation) a passage[44] already given in the original:

The metaphysical proofs of God are so remote (éloignées) from the reasoning of men, and so contradictory (impliquées, far-fetched) that they make little impression; and even if they served to convince some people, it would only be during the instant that they see the demonstration; an hour afterwards they fear to have deceived themselves.[45]

Adams continues to paraphrase Pascal, as follows:

Moreover, this kind of proof could lead only to a speculative knowledge, and to know God only in that way was not to know Him at all. The only way to reach God was to deny the value of reason, and to deny reason was scepticism.

Then follows Adams's translation of the famous passage in the *Pensées*, starting with the words "En voyant l'aveuglement et la misère de l'homme" and ending "afin que je visse quel parti je dois suivre," which he calls "the true Prometheus lyric."[46]

Adams has a remark, following close upon the long passage from Pascal, which has a kind of oblique meaning for us who are interested in what he thought of its author:

The mind that recoils from itself can only commit a sort of ecstatic suicide; it must absorb itself in God; and in the bankruptcy of twelfth-century science the Western Christian seemed actually on the point of attainment; he, like Pascal, touched God behind the veil of scepticism.[47]

Pascal could not be satisfied with Saint Thomas's proof of God as a true cause.[48] Also, for Pascal, whom Adams calls "the finest religious mind of the time,"[49] Descartes seemed to want to prove too much, when he argued that the existence of the idea of God within us proved His real existence. In this, Pascal and Saint Thomas were in agreement.

On the Augustinian doctrine of the Church, that evil is an *amissio boni*—a privation of good—that it (evil) might be "an excess of good as well as absence of it," Adams quotes Pascal:

three degrees of polar elevation upset all jurisprudence; a meridian decides truth; fundamental laws change; rights have epochs. Pleasing Justice! Bounded by a river or a mountain! Truths on this side of the Pyrenees! Errors beyond![50]

The Thomistic tour de force of herding God and man under the same roof, as Adams put it, shocked a good many Christians as well as heretics; and mystics like Saint Bernard, Saint Francis, Saint Bonaventure, or Pascal . . . "felt the nearness of God without caring to see the mechanism"[51] of the scientific proof of solemn truths.

The direct references to Pascal in *The Education* are distributed over three different chapters—"The Dynamo and the Virgin," "The Abyss of Ignorance," and "A Dynamic Theory of History."

Poetry is the only satisfying form of expression for a soul in crisis; for in it and through it the catastrophic impact of opposing forces is resolved in lyrical outflow. Adams had need of such expression, especially after his "long and tortuous" excursions through fields of knowledge, including the "vast forests of scholastic science." And in the chapter on "The Dynamo and the Virgin" he tells us that Pascal was one of those spirits he encountered on the long road from Zeno to Descartes, through Thomas Aquinas and Montaigne.[52] He now had crying need for "the true Prometheus lyric" to relieve the critical state of his own soul. Implicitly, Pascal's lyric suggests, at least in part, Adams's prayer to the Virgin and the Dynamo; for it too cries out from the midst

of the "aveuglement et la misère de l'homme et ces contrariétés qui se découvrent dans sa nature."

In spirit Adams's *Prayer to the Virgin of Chartres* is a
metrical stylization of Pascal's prose-lyric. It is as if Adams's
translation of the "Aveuglement" passage trained his poetic
vision on a poem of his own making. But the poem is subtly
bound to the passage that helped to inspire it. In both there
is the image of a lost, truant child, with its bulging eyes
looking out contritely on a shadowy vastness, in search for
the mother. The "murmurs" of this child are the outcries
of humanity stricken with blindness and misery, trying to
act bravely.

> Brave though we be, we dread to face the Sphinx,
> Or answer the old riddle she asks.
> Strong as we are, our reckless courage shrinks
> To look beyond the piece-work of our tasks.

Here are the "contrariétés étonnantes qui se découvrent dans
sa nature"—man in the presence of his own thought dwarfed
by the realization of the "finite sphere that bounds the
impotence of thought," in search of "an outlet everywhere"
but finding himself arrested by a transcendent force which
he can neither see nor understand—"sans savoir qui l'y
a mis, ce qu'il y est venu faire, ce qu'il deviendra en mourant."
"Still silence! Still no end in sight! No sound in answer to
our cry!" Something exists beyond what man can see but
"We see/Only our certain destiny/And the last word of Fate."[53]

Ainsi, considérant combien il y a d'apparence qu'il y a autre chose
que ce que je vois, j'ai recherché si ce Dieu dont tout le monde
parle n'aurait pas laissé quelques marques de lui. *Je regarde de
toutes parts et ne vois partout qu'obscurité.*

Pascal calls out *de profundis* for a light, "afin que je visse
quel parti je dois suivre." In antiphonal fashion Adams
prays:

Help me to Know! not with my mocking art . . .
Help me to feel! not with my insect sense . . .
Help me to bear! not my own baby load. . . .

Now that Henry Adams's theological history is beginning to
interest the world ("Did he or did he not turn to Cathol-
icism?"), we find a new significance in a passage he read in
John Morley's *Life of William Ewart Gladstone:*

His [Gladstone's] is not one of the cases, like Pascal, or Baxter, or
Rutherford, or a hundred others, where a man's theological history is to the world, however it may seem to himself, the most important aspect of his career or character.[54]

Whether the case of Adams had reached the peak of a
crisis or not, one thing is certain, that he found himself
carried along in the maelstrom of the warfare between religion and science—a warfare in which, as it advanced, religion tried to adopt the methods of science for its own uses
and science made a desperate effort to orient itself in the
mysterious regions of religion. In the melee that ensued
between these two realms, he encountered, among the
"hundred others," Renan and Taine in France, Symonds
(to take but one example there) in England, who underwent
spiritual crises. In their story and in the general history of
conflict between religion and science, reaching back to the
Renaissance and extending forward into the twentieth
century, Adams perceived the story of his own quest for
unity in a world of multiplicity. And in this story, the figure
of Pascal assumed for him both poetic and dramatic importance.

Adams found in the *Pensées* an admission that the search
for "elusive personal music" (Miss Eastwood's phrase) was
bound to end in failure unless it could be apprehended as a
phase of a universal harmony, or God. He further saw in it
the *locus classicus* of anti-intellectualist reaction, which he

presently found vigorously renewed in Bergson—a reaction which refused to admit that it was unreasonable to question the primacy of Reason in all things. Also, he found there a new cult of personality which relieved the "moi haïssable" in its pursuit of "an exquisite intensity of feeling" (compare Pater's "gemlike flame") of its insularity by merging it in a universal whole. Thus, the cult of personality becomes a method of pursuing one's way to God, with whom alone rests all salvation. Adams is revealed here as a man of his time, tapping with his fingertip in unison with the music of contemporary pan-lyricism.

In the chapter entitled "The Abyss of Ignorance," we find the next reference to the author of the *Pensées*. Whereas in the *Mont-Saint-Michel* he called Pascal "the finest religious mind of the time," he now characterizes him as "one of the greatest minds between Descartes and Newton"[55] and adds that he (Pascal) saw the master-motor of man in ennui—restlessness forcing action. Pascal's references to *ennui* comported only too well with Adams's cultivation of it. The recurrence of that word in his correspondence indicates that for him it had become a cult comparable to *la noia* in Leopardi and *Spleen* in Baudelaire. In the three of them, Leopardi, Baudelaire, Adams, ennui is the resultant of the struggle between reason and will—a struggle which found its classic expression in Pascal. Ennui, then, becomes the popular expression of philosophic dualism—the swinging on two horns of an age-old dilemma over "the abyss of ignorance."

We bid a fond farewell to Pascal in the ideational cauldron, "A Dynamic Theory of History"—where other names toil and trouble, such as those of Archimedes, Aristarchus, Ptolemy, Euclid, Plato; Joinville, Turgot, Auguste Comte; Giordano Bruno, Galileo, Kepler, Spinoza, Descartes, Leibnitz, Newton, Lord Bacon; Voltaire, Schopenhauer,

Nietzsche; Priestley, Jenner, and Franklin. That in this galaxy Pascal's name should be juxtaposed to Montaigne is quite understandable, since the connection in which their names occur is *skepticism* or the "persistence of thought inertia" as the "leading idea of modern history." As philosopher and scientist, Pascal was in a position to realize the expanding complexity of man's mind. As Christian poet he expressed his, and Man's bewilderment in its awesome presence—the bewilderment of "a priest of Isis before the Cross of Christ."[56] Against this growing metaphysical shadow, no help is to be found in man. Adams underlined the following directive in the *Pensées:*

C'est en vain, ô hommes, que vous cherchez dans vous-mêmes le remède à vos misères. Toutes vos lumières ne peuvent arriver qu'à connoître que ce n'est point dans vous-mêmes que vous trouverez ni la vérité, ni le bien. Les philosophes vous l'ont promis, et ils n'ont pu le faire.[57]

Since Pascal cries out poetically against mind as mechanism, one may well wonder why Adams, in search of a dynamic theory of history, draws Pascal's name into the circle of his discussion. A clipped statement in the *Mont-Saint-Michel* gives us the answer: "For us the poetry is history, and the facts are false."[58] Clearly, in his oscillation between the *esprit de géométrie* and the *esprit de finesse* Adams leaned toward the latter. In the opening year of the twentieth century, with two classics taking shape in his mind, he echoed Pascal in some *pensées* of his own.

The wit of man is . . . a sheer encumbrance, given him to show his idiocy. At least once a week, I lie down and roll in the dirt, to expiate my sins of reason. . . . I know I'm a fool, but the more I get folly, the more I wonder at the obstinacy with which the human being clings to the belief in reason. Who is right? Who isn't wrong?[59]

Touching his brother's *Law of Civilization and Decay*, he

spoke of man's *"profound helplessness and dependence on an infinite force that is to us incomprehensible and omnipotent."*[60]

Because the following sentence is often read without proper allowance for Adams's brand of humour, it has been responsible for the assumption that he embraced the Catholic faith: "There is no help for me except in the bosom of the Church."[61] These words were written in 1900, when he was deep in Saint Thomas Aquinas and Pascal, Saint Francis, and Saint Bonaventure.[62] His mind was then considerably exercised over the consequence and logicality of the *Pensées*. He adopted the paradoxical stand of Matthew Arnold (in whom one finds many echoes of Pascal), that the French mystics were never mystical; but was irritated by the fact that this idea "never has got lodgment in the English or German mind." [63]

Had Adams followed Renan in the study of Pascal, as he followed him otherwise, he would have been led out of his dilemma. In a letter congratulating Ernest Havet on the erudition of his "Étude" on the *Pensées*, Renan wrote:

Votre jugement sur l'état moral et intellectuel où furent composées les *Pensées* me semble de la plus parfaite vérité. . . . Je crois pour ma part que le livre de Pascal, s'il l'eût mené à fin, eût été de tout point faux et insupportable; car il n'est pas probable que la sagesse de Port-Royal eût laissé passer dans un ouvrage dogmatique les hardiesses que nous admirons. L'essentiel eût été cette vaine argumentation par les prophètes et les miracles, dont les matériaux informes sont avec raison relégués dans les appendices de votre édition. Les *Pensées* proprement dites n'eussent été, je crois, que l'accessoire et comme le préambule.[64]

As for dragging "the French mind far from line and logic,"[65] if by logic Adams meant science, there again Renan's answer was direct and clear: "La science viendrait à détruire en apparence Dieu et l'âme immortelle, que le livre des *Pensées* resterait jeune encore de vie et de vérité." Unlike Renan, Adams viewed Pascal with the eyes of a nineteenth-cen-

tury romantic and thus there arose in his mind the problem
of *consequence*—it was a problem that applied to himself
more than to Pascal, who together with Bossuet upheld the
"juste milieu,"[66] just as the inebriety of Novalis created the
image of a God-intoxicated Spinoza. But what is God? He
is the One—the one in whom all opposites are resolved. In
their hunger for unity, all thinkers and poets are God-intoxicated men. Of this Adams was fully aware.

Pascal's theory of orders and his *Mémorial* attest to
Adams's correctness in placing him among the mystics.
Adams's own development paralleled the ascending hierarchy
of Pascal's orders: 1) the order of matter, 2) the order of
minds, 3) the order of grace or holiness.[67] Starting with the
order of *matter* (his early interest in geology), he had gone on
to the order of mind (witness his growing interest in psychology) and had progressed to the order of grace in his study
of Maumus, Régnon, and the mystics (including Pascal).
Pascal's *Mémorial* finds its literary analogue in Adams's
Prayer to the Virgin. Ultimately, the coherence of the arts
and the sciences, man's varying responses to the mystery of
the universe, must be sought—if it is to be found at all—in
contemporary pan-lyricism, which may be traced back to
Pascal, who, in the rich variety of his spirit, exhibited at
different times both the method of the scientist and the
intuitive approach of the artist.

The *Pensées* are a collection of *poèmes en prose* which de-
rive their unity not from any subject inherent in them, but
from the troubled spirit that puts them into motion, like
an unseen zephyr that is made manifest by rippled waters.
The mind is caught by the blandishment of rhythmic
motion.

But there is one thing that in the nineteenth century gave
coherent meaning to readers of the *Pensées*: the interfusion
of man's pain, in the presence of the inscrutable forces of

nature, in a pattern of reflective irony. This reflective irony, manifest throughout Adams's work, especially attracted him to Pascal.

Adams may have come originally to the author of the *Pensées* to get certain answers to certain questions ("What is the nature of God?" "Can we prove God?"). He left enriched with the art of contemplating the vastness of man's hunger for the unknown, and the immeasurable reserves in his heart and brain which sustain him in his quest for the appeasement of that hunger. But, if close study of Pascal enriched his imagination, contact with the thought of Descartes yielded him, at once, a vision of the variety of problems confronting the rational mind and an insight into the doubts that inhere in its very operation. In a sense, therefore, Pascal was to prepare Adams, as he did many others, for the intuition of Bergson, while Descartes pointed the way to the scientific criticism of the Poincarés.

VII

The Belated Romantic: Exoticism

RESTLESSNESS was a family trait among the Adamses.
Henry was no exception. From his reading, he learned how
he might capitalize on his *nostalgie*. John La Farge helped
him with artistic companionship in travels to far-off Japan and
Tahiti. Tired of the "wearisome disease of past and present,"[1]— his *History* was not yet completed[2]—he wrote from
San Francisco on June 11, 1886, "My ship is in the bay."[3]
He was bound for Japan. While there he recalled his youthful
reading of Musset and spoke of his "melancholy little
Esther." He knew and recognized very easily the literary
value of "melancholy," for he was to repeat the word often
in his letters from Tahiti. Some of this melancholy really
came from his reading of Chateaubriand, Maurice de Guérin,
Senancour and Pierre Loti. Though he read the latter's
Madame Chrysanthème after his experiences in Japan, the
dedicatory "Préface" of Loti's book[4] very conveniently seems
to speak for Adams: "Bien que le rôle le plus long soit en apparence à Madame Chrysanthème, il est bien certain que les
trois principaux personnages sont *Moi*, le *Japon*, et l'*Effet*
que ce pays m'a produit."

Instead of Nirvana, which he went to seek "late in this season of the world,"[5] Adams found the cackle of women who were "obviously wooden dolls badly made," and everywhere "the same eternal and meaningless laughter, as though death were the pleasantest jest of all." To him this was a dream world suggestive of fairy books and the nursery.[6] Attendance at a Geisha ball reinforced this impression. He was "lost in astonishment at this flower of eastern culture."[7]

So strong was his affinity for exotic literature that the parallelism in tone and feeling do not surprise us. Nor should we be surprised at his mention of Loti in writing from Papeete, in the South Sea Isles.[8] Loti's treatment of exotic love could now serve Adams's purpose: to give literary form to his experience in Tahiti.[9]

Professor Gilbert Chinard has shown that there was a rich literature dealing with Tahiti.[10] Adams starts his work with Bougainville who had the practical objective of establishing a French colony there.[11] In his *Voyage autour du Monde* (first published in Paris in 1771, 2 vols.), it is the description of the people and the island of Otahiti[12] that has become most current.[13] According to Adams, Bougainville touched at Hitiaa, on the eastern side of Tahiti, in April, 1768.

In addition to Bougainville's *Voyage*, Adams made use of an "Essai sur l'île d'Otahiti" (1779), falsely attributed to the same author.[14] This essay, which offers "a pleasant jumble of Montesquieu, Rousseau and Hawkesworth" was pointed out to Adams (so he tells us), by a friend.[15] Adams does not mention that the author of this work was a certain Taitbout, a scientist and mathematician, who died in 1799.[16] He quotes the following reflection from Taitbout's work:

Il est doux de penser que la philanthropie semble naturelle à tous les hommes, et que les idées sauvages de défiance et de haine ne sont que la suite de la dépravation de moeurs, qui ne peut exister chez un peuple qui n'en a pas même l'idée.[17]

The source of most misunderstandings about Tahiti, according to Adams, was the naturalist Commerson[18] who was of Bougainville's party on his voyage. It was he who called the island Utopia, and declared, Rousseauistically, that in Tahiti "l'acte de créer son semblable est un acte de religion." Adams quotes further from Commerson:

Je ne les quitterai pas, ces chers Taïtiens, sans les avoir lavés d'une injure qu'on leur a faite en les traitant de voleurs. Il est vrai qu'ils nous ont enlevé beaucoup de choses, et cela même avec une dextérité qui ferait honneur au plus habile filou de Paris; mais méritent-ils pour cela le nom de voleurs? Voyons ce que c'est que le vol? c'est l'enlèvement d'une chose qui est en propriété à un autre, il faut donc que ce quelqu'un se plaigne justement d'avoir été volé, qu'il lui ait été enlevé un effet sur lequel son droit de propriété était préétabli; mais ce droit de propriété est-il dans la nature? non: il est de pure convention; or, aucune convention n'oblige qu'elle ne soit connue et acceptée. Or, le Taïtien qui n'a rien à lui, qui offre et donne généreusement tout ce qu'il voit désirer, ne l'a jamais connu ce droit exclusif! donc l'acte d'enlèvement qu'il vous a fait d'une chose qui excite sa curiosité, n'est, selon lui, qu'un acte d'équité naturelle. . . . Je ne vois pas l'ombre d'un vol là-dedans.[19]

This sentimental casuistry is perfect Rousseau and by contrast reveals all of Bougainville's society as corrupt. The following quotation from Adams further emphasizes this point:

The French philosophers seriously used Tahiti for this purpose, and with effect, as every one knows. Wallis's queen played a chief part in the European play, by exciting interest and sympathy; for the years before and after 1770 were sentimental, and, between Diderot's Orou[20] and Goethe's *Werter*, the sentimental princess of Hawkesworth's voyages was at home. . . . Dr. Hawkesworth may have added some color to the story that Wallis had to tell. . . . [The] queen was, without her own knowledge or consent, directly concerned in causing the French Revolution and costing the head of her sister-queen, Marie Antoinette.[21]

But Adams's reading was not confined to these authors.
He also read J. A. Moerenhout's *Voyages aux Iles du Grand
Océan*,[22] and while he finds Moerenhout confusing in the
matter of sources and names, he credits him with being
"the only writer about Tahiti who knew Papara well."[23]
Still another source was Vincendon-Dumoulin's *Iles Taïti;
esquisse historique et géographique*.[24]

Belonging, in his sophistication, among Loti's "les désen-
chantés," Adams tried to make of his experiences works of
enchantment, as did the author of *Madame Chrysanthème*
and more especially of *Le Mariage de Loti*, which has its
setting in Tahiti. Like his favorite author, Henry dreamt of
canalizing his *ennui*, his *pessimism*, his *sensibility*, and perhaps even his fear of death into a book of "sensuous glam-
our." "Tahiti! does the word mean anything to you?" he
wrote to Elizabeth Cameron from Papeete in 1891. "To me
it has a perfume of its own, made up of utterly inconsequent
associations; essence of the South Seas mixed with imaginations of at least forty years ago; Herman Melville and
Captain Cook head and heels with the French opera and
Pierre Loti."[25]

Adams's letters were written with an eye for literary effect,
and this was especially true when he communicated his
impressions of the South Seas. "To me the atmosphere is
more than tinged by a South Sea melancholy. . . . Melancholy in such air and with blues so very ultramarine, has
charm. . . . The melancholy of it quite oppresses me."[26] By
comparison, he finds Samoa "never melancholy"; whereas
Tahiti, or at least Papeete, is "distinctly sad." His favorite
stroll is to the decaying parapet of a fort, where he "can lie
down—and watch the sunset without society." What
strikes him more and more with every visit is "the invariable
tone of pathos in the scenery." At least, he reveals his true
purpose in all this:

If I could only paint it,[27] *or express it in poetry or prose,*[28] or do any-thing with it, or even shake it out of its exasperating repose, the feeling would be a pleasant one, and I should fall in love with the very wrinkles of my venerable and spiritual Tahitian grand-mother.[29]

Here we have, then, his craving for the mastery of his mel-ancholy in literary form. In his "rêve exotique," he had before him the remote example of Chateaubriand and the more proximate one of Loti. How much Adams would have loved to sign his name to this *poëme en prose:*

Moi qui ai conservé tant de fleurs fanées, tombées en poussière, que j'avais prises, ça et là, au moment des départs, dans différents lieux du monde; moi qui en ai tant conservé que cela tourne à l'herbier, à la collection incohérente et ridicule,—j'ai beau faire, non, je ne tiens point à ces lotus, bien qu'ils soient les derniers souvenirs vivants de mon été à Nagusaki.[30]

Occasionally Adams approaches his model in tonality—as in this bit:

Take, then, your wife! Taurua! my friend! we are separated, she and I! Taurua, the morning star to me. For her beauty I would die. You were mine, but now—take, then, Taurua! my friend! We are separated, she and I![31]

Later Adams adds: "Beauty does not last long in Tahiti."[32] But at all times he has the literary awareness that "perfect simplicity is a beauty" and that "homesickness is poetic."[33]

Adams met Stevenson at Samoa in 1890. While there, Stevenson had reread Dumas's works; he corresponded with Marcel Schwob;[34] and among his favorite authors were Renan, Taine, and Bourget. The latter's *Essais de psy-chologie contemporaine,* Stevenson read with delight; but he enjoyed even more Bourget's *Sensations d'Italie,* sent to him by Adams's close friend, Henry James. In 1893 Stevenson lamented: "Taine gone, and Renan, and Symonds, and

Tennyson, and Browning; the Suns go swiftly out, and I see no suns to follow."[35]

When Adams, together with La Farge, came to see Stevenson (Oct. 17, 1890) he found the latter "extremely entertaining" in conversation. "He has the nervous restlessness of his disease."[36] Stevenson spoke of his place as " 'full of Rousseaus,' meaning picturesque landscapes."[37] The last time they saw each other, they parted "on the beach, in the Samoan moonlight."[38] What better stage-setting could one ask for the belated romantic that Adams was!

Students have recognized the fact that *exoticism* belongs to the history of the Romantic movement, and that poetic loneliness and cosmic loneliness are elements of exoticism. Associated with these elements also is the notion of *heroic* failure and the personality image which grows out of it. It is interesting to examine the growth of this image in Adams.

Henry himself started the legend of his failure. On close inspection, the actual references to it in his autobiography are not so many as they first appear to be. In the chiaroscuro of his thought, what he made to look like failures could be interpreted, with justification, as successes. The very first page of the *Education* strikes the romantic note of a man who feels out of joint with his environment:

Had he been born in Jerusalem under the shadow of the Temple and circumcised in the Synagogue by his uncle the high priest, under the name of Israel Cohen, he would scarcely have been . . . more heavily handicapped in the races of the coming century.[39]

Early in life, he saw himself as one of "a million young men planted in the mud of a lawless world."[40] He found himself constantly "tossed between the horns of successive dilemmas."[41] He "could see easy ways of making a hundred blunders; he could see no likely way of making a legitimate success."[42]

Not without conscious conformity to his design of himself as a failure does he adduce the incident of the discovery,
with the aid of the famous Libri at the British Museum, of
lines scribbled by the artist on the back of a drawing that
Adams had bought as Raphael's:

> Perche sei grande nol sei in tua volia;
> Tu vedi e gia non credi il tuo valore. . . .[43]

Regarding himself as an Hamletesque figure, he "had no
need to learn from Hamlet the fatal effect of the pale cast of
thought on enterprises great or small."[44] He thought that
"he knew no more in 1868 than in 1858,"[45] and concluded,
therefore, that "at thirty years old, the man who has not
yet got further than to study the situation, is lost, or near
it."[46] He felt completely lost, as "a belated reveller, or a
scholar-gipsy like Matthew Arnold's. His world was dead."[47]
Considering himself as an *âme damnée*, "he found a personal
grief in every tree."[48]

The blow of mortality which Adams felt after his sister's
death in Italy, conspired to intensify his sense of failure. Like
a stricken Rousseau, Senancour, or Musset he sought solace
among mountains and lakes. Writing of that period, he says
(very much in their manner):

The fantastic mystery of coincidences had made the world, which
he thought real, mimic and reproduce the distorted nightmare of
his personal horror. He did not yet know it, and he was twenty
years in finding it out; but he had need of all the beauty of the
Lake below and of the Alps above, to restore the finite to its place.
For the first time in his life, Mont Blanc for a moment looked to
him what it was—a chaos of anarchic and purposeless forces—
and he needed days of repose to see it clothe itself again with the
illusions of his senses, the white purity of its snows, the splendor of
its light, and the infinity of its heavenly peace.[49]

Here is how he characterizes his advent as a professor of
history at Harvard: "Crushed by his own ignorance—lost

in the darkness of his own gropings—the scholar finds himself jostled of a sudden by a crowd of men who seem to him ignorant that there is a thing called ignorance."

Chapter XX deals specifically with his teaching experience and is entitled "Failure." His confidence in his own abilities as a teacher was somewhat shaken by his high conception of the pedagogue: "A teacher affects eternity; he can never tell where his influence stops."[50] As for the teaching of history, "In essence incoherent and immoral, history had either to be taught as such—or falsified. . . . Adams wanted to do neither."[51] Ergo, his failure as a teacher. To be sure, "his was among the failures which were respectable enough to deserve self-respect."[52]

Somewhere Emerson makes the point that sooner or later a man must choose between rest and truth. And, according to Adams, "Nothing is easier, if a man wants it, than rest, profound as the grave."[53] Taking, perhaps, Vigny's dictum, "Seul le silence est grand," as a motto, he lost himself in "the Pursuit of Ignorance in Silence . . . *futilitarian* silence."[54]

Science itself, as the nineteenth century was expiring, contributed to his design of failure. It "warned him to begin again from the beginning."[55] As for art, "He knew that his artistic standard was the illusion of his own mind."[56]

Finally, thrown into "Hamlet's Shakespearean silence" by the death of Hay, it pleased Adams to see himself as "an ignorant old man [who] felt no motive for trying to escape, seeing that the only escape possible lay in the form of *vis a tergo* commonly called Death."[57]

Here, then, in these quotations we have the source of the legend of Adams's so-called failure. However, the critics who have used this source for their further elaboration of his lack of success, have ignored those passages in the *Education* which actually contradict and cancel the notion of failure. Indeed, very often the contradiction will be found in the same passage side by side with the affirmation.

Even a superficial analysis reveals Henry Adams as a romantic individual who, given his background and tradition, was bound to develop a romantic personality image of himself. This image, that of the *heroic failure* or the *failure as hero* would naturally enhance his own value, at least in his own view of himself. However, this artistic construct, as we shall presently show, was mistaken by some people for autobiographical truth.

In a letter written to Waldo Frank on December 9, 1919, Amy Lowell said:

I wish you had known him as I did. It was a lesson in what not to make of your life, as he recognized himself, poor old fellow, recognized to the extent of pen and paper but never to any further extent. Seeing himself clearly and uncompromisingly, he wrote for his own private instruction and the eyes of a few sympathetic friends the terribly ironic estimate of himself. . . . It was not an inspiring spectacle in the life, however it may be in the book.[58]

"Recognized to the extent of pen and paper," indeed! But what did she make of page 316 of the *Education*, where Adams distinctly says that "He had enjoyed his life amazingly, and [what is more] would not have exchanged it for any other that came in his way." And did Amy Lowell reach page 451 of Adams's *Education* where he asserts that "No one means all he says, and yet very few say all they mean, for words are slippery and thought is viscous"?

Parrington followed the work and thought of Henry Adams very acutely. Yet he, too, ruminated over the *failure*. Referring to the period when Adams was engaged in writing his *Mont-Saint-Michel and Chartres*, he says: "Thus at last, in another land and at a remote age, Henry Adams found the clue that explained for him his own failure and the source of the dissatisfactions that had tracked him doggedly through his far wanderings."[59] The idea of failure is implicit in Parrington's exposition of Adams's career:

> To Henry Adams, skepticism early became a habit. . . . A rationalist, he followed his intellect in an eager quest for the law of historical evolution, and he ended fifty years later in mysticism. It was a natural outcome for a lifetime of rationalizing—a compensation for the mordant dissatisfactions that issued from the restless play of mind.[60]

He charges Adams with a want of substantial realism in dealing with political corruption (as instanced in the novel *Democracy*), because of his "curious failure to take into account the economic springs of action."[61] And it was this want that prevented Adams from feeling at home in the new world of the Gilded Age, or from embracing a socialistic view of society. That our author should, in consequence, have regarded himself as a misfit, or as a failure, was inevitable.

However, Parrington's wisdom, coupled with his amazing learning, prevents him from misunderstanding to the extent that Amy Lowell—and Carl Becker—did. Says Becker:

> The *Education* is in fact the record, tragic and pathetic underneath its genial irony, of the defeat of fine aspirations and laudable ambitions. It is the story of a life which the man himself, in his old age, looked back upon as a broken arch.[62]

As students of literary history, we recognize in *the broken arch* an image closely associated with the *broken column* and *broken stone*, two distinctly romantic images. While Dr. Becker admits that "No sane man would call [Adams's career] a failure," he nevertheless argues:

> The chief question which the *Education* presents to the critic is therefore this: why did Henry Adams look back upon his life, which to other men was so enviable in itself and so notable in its achievements, as a failure?

Becker finds the answer to this question in Adams's own words: "To be educated is to be able to identify one self and one's work with the main stream or tendency of one's time; . . . to possess a philosophy which will solve the mystery of life."[63] Naturally, Adams failed in getting the sort of education which would possess him of such a philosophy; but who, between Plato and Einstein, hasn't failed in that sense? Towards the end of his article, Dr. Becker tells us that, "It is not likely that many readers will see the tragedy of a failure that looks like success."[64] To elucidate or to resolve this paradox is precisely what constitutes our problem.

Unlike Amy Lowell, Parrington, and Becker, Paul Elmer More doesn't actually use the word "failure." Instead, he resorts to a few assertions which imply the idea: "Adams ends his career in sentimental nihilism. . . . he could not rest easy in negation, yet he could find no positive faith to take its place."[65] For Paul Elmer More it is all a question of faith. Here is how he traces the career of Adams's ultimate failure:

By a gradual elimination of its positive content, the faith of the people—i.e. of this breed of New England of whom Adams was so consciously a part—had passed from Calvinism to Unitarianism, and from this to free thinking, until in the days of our Adams there was little left to the intellect but a great denial.

Here, then, is the story of a man "whose conscience was moving, so to speak, *in vacuo*, like a dispossessed ghost seeking a substantial habitation."[66] The question is, did Adams have the need for the kind of habitation More had in mind?

The same attitude is found among critics abroad. In an article entitled "Les Scrupules d'un Américain attardé," which is, in fact, a review of the *Education*, by Fernand Baldensperger, we read:

Henry Adams éprouva de bonne heure pour la retrouver sans
cesse, la poignante impression d'un homme qui, sans ombre de
pose romantique, et par le plus sincère des scrupules, se plaindra
d'être venu trop tard dans un monde trop vieux.[67]

In the romantic allusiveness of the last phrase, we have at
least a hint at Adams's failure, his failure to adjust himself
to the world in which he had to live. The assertion, "sans
ombre de pose romantique," I shall have occasion to question
later. Considering the *Education* as personal revelation, M.
Baldensperger remarks with quizzical surprise: "Quoi! dans
un genre où les *Confessions, Vérité et Fiction, les Mémoires
d'outretombe*, semblent offrir des modèles incontestés, pas
la moindre silhouette féminine un peu poussée!"[68] There *are*
as a matter of fact some *silhouettes féminines* in the *Education;*
but as for purple passions, they are all concealed in the image
of the Virgin in *Mont-Saint-Michel and Chartres.*

Actually, Adams's despair was of a purely *literary* nature,
and as such it was no more "overstated" than was that of
Alfred de Musset in *Les Nuits*, of Lamartine in *Le Lac*, of
Victor Hugo in his *Tristesse d'Olympio*, or of any of the
English romantics. And just as his despair was of the pattern
of these poets, his skepticism may also be traced back to its
one great modern source—Michel de Montaigne. In his
"parade of erudition, irony, derision, self-mockery, occasional
pathos,"[69] Adams was of the company of many outstanding
poets, ancient and modern.

It was Henry Adams himself who was responsible for the
notion, later elaborated and expanded by others, that he was
a failure. The theme-song of the whole *Education* is his own
so-called failure. I say "so-called" because the conception
of himself as such comported with his idea (itself a composite
of ideas) that if there is one thing that makes the individual
life worthy of notice at all, it is the heroic element in it, which,
as in a tragedy, carries with it the notion of doom.

In a letter addressed to John Hay, he wrote: "I am clear that you should write autobiography. I mean to do mine. After seeing how coolly and neatly a man like Trollope can destroy the last vestige of heroism in his own life, I object to allowing mine to be murdered by any one except myself."[70] Thus we are given, from his own pen, a hint at the heroic element of which mention was made a moment ago.

Adams visioned his own mind, as well as all human thought, "caught and whirled about in the vortex of infinite forces." He saw himself almost in the manner of Alfred de Musset—romantically enough—as "drifting in the deadwater of the *fin-de-siècle*," as "a stranded Tannhäuser" in his household at St. Germain in the late '90s, slowly beginning "to feel at home in France."[71]

If we follow the *marche-route* of our stranded Tannhäuser, we find that it reached from the winged meliorism of Hugo and Shelley, through Leopardi, Von Hartmann, Schopenhauer, benevolent evolutionism, the symbolic languor of "The Lotus Eaters," to Walter Pater, who, in the unforgettable "Conclusion" to his *Renaissance*, quotes Novalis: "Philosophiren ist dephlegmatisiren, vivificiren."[72] We see that Adams's quest led him over the full length of the way of romanticism, right into the whirlpool of *Energy*. "How shall we pass most swiftly," asked Pater, "from point to point and be present always at the focus where the greatest number of vital forces unite in their purest energy?" The senses are challenged to become and stay electric with a "gemlike flame." Success is equated with sustained ecstasy. Science itself is enlisted for the purpose of maintaining "this ecstasy."

While all melts under our feet, we may well grasp at any exquisite passion, or any contribution to knowledge that seems by a lifted horizon to set the spirit free for a moment, or any stirring of the senses, strange dyes, strange colours, and curious odours, or work of the artist's hands, or the face of one's friend.

But in the heart of all this was "some tragic dividing of forces"—failure. Adams, too, could not "on this short day of frost and sun . . . sleep before evening," nor would he acquiesce "in a facile orthodoxy of Comte or of Hegel."[73] His ego would have its full play in a field of running-down energies—a perfectly romantic picture of heroic failure. This *mal romantique* is very often disguised in his quest for a science of history; in reality, science is for him another form of aesthetic contemplation; his religious skepticism is another facet of his romantic disease.

Janko Lavrin says, rightly, we believe, that "we are all romantics whatever else we may be besides"; and it is interesting to note that Adams answers to—in fact, combines— every one of the ten romantic types enumerated by the former.[74] One image which emerges from the conflict between desire and restraint and crystallizes into a personality image, in one who combines the Lavrin types, is that of the *heroic failure* or the *failure as hero* (Vigny, Musset, Hugo). It is this image that Adams wrote into his theory of history. In fact, his activity as an historian might be cited as the best exemplification of his romanticism. His conception of the catastrophic march of experience certainly derives in great measure from his personality image. Incidentally, Michelet's influence on Adams might account for a good deal in the latter's conception of history. Both sought to "understand and welcome eagerly the diverse manifestations of the human spirit." None the less, there is a basic difference in the type of romantic idealism that informed each historian.

As for purposelessness in history, to the Romanticists, it was another name for romantic genius.[75] What would differentiate Adams from the older romantics would be his interest in experimental methods in science (though, of course, there is Goethe); but here, too, he sought the results which bolstered up his idea of dissipation of energy—of failure.

It must be remembered also that Henry Adams was nurtured on the romantic personality image in his grandfather's library; for John Quincy Adams not only possessed a copy of *The Sorrows of Werther*, but had made his own translation of it. "There have been men in all ages," says Coleridge in his *Biographia*, "who have been impelled as by an instinct to propose their own nature as a problem, and who devote their attempts to its solution."[76] *The Education of Henry Adams* becomes more intelligible in the light of the *Confessions* of Jean Jacques and *The Sorrows of Werther;* it, too, is the product of a man who definitely belongs to the romantic tradition.

Ultimately, the romantic "values the world which is created by his imaginative will more highly than the world of which his senses bring him their crudely literal reports."[77] It is of more than parenthetic interest to cast a glance at a notation in Adams's copy of *Les Confessions de Saint Augustin*. On page 361, Adams read: "Ergo animus ad habendum seipsum angustus est"; next to it he questioned: "Does this mean: 'The mind is too narrow to contain itself?' "[78] Again, on page 591 he read, "Vous êtes vous-même votre repos" for "Tua quies tu ipse es" and he pencilled this query: "Or is it:—votre repos, c'est vous." Note the emphasis thrown on the all-containing Ego. We are reminded of Novalis, with whom everything tended inwards; whose soul (*Gemuth*) is the centripetal force of the spiritual life.[79] So many of the romantics thought that "Leben ist eine Krankheit des Geistes" and that the "World-spirit in living individuals attains to self-consciousness."[80] Adams's thought wore a good deal of that stripe.

John Cournos has compared Adams, in certain external

aspects, with Amiel.[81] Amiel was also regarded as a "failure" by his friends, and his posthumous *Journal intime*
seemed to confirm their belief. For both Adams and Amiel
reality seemed to fall short of that ideal in which they preferred to luxuriate. Despair followed—despair both of the
world and of oneself. Thus the failure image comes into the
foreground and itself usurps the place of the lost ideal—an
image which hovers on the verge of a new synthesis—perhaps a return to God. The succession which Cournos indicates, while not as yet fully documented, seems none the
less sound: namely, that Amiel, in some respects, had an-
ticipated Adams, and that Adams, in his turn, had antic-
ipated Oswald Spengler.[82]

We are now ready for a revaluation of Adams's "failure."
Seemingly he recapitulated here in America the whole
romantic tradition of Europe. This tradition included aesthetic pessimism, in whose framework he built up a personality image which he came to enjoy artistically. The
image was that of the failure, the heroic failure. He came
to enjoy the spectacle doubly: on the stage as an actor; from
the wings as an onlooker who revels in the gaping of the
audiences in the galleries and in the pit.

In the intensification of his ego, Adams ran the gauntlet
of romantic subjectivism: "scientificism", sentimentalism,
sensualism.[83] Most frequently, the three make up the web
of his literary fabric. Thus, *The Degradation of the Democratic
Dogma*, most of his *Essays*, and his *History* reveal his scientific interest; his *Letters*, his two novels (*Esther* and *Democracy*), and his life of George Cabot Lodge comprise his
sentimentalism; his poems and his book on Tahiti embody
his sensualism; while his *Education* and his *Mont-Saint-
Michel* (which, after all is said, constitute his greatest claim
to fame) comprehend the three. One romantic by-product of

such an amalgam is, of course, mysticism; and we do find its particular manifestation in his Brahma poem. Here he touches the American phase of romanticism, the transcendentalism of Emerson, Channing, Alcott.

Adams's failure was only a pen and paper failure. He wrote "a terribly ironic estimate of himself" because it pleased his artistic fancy to do so. Corresponding to Rousseau's "chain of feelings" reaching out for logical continuity in thought, we have in Adams a *chain of thoughts* reaching out for artistic cohesiveness in feelings expressed and precipitating an emotional amalgam to give them unity. In both, the aesthetic bias is at work in the creation of a personality image.

Using Parrington's words, we ask: What did Adams find "in another land and at a remote age"? Did he find there "the clue that explained for him his own failure and the source of the dissatisfactions that had tracked him doggedly through his far wanderings?"[84] Or did he rather find there (in the Middle Ages and at Chartres) what all romantics have found there, namely, an escape from the onslaught of an iron-clad, machine-cluttered, money-changing world? Discontent? Adams manifests the romantic, nay, even the "divine" discontent; for no person with creative imagination has ever been satisfied that his efforts have resulted in works which, in their impact on society, have been commensurate with his ability or aspirations. The product always falls pathetically short of the heroic image which projects it. In the light of this interpretation, the "ombre de pose romantique,"[85] denied to Adams, becomes his constant abode.

Adams's sense of success beneath seeming failure rings within his proud though characteristically ironic statement:

I've managed to drag on a degraded existence for the last thirty years without an office or an honor to my family-back, as far as I can see, all the better for the freedom. We have outlived dynasties and are still on top, while a thousand Congressmen, Cabinets and Presidents have vanished.[86]

Adams's failure image was in full consonance with the knowledge that "the only competition worthy of a wise man is with himself."[87] It was this self that he took to far-off places and that he brought back enriched with exotic vision and historic lore. But here again, a literary tradition, found for the most part in French literature, helped to sharpen his vision; especially as he sought to articulate it in a work of his own.

VIII

Conclusion

In any account of Franco-American cultural relations, the Adamses must occupy an important place. This is especially true of Henry Adams. Indeed, between the time that *L'Amérique délivrée, Esquisse d'un poème sur l'Indépendance de l'Amérique* was published with an *Épître dédicatoire à Monsieur John Adams*[1] and the Harvard Tercentenary celebration when Le Breton spoke on "Henry Adams et la France,"[2] French thought had been part of the Adams tradition. In his avid absorption of French literature Henry Adams followed in the tracks of his family. Furthermore, the romantic personality traits of Henry, which were amplified by his reading of Rousseau and the literature which followed, are revealed as latent in John's dualism and as coming to flower in John Quincy Adams. Certain problems relating to the Romantic movement, like the conjugate ideas of democracy and chaos, recurred in the Adams family.

Henry's interest in science was nurtured and stimulated by French thinkers. This interest received its formulation and clarification from the works of men like Delambre and Cuvier. The latter's catastrophism was to play an important role in Adams's thinking, while his vital interest in psychology may be traced back to Cabanis, Condillac and Helvétius, and the idéologue Destutt de Tracy. It is to them that he owed, in a great measure, his rapprochement between philosophy and science. Alongside the idealistic movement (Kant and Hegel) which Adams could not escape, he was subject to the influence of French Naturalism which adapted under the name of Materialism the content of physics to the purposes of metaphysics. The movement had its rise in the idéologues. In Saint-Simon the naturalistic philosophy was applied to history. The consequence of this movement was the positivistic system (of Auguste Comte) which manifested itself, after 1857, in Littré, Taine, and Renan. This chain of ideas had a great fascination for Henry Adams and made its mark in his attempt at a philosophy of history. But, in his penchant for French ideas, Adams was saved from the dogmatic materialism of Germany.

The two phases of historical awareness in Adams—the factual and the aesthetic—were enriched in contact with French currents of thought. One gains an idea of the French sources used by Henry in the writing of his *History* by examining his transcripts of the *Affaires étrangères* now at the Library of Congress, and the works now deposited at Western Reserve University and at the Massachusetts Historical Society.

In his groping for a philosophy of history, Adams found help not only in the French philosophers of the eighteenth century, but in those of the nineteenth—among them men of science like Carnot, Dastre, Lapparent, Tropinard, Vuplian, and the Poincarés. Avidly he turned the pages of *La Revue des idées* for clues that would lead to a nexus between the moral and physical sciences. With this end in view he read Le Bon's *Physiologie des foules* and *La Psychologie politique* as well as Grasset's *Idées médicales* and Brunhes' *Dégradation.*[3]

Adams's acquaintance with French literature covered the full length of its history, from the *Chanson de Roland* through the nineteenth century; we find echoes of this extensive reading throughout his own work. This is especially true of the literature of the Middle Ages which he masterfully wove into the fabric of his *Mont-Saint-Michel and Chartres.* There he is indebted not only to the literature but also to scholarly works which dealt with it.

As a literary student and as an historian he appreciated the eighteenth century; but his approach to the nineteenth was that of an *enfant du siècle.* It is as such that he displayed "an affection for Alfred de Musset," fell under the spell of Victor Hugo's poetry of the sea, and was captivated by the literature of French exoticism. A belated romantic, he was working in a literary tradition of exoticism. The nostalgic impulse at once mastered him and was mastered by him when he made literature of it. In this tradition, *melancholy* and the image of oneself as an *heroic failure* were necessary stock-in-trade. They had positive artistic value which had been given currency by the writers who appealed to Adams—Chateaubriand, Maurice de Guérin, Senancour, and Pierre Loti. And very often one finds the spirit of the following lines of Amiel's *Journal intime* in Adams's own work:

J'entends distinctement tomber les gouttes de ma vie dans le gouffre dévorant de l'éternité. Je sens fuir mes jours au-devant de la mort. Tout ce qui me reste de semaines, de mois ou d'années à boire la lumière du soleil ne me paraît guère qu'une nuit, une nuit d'été qui ne compte pas, car elle va finir.—La mort! le silence! l'abîme!—Effrayants mystères pour l'être qui aspire à l'immortalité, au bonheur, à la perfection![4]

To be sure, these sentiments are presented in more restrained form in Adams's letters and in his *Education,* but they are the very ones which led him to exclaim pathetically towards the end, "Dear child, keep me alive."[5] Thus, his poetic loneliness and what was a lifelong *pose romantique* ended as a passionate cry of the heart.

For Adams, history, literature, philosophy, and even science were correlative processes of the human spirit in quest of form and unity. Descartes and Pascal demonstrated for him this correlativity. Without an understanding of this interdependence in the filiations of the creative imagination one can barely hope to grasp the meaning of the *Education* or of the *Mont-Saint-Michel and Chartres*.

From the time that he offered his "Prayer to the Virgin of Chartres" to Elizabeth Cameron in 1901, to the moment when he was stricken with paralysis, Henry Adams was occupied with writing and revising *Mont-Saint-Michel and Chartres*,[6] the first version of which appeared privately in 1904, the last under the imprint of Houghton Mifflin in 1913. This was the flower that bloomed on French soil in the atmosphere of French aspiration to Unity and Peace. The rest was a matter of learning how to die—of pondering the eternal bond of "La Vie et la mort." Here again a distinguished member of the Institute served as his guide. Adams was still cogitating the problems of energy, of a *quid proprium* called life, and of a philosophy of knowledge or science.

Adams spoke of *Euthanasia* while he read in Dastre's book

L'instinct de la mort survenant à la fin d'un cycle normal et bien rempli, facilitera sans doute au vieillard le départ pour le grand voyage. Le Déchirement n'existera plus pour lui; n'existera-t-il point pour ceux qu'il laisse?[7]

Thus we have reached our point of conclusion. The growth in Adams's mind of the scope and design of his monumental *History* was largely dependent on his mastery of

French sources. At the same time that he was hard at work
on his *History* he was already reaching out for history of
another sort,—*Mont-Saint-Michel and Chartres*. Because
of the historic pattern he was to undertake, and also because
of an inbred taste for *belles-lettres*, he turned to the full
circuit of French literature and French philology. We have
seen how his studies were translated into works of his own:
the *Mont-Saint-Michel*, the *Education*, his book on *Tahiti*,
and his *Poems;* how, indeed, he whose prose is cluttered with
French words and phrases, and who made upwards of
twenty-five trips to France, derived a personality image of
himself as artist by intimate contact with the creative spirit
of France. It is there that we trace, in good part, his epigrammatic incisiveness, his flashes of irony and fits of satire,
his quest of unity and his exposure of chaos; his wistful
moments in the midst of philosophic reflection; his poetic
insight into the realm of science; and finally, his failure image
of himself which goes hand in hand with his exoticism. In
all these aspects we see him walking on the high road of the
imagination, accompanied, as it were, by the spirits of Pascal,
Descartes, La Bruyère, Voltaire, Michelet, Renan and the
whole cycle of French poetry from the Chanson de Roland
to Mallarmé. The high road led to *Mont-Saint-Michel and
Chartres*.

Notes

Chapter I. ANCESTRAL BACKGROUND

1. See *John Adams's Book*, ed. Henry Adams II.
2. We find the same oscillation, in this regard, in John Adams.
3. Henry Adams, *The Education of Henry Adams*, p. 16.
4. See *Works of John Adams*, I, 40, 46; Harvey Gates Townsend, *Philosophical Ideas in the United States*, p. 634; Howard Mumford Jones, *America and French Culture*, pp. 375–376; Isaac Woodbridge Riley, *American Philosophy: the Early Schools*, pp. 10–11.
5. Jacob Salwyn Schapiro, *Condorcet and the Rise of Liberalism*, p. 238.
6. *Works of John Adams*, I, 84–85; Gilbert Chinard, *Honest John Adams*, p. 320.
7. Chinard, *op. cit.*, p. 125.
8. *Works of John Adams*, I, 148.
9. He described Condorcet in a letter to his wife. He also met Turgot and attended a meeting of the Academy of Sciences at which both Voltaire and Franklin were present. He saw plays by the former as well as by Molière. In Paris, Jefferson had become his colleague and had undertaken to have a French translation made of John Adams's book on the "Defense of the Constitutions of the Government of the United States of America against the attack of M. Turgot, in his letter to Dr. Price dated the twenty-

second of March, 1778." The first volume of the *Defense* was printed in January, 1787. Taking his stand against Rousseau and Montesquieu, the main burden of his work is this: "No democracy ever did exist or can exist. . . . No such passion as a love of democracy, stronger than self-love, or superior to the love of private interest, ever did, or ever can prevail in the minds of citizens in general. . . . No love of equality, at least since Adam's fall, ever existed in human nature. . . . The democracy of Montesquieu and its principles of virtue, equality, frugality, [are all] figments of the brain, delusive imaginations, delirious reveries." (*Works of John Adams*, VI, 210; Chinard, *Honest John Adams*, p. 214).

10. Schapiro, *Condorcet*, p. 243.

11. It was against his "Quatre Lettres d'un Bourgeois de New Haven, sur l'Unité de la Législation" that Adams directed his "Discourses on Davila." Here again, we encounter the names of Rousseau, Voltaire, *et al.* In a moment of temperamental expansiveness John Adams called Condorcet a fool—in a marginal footnote in his copy of the Frenchman's *Sketch of the Intellectual Progress of Mankind* (Schapiro, p. 227). Yet he was far more indebted to the "fool" than wise old John took the trouble to admit—and not only he, but his son and his great-grandson.

12. *Correspondence of John Adams with Benjamin Waterhouse, 1784-1822*, ed. W. C. Ford, pp. 29–31.

13. *Correspondence of John Adams and Thomas Jefferson, 1812-1826*, p. 47.

14. *Ibid.*, pp. 112, 113.

15. *Ibid.*, p. 118.

16. *Ibid.*, pp. 124–125.

17. *Ibid.*, pp. 143–145.

18. Henry Adams later put in the mouth of one of the characters in his novel *Esther* the remark, "I don't go to church because I would feel so unchristian."

19. *Correspondence of John Adams and Thomas Jefferson*, pp. 146–147.

20. *Ibid.*, pp. 149–150.

21. *Ibid.*, pp. 156, 157.

22. *Ibid.*, pp. 123–124.

23. *Ibid.*, p. 155.

24. *Ibid.*, p. 193.

25. *Ibid.*, p. 193.

26. In a letter to Jefferson (Dec. 16, 1816) John Adams has the following to say of Ideology: "Three vols. of Ideology! Pray explain to me this Neological title! What does it mean? When Bonaparte used it, I was delighted with it, upon the Common principle of delight in everything we cannot understand. Does it mean Idiotism? The science of *non composmentuism?* The science of Lunacy? The theory of delirium? Or does it mean the science of self-love? Of *Amour-propre?* Or the element of vanity?" *Ibid.*, p. 150.

27. Chinard, *op. cit.*, p. 47.

28. *Ibid.*, p. 206.

29. See his *Life in a New England Town: 1787, 1788*, p. 148.

30. During a period of two months John Quincy Adams had read the *Esprit des lois* besides other works (*ibid.*).

31. *Life in a New England Town*, pp. 31, 60, 63.

32. *Ibid.*, p. 112. Towards the end of June, 1788, he expressed the desire to read Gibbon's continuation of the *Decline*, "which is not, however, yet completed" (*Ibid.*, p. 146). Paine's *Rights of Man* he read promptly on its appearance and wrote a reply to it.

33. Howard Mumford Jones, *America and French Culture, 1750-1848*, p. 260.

34. *Writings* (Ford ed.) II, 255. (Letter to John Adams, Feb. 17, 1798.)

35. *Life in a New England Town*, p. 113.

36. *Memoirs*, 12 vols., Philadelphia, 1874–1877.

37. *Ibid.*, I, vi.

38. *Memoirs*, II, 553: "I feel the sentiment with which Tycho Brahe died, perhaps as strongly as he did. His 'ne frustra vixisse videar' was a noble feeling, and in him had produced its fruits."

39. *Ibid.*, V, 219, 220.

40. Printed by order of the Senate of the United States, Washington, 1821.

41. Like his father, he was interested in silvaculture, and owned Michaux's *North American Sylva*. He also read in part Du Hamel on "Plantation," *Memoirs*, VII, 284, 287.

42. *Report*, pp. 13, 14, 129.

43. *Ibid.*, p. 7: It is interesting to note that John Quincy Adams also talks of "the man of nature."

44. *Ibid.*, pp. 5, 6.

45. *Ibid.*, p. 12.

46. Apropos the question of linguistic barriers or aversion to new nomenclature, John Quincy Adams has this to say: "Human nature, in its broadest features, is everywhere the same." He cites the repugnance of the French people to new nomenclature, "In the ordinary operations of the mind, distinctness of idea is, by the laws of nature, linked with the chain of association between sensible images and their habitual denominations, more closely than with the exactness of logical analysis" (*ibid.*, p. 56). The psychologic insight here is modern in its expression and reminds one of Henry Adams reading James's *Principles of Psychology*.

47. *Report*, p. 13.
48. *Ibid.* See note 46, above.
49. *Report*, p. 88.
50. *Ibid.*, p. 129.
51. *Memoirs*, V, 290.
52. *Ibid.*, pp. 265, 286, 311–312.
53. Henry Adams, *Education*, p. 389.
54. *Ibid.*, p. 427.
55. *Memoirs*, VII, 459.
56. *Ibid.*, VIII, 123.
57. One recalls his essay on *Othello*.
58. *Memoirs*, VIII, 218, 235, 241.
59. *Memoirs*, XI, 384.
60. *Ibid.*, XI, 408, 409.
61. *Ibid.*, XI, 385.

Chapter II. INITIATION

1. Author of *Arnoult's Pronouncing French Reader*.
2. It is not unlikely that as a little boy Henry was taught French by his grandparents, John Quincy and Louisa Catherine Adams— she who was "Louis Seize" (*Education*, 19). Whether the program at Mr. Dixwell's school, where Henry was prepared for college, included the study of French, the present writer is unprepared to say. (George McKee Elsey says nothing about it in his article, "The First Education of Henry Adams," *NEQ*, XIV, December, 1941). We do know that "his father rendered him a great service by trying to teach him French and giving him some idea of a French accent" (*Education*, 36). It is quite clear, however, that by his

junior year Adams could read French with considerable fluency, enough to appreciate the poetry of Alfred de Musset and Sainte-Beuve's criticism of that poet (see pp. 146–147). The English-French dictionary he possessed postdates his graduation from Harvard. (*Dictionnaire générale Anglais-Français*. Nouvellement rédigé d'après Johnson, Webster, Richardson, etc. Les Dictionnaires français de l'Académie de Laveaux, de Baiste, etc. . . . Par A. Spiers. . . . 12th ed. 2 vols. Paris, 1859).

3. See Richmond L. Hawkins, *Auguste Comte and the United States, 1816-1853*, pp. 25, 27, 61, and *passim*.

4. *Harvard Magazine*, III (1855–58), 314.

5. *Ibid.*, p. 398.

6. Adams continues: "According to D'Israeli, the following is a part of its preface," *Ibid.*, p. 401.

7. *Ibid.*, III, 404.

8. Henry Adams, *Education*, pp. 76, 81; *Letters, 1858-91*, pp. 3, 8, 27, 41. In 1858 Mommsen (who had said that one could not know any history without a knowledge of French) occupied his Chair at Berlin. French admiration for German scholarship was marked that year by the establishment of the *Revue germanique* with Renan as one of the leaders.

9. *Letters, 1858-91*, pp. 55, 56.

10. Henry Adams, *Education*, p. 119.

11. See Lionel Trilling, *Matthew Arnold*, p. 401. Arnold was also of Lord Houghton's circle.

12. T. Wemyss Reid, *The Life, Letters and Friendships of Richard Monckton Milnes*, I, xi, xii, and *passim*.

13. This account is taken substantially from Reid, *Life and Letters . . . of Milnes* II, 167–174, also pp. 32, 64, and Vol. I, *passim*. We should add to those Frenchmen whom Milnes knew the Comte de Paris, Labouchère—"one of the few British who know Frenchmen"—Waddington, Gambetta, D'Haussonville. In the war of 1870 between Germany and France Milnes was against Napoleon. *Ibid.*, II, 230–237, 366.

14. *Ibid.*, *passim*.

15. For the story of their meeting see *Education*, Ch. IX, "Foes or Friends (1862)"; Edmund William Gosse, *Life of Algernon C. Swinburne*, p. 286; *Letters, 1892-1918*, p. 638, Ford's note 2: "I was quite knocked silly when Eddie [Hoyt] who was reading to me from Gosse's *Life of Swinburne*, calmly read out a quotation from

myself which was attributed to some apparently well known Mr·
Adams who turns out to be, in all probability, my own father"
(To Elizabeth Cameron, 3 August, 1917).

16. T. Earle Welby, *A Study of Swinburne*, p. 258.

17. *Ibid.*, pp. 259, 260, 261, 262.

18. *Education*, p. 142.

19. *Letters 1858-91*, pp. 123, 124.

20. *The Letters of Algernon C. Swinburne*, p. 289, editor's footnote: "This refers to the Royal Literary Fund Dinner of May 2,
1866."

21. *Ibid.*, pp. 147–149.

22. There is a copy of this book in the Adams Collection. "William Blake" made its first appearance in 1867. The Collection also
contains Gilchrist's *Life of William Blake*.

23. "Blake," p. 3.

24. So many names of importance in French literature were encountered by Adams in Swinburne's "Blake": Hugo, Rabelais,
Ronsard, Rousseau; Aucassin et Nicolette. Also the expressions
"Art for Art's sake" (p. 99), and Baudelaire's "Art for Art's sake
first of all" (p. 100).

25. *Ibid.*, p. 100.

26. Henry Adams, *Life of George Cabot Lodge*, pp. 126, 133.

27. *A Study of Swinburne*, p. 198.

28. *Ibid.*, pp. 194, 198, 208.

29. Gosse, *Life of Swinburne*, p. 168.

30. *Op. cit.*, p. 113: "The reader who cares to remember that
everything here set down is of immediate importance and necessity
for the understanding of the matter in hand [namely the life of
Blake, and the faith and works which made that life what it was]
may as well take here a word of comment. It will soon be necessary
for even the very hack-writers and ingenuous people of ready pens
and wits, who now babble about Balzac in English and French as a
splendid specimen of their craft, fertile but faulty, and so forth—to
understand that they have nothing to do with Balzac; that he is
not of their craft, nor of any but the common craft of all great
men—the guild of godlike things and people; that a shelf holding
'all Balzac's novels forty volumes long,' is not 'cabin-furniture'
for any chance 'passenger' to select or reject. Error and deficiency
there may be in his work; but none such as they can be aware of.
Of poetic form, for example, we know that he knew nothing; the

error would be theirs who should think his kind of work the worse for that. Among men equally great, the distinctive supremacy of Balzac is this: that whereas the great men who are pure artists (Shakespeare for instance) work by implication only, and hardly care about descending to the level of a preacher's or interpreter's work, he is the only man not of their kind who is great enough to supply their place in his own way—to be their correlative in a different class of workmen; being from his personal point of view simply impeccable and infallible. The pure artist never asserts; he suggests and therefore his meaning is totally lost upon moralists and sciolists—is indeed irreparably wasted upon the run of men who cannot work out suggestions. Balzac asserts and Balzac can not blunder or lie. So profound and extensive a capacity of moral apprehension no other prose writer, no man of mere analytic faculty, ever had or can have. This assuredly, when men become (as they will have to become) capable of looking beyond the mere clothes and skin of his work, will be always, as we said, his great especial praise; that he was, beyond any other man, the master of morals—the greatest direct expounder of actual moral fact. Once consent to forget or overlook the mere *entourage* and social habiliment of Balzac's intense and illimitable intellect, you cannot fail of seeing that he of all men was fittest to grapple with all strange things and words, and compel them by divine violence of spiritual rape to bring forth flowers and fruits good for food and available for use."

31. Throughout the 1860s Henry Adams often refers to Mill and it is clear that Mill had become for him a standard of comparison in high scholarship. See Adams, *Cycle of Letters*, I, 252, 253; II, 95.

32. *Letters, 1892-1918*, pp. 55, 56, 123.

33. *Education*, p. 33.

34. John Stuart Mill, *Autobiography*, pp. 162–164.

35. Avignon is referred to sentimentally in *Esther*.

Chapter III. INTRODUCTION TO HISTORY

1. "I have already a dozen ideas in my head which if elaborated would occupy me years." *Letters, 1858-91*, p. 151, to Edward Atkinson, Washington, February, 1869.

2. *Ibid.*, p. 169. The Adams Collection contains Gibbon, *Decline and Fall of the Roman Empire*, notes by Guizot, 5 vols.

3. *Education*, p. 307.

4. *Letters, 1858-91*, p. 194: "My predecessor was turned out of Harvard because he was a Comtist"; Benjamin Rand, "Philosophical Instruction in Harvard University from 1636 to 1900," *The Harvard Graduate Magazine* (September, 1928), pp. 199, 200.

5. S. E. Morison, ed., *The Development of Harvard University, 1869-1929*, p. 332.

6. Adams's interest in Descartes was both keen and deep; but we reserve the discussion of it for a separate chapter.

7. See R. B. Perry, *The Thought and Character of William James*, II, 52.

8. *North American Review*, CIX (1869), 1.

9. *Ibid.*, CXVII (1873), 401.

10. *Ibid.*, CXIX (1874), 561.

11. *Ibid.*, CVII (1868), 460.

12. *Ibid.*

13. *Ibid.*, CXI (1870), 377.

14. "In short," says the review, "the Cosmic Philosophy seems to us to be an attempt to convert Mr. Darwin's principle of natural selection into a philosophy" (*ibid.*, CXX, 1875, 203).

15. *Ibid.*, CXX (1875), 237.

16. *Ibid.*, CVII (1868), 322.

17. *Ibid.*, CXIX (1874), 166.

18. *Ibid.*, CXV (1872), 460.

19. *Ibid.*, CXVIII (1874), 390-397.

20. *Ibid.*, CXX (1875), 455.

21. *Ibid.*, CXIX (1874), 406.

22. *Ibid.*, CXXIV (1877), 156.

23. *Ibid.*, CXXIV (1877), 506.

24. *Ibid.*, CLXVI (1873), 483.

25. In 1857-58, Henry Adams (then a senior) recited to Bowen on Reid's *Intellectual Powers of Man* and on Bowen's *Ethics and Metaphysics*. See *Rand*, p. 194; *Harvard Catalogue*, 1857-58.

26. Adams, *Cycle of Letters*, II, 95-96.

27. *Letters, 1858-91*, p. 236.

28. *Charge Books*, 1870-71 (Harvard College Archives), pp. 156, 215.

29. Joseph de Claude, 1785-1872, who wrote, c. 1858, *Histoire*

de la lutte des papes et des empereurs de la maison de Souabe, de ses causes et de ses effets.

30. He did not consider Freeman a very solid writer, for all his parade of knowledge. "I had reviewed very sharply two of [his] books when I edited the *North American Review*, and he knew it . . . he told me he had replied to my charges, as I would see in the preface to the first volume of his third edition of the *Norman Conquest*. I feel not the slightest curiosity to see the reply" (*Letters, 1858-91*, p. 334).

31. *Letters, 1858-91*, p. 194.

32. Fiske, *Letters*, p. 193. For Auguste Comte and the United States, before Fiske, see *A. Comte and the U.S.* (1816–1853) by Richmond L. Hawkins.

33. Fiske, *Letters*, p. 185.

34. Appointed October 19, 1869.

35. Fiske, *Letters*, p. 194.

36. *Documents Relating to New England Federalism* (1800–1815), ed. Henry Adams, 1877.

37. *Letters, 1858-91*, p. 314.

38. Max I. Baym, "Henry Adams and Henry Vignaud," *The New England Quarterly*, XVII, No. 3 (September, 1944), 442–449. We repeat here the facts as given in this article. For Vignaud, see Waldo Leland's excellent article in the *Dictionary of American Biography*. I have had the further benefit of Dr. Leland's personal recollections of both Vignaud and Adams. For permission to use hitherto unpublished letters of Adams to Vignaud, and for valuable aid, I am indebted to Dr. R. G. Adams, Director of the William L. Clements Library at the University of Michigan, and to his associate Miss Elizabeth B. Steere.

39. Charles Francis Adams, Jr., later made use of Henry's "copy of the rebel organ in London" (*Letters, 1892-1918*, p. 101).

40. Records of the Dept. of State, Diplomatic Posts, France, Press Copies of Miscellaneous Corr. sent, August 9, 1879–May 21, 1880, pp. 120–121. For permission to reproduce manuscripts and for valuable assistance, I acknowledge my gratitude to the authorities of the various divisions of the National Archives.

41. See Adams's "Napoleon I et St. Domingue," *La Revue Historique*, XXIV (April, 1884), 92–130.

42. Letter to C. M. Gaskell, Paris, Dec. 20, 1879; *Letters, 1858-91*, p. 317.

43. Adams's transcripts are at the Library of Congress.

44. Letter to Henry Cabot Lodge, Feb. 22, 1880, *Letters, 1858-91*, p. 319.

45. This letter is pasted in Vignaud's copy of *New England Federalism, 1800-15* (Boston, 1877), edited by Henry Adams.

46. Brown was Chief Clerk at the State Dept. (See Reg. of the Dept. of State.)

47. Obviously, someone who had lost his job in the Marine Archives.

48. The volume is Adams's *Life of Albert Gallatin*, 1879. The flyleaf bears the following inscription: "To: Henry Vignaud with the author's compliments—Témoignage de reconnaissance 8 Jan. 1880."

49. National Archives: Records of the Dept. of State Diplomatic Posts, French Press Copies of Miscellaneous Corr. sent, May 21, 1880–March 17, 1881, p. 119; p. 120 is the copyist's receipt.

50. Letter to Elizabeth Cameron, Aug. 16, 1890, *Letters, 1858-91*, pp. 403–404. Theo. Frelinghuysen Dwight (1846–1917), one-time secretary and librarian to George Bancroft; translator and librarian for 13 years at the State Dept. Library in Washington, became a companion and, in Adams's own words, "a sort of literary factotum" to the Adamses, and helped to usher in the *History* in 1891 by reading the proof sheets. In April, 1892, he became librarian of the Boston Public Library.

51. As witnessed by such articles in the Mémorial Diplomatique as "La Relativité de la connaissance," "Les Procédés métaphysiques dans l'école révolutionnaire," and "La Philosophie positive et M. Littré."

52. James Truslow Adams errs when he says (*The Adams Family*, p. 536) that "by the end of 1891 [Adams] was again in Washington." Henry Adams was in Paris through January 7, 1892, after which he went to London. (See *Letters 1858-91*, pp. 534–535.)

53. This letter was inserted in Vignaud's copy of Adams's *Historical Essays*.

54. The Bering Sea Controversy was on at this time, and Minister T. Jefferson Coolidge, in calling on M. Ribot, the Minister of Foreign Affairs, or on M. Le Royer, the President of the Senate, had his First Secretary, M. Vignaud, always with him. At the American Legation, Coolidge discussed the controversy with Vignaud, as well as with other members of the Staff. See *Thomas*

Jefferson Coolidge, 1831-1920: an Autobiography (Mass. Hist. Soc., 1923), pp. 142, 148, 151, and *passim;* also *Diplomatic Memoirs,* by John Watson Foster, II, 32–42.

55. This letter, like the preceding one of September, was also inserted in Vignaud's copy of Adams's *Historical Essays.*

56. See R. G. Adams, *Three Americanists, passim,* and S. E. Morison, *Admiral of the Ocean Sea, passim;* as well as Vignaud's *Études sur la vie de Colomb.*

57. This letter was inserted in Vignaud's copy of Brooks Adams's *The Emancipation of Massachusetts* (Boston, 1887).

58. Levi Parsons Morton, Minister to France, with whom Vignaud went in 1883 as a delegate to the international convention for the protection of submarine cables. (See Henry Adams, *Letters, 1892-1918,* p. 313.)

59. The Vignaud Collection at the Clements Library includes the following books by Adams, each with the Vignaud book plate: *Démocratie: Roman Américain* (Paris, 1883; a clipping inserted asserts that the "real author" is Mrs. Henry Adams); *Documents Relating to New England Federalism, 1800-15* (Boston, 1877; signature of Vignaud in pencil on front cover, verso); *Historical Essays* (New York, 1891); *History of the United States of America* (New York, 1889–91); and *The Life of Albert Gallatin* (Philadelphia, 1879).

60. So described in a letter by W. W. Bishop, as Librarian, to the late President Burton of the University of Michigan, Dec. 29, 1922, containing details of the purchase of the Vignaud Collection. Used by permission of Mr. Bishop.

61. See Appendix II–A.

62. *History,* I, 157, 161.

63. *Ibid.,* pp. 42, 93–94.

64. *Ibid.,* pp. 143 f.

65. I, 334. Adams warns us that not less than 32 vols. of fragmentary writings of Napoleon are necessary for the comprehension of his mind.

66. II, 33.

67. IV, 59.

68. IV, 60.

69. IV, 66.

70. V, 22.

71. V, 235.

72. I, 198, 277.
73. I, 335, 352.
74. II, 310, 376.
75. This was reprinted in *Historical Essays*. At the Mass. Hist. Soc. there is a black notebook full of notes and citations in French for a study of Toussaint. Adams used A. Thier's *Consulat et empire* (20 vols.; at Mass. Hist. Soc.) and the *Vie de Toussaint*, by Saint-Rémy.
76. *Historical Essays*, pp. 154–156, 157. "The French people prided themselves in their keen sense of the ridiculous" (p. 157).
77. See Appendix II. It is amusing to witness Adams in the role of translator thinking out loud, as it were, in parentheses. "You will even let him perceive (vous lui laisserez même entrevoir) . . . I shall not be unwilling (éloigné) to intervene" (*History*, IV, 293); "Caisse de l'amortissement (sinking fund)"; "de transiger (compromise)" (*Ibid.*, V, 144, 255); "The party most nearly in sympathy with us (le parti qui se rapproche le plus de nous)" (*Ibid.*, VI, 47).

Chapter IV. THE LITERARY USE OF THREE FRENCH
HISTORIANS

1. *Letters, 1858-91*, p. 305.
2. A more detailed attempt at tracing the reputation of Michelet's work in America has been undertaken in a paper to be published elsewhere.
3. See article by the present writer, "The 1858 Catalogue of Henry Adams's Library," *The Colophon* III, n.s., No. 4 (Autumn, 1938), 487.
4. *The Harvard University Catalogue of Officers and Students*, 1871–72, p. 39, indicates that in 1870–71 the course in Mediaeval History (Hist. II) required as texts Sismondi's or Michelet's *History of France*. One of Adams's distinguished students, Lindsay Swift, recalls that in 1871–72 Adams gave a course on the history of Germany, France, and the Church (8th to 15th century) and that the assigned text on France was the so-called *Student's History of France*. (See *Proceedings of the Mass. Hist. Soc.*, LII, 1918–19, 69–77.) I have found that this text was by William Henley P. Jervis (author's name does not appear on title page) and was part

of a popular series of Students' histories on various subjects, published by Harper & Bros. in the early 70s. In the Preface, Jervis says that the writer on whom chief reliance has been placed is Henri Martin, "the most valuable of all French historians." Other authorities are mentioned, such as Guizot and Thierry. Michelet's name, however, is not included. For scholars acquainted with the Adams-Freeman feud (see Cargill, *The Mediaevalism of Henry Adams*), Jervis's further remarks in the Preface are not without interest: he (Jervis) claims that he has given a sympathetic account and has, above all, avoided the "capital error of writing the *History of France* from an English point of view." The *History of France* occupied practically Michelet's whole life, from 1831–74. Of this work Carré says: "C'est Michelet tout entier" (Jean-Marie Carré, *Michelet et son temps*, p. xiv.)

5. Gabriel Monod (1844–1912), who said that he owed his vocation for history to his teacher Michelet, was the custodian of the latter's papers after the death of the second Madame Michelet. Monod's 2-volume work on the historian was published posthumously in 1924, the year of the celebration of the 50th anniversary of Michelet's death. In 1875 Monod had published his *Jules Michelet*. According to Monod, Michelet was dissatisfied both with the *pictorial school* which neglects psychology and the *philosophic school* which analyzes too much and barely gets down to the events (Monod, *La Vie et la pensée de Jules Michelet, 1798-1852*, p. 265). Michelet aimed at a synthesis. Most likely Henry Adams got to know Professor Monod early in the 1870s; for Marian Adams referred to Monod in 1879 as "an old acquaintance of Henry's" (*The Letters of Mrs. Henry Adams*, 1865 83, p. 222). In the spring of 1884 Adams published an article on "Napoleon I at St. Domingo" (in French) in the *Revue historique*, founded by Monod, in 1876. Whether Adams discussed Michelet with Monod or read what the latter had to say about Michelet remains for the present a matter of conjecture. One may, however, venture a guess that together with other scholars reading the *Revue* Adams read, in the *Revue* for 1876, Monod's "Du progrès des études historiques en France depuis le XVIe siècle." In a letter addressed to Elizabeth Cameron from Paris, 5 Sept. 1899 (while the Dreyfus affair was raging), Adams writes of Monod as follows: "My idiot friend, Gabriel Monod, who is as near to being an ideal Harvard professor as I know, and as little a Frenchman, makes a fool of himself whenever

he is given the smallest opportunity" (*Letters, 1892-1918*, p. 238).

6. The year that Adams entered Harvard (1854), the foundation of the Historical Institute at Vienna, on the model of the École des Chartes, inaugurated the systematic study of the Middle Ages. (G. P. Gooch, *History and Historians in the Nineteenth Century*, p. 428.) In France a lively interest in the mediaeval history of the country was aroused by Thierry and Barante, Guizot, and Michelet; but its systematic study owed most to the École des Chartes. It was there that Michelet's pupil Quicherat learned more exact methods. (Gooch, p. 207.)

7. This book is in the Adams Collection at the Mass. Hist. Soc. and is entitled, in full: *History of France from the Earliest Period to the Present Time*, by M. Michelet, Professeur-Suppléant à la Faculté des Lettres, Professeur à l'École Normale, Chef de la Section Historique aux Archives du Royaume; Vol. I, translated by G. H. Smith, F. G. S.; Vol. I bears on the flyleaf, "Henry B. Adams," in a script characteristic of his youth. Vol. II is inscribed on the flyleaf, "Henry Brooks Adams, Quincy."

8. P. 85 is turned down at the upper edge, at the place where the "March of the English" is described.

9. There are small pieces of white paper, serving as bookmarks, inserted between pp. 120 and 121 which bear the caption "Character of Charlemagne," and pp. 144 and 145, which have as captions (respectively) "Charles the Simple" and "Louis D'Outremer and Lothaire."

10. In the left margin Adams wrote "Eudes 888."

11. *Syllabus: History II France*, Items 223–292 (Archives, Harvard).

12. In the left margin Adams wrote, "Charles 898."

13. In the left margin Adams wrote, "Robert 922."

14. The italics represent Adams's sublineations.

15. *Idem.*

16. Adams's scoring.

17. Italics represent Adams's sublineations.

18. The items are as follows. 230: The first line of the dukes of Burgundy. 231: How did the Capetian family acquire Burgundy? 232: The duchy, the county, and the kingdoms of Burgundy; Hugh the Great. 233: Lothaire; his war with Germany. 234: Circumstances of the election of Hugh Capet as king. 235: Fate of the Carlovingian family.

19. Between pp. 184 and 185 there is a piece of paper that served as a bookmark. The captions on the respective pages are: "The Year One Thousand" and "The Church, The General Refuge."

20. Between pages 192 and 193 there is a bookmark (a small piece of paper). The captions on these pages, respectively, are: "The Holy See and Holy Empire" and "Materialism of the Feudal World." Another bookmark is inserted between pages 196 and 197. There the captions, in order, are: "Contest between Church and Empire" and "Character of the Normans."

21. Michelet quotes in a footnote: Guill, Apulus, l.ii ap. Muratori, V. 259. "Corpora derident Normannica, quae breviora Esse videbantur."

22. Michelet refers to Gibbon, X, 289.

23. Again we find a small paper bookmark between pages 198 and 199 where the respective captions are: "Norman Settlement in Italy" and "William the Bastard."

24. See Appendix IIB, item 22.

25. "Every one knows that there is war between the two! The thirteenth century has few secrets. There are no outsiders. We are one family as we are one Church. Every man and woman here, from Mary on her throne to the beggar on the porch, knows that Pierre de Dreux detests Blanche of Castile, and that their two windows carry on war across the very heart of the Cathedral" (*op. cit.*, p. 184).

26. *Mont-Saint-Michel*, p. 186.

27. Michelet, *History*, I, 222–229.

28. Adams also read and made notations in Rémusat's *Abélard*. Of this I shall treat elsewhere.

29. Adams, p. 286; Michelet, pp. 223–224. Here Michelet gives us a note, a reference to the *Liber Calamitatum* (a letter to Heloise): "Now [he alludes to the time of his love] whatever songs I devised were amatory, not the secrets of philosophy. Many of these songs, as thyself knowest, are yet commonly sung in many countries; chiefly by those who find enjoyment in existence." Abelard joined his [i.e., William of Champeaux's] pupils, submitted to him his doubts, "puzzled him, laughed at him, and closed his mouth."

30. *Mont-Saint-Michel*, pp. 286–287.

31. *Ibid.*, p. 287.

32. Michelet, p. 224.

33. Adams, p. 287.

34. Michelet, p. 225.

35. Adams, p. 287.

36. And with J. S. Mill. Most likely Adams read Michelet's essay on *Woman, Love and Woman*.

37. Compare Michelet's *History*, pp. 293–295 with *Mont-Saint-Michel*, pp. 81–82.

38. The actual words in Michelet are, "She is said to have written to him as follows."

39. The English text of Michelet reads "Bretagne."

40. *Mont-Saint-Michel*, p. 189; Michelet, p. 295. Michelet takes the quotation from D. Morice, *Preuves de l'histoire de Bretagne*, I, 158.

41. Michelet, *History*, I (Ch. VIII), 291–294.

42. *Ibid.* (Ch. IX), pp. 316–317.

43. *Ibid.*, p. 316.

44. *Mont-Saint-Michel*, p. 348.

45. Michelet, p. 316.

46. *Mont-Saint-Michel*, p. 348. Michelet quotes (in a footnote, p. 316): "He was fat" (Grossus fuit)—Processus de St. Thomas (from Guill. de Thoro, Vit. S. Thomae, ap. Acta SS. Martis, i).

47. Michelet, pp. 324–325.

48. *Mont-Saint-Michel*, p. 29.

49. Michelet, p. 325. The italics are mine.

50. *Mont-Saint-Michel*, p. 29. Italics mine.

51. This is well expressed in George H. Mead's *Movements of Thought in the Nineteenth Century*, p. 72. The interest of the individual "lay in the ritual, the form which united people together in the process of worship, which was expressed in the architecture of the Church, in the pageantry of the ritual itself. This appealed directly to the religious response during the Romantic period. This response comes back to the individual, to his aesthetic approval or disapproval."

52. *History*, I, 327–335.

53. See Michelet, pp. 311–315; Adams, pp. 199, 201, 253, 254. One might add that Walter Pater joins the two voices.

54. For the possible relationship between Michelet and Scott, cf. the work of Carré, Halphen, Monod, Moreau, and Partridge, *passim*, indicated in the Bibliography below. For Adams and Scott, cf. indexes of the *Letters* and *Mont-Saint-Michel*. In the *Education* (p. 39) Adams says: ". . . the happiest hours of the

boy's education were passed in summer lying on a musty heap of Congressional Documents in the old farmhouse at Quincy, reading 'Quentin Durward,' 'Ivanhoe,' and the 'Talisman.' "

55. Halphen, *L'Histoire en France depuis cent ans*, p. 39.

56. *Ibid.*, p. 82; *Education* and "The Tendency of History," *passim*.

57. Edmund Wilson, *To the Finland Station*, pp. 11–12. One recalls that Goethe, before Michelet, remarked that the romantic is the sickly and that the classic is that which is healthy.

58. Gabriel Monod, *La Vie et la pensée de Jules Michelet, 1789-1852*, I, 265, note 1.

59. Notice the poetically humorous identification of the self, in each, with the period he was recreating—

Adams: "I am rococo—I am twelfth century—I have invented Albert Gallatin."

Michelet: "I have just gone through [he is talking of the French Revolution] *September* and all the terrors of death; massacred the Abbaye, I am on the way to the revolutionary tribunal, that is to say, to the guillotine."

60. Certain values of Michelet's *History* have continued to be recognized. Indeed, with regard to his treatment of the medieval period G. P. Gooch says: "Of general histories on the Middle Ages none have approached the opening volumes of Michelet in brilliance and suggestion" (*History and Historians in the 19th Century*, p 213).

61. *Education*, p. 403. Even in 1872, when he was busy with "fearful German books" and he was advising H. C. Lodge to learn to appreciate and use the German historical method (which the French historians themselves were doing at the time), his ideal was unconsciously becoming molded on the French line. "I have, no doubt," he wrote to Lodge on June 2, 1872, "the more respect for knowledge, even when knowledge is useless and worthless, than for mere style, even where style is good; but unless one learns beforehand to be logically accurate and habitually thorough, mere knowledge is worth very little. At best it never can be more than relative ignorance, at least in the study of history" (*Letters, 1858-91*, p. 253). This ideal, stated in a phrase, is *la clarté française*.

62. See "Henry Adams et la France" by Maurice Le Breton in *Harvard et la France*.

63. *Letters, 1892-1918*, p. 304, letter to Chas. F. Adams, Jr.,

Dec. 18, 1900. The index of this volume needs correction; Michelet, for example, is not listed at all, where he should be (on p. 304).

64. See p. 68, above.

65. *Letters, 1858-91*, pp. 55–56, letter to his mother, Dresden, March 4, 1860.

66. The first two volumes of the *Cosmos* were published between 1845 and 1847; the 3d and 4th vols. between 1850 and 1858; and the 5th, posthumously, in 1862 (see *Encylopaedia Britannica*, 14th ed., p. 878).

67. Renan, *Correspondance 1846-71*, Vol. I. Renan reviewed Humboldt's book in the *Revue philosophique* and sent him the review (I, 11, 12).

68. "La Vie de Jésus," Sept. 7, 1863; "M. Ernest Renan," June 2 and 29, 1862.

69. *Letters, 1858-91*, p. 202, letter to Charles M. Gaskell, Harvard, Feb. 13, 1871.

70. *Correspondance*, II, 3.

71. See Tronchon, *Ernest Renan à l'étranger*, p. 300; Adams, *Letters 1858-91*, p. 295.

72. Renan, *Correspondance*, II, 156, letter to C. Ritter, Paris, 26 December 1878.

73. *Letters, 1858-91*, p. 273.

74. See G. G. Colton's "Introduction" to Renan's *Recollections of My Youth*, p. xv.

75. *Education*, p. 91.

76. *Ibid.*

77. *Ibid.* See Amy Lowell, *Keats*, I, 587; Byron, *Poetical Works* (Oxford, 1914), pp. 97, 217–218.

78. *Correspondance*, I, 64.

79. *Education*, p. 386.

80. *Correspondance*, I, 16.

81. *Correspondance*, II, 65 (Rome, 26 Dec. 1849).

82. *Education*, p. 386.

83. *Ibid.*, p. 434.

84. *Correspondance*, I, 284, letter, 12 Sept. 1861.

85. Both Adams and Renan read George Eliot, as has already been indicated. George Eliot and George Lewes met Renan on the last day of the year 1866 at Mme Mohl's. There Scherer and his wife, Jules Simon and others were invited to meet the Spain-bound pair (see *George Eliot: a Biography*, by Blanche Colton

Williams, p. 229). Eliot read the *Vie de Jésus* in 1863 upon its appearance and had some enthusiastic things to say about it, with qualifications. (See *George Eliot's Life as Related in Her Letters and Journals*, II, 359, 360, 372; III, 5.)

86. Meredith called the *Vie de Jésus* "one of the finest works of this generation." *Letters of George Meredith*, I, 121 (Aug. 20, 1863); and p. 127.

87. Iris Esther Sells, *Matthew Arnold and France*, p. xlii. Unlike the Englishman, Adams was never made the subject of conversation between Renan and his friend George Sand, nor did he ever meet the author of *La Vie de Jésus*, as Arnold had done in 1849, or got his name into the letters of Sainte-Beuve (1860). (Sells, pp. 36, 221, 225.)

88. Alexander P. Kelso, *Matthew Arnold on Continental Life and Literature, passim.*

89. Adams's library at the Mass. Hist. Soc. contains the following books by Matthew Arnold: *Culture and Anarchy*, New York, 1883; *Essays in Criticism*, London, 1865; *Essays in Criticism*, New York, 1883 (Preface marked, top of p. 7 "re Philistinism"); *God and the Bible*, New York, 1883 (pages uncut); *Literature and Dogma*, New York, 1883; *Mixed Essays*, New York, 1883; *Arnold's Notebooks*, with a Preface by the Honorable Mrs. Wodehouse and a portrait, London, 1902; *On the Study of Celtic Literature and on Translating Homer*, New York, 1883; *Poems*, 3d ed. London, 1857 (in *Collection of British Poets*, Vol. II); *Poetical Works of Matthew Arnold*, London, 1890; *Saint Paul and Protestantism* . . . New York, 1883.

90. See *The Poetry of M. Arnold: a Commentary* by C. B. Tinker and H. F. Lowry: "Arnold's attention was first drawn to the legend of Saint Brandon by Renan's *La Poésie des races celtiques*" (p. 125). "The 'Paladium' poem represents very well the advanced thought of 1852, particularly that of Renan, which aspired to keep the spirit of Christianity without the specific articles of its creeds" (p. 191). The idea that faith must be based "on something more spiritual than dogma or superstition" (see Sells, p. 197) was shared alike by Sénancour (see his *Obermann*), Renan, Arnold, and Henry Adams.

91. In 1863 Arnold read the *Vie de Jésus* and in 1866 he was finishing Renan's *Averroës* and *Les Apôtres* (see Tinker and Lowry, p. 269).

92. Kelso, p. 24. See Renan's *Réforme intellectuelle et morale de la France* (1871).

93. *Letters, 1892-1918*, p. 94, letter, Jan. 23, 1896.

94. *Ibid.*, p. 610.

95. "But, if you need other evidence, you can consult Renan, who is the highest authority" (*Mont-Saint-Michel*, p. 140).

96. His diary fell into Arnold's hands late in life (see Kelso, p. 17). Both Arnold and Adams may have received their desire to read Amiel from Renan.

97. Symonds, *Autobiography*, pp. 128, 129, 130.

98. Circa 1892.

99. "Some Recollections of Ernest Renan," *The Nineteenth Century*, XXXII (1892), 718, 719.

100. To Charles Milnes Gaskell, Paris, 15 Nov. 1903 (*Letters, 1892-1918*, p. 413).

101. Completed by March 15, 1903 (see *Letters, 1892-1918*, p. 403, note 1).

102. *Averroès et l'averroïsme*, pp. 201–202. It is obvious that Adams derived from Renan his information on Averroes and the intellectual commerce between Alexandria, Syria, and the continent. *Mont-Saint-Michel*, p. 140; see also pp. 304 and 315.

103. *Mont-Saint-Michel*, pp. 140–141.

104. *Ibid.* Adams mentions Renan again on p. 354: "Between Norman blood and Breton blood was a singular gap, as Renan and every other Breton has delighted to point out. Both Abélard and Descartes were Breton." (Note: Adams is in error here. Descartes is Tourangian—i.e. from the former Province of Touraine.)

105. P. xi; see also Renan, *Correspondance*, II, 315.

106. Pp. 320, 357.

107. See section on Descartes, above, p. 188.

108. Ch. XVI, pp. 347–383.

109. Renan, *Averroës*, pp. 107–152.

110. Compare *Averroës*, pp. 107–142 *passim* and *Mont-Saint-Michel*, pp. 350–351, 360.

111. *Averroës*, p. 236.

112. *Mont-Saint-Michel*, pp. 361–362.

113. See above, p. 188.

114. *Mont-Saint-Michel*, pp. 361–362.

115. *Averroès*, pp. 239, 241.

116. *Mont-Saint-Michel*, p. 341.

117. *Vie de Jésus*, pp. 468, 475; see also p. 129: "N'imposons pas nos petits programmes de bourgeois sensés à ces mouvements extraordinaires si fort audessus de notre taille." Compare *Mont-Saint-Michel*, p. 306: "it is clear that tourists and heretics had best leave the Church to deal with its 'substances propres' and with its own members in its own way."

118. *Mont-Saint-Michel*, p. 344.

119. *Saint Paul*, pp. 10, 103.

120. *Mont-Saint-Michel*, p. 187.

121. *Saint Paul*, p. 281.

122. *Mont-Saint-Michel*, p. 164.

123. *Saint Paul*, p. 291.

124. *Les Apôtres*, p. XLIV.

125. *L'Antechrist*, p. 323.

126. *Mont-Saint-Michel*, pp. 251–252.

127. *L'Antechrist*, p. v. Italics are mine.

128. *Mont-Saint-Michel*, p. 226.

129. Renan is referring here to Havet's *Origines du Christianisme*.

130. *Feuilles détachées*, p. 333. The italics represent Adams's sublineations.

131. Amiel expressed this indignation in II, 123, of his *Journal* (see *Feuilles détachées*, pp. 394–395).

132. *Feuilles*, pp. 394–395. Compare "if humanity has any goal, etc." in *Mont-Saint-Michel*, p. 344.

133. See *Letters, 1892-1918*, p. 295 and note.

134. *Feuilles*, p. 360. For discussion of Hugo see Ch. V, above, on French *Belles-lettres*.

135. *Vie de Jésus*, p. 58.

136. We might cite here the parallel case of Mallarmé.

137. *Feuilles*, p. 362.

138. This introspection gives rise to a sense of spiritual isolation and loneliness. (See René Canat, *Une forme de mal du siècle*).

139. *Conférences d'Angleterre*, p. 214.

140. *Education*, p. 432.

141. See *Feuilles*, p. 417.

142. Here Renan has this footnote: "Je parle au sens relatif. Un être nous dépassant de l'infini et se décelant à nous par des actes comme l'homme est le dieu de l'animal."

143. *Feuilles*, p. 417.

144. The subject of Renan and America has been treated in a separate paper to be published in the near future.

145. *Feuilles*, p. 417.

146. See Maurice Mandelbaum, *Problem of Historical Knowledge*.

147. *Education*, p. 432.

148. Letter to Charles Ritter, 12 Sept. 1876 (*Correspondance*, II, 99).

149. Letter to C. M. Gaskell, Washington, 17 Feb. 1910 (*Letters, 1892–1918*, p. 835). For other references to Schopenhauer see letter to Margaret Chanler, Paris, 9 Sept. 1909 (*ibid.*, p. 524). *Education*, pp. 405–406, 432, 484–485.

150. See Francis Espinasse, *Life of Renan*, pp. 120–121, 176–177. See also Renan, *Correspondance*, letter to Marcellin Berthelot, and his *Caliban* and *Dialogues et fragments philosophiques* (1876).

151. See Max Nordau, *The Interpretation of History*, pp. 318–319.

152. *Ibid.*, p. 319.

153. "The Tendency of History," from the *Annual Report of the Am. Hist. Ass'n, 1894*, Washington, 1895, p. 18.

154. See Renan's letter on this subject to Berthelot; and see also Adams, *Education, passim*.

155. "I . . . always had a weakness for science mixed with metaphysics. I am a dilution of Lord Kelvin and St. Thomas Aquinas" (*Letters, 1892–1918*, p. 392).

156. *Avenir de la science*, 8th ed., 1894, pp. xii–xiii.

157. "L'histoire est pour moi ce que la raison est pour vous"— he is writing this to his friend Berthelot.—"Par l'histoire je n'entends pas, vous comprenez, l'histoire politique dans le sens ordinaire du mot; mais l'esprit humain, son évolution, ses phases accomplies" (*Correspondance*, I, 122).

158. "Les Sciences de la nature et les sciences historiques," letter to M. Marcellin Berthelot, Dinard près Saint-Malo, août 1863 (in *Dialogues et fragments*, pp. 160–161).

159. *Ibid.*, p. 154.

160. *Ibid.*, pp. 155–173.

161. *The Tendency of History*, p. 18.

162. Henry Adams, *The Degradation of the Democratic Dogma*, p. 196.

163. *Conférences*, p. 147.

164. *Mont-Saint-Michel*, p. 381. The elegiac wistfulness in

these two passages (and others one might cite) has its dual literary source in Shakespeare and Ronsard. See Max I. Baym, "Recurrent Poetic Theme," *The Shakespeare Association Bulletin*, XII, No. 3 (July, 1937), 155-158.

165. Baym, *loc. cit.*
166. *Education*, p. 85.
167. *Ibid.*, pp. 287-288.
168. Edward Gibbon, *Autobiography*, p. 160.
169. Walter Pater, *Marius the Epicurean* (London ed., 1924), p. 213; *Correspondance, Renan et Berthelot*, p. 43 (Rome, 9 Nov. 1849); *Education*, p. 90.
170. *Correspondance, Renan et Berthelot*, p. 64.
171. *Education*, p. 91. "In Feb., 1868, he was back in Rome, and sat once more on the steps of Ara Coeli, as had become with him almost a superstitution" (p. 235). Towards the end of the book he pictures himself as going back "in 1964, to sit with Gibbon on the steps of Ara Coeli" (p. 497).
172. *Ibid.*, p. 90; *Correspondance, Renan et Berthelot*, p. 72.
173. *Correspondance, Renan et Berthelot*, p. 80; *Education*, p. 94.
174. *Childe Harold*, Canto III, Stanzas cvi, cvii, cx. "I am reading Voltaire and Gibbon, although I wrote to Reynolds the other day to prove reading of no use," John Keats wrote to his brothers George and Tom, mentioning in the same letter that Lord Byron's Fourth Canto of Childe Harold is expected out. Apparently, he had just read Canto III where he found the names of the two historians whom he was now reading (see Amy Lowell, *John Keats*, I, 587-588).
175. William James, *A Plurastic Universe*, p. 144.
176. *Souvenirs d'enfance et de jeunesse*, pp. viii, ix.
177. He could have read the prayer in the *Revue des deux mondes* for Dec. 1, 1876.
178. Ernest Renan, *Prière sur l'Acropole*, ed. Eugène Vinaver and T. B. L. Webster (Manchester Univ. Press, 1934), p. 15.
179. *Souvenirs d'enfance et de jeunesse*, p. 60.
180. *Ibid.*, pp. 62-72 (compare "Un immense fleuve . . . ," with M. Arnold).
181. Compare "Je suis né, déesse, . . . de parents barbares, chez les Cimmeriens . . . au bord d'une mer sombre. . . . Mes pères, . . . étaient voués aux navigations lointaines. . . . Je fus bercé au souvenir des glaces flottantes."

182. Compare "Des prêtres d'un culte étranger, venu des Syriens de Palestine, prirent soin de m'élever."

183. Compare "Et puis si tu savais combien il est devenu difficile de te servir! Toute noblesse a disparu. Les Scythes ont conquis le monde. Il n'y a plus de république d'hommes libres. Une pambéotie redoutable, une ligue de toutes les sottises, étend sur le monde un couvercle de plomb, sous lequel on étouffe."

184. See Adams, *Letters to a Niece*.

185. Quoted in Espinasse, *Life of Renan*, p. 77.

186. See Matthew Arnold's *Culture and Anarchy*.

187. The year in which he completed his novel *Democracy* and began work on his *History*.—Both Taine and Renan may have read Adams's novel which appeared in a French translation, under the imprint of Plon, in 1883. It ran through two editions. One copy that Hay sent him, inscribed "From John Hay, February 1883," was a second edition; another, a second edition, picked up many years later, is inscribed by Adams: "Bought on the Quai Malaquais, August 26, 1908, fr. 1.25." Both copies are at the Mass. Hist. Soc.

188. See the Harvard Catalogues, 1854–58.

189. As part of a gift from Thomas Lee of Brookline, Mass.

190. *North American Review*, XCIII (July-October, 1861), 99–107. *La Fontaine* was in the third edition; the others in the second edition.

191. April, 1864, and January, 1865.

192. In this review Rae asserted that Taine's work compared very favorably indeed with Buckle's *History of Civilization in England*, which had appeared in 1857. Thus it was (perhaps) in conjunction with his study of Taine, that Adams's attention was drawn to Buckle.

193. See *A Cycle of Letters*, II, 95; Mill's review of *De l'intelligence* in *Dissertations*.

194. In 1860 Taine went to England and there met Palgrave.

195. *Cycle of Letters*, I, 135.

196. *Esther*, p. 256.

197. *Democracy*, p. 9.

198. In 1872 the *Atlantic* carried Henry James's review of Van Laun's translation of the *Histoire de la littérature anglaise*. Adams followed closely everything Henry James wrote. See *Atlantic Monthly*, XXIX (April, 1872), 469.

199. See my article "William James and Henry Adams," *New England Quarterly*, X, No. 4 (December, 1937), 718–719; *Education*, p. 231.

200. *On Intelligence*, reviewed by James T. Bixby, *North American Review*, CXVII (1873), 401.

201. *Education*, p. 432.

202. Philosophy 4: Psychology—Taine on Intelligence. See my article, "James and Adams," *New England Quarterly*, X, No. 4 (December, 1937), 721.

203. *De l'intelligence*, II, 192. This essay was reprinted in Fiske's *The Unseen World, and Other Essays*.

204. Fiske, *Classroom Taine*, pp. iii, iv. In 1874 Fiske made use again of *De l'intelligence* in his analysis of sound. (See *Outline of Cosmic Philosophy*, III, 179–184.)

205. After 1830 Cousin's philosophic career was practically over.

206. George H. Mead, *Movements of Thought in the 19th Century*, ed. Merritt H. Moore. See also John T. Merz, *A History of European Thought in the Nineteenth Century*.

207. André Chevrillon, *Taine, formation de sa pensée*, p. 128.

208. See A. Fouillée, *Le Mouvement idéaliste et la réaction contre la science positive*, p. xvi. "Taine devait être de ceux qui favorisèrent le mouvement idéaliste, parce qu'il avait lui-même préparé la voie dans son beau livre *De l'Intelligence*" (*ibid.*, quoted in Giraud, *Essai sur Taine*, p. 147).

In the Adams collection, there is a copy of Alfred Fouillée's *Histoire de la philosophie* (6th ed., Paris, 1891) with the following passage (on pp. 445–446) underscored by Henry Adams: "Maintenant, comment faut-il se représenter cet absolu? Selon Hegel, il est la pensée, la raison, non une volonté supérieure à la pensée même. N'est-ce point là, dira-t-on, identifier les contraires; absolu et relatif, liberté et nécessité, idéal et réel?—Oui, sans doute, répond Hegel; mais l'identité des contraires est précisément le secret du progrès universel, le secret de la vie."

209. Boutroux wrote: "Il est probable qu'en métaphysique il n'a pas seulement contribué au développement du mouvement positiviste, mais que, par le mélange de spéculation et d'observation qui caractérise son oeuvre, par la disproportion visible de ses premisses et de ses conclusions, il a amené plus d'un esprit à réagir contre le positivisme, et contribué, indirectement, à la renaissance de l'idéalisme" (quoted in Giraud, *Essai sur Taine*, p. 148).

210. Giraud, *op. cit.*, p. 76.

211. In this regard see the work of George Sarton, in general.

212. See Woodbridge Riley, "La Philosophie française en Amérique," *Revue philosophique de la France et de l'étranger*, Nos. 5–6, May-June, 1919, pp. 369–423.

213. See her *Society in America*.

214. Chevrillon, p. 122; see also Appendix VI: "Philosophy of History," pp. 399, 400.

215. *Education*, p. 432.

216. See, for example, his analysis of Sumner (*Education*, p. 252).

217. *Gallatin*, p. 171.

218. *John Randolph*, p. 305.

219. Among others, he was then reading Henry Maudsley's *Body and Will*.

220. *History*, I, 172; II, 34; V, 54.

221. *Education*, pp. 399–401.

222. *Gallatin*, p. 171.

223. Now found among the books he presented to Western Reserve University. *La Révolution*, Vol. II, Book I.

224. *La Révolution*, I, 4.

225. *Ibid.*, pp. 189, 190, 191.

226. *Ibid.*, p. 211.

227. *Ibid.*, pp. 245, 246.—On p. 247 Taine has a footnote (note 1) consisting of the following quotation and comment, next to which Adams put a questionmark in the margin: "Toute société dans laquelle la séparation des pouvoirs n'est pas déterminée n'a point de Constitution." (Déclaration des Droits, Article 16.)

"Ce principe est emprunté à une texte de Montesquieu et à la Constitution Américaine. Pour tout le reste on a suivi la théorie de Rousseau."

228. *Letters, 1892-1918* (1603 H St., 16 June 1892), pp. 10, 11.

229. *Essai sur Taine*, 2d ed., pp. xxi, 311.

230. By W. P. Trent, in VII, No. 4 (July, 1902), 796–798.

231. Aulard, pp. ix, x.

232. 4 Vols., Riga and Leipzig, 1784–91. We are disregarding here the political implications which put the Sorbonne under fire.

233. Aulard, pp. 4–11.

234. Both read the *Causeries du lundi* to this effect: "Entre un fait aussi général et aussi commun à tous que le sol et le climat, et un résultat aussi compliqué et aussi divers que la variété des

espèces et des individus qui y vivent, il y a place pour quantité de causes et de forces plus particulières, plus immédiates, et tant qu'on ne les a pas saisies, on n'a rien expliqué" (*Causeries du lundi*, XIII, 56). This passage is quoted in Emerson's *Journals* (IX, 1856–63, 530) as a substantiating remark to this statement of Emerson's: "Taine generalizes rashly, and writes: 'La race façonne l'individu, le pays façonne la race. Un degré de chaleur dans l'air et d'inclination dans le sol est la cause première de nos facultés, et de nos passions . . .'" (p. 529). Emerson adds: "See also a just censure in the like spirit on Taine's proposed formula of each mind, as of Livy—*Ibid*. [*Causeries du lundi*, Vol. XIII]." Emerson wrote this in 1863 when he was sixty years old.

235. "C'est une pyrotechnic littéraire. La vérité historique s'y trouve sacrifiée, à chaque instant, aux nécessités de l'art" (p. 327).

236. Aulard, p. 330. Also "Le document ne lui parle pas. C'est lui qui parle, et tout le temps, au document" (*Ibid*., p. 328).

237. *Letters, 1892-1918*, pp. 501–502.

238. William Henry Smith, 1833–96. *A Case of Hereditary Bias. Henry Adams as an Historian. Some Strictures on the "History of the United States of America"* by Housatonic. New York, 1891.

239. Chevrillon, p. 388. At age of 19, Taine had written, in an essay on the "Destiny of Man," that man aspired to that interior unity which would put an end to his inner disturbances and impotence.

240. See *The Degradation of the Democratic Dogma*, pp. 114–127. We know that at twenty Taine was under the influence of Spinoza and Hegel and that he then adhered to universal determinism and to an equation of philosophy and science (Giraud, p. 55).

241. Emerson, *Works* (in one volume), p. 213.

242. Un concert vague emplit l'espace illimité;
      Les ondes de l'éther palpitent en cadence,
      L'atome imperceptible exécute sa danse,
      Sur un rhythme savant, à sa forme adapté.

      Par son premier élan et son poids emporté,
      L'astre roule, décrit son orbe et recommence;
      Le monde harmonieux, sous un archet immense,
      Vibre, et chante tout bas l'hymne de sa beauté.

      O mes bienheureux chats! Votre rouet paisible
      Nous apporte une voix de ce choeur invisible
      Où se dit le secret du mystique univers.

O grave mélopée! O musique discrète!
J'écoute, je comprends; mon coeur devient poète,
Et mon coeur tout entier a frémi dans mes vers.

(Quoted in *Giraud*, p. 103.)

243. Ludwig Lewisohn, *The Story of American Literature*, pp. 310, 311.

244. Monod, *Renan, Taine, Michelet*, p. 131.

245. See Giraud, pp. 120, 121.

246. *Ibid.*, p. 110.

Chapter V. BELLES LETTRES

1. These three books and one other by Gaston Paris, are in the Adams Collection. See Appendix I, below.

2. Since Adams's attempts at philology form a subject calling for specialized treatment, we are at present omitting it. We offer, however, in Appendix I, a complete list of the *studies* Adams used.

3. See Appendix I, below.

4. Editions of *Aucassin and Nicolette* in the Adams Collection are those of F. W. Bourdillon (see *Mont-Saint-Michel*, p. 231), L. Moland and C. D'Héricault, and Hermann Suchier. For full imprint data, see Appendix I below.

5. *Mont-Saint-Michel*, p. 13.

6. *Ibid.*, p. 120.

7. In Adams's library and now in the Collection (see Appendix I, below) are texts of the *Chanson de Roland* by Léon Gautier (1872), Wendelin Foerster (1883, 1886), and F. B. Luquiens (1909).

8. *Mont-Saint-Michel*, pp. 242 f.

9. *Ibid.*, pp. 251–284. See Appendix I, below.

10. The following chapters in *Mont-Saint-Michel* are devoted to early French poetry: Ch. II, "Chanson de Roland," pp. 14–31; Ch. XI, "The Three Queens," pp. 198–229; Ch. XII, "Nicolette and Marion," pp. 230–250; Ch. XIII, "Les Miracles de Notre Dame," pp. 251–284. A conservative estimate reveals that 27 percent of the work is constructed of excerpts from and discussions of medieval French poetry.

11. *Mont-Saint-Michel*, p. 214.

12. *Ibid.*, p. 220.

13. Guillaume de Saint-Pair, *Le Roman du Mont-Saint-Michel*.

14. *Mont-Saint-Michel*, pp. 272, 273.
15. *Ibid.*, pp. 249, 250.
16. Consult *Harvard College Catalogue*, 1857–58.
17. Cf. Henry Adams, *Syllabus History II*, p. 5 (items 250 f.) (Harvard Archives).
18. *Mont-Saint-Michel*, p. 253.
19. *Ibid.*, p. 254: "Ung jour moi estant devant le roi lui deman- day congie d'aller en pelerinage a nostre Dame de Tourtouze [Tortosa in Syria] qui estoit ung veage tres fort requis. Et y avoit grant quantite de pelerins par chacun jour pour ce que c'est le premier autel qui onques fust fait en l'onneur de la Mere de Dieu ainsi qu'on disoit lors. Et y faisoit nostre Dame de grans miracles a merveilles. Entre lesquelz elle en fist ung d'un pouvre homme qui estoit hors de son sens et demoniacle. Car il avoit le maling esperit dedans le corps. Et advint par ung jour qu'il fut amene a icelui autel de nostre Dame de Tourtouze. Et ainsi que ses amys qui l'avoient la amene prioient a nostre Dame qu'elle lui voulsist re- couvrer sante et guerison le diable que la pouvre creature avoit ou corps respondit: 'Nostre Dame n'est pas ici; elle est en Egipte pour aider au Roi de France et aux Chrestiens qui aujourdhui arrivent en la Terre sainte contre toute paiennie qui sont a cheval.' Et fut mis en escript le jour que le deable profera ces motz et fut apporte au legat qui estoit avecques le roi de France; lequel me dist depuis que a celui jour nous estion arrivez en la terre d'Egipte. Et suis bien certain que la bonne Dame Marie nous y eut bien besoin."
20. In Adams Collection: John Froissart, *Chronicles*, 2 vols., 1868.
21. See A. Molinier, *Les Sources de l'histoire de France*, Vols. IV and V (1904); Adams refers to the same author's *Histoire générale des arts appliqués*, 4 vols., Paris, 1896; cf. *Mont-Saint-Michel*, p. 107.
22. *Mont-Saint-Michel*, p. 255.
23. This is found in the Adams Collection.
24. *Ibid.*
25. Both the *Annales* and the *Théâtre indien* are in the Adams Collection.
26. See, for example, *Mont-Saint-Michel*, pp. 205–206.
27. The only Sainte-Beuve books in the Adams Collection are *Causeries du lundi* (markings in Vol. I only); *Nouveaux lundis*; *M. de Talleyrand* and *Le Général Jomini*, 2d. ed., 1869. There are,

curiously, no references to Sainte-Beuve in any of Adams's own
writings.

28. Pp. 41, 126.

29. The Adams Collection has Jusserand's 2-volume *Histoire
littéraire du peuple anglais, des origines à la renaissance.* 2d ed.,
Paris, 1896. Vol. I has this inscription: "A monsieur Henry Adams
cordial hommage d'un auteur confus de n'en avoir pas dit plus
long sur le XII siècle, J. J. Jusserand." And Vol. II: "A monsieur
Henry Adams, 'Pur remembrer des ancesseirs. Les diz, e les faize
les murs' (Wace). Jusserand. Washington, Jer, 1905." The *Ronsard* (in Les grands écrivains français series) is dated Paris, 1913.

30. See *Letters, 1892-1918,* pp. 520–521.

31. *Ibid.,* p. 521.

32. See Chapter on John and J. Q. Adams.

33. *Education,* p. 229. On p. 330 Adams quotes the following
lines:

> Tout bien considéré, je te soutiens en somme,
>   Que scélérat pour scélérat,
> Il vaut mieux être un loup qu'un homme.

These verses are not, as some might take for granted, from any
of the fables having "loup" as part of the title, but from "Les
Compagnons d'Ulysse" (Livre xii.1).

34. *Essais,* I, 193.

35. I, 215, 216.

36. I, 216.

37. The rest of the passage that follows was underlined by
Adams.

38. I, 217.

39. III, 93.

40. III, 96.

41. IV, 260.

42. IV, 262, 263.

43. *Education,* pp. 389, 454, 485, 492.

44. *Letters, 1892-1918,* p. 477.

45. Montaigne, *Textes choisis,* p. 96.

46. This series can, of course, be filled out by including St.
Augustine's *Confessions*; Alfred de Musset, *La Confession d'un
enfant du siècle*; Amiel's *Journal intime;* the *Journal* of Maurice de
Guérin; and the *Mémoires* of Mme de Staël. All these works are
in the Adams Library.

47. Rousseau, *Confessions* (Plon, ed., Paris), I, 3. Italics mine.
48. *Education*, p. ix.
49. *Ibid.*, p. 435.
50. *Ibid.*, p. 4.
51. *Ibid.*, p. 5.
52. *Ibid.*, p. 441.
53. *Ibid.*, p. 433.
54. *Ibid.*, p. 434.
55. *Ibid.*, p. 382.
56. *Ibid.*, pp. 476, 487.
57. *Ibid.*, p. 420.
58. *Essais*, III, xiii.
59. *Education*, pp. 472, 471.
60. "The life that Brantôme describes" (*Letters, 1892-1918*, p. 81, letter to Eliz. Cameron, Paris, 12 Sept. 1895).
61. "No Frenchman except Rabelais, and Montaigne had ever taught anarchy other than as a path to order" (*Education*, p. 454).
62. *Esther*, p. 197.
63. *Letters, 1892-1918*, pp. 84, 85.
64. *Ibid.*, p. 133 (Paris, 19 Oct. 1897).
65. *Education*, pp. 4, 5.
66. The following works are in the Adams Collection: Charles Perrault, *Contes;* Jean de La Bruyère, *Caractères*—Suivis des Caractères de Théophraste, trad. du grec par La Bruyère, Paris, 1847; La Rochefoucauld, *Maximes* (see note 68, below).
67. *Education*, p. 15.
68. This book is in the Adams Collection. The flyleaf bears the inscription, "To My Esteemed Friend, H. B. Adams, from his classmate James May. April 9th, 1857." This is obviously the copy referred to by Henry Adams in the 1858 Catalogue.
69. *Education*, p. 4.
70. *Letters, 1892-1918*, p. 89. For the vivid pictures of her times, in her letters Abigail Adams challenges comparison with Mme de Sévigné, whose *Lettres* are in the Adams Collection.
71. *Letters to a Niece*, p. 81.
72. In the Adams Collection. Vol. I, *Les Antiques, I:* Eschyle (troisième éd., Paris, Calmann Lévy Editeur, Ancienne Maison Michel Lévy Frères, 3, Rue Auber, 3. 1881); Vol. II, *Les Antiques, II:* Sophocle, Euripide, Aristophane, Calidasa (Paris, 1882); Vol. III, *Les Modernes, III:* Shakespeare, Le Théâtre français depuis ses

origines jusqu'à Beaumarchais (Paris, 1884). It is possible that Adams first heard of P. de Saint-Victor from Swinburne and that years later his interest in this writer was strengthened through his study of Taine. The latter spoke enthusiastically of Saint-Victor's classic style and of his "goût de la grandeur." See Taine, *Dernières essais de critique et d'histoire* (*Débats du 24 décembre 1869*); and see also Giraud, pp. iii, 254.

73. *Harvard Magazine*, III (December, 1857), 401.

74. "The classic and promiscuous turmoil of the forum, the theatre, or the bath, which trained the Greeks and the Romans, or the narrower contact of the church and the coffee-house, which bred the polished standards of Dryden and Racine, were unknown in America." (*Life of Lodge*, p. 8).

75. In the Adams Collection: Jean Baptiste Molière, *Oeuvres complètes*, Edition variorum, etc., par Charles Louandre, Ed., ornée du portrait de Molière (3 vols. Paris, G. Charpentier et Cie, n. d.). Also, two plays by Fabre d'Eglantine, *Le Philintine de Molière* (ou suite du *Misanthrope*), 1790; *L'Intrigue épistolaire*, 1791.

76. *History*, I, 243.

77. *Democracy*, p. 110.

78. *Mont-Saint-Michel*, p. 15.

79. *Life of Lodge*, pp. 25, 37.

80. *Harvard Charge Books*, March 22, 1876, p. 3.

81. Charles Batteux, 1713–1780, *Les Quatre Poétiques d'Aristote, d'Horace, de Vida, de Despreaux*, avec les traductions et des remarques par M. L'Abbé Batteux, Professeur royal, de l'Académie françoise, et de celle des Inscriptions et Belles Lettres. A Paris Chez Saillant et Noyon, Libraires rue Saint-Jean-de-Beauvais. Dessaint Libraire, rue de Foin. MDCCLXXI.

82. *Mont-Saint-Michel*, p. 141 and *passim*.

83. However, the Diderot books in the Adams Collection are of a later date than that on which he withdrew the Batteux work. But his general acquaintance with French Literature of the 18th century is at least contemporaneous with, and even antedates, his knowledge of Batteux. The Diderot books in the collection are *Jacques le Fataliste* (lineation on p. 213), and John Morley, *Diderot and the Encyclopaedists*. Adams's only direct reference to Diderot is to be found in *Mont-Saint-Michel*, p. 107. In reading Paul de Saint-Victor's *Trois Masques*, his attention was once more drawn to Diderot.

84. See Ch. I, above.

85. *Works*, I, 429.

86. Adams's copy was dated Paris, 1844. The flyleaf bears the following inscription: "To My esteemed Friend, H. B. Adams, from his classmate, April 9th '57—James May."

87. The italicized passages represent those Adams underscored. *Romans*, p. 3.

88. *Ibid.*, p. 10.

89. *Ibid.*, p. 70.

90. *Ibid.*, p. 74.

91. *Ibid.*, p. 78.

92. *Ibid.*, p. 250.

93. *Education*, p. 460.

94. *Romans*, p. 276.

95. *Ibid.*

96. *Letters, 1858-91*, pp. 498–499.

97. *Romans*, p 277

98. *Ibid.*, p. 307.

99. *Ibid.*, p. 456.

100. *Ibid.*, p. 487.

101. *Ibid.*, p. 487. Compare Goethe, *Natur und Kunst*. Adams read Goethe and was greatly familiar with all his work.

102. *Ibid.*, p. 490.

103. See section on "Taine," above; see also my article on "William James and Henry Adams."

104. *Romans*, p. 495.

105. *Ibid.*, p. 526.

106. *Ibid.*, p. 506.

107. *Ibid.*, p. 508.

108. *Ibid.*, p. 524.

109. *Ibid.*, p. 526.

110. *Letters, 1892-1918*, p. 121 (Letter to C. M. Gaskell, Washington, 4 Jan., 1897).

111. Adams used an 1819 edition of Voltaire's works. See *Gallatin*, p. 7.

112. "9 février, 1761.—Voici la plus belle occasion, mon cher ange, d'exercer votre ministère céleste. Il s'agit du meilleur office que je puisse recevoir de vos bontés.—Je vous conjure, mon cher et respectable ami, d'employer tout votre crédit auprès de M. le Duc de Choiseul; auprès de ses amis; s'il le faut, auprès de sa maîtresse,

etc., etc. Et pourquoi osé-je vous demander tant d'appui, tant de
zèle, tant de vivacité, et surtout un prompt succès? Pour le bien
du service, mon cher ange; pour battre le Duc de Brunsvick. M.
Gallatin, officier aux gardes suisses, qui vous présentera ma très-
humble requête, est de la plus ancienne famille de Genève; ils se
font tuer pour nous de père en fils depuis Henri Quatre. L'oncle de
celui-ci a été tué devant Ostende; son frère l'a été à la malheureuse
et abominable journée de Rosbach, à ce que je crois; journée où les
régiments suisses firent seuls leur devoir. Si ce n'est pas à Rosbach,
c'est ailleurs; le fait est qu'il a été tué; celui-ci a été blessé. Il sert
depuis dix ans; il a été aide-major; il veut l'être. Il faut des aides-
major qui parlent bien allemand, qui soient actifs, intelligens;
il est tout cela. Enfin vous saurez de lui précisément ce qu'il lui
faut; c'est en général la permission d'aller vite chercher la mort à
votre service. Faites-lui cette grâce, et qu'il ne soit point tué,
car il est fort aimable et il est neveu de cette Mme. Calendrin que
vous avez vue étant enfant. Mme. sa mère est bien aussi aimable
que Mme. Calendrin" (*Gallatin*, pp. 3 and 4).

113. *Ibid.*, p. 6.
114. *Ibid.*, pp. 7, 8 (Voltaire, *Works*, 1819 ed., XII, 371).
115. See p. 124, above.
116. *Randolph*, pp. 13, 14.
117. *History*, I, 97.
118. *Ibid.*, I, 161.
119. *The Letters of Mrs. Henry Adams, 1865-1883*, pp. 32, 33
(letter from Nuremberg Sept. 5, 1872).
120. *Education*, p. 391.
121. "This persistence of thought-inertia is the leading idea of
modern history." *Ibid.*, p. 484.
122. Henry Adams, *Degradation of the Democratic Dogma*,
p. 230.
123. *Letters, 1892-1918*, p. 532. Candide, one recalls, is sub-
titled "Ou l'Optimisme."
124. "Zadig voulut se consoler, par la philosophie et par l'amitié,
des maux que lui avait faits la fortune. Il avait dans un faubourg
de Babylone une maison ornée avec goût, où il rassemblait tous
les arts et tous les plaisirs dignes d'un honnete homme. Le matin,
sa bibliothèque était ouverte à tous les savants; le soir sa table
l'était à la bonne compagnie" (*Romans*, p. 10).—*Letters, 1892-
1918*, p. 639.

125. *Candide*, p. 241.
126. *John Randolph*, p. 215.
127. *Historical Essays*, p. 96; J. Q. Adams, *Works*, I, 429.
128. Cf. *Harvard Magazine*, III (December, 1857), 403–404.
Recall that John Adams had spoken of the "epigrammatic wit of
Voltaire" and of "the dreamy enthusiasm of Rousseau" (*Works*, I,
429) and that John Quincy Adams had read the latter while he
was a law student in the office of Theophilus Parson at Newburyport in the year 1787–88. In his diary for that year he wrote that
[one stormy night] "I was at home all the evening, reading Rousseau's *Confessions* (1st ed. Geneva, 1782). This is the most extraordinary book I ever read in my life" (*Life in a New England
Town*, p. 36).
129. *Albert Gallatin*, pp. 16, 17.
130. *Ibid.*, p. 25.
131. *John Randolph*, pp. 13, 14.
132. *Ibid.*, p. 13.
133. *Ibid.*, p. 46.
134. Rousseau, *Confessions*, Paris, p. 232; *Classiques*, Plon ed.,
II, 60, 61.
135. 1886 ed., p. 233; Plon ed., p. 62.
136. *Ibid.*
137. 1886 ed., p. 407; Plon ed., p. 368; the italics at the end of
the passage represent Adams's underscorings. The play referred to
is the *Fils naturel*.
138. 1886 ed., p. 494; Plon ed., III, 107.
139. 1886 ed., p. 493; Plon ed., III, 105, 106.
140. *History*, I, 98.
141. "The Tendency of History: Communication from Henry
Adams, President of the Amer. Hist. Asso.," *Annual Report of the
Amer. Hist. Asso. 1894*, pp. 17–23.
142. *Ibid.*, p. 19.
143. In Samoa he went to see Robert Louis Stevenson, whose
interest in French literature has been studied by Jean-Marie
Carré.
144. There is one exception. The statement, "Whatever pleased
the French from Rousseau downward, was pretty sure to displease
the English" (p. 8, 1893 ed.) reads in the 1901 ed., p. 56, "Whatever pleased the French was pretty sure to displease the English."
145. 1893 ed., pp. 5, 6; (1901 ed., pp. 53, 54). The author of the

268 Notes: Belles Lettres
"Essai" in question was a certain Taitbout, who died in 1799 and who in 1727 (?) had written an *Abrégé élémentaire d'astronomie, de physique, d'histoire naturelle, de chymie, d'anatomie, de géométrie et de mécanique*, 8 vols., Paris 1777 (?). The title of the "Essai" in full is: *Essai sur l'isle d'Otahiti située dans la mer du sud; et sur l'esprit et les moeurs de ses habitants* (Avignon, Froullé, 1779, 125 pp.).

146. *Memoirs of Marau*, 1893 ed., p. 7; 1901 ed., p. 55.

147. *Ibid.*, 1893 ed., p. 101; 1901 ed., p. 136.

148. *Letters, 1892-1918*, p. 490.

149. *Ibid.*, p. 569 (to C. M. Gaskell, Paris, 15 July 1911).

150. Henry Adams, *Degradation*, p. 203.

151. Rousseau, *Confessions*, Bk. 7.

152. Henry Adams, *Education*, p. 221.

153. In the *Mont-Saint-Michel* (p. 107), Adams talks of the "bourgeois taste of Voltaire and Diderot" with regard to matters touching the Virgin and the worship of her. In *Jacques le fataliste*, p. 213, Adams underlined: ". . . il était prudent, avec le plus grand mépris pour la prudence."

154. Adams Collection: Jean François Regnard, *Théâtre, suivi des poésies diverses de la Provençale, des Voyages en Laponie, en Suède, etc., avec une introduction par M. Louis Moland* (5 vols., Paris, n.d.). Signature (1902) on the title page is not in Henry Adams's handwriting.

155. Adams Collection: Pierre Auguste de Beaumarchais, *Théâtre de Beaumarchais, suivi de ses poésies diverses et précédé d'observations littéraires par M. Sainte-Beuve* (Paris, 1883).

156. Adams, *History*, Vol. I, Ch. IV. There is also a reference to *Gil Blas* in *ibid.*, I, 347.

157. Adams, *Letters, 1858-91*, p. 338.

158. Vol. CXIX (1874). Gautier's posthumous works, *Souvenirs intimes* and *Histoire du romantisme*.

159. *Hist. du Romantisme*, p. 297.

160. Adams seems to have bought, soon after its appearance, Musset's *Comédies et proverbes*. This is in the Adams Collection. The other Musset items there are: *Poésies nouvelles*, 1836–1852 (Paris, 1860); *Nouvelles* (Paris, 1860); *Oeuvres posthumes d'Alfred de Musset* (Paris, 1860); *Premières poésies*, 1829–1835 (new ed., Paris, 1861); *La Confession d'un enfant du siècle* (new ed., Paris, 1861); *Contes* (Paris, 1865).

161. *Education*, pp. 142, 143.
162. "Wandering between two worlds, one dead,
     The other powerless to be born,
     With nowhere yet to rest my head. . . ."
     (*Stanzas from the Grande Chartreuse.*)
163. *Letters, 1858-1891*, p. 176 (13 Dec. 1869, Letter to C. M. Gaskell).
164. Italics mine.
165. *Letters, 1858-91* (Letter to C. M. Gaskell, 13 Jan. 1870, 2017 G St., Washington), pp. 177, 178. This sounds much like *La Confession d'un enfant du siècle.*
166. See Max I. Baym, "Emma Lazarus and Renan," *Publications of American Jewish Historical Society*, XXXVII (1947), 17–29.
167. Cf. *Atlantic Monthly*, XXXVI (1875), 757.
168. *Letters, 1858-91*, p. 368.
169. In Henry Adams Collection, Mass. Hist. Soc.
170. The lines Adams wrote are:

> Beatrix Donato fut ce doux nom de celle
> Dont la forme terrestre eut ces divins contours
> Dans son corps sans tache était une ame fidèle,
> Dans sa blanche poitrine un esprit sans détours
>
> Le fils du Titien pour la rendre immortelle
> En fit ce portrait, témoin d'un mutuel amour
> Puis cessa de peindre, à compter de ce jour
> Ne voulant de sa main illustrer d'autre qu'elle.

(In black notebook, pp. numbered by Henry Adams.)
171. Adams, *Letters 1858-91*, p. 377.
172. "Henry Adams insisted that when his wife died [in 1884], he also died to the world." *Degradation*, p. 1.
173. There are many references to Titian in Adams's writings: Musset himself frequented art galleries and among his preferences was Titian. (Cf. Pierre Gastinel, *Romantisme d'Alfred de Musset*, p. 234.)
174. *Letters, 1858-1891*, pp. 352, 357.
175. See "A Bibliography of the Writings in Prose and Verse of Algernon Charles Swinburne," by Thomas James Wise, in *Works of Swinburne*, Bonchurch ed., Vol. XX.
176. Swinburne, *Works*, Bonchurch ed., XIV, 314.

177. *Poésies nouvelles*, 1838, p. 192; *Nouvelles et contes*, Vol. I.
According to Musset's short story, *Le Fils du Titien*, a son of the
great Venetian painter Titian (1477–1576) fell deeply in love with
the beautiful Beatrix Donato, and after painting her portrait
abandoned his art for the superior reality of his love. On the portrait he inscribed this sonnet. Titian's son and Beatrix are really
Musset and Aimée d'Alton, with whom he had a love episode in
1837–38. (Diller and Guthrie, *Anthology*, p. 132.)

Here are some pertinent passages from *Le Fils du Titien* (Musset,
Oeuvres Complètes, Vol. VI; *Nouvelles et contes*, Vol. I).

Le Fils du Titien, p. 306: "Elle ne dormit pas de la nuit; les plus
riants projets, les douces espérances l'agitèrent. Elle voyait déjà
ses rêves réalisés, son amant vanté et envié par tout l'Italie, et
Venise lui devant une gloire nouvelle. Le lendemain, elle se rendit,
comme d'ordinaire, la première au rendez-vous, et elle commença,
en attendant Pippo, par regarder son cher portrait. Le fond de ce
portrait était un paysage, et il y avait sur le premier plan une
roche. Sur cette roche, Béatrice aperçut quelques lignes tracées
avec du cinabre. Elle se pencha avec inquiétude pour les lire; en
caractères gothiques très-fins, était écrit le sonnet suivant." *Ibid.*,
p. 307: "Quelque effort que Béatrice pût faire par la suite, elle
n'obtint jamais de son amant qu'il travaillât de nouveau; il fut
inflexible à toutes ses prières, et, quand elle le pressait trop vive-
ment, il lui récitait son sonnet. Il resta ainsi jusqu'à sa mort fidèle à
sa paresse; et Béatrice, dit-on, le fut à son amour. Ils vécurent
longtemps comme deux époux, et il est à regretter que l'orgueil des
Lorédans, blessé de cette liaison publique, ait détruit le portrait de
Béatrice, comme le hasard avait détruit le premier tableau du
Tizianello." (Note de l'auteur: "C'est aux recherches d'un amateur
célèbre, M. Doglioni, qu'on doit de savoir que ce tableau a existé.")

178. Adams was an ardent reader of Goethe.

179. Cf. Max I. Baym, "Henry Adams and the Critics," *The
American Scholar*, Vol. XV, No. 1 (Winter 1945–46).

180. Adams, *Letters, 1858-91*, p. 468, letter to Elizabeth Cameron, Tahiti, Feb. 13, 1891.

181. In a letter to Gaskell, 8 March, 1888, he complains, "Meanwhile history has made little progress" (*Letters, 1858-91*, p. 388).

182. *Ibid.*, p. 389, letter to Elizabeth Cameron, Quincy, 10
June 1888.

183. Adams, *Letters to a Niece*, pp. 18, 19.

184. See *The Life, Letters, and Friendships of Richard Monckton Milnes*, by T. Wemyss Reid, I, 463; *Education*, p. 139.

185. A compliment paid to Milnes in a letter by Matthew Arnold, who borrowed the phrase from Sainte-Beuve. See *Life of Milnes*, II, 40.

186. *Ibid.*, I, 116.

187. *Ibid.*, II, 32.

188. See Max I. Baym, "Baudelaire and Shakespeare," *Shakespeare Association Bulletin*, XV, No. 3 (July, 1940), 131–148; XV, No. 4 (October, 1940), 195–205.

189. In neither case is the name of the poet actually mentioned. Here are the opening sentences of the respective books. "The greatest poet of our age has drawn a parallel of elaborate eloquence between Shakespeare and the sea; and the likeness holds good in many points of less significance than those which have been set down by the master-hand" (*A Study of Shakespeare* by A. C. Swinburne, p. 1).

"In the spring of 1616 the greatest Englishman of all time passed away with no public homage of notice, and the first tributes paid to his memory were prefixed to the miserably garbled and inaccurate edition of his works which was issued seven years later by a brace of players under the patronage of a brace of peers." And in the next sentence, "In the spring of 1885 the greatest Frenchman had passed away" (*Victor Hugo* by Algernon Charles Swinburne, p. 5). We add here an excerpt from the parallel drawn by Hugo between Shakespeare and the sea, and of which Swinburne speaks: "Il y a des hommes Océans en effet. . . . Cet infini, cet insondable, tout cela peut être dans un esprit, et alors cet esprit s'appelle génie, et vous avez Eschyle, vous avez Isaïe, vous avez Juvénal, vous avez Dante, vous avez Michel-Ange, vous avez Shakespeare, et c'est la même chose de regarder ces âmes ou de regarder l'Océan" (Hugo, *William Shakespeare*, pp. xv, xvi).

190. Swinburne, *Hugo*, p. 175.

191. *Mont-Saint-Michel*, p. 1.

192. Swinburne, *Hugo*, p. 175.

193. Quoted in T. Earle Welby, *A Study of Swinburne*, p. 84.

194. *Mont-Saint-Michel*, p. 1.

195. *Ibid.*

196. *Tempest*, III, iii, 9–10.

197. Items in Henry Adams Collection: *Les Châtiments*, 1882,

and *La Légende des siècles* contain no inscriptions. Incidentally, Hugo's work received notice in America in such magazines as the *Atlantic Monthly* and the *North American Review*. For Hugo in England, see Kenneth Ward Hooker, *The Fortunes of Victor Hugo in England*.

198. Ernest Renan, *Feuilles Détachées*. (See General Bibliography.)

199. Adams, *Letters, 1858-91*, p. 383, letter to John Hay, Washington, 1 May, 1887.

200. *Education*, p. 143.

201. *Letters, 1858-91*, p. 189.

202. See Renan Chapter, p. 77. (Also compare the Rossettis and the Lambs, as well as Wordsworth.)

203. Inscription on flyleaf: "H. B. Adams, Florence, 15 July 1870." Greatly inspired by "La tumulte immense de la mer," Guérin had read Victor Hugo ("J'ai lu avec la plus vive délectation *Lucrèce Borgia*"). He notes Hugo's *dualism:* his tendency to be impetuous, fiery; at the same time, calm, plaintive. Then there is a reference to *Hernani*. "Ici, royalistes, libéraux, romantiques, classiques, tout se mêle, s'entrechoque, se combat et donne au monde le spectacle le plus curieux et quelquefois le plus burlesque." (The year of this entry is 1830.) In one of his letters to his sister (in 1832) he begs her to bring him a copy of "Les Orientales" on her next visit. (*Journal*, pp. 26, 59, 70, 149, 198.)

204. *Ibid.*, p. 70.

205. *Ibid.*, pp. 74, 76.

206. 1810–1839.

207. *Causeries du Lundi*, xv, 1.

208. Vol. XII.

209. "Ce volume, tiré à petit nombre, ne se vend pas" (*Causeries*, XII, 2).

210. *Ibid.*, p. 4.

211. *Ibid.*, pp. 4–7.

212. *Ibid.*, pp. 9, 10, 12.

213. *Ibid.*, p. 13.

214. See p. 154 above.

215. Guérin, *Journal*, pp. 144, 145.

216. *Education*, pp. 287–289 (italics mine).

217. Guérin, *Journal*, p. 6.

218. *Education*, pp. 54, 55.

219. Guérin, *Journal*, p. 6. (Italics mine.)
220. *Ibid.*, p. 39.
221. *Education*, p. 282.
222. *Journal*, p. 12.
223. Pierre Jean de Béranger, *Oeuvres complètes*, 2 vols., Paris, 1858; Chateaubriand, *Voyages en Amérique, en Italie, au Mont Blanc*, new ed., Paris, 1873.
224. I, 325.
225. P. 567.
226. Following are the writers taken up by Faguet in his *Dix-neuvième siècle, Études littéraires* (9th ed., Paris, 1892): Chateau-briand, Lamartine, Vigny (the line quoted from Vigny is on p. 136), Hugo, Musset, Gautier, Mérimée, Michelet, Sand, Balzac.
227. "The highest results flow from silence" (*Letters, 1858-91*, p. 301). "I believe silence to be now the only sensible form of expression" (*Letters, 1892-1918*, p. 69). "My destiny . . . lies in silence, which I hold to be alone sense" (*Ibid.*). "At least I can hold my tongue, the only valuable result of 40 years of education in the most cultivated human society" (*Ibid.*, p. 215).

In *Esther:* "The dignity of silence which respected itself: the presence which was not to be touched or seen" (p. 74); "Buddhist Saints stand for years silent on one leg" (p. 92); "Women cannot work without company. Do you like solitude?" (p. 117); "I would like to own a private desert and live alone in the middle of it, with lions and tigers to eat intruders" (p. 117); "The sea is capricious, fickle, angry, fawning, violent, savage and wanting; it caresses and raves in a breath, and it has its moods of silence" (p. 258).
228. Cf. Max I. Baym, "Adams and the Critics."
229. There are several references to Vigny in Adams's *Life of Lodge* (pp. 23, 24, 25), a young poet who reflected this loneliness in America.
230. See Canat for the treatment of *Solitude* in French literature.
231. Cf. Prudhomme's *Les Solitudes*.
232. *Oeuvres de poésies* (5 vols., Paris, 1865–66); Vol. IV is the translation of *De rerum natura* (*De la nature des choses*); Vol. V: *Harmonie et beauté, La Philosophie antique*, and *Les Sciences*.
233. There are references to Sully Prudhomme in the *Life of Lodge*, pp. 23–24.
234. René Taupin, *L'Influence du symbolisme français sur la poésie américaine*, p. 35.

235. The Adams Collection contains Verlaine's *Choix de poésies*, Paris, 1891, with a sketch of the author by Eugène Carrière.

236. Adams, *Letters, 1892-1918*, pp. 115, 116.

237. *Ibid.*, p. 72 (to C. M. Gaskell, Washington, 20 June, 1895).

238. Jean Carrère's book, *Les Mauvais Maîtres*, which appeared in weekly installments in the *Revue heldcmadaire* frcm 1902 to 1904, was, in many respects, an echo of Nordau's book.

239. *Mont-Saint-Michel*, p. 14.

240. *Life of Lodge*, pp. 9, 21.

241. Mallarmé, *Vers et prose*. Morceaux choisis, Avec un portrait par James McNeill Whistler. Deuxième édition. Paris, 1893. In the Adams Collection.

242. *Letters, 1858-91*, p. 404.

243. *Ibid.*, p. 388.

244. *Ibid.*, p. 365.

245. *Ibid.*, p. 366.

246. One should add this to the collection of Mallarméesque tones in Adams: "I have composed the last page of my history and the weather is so wet that for a week I've been in vain trying to do Gibbon and walk up and down my garden. I wish Gibbon had been subjected to twelve inches of rain in six weeks, in which case he would not have waited to hear the barefooted monks sing in the Temple of Jupiter, and would have avoided arbors as he would rheumatics. I am sodden with cold and damp, and hunger for a change." *Letters, 1858-91*, p. 392 (to J. Hay, Quincy, 23 Sept. 1888).

247. In June, 1894, he wrote: "How much Petronius could give Zola, and yet need no odds! I am now preparing to start into the Rocky Mountains for the summer . . . and I am going to carry with me a small library of the Roman decadents. The contrast should be entertaining" (*Ibid.*, p. 48).

248. *Letters, 1892-1918*, pp. 87–88 (Paris, 25 Sept. 1895).

249. *Ibid.*, p. 72.

250. *Mont-Saint-Michel*, p. 2.

251. *Studies in European Literature*, the Taylorian Lectures, 1889-1899 (delivered by S. Mallarmé, W. Pater, E. Dowden, W. M. Rossetti, I. W. Rolleston, A. Morel-Fatio, H. Brown, P. Bourget, C. H. Herford, H. Butler-Clarke, W. P. Ker); Mallarmé, *La Musique et les lettres*, p. 142.

252. "Of course you know what Bourget and the psychologists

do." *Letters, 1892-1918*, p. 115 (to C. M. Gaskell, Hamburg, 24 Aug. 1896).

253. *Studies in European Literature*, "Flaubert," 1897, pp. 253–274.

254. *Life of Lodge*, p. 22.

255. All of these works are in the Adams Collection. Sainte-Beuve—*Causeries du lundi*, 15 vols., Paris, 1853–62 (Markings in 1st vol. only); *Nouveaux Lundis*, 13 vols., Paris, 1864–1870. Jules Lemaître, *Les Contemporains*; études et portraits littéraires, sixième série, quatrième édition, Paris, 1896. Abel François Villemain, *Choix d'études sur la littérature contemporaine* . . . Paris, 1857. Emile Zola, *Documents Littéraires*. . . . Paris, 1881. Gustave Vapereau, *Dictionnaire universel des contemporains*, quatrième édition, Paris, 1870; Supplément par Léon Garnier, Paris, 1873. A. Jal, *Dictionnaire critique de biographie et d'histoire* . . . Deuxième édition, Paris, 1872. *Nouvelle biographie générale*, 46 vols.

256. Zola's *Documents littéraires*: Chateaubriand, Victor Hugo, Alfred de Musset, Théophile Gautier, Les Poëtes Contemporains (Here he mentions "les trois grands générateurs"—Hugo, Musset, Lamartine—of contemporary lyricism. Of these Hugo continues to be "le souverain maître de la jeune génération." Mentions Vigny, Béranger, Gautier, Baudelaire, Banville, and Leconte de Lisle. Leconte de Lisle's influence has been considerable. Baudelaire has lot of imitators. "Vers 1860, sous le second Empire, la poésie n'était pas en grand honneur."), George Sand, Dumas fils, Sainte-Beuve, La Critique Contemporaine, De la Moralité dans la littérature.

257. I found inserted in this volume, between pp. 86 and 87, a green ticket as follows:

Sièges des Promenades de Paris
Chaise *Of*. 10
Présenter ce Bulletin à toute réquisition du Contrôle
Adn. Rue de Ponthieu, 24

Apparently, Adams read the book while in Paris.

258. In the Adams Collection. Talleyrand had wandered through America in 1794 (*History*, I, 352). Three years earlier Chateaubriand had been here.

259. *History*, I, 352.

260. *Gallatin*, p. 567.

261. *Letters, 1892-1918*, p. 614 (to Eliz. Cameron from Château de Marivault, St. Crépin, Oise [July, 1913]?).

262. In Adams Collection: *Mémoires de Mme de Staël*, 3 vols., 1864.

263. *Gallatin*, p. 531 (letter of July 31, 1814).

264. *Ibid.*, p. 530.

265. *Ibid.*, pp. 531, 532.

266. *Ibid.*, pp. 533, 534.

267. *Ibid.*, p. 563.

268. *Ibid.*, p. 566 (Paris, 17th July 1817).

269. *Daniella* (2 vols.), could not be located in the Adams Collection.

270. *Atlantic Monthly*, XXXVIII (1876), 444-451.

271. "George Sand and Her Works," *The Galaxy*, January-April, 1867, pp. 240-249, 618-625.

272. See article on the *Galaxy* by Mott in *Sewanee Review*, Vol. XXXVI.

273. "Nebulae," *Galaxy*, January-April, 1867, p. 334.

274. *Ibid.*, p. 335.

275. Incidentally, Benson gives us an occasional bit of beautiful English prose as a rendering of some of G. S.'s French. This, for example: "Sing, Beppa, sing. . . . Tell your friends to move their oars like the wings of a bird of the sea, and to carry you away in your gondola like a white Leda upon the brown back of a wild swan" (*Ibid.*, p. 621).

276. *Galaxy*, January-April, 1867, pp. 618-625.

277. *Ibid.*, p. 622.

278. See *Letters of Marian Adams*, pp. 156, 182, 188. The Adams Collection contains Eugène Fromentin's *Les Maîtres d'autrefois*, 14th ed., 1882.

279. *Letters of Marian Adams*, pp. 405, 410, 412.

280. *Ibid.*, pp. 414, 415.

281. Benson, *Galaxy*, January-June, 1867, p. 620.

282. In the Adams Collection may be found: Stendhal, *La Chartreuse de Parme*, nouvelle édition entièrement revue et corrigée, Paris, 1882 (inscribed "Mr. Adams, Jan. 1885"); *Promenades dans Rome*. Paris, 1858.

283. See my article "William James and Henry Adams," *New England Quarterly*, X, No. 4 (December, 1937), 717-742.

284. G. Lanson and Paul Tuffran, *Manuel d'histoire de la littérature française*, p. 626.
285. Cf. my article, "Henry Adams and the Critics," *The American Scholar*, Vol. XV, No. 1 (Winter 1945–46).
286. Cf. *Letters, 1892-1918*, pp. 84, 85.
287. *Ibid.*, p. 85 (in the Adams Collection).
288. Balzac, *Oeuvres complètes*. Paris (Librairie Nouvelle), 1856–1860. 45 Vols., 16°. [Vol. 29—Scènes de la Vie militaire: "Les Chouans ou la Bretagne en 1799"; "Une passion dans le désert" is missing.]
289. Adams, *Historical Essays*, pp. 325, 326.
290. *Letters, 1892-1918*, p. 35 (to C. M. Gaskell, 23 Jan. 1894); this reference to Flaubert is not indicated in the Index. See Ch. VII, above, on "Exoticism."
291. In the Adams Collection: Flaubert, *Correspondance, 1830-1880*, 4 vols., 1889–1893.
292. In Adams Collection: *Madame Bovary*, Paris, 1891; *Salambô*, Paris, 1892; *Trois contes:* (Un Coeur simple; La Légende de Saint-Julien L'Hospitalier; Hérodias), 1890; *Bouvard et Pécuchet*, Paris, 1891; *La Tentation de Saint Antoine*, 1895 (signed "Henry Adams"); *Par les champs et par les grèves* (Voyage en Bretagne), 1886 (see in this: "Le Chant de la mort"; also "Rabelais").
293. Italics mine. Note Adams's repetition of this paradox when he speaks of George Cabot Lodge: "Lodge has what the French call the faults of his qualities." (*Life of Lodge*, p. 111). G.C.L. read Flaubert (*Ibid*, p.24).
294. *Mont-Saint-Michel*, p. 55.
295. The other writers discussed in this book are: Banville, Baudelaire, Brunetière, Coppée, Alphonse Daudet, Ferdinand Fabre, Octave Feuillet, Anatole France, Goncourt, Hérédia, Hugo, Huysmans, Lamartine, De Lisle, Loti, Maupassant, Mérimée, Michelet, Gaston Paris, Prudhomme, Racine (Romantisme de), Renan, Henri Rochefort, Sarcey, Stendhal, Taine, Verlaine, Zola.
296. In Adams Collection: *Outre mer* (Notes sur l'Amérique), 2 vols., 1895.
297. *Studies in European Literature* (Bourget on Flaubert), p. 263.
298. Maupassant items in Adams Collection: *La Vie errante*, 17th ed., 1890; *Sur l'eau*, n.d.; *Mlle Fifi, nouveaux contes*, 15th ed., 1890 (18 short stories); *L'Inutile Beauté*, 23d ed., 1890 (11 short

stories); *Le Horla*, 27th ed., 1892 (14 stories); *Clair de lune*, 16th ed., Paris (17 stories); *La Petite Rogue*, 17th ed., Paris, 1886 (10 short stories); *Miss Harriet*, 15th ed., 1891 (12 stories; contains *Mon Oncle Jules*); *Contes de la Bécasse*, 14th ed., 1887 (17 stories); *Monsieur Parent*, 27th ed., 1891 (17 short stories); *Toine*, n.d.; *Bel-Ami*, 64th ed., 1891; *Au soleil*, 11th ed., 1888.

299. Adams, *Letters, 1858-91*, p. 534.

300. *Ibid.*, p. 535.

301. *Ibid.*, p. 534.

302. Adams, *Letters, 1892-1918*, p. 81 (Paris, 12 Sept. 1895). In a footnote, W. C. Ford points out that while "there are a number of references in the *Journals* to this Hôtel on the Champs Elysées, notably in the First Series, II and III, Madame de Paiva could not have been in possession at this time." (*Ibid.*, p. 81, note 1.)

303. *Ibid.*, p. 105 (to Elizabeth Cameron, 18 June 1896). Following are the Goncourt items in the Adams Collection: *Journal des Goncourt, mémoires de la vie littéraire, 1851-84*, 6 vols., 1889; *Histoire de la société française pendant le directoire*, new ed., 1895; *Manette Salomon*, new ed., 1889; *La Dubarry*, new ed., 1891; *Renée Mauperin*, new ed., 1890.

304. 13th ed., 2 vols., 1889; contains many references to England, and English expressions.

305. *Studies in European Literature*, p. 49.

306. In the Adams Collection: Feuillet, *Histoire de Sibylle*, 5th ed., 1863.

307. *Letters, 1858-91*, pp. 101, 102.

308. *Historical Essays*, p. 323; *Life of Lodge*, pp. 23–25. In the Adams Collection: Alexandre Dumas, *Le demi-monde*, 6th ed., 1855; *L'Envers d'une conspiration*, 1860; *Histoire du supplice d'une femme* (Réponse à M. Émile de Girardin par Alexandre Dumas, fils), 2d ed., 1865 (bound with Girardin's *Supplice d'une femme*); *Les Quarante-cinq*, new ed., 3 vols., 1894–96.

309. In Adams Collection: F. Fabre, *Le Chevrier*, 1879; *Mon Oncle Célestin, moeurs cléricales*, 3d ed., 1881; *Barnabé*, 1891; *L'Abbé Tigrane, candidat à la papauté*, 1891; *Lucifer*, 1891.

310. *Le Capitaine Fracasse*, 2 vols., 1889.

311. Signed "Henry Adams, Oct. '98"; see p. 86, "At Chartres. . . ."

312. *La Bièvre et Saint Séverin*, 1898.

313. *Letters, 1892-1918*, p. 115 (to C. M. Gaskell, 24 Aug. 1896).

In this letter he also mentions some other authors treated by Lemaître: Zola, Bourget, Verlaine, Rochefort.

314. *Mont-Saint-Michel*, pp. 76–77. The other citation (pp. 83–84) concerns the relative values of 12th and 13th century sculpture.

315. *Letters, 1892-1918*, p. 181 (to Sir Robert Cunliffe, Paris, 1898).

316. In a letter dated in 1888, he does mention Zola: "what our friend Zola calls *la joie de vivre.*" Cf. *Henry Adams and His Friends: a Collection of His Unpublished Letters*, comp. Harold Dean Cater, p. 180 (the item is not in the index).

317. *Letters, 1892-1918*, p. 48.

318. *Ibid.*, p. 105. In the same letter (to Elizabeth Cameron, 18 June 1896) Adams uses the expression "la bêtise humaine," perhaps reminiscent of *La Bête humaine*.

319. *Ibid.*, p. 115.

320. *Ibid.*, pp. 114–115 (note).

321. On this subject, see Lee M. Friedman, *Zola and the Dreyfus Case: His Defense of Liberty and Its Enduring Significance*, Boston, 1937.

322. *Letters, 1892-1918*, pp. 150–151.

323. Cf., *Henry Adams and His Friends*, p. 544.

324. All these are in the Adams Collection: *Au bonheur des dames*, 1883; *Son excellence Eugène Rougon*, 16th ed., 1881 (the signature is not in Adams's hand, 1895); *Les Trois Villes—Lourdes*, 1894; *Rome*, 1896; *Paris*, 1898; *Documents littéraires*.

325. *Letters, 1892-1918*, p. 133 (to Sir Robert Cunliffe, 19 Oct. 1897).

326. Edouard Ourliac, *Théâtre du Seigneur Croquignole*, 1866. *La Première Tragédie de Goethe* (in the Adams Collection).

327. Alfred de Musset, *Comédies et proverbes*. (See General Bibliography.)

328. Eugène Scribe, *Oeuvres choisies*, 5 vols., 1845.

329. See *1858 Catalogue* by M. I. Baym.

330. In *Nouveau théâtre de Salon* . . . , 1865 and 1873.

331. Charles Bataille and E. Rasetti, *Les Drames de village*, 1st ser., 2 vols., 1862.

332. 6th ed., 1859.

333. *L'Homme à l'oreille cassée*, 1862; *Théâtre impossible* (Guil-

lery; *L'Assassin; L'Education d'un prince*); *Le Chapeau de Sainte Catherine*, 2d ed., 1864; *Madelon*, 4th ed., 1865.

334. 1881–83. Vol. II is missing.

335. 4th ed., 1861 (bound with Sardou's *Nos intimes*). The Collection also contains Augier's *Le Fils de Giboyer*, 8th ed., 1863 (bound with Sardou's *Les Ganaches*).

336. The Feuillet items in the Collection are: *Le Roman d'un jeune homme pauvre*, 3d ed., 1859 (bound with Feuillet's *Scènes et comédies*); *Scènes et proverbes*, new ed., 1859; *La Tentation*, 2d ed., 1860; *Montjoye*, 2d ed., 1864; *Monsieur de Camors*, 1867.

337. 19th ed., 1895.

338. *Théâtre de campagne*, 1881–84.

339. *Letters, 1892-1918*, p. 243.

340. *L'Aiglon* was produced by Sarah Bernhardt on March 15, 1900; *Madame Sans Gêne* was presented in 1893, and *Cyrano de Bergerac* dated from 1897. (See footnote, p. 298, *Letters, 1892-1918*.)

341. In the Adams Collection: Sardou, *Oeuvres*, 10 vols., 1864–85; *Les Poètes de mouche*, 1860; *Les Diables noirs*, new ed., 1881; *Seraphine*, 5th ed., 1879; *Les Ganaches*, 1863; *Le Giboyer*, 1863; *Nos intimes*, 1862. Adams had heard lectures by Francisque Sarcey, who thought highly of the dramatic work of Sardou (*Letters, 1892-1918*, pp. 141–142).

342. *A Letter to American Teachers of History* (1910), in the *Degradation of the Democratic Dogma*, p. 244. He had read Rostand's Academy speech soon after its delivery (June 4, 1903). (See *Letters, 1892-1918*, p. 409, note 1.) That speech of Rostand's—a eulogy of Henri de Bornier, author of *La Fille de Roland* and other plays—is worth reading mainly for those passages where the style becomes memorable. See, for instance, his exordium on the true function of the theatre; his definition of *le panache*, his elaboration on the Provençal Chanson, "Les gens de Lunel ont pêché à la lune." The names mentioned throughout the speech surely interested Adams: Daudet, Hugo, Gautier, Paul de Saint-Victor, Feuillet, Gaston Paris ("Messieurs, on n'écrit pas *la Fille de Roland* sans devoir quelque chose à Gaston Paris"). *Degradation*, p. 22.

343. *Letters, 1892-1918*, pp. 539, 542.

344. Marian Adams, *Letters*, p. 223.

345. *Ibid.* (1880), p. 239.

346. *Ibid.* (1881), p. 282.

347. He had seen her before in a French adaptation from Aristophanes' *Lysistrata*, which (he said) "annoyed his *historic nerves.*" *Letters, 1892-1918*, p. 104.
348. *Ibid.*, p. 291.
349. *Ibid.* (1905), p. 450.
350. *Ibid.*, p. 451.

Chapter VI. PHILOSOPHIC EXCURSION:
DESCARTES AND PASCAL

1. *Mont-Saint-Michel*, p. 323.
2. In a letter to Margaret Chanler (*Letters, 1892-1918* Paris, 9 Sept. 1909) he wrote: "I rather agree with you and your friend Bergson that St. Thomas said all there was to say . . . What I like most in the schoolmen is their rule of cutting infinite sequences short. They insist on stopping at the prime motor at once. Bergson and all the speculators who follow Kant, start with Space, and then merge that Space in Thought, and are bound to merge that Thought-space in Hyper-thought-space and so on to infinity . . . but become scared and stop, without explaining the reason for stopping. . . . I like best Bergson's frank surrender to the superiority of Instinct over Intellect. You know how I have preached that principle, and how I have studied the facts of it. In fact I wrote once a whole volume—called my *Education* . . . in order to recall how Education may be shown to consist in following the intuitions of instinct" (pp. 523-524). To William James he declared (Paris, 20 June, 1910): "With humble heart I have chased the flying philosopher, trying to find out *his* opinion that I might guide my own steps. . . . Therefore . . . I am trying to find out what your friend Ostwald—or Bergson or Dastre or Loeb (Brunhes is just dead)—thinks or teaches or intends" (p. 543). Writing of his *Chartres* volume to Professor Albert Stanburrough Cook (Paris, 6 Aug. 1910) he said: "My idea is that the world outside—the so-called modern world—can only pervert and degrade the conceptions of the primitive instinct of art and feeling. . . . If you are curious to see the theory stated as official instruction, you have only to look over Bergson's *Evolution Créatrice* (pp. 288, 289). The tendencies of thought in Europe seem to me very strongly

that way" (p. 547). Adams had quoted from these pages of Bergson, in his *Letter to American Teachers of History*, 1910: "Intuition is almost completely sacrificed to intelligence. . . . Intuition is a lamp, almost extinguished. . . . On our personality, on our liberty, on the place we occupy in nature as a whole, on our origin, and perhaps also on our destiny it casts a feeble and flickering light, but a light which pierces, none the less, the darkness of the night in which our intelligence leaves us." (How much these words of Bergson came full circle with the words Henry Adams, as an undergraduate, read in Lewes: "Nature is an eternal darkness. . . . An eternal silence!") On the basis of this (and many other corroborating authorities quoted in the *Letter*) Adams is forced to conclude: "The last traces of an instinct now wholly dead or dying, nothing remains for the historian to describe or develop except the history of a more or less mechanical dissolution." (*Degradation*, pp. 204–206.)

3. We enumerate later some of the histories of philosophy Adams used in his study.

4. The flyleaf of the first two volumes, which are bound together, bears the inscription, "Henry B. Adams. Oct. 20, '57." Cf. *1858 Catalogue*. The inscription on the flyleaf of Vols. III and IV (which are also bound together) is: "Henry Brooks Adams, Quincy."

5. Footnote by Lewes: "In his work 'De l'Humanité'. Without explicitly avowing Realism, his conception of Humanity, as distinct from human individuals, implies it."

6. Lewes, II (Ch. IV, "The New Academy: Accesilaus and Carneades"), p. 176; (Ch. V, "Ninth Epoch: the Alexandrian Dialectics"), p. 199.

7. In his senior year, Adams recited to Bowen on the latter's *Ethics and Metaphysics*, through which he was introduced to Descartes and Pascal.

8. The conflict of religion and science, so much a part of the history of nineteenth-century thought, interested Adams. In both Descartes and Bacon he found two philosophers who tried to keep religion and science apart in order to avert confusion and chaos from the field of philosophy. Mind was the starting point of the one; nature, of the other. To effect a nexus between the two has been the classic problem in philosophy and Adams was concerned with this problem in its application to a philosophy of history. Here are some of the passages in Bacon in which Adams made his

pencilings, and the ideas which he underlined: "Being convinced
that the human intellect makes its own difficulties, not using the
true helps which are at man's disposal, soberly and judiciously;
whence follows manifold ignorance of things, and by reason of that
ignorance mischiefs innumerable; he thought all trials should be
made; whether that commerce between the mind of man and the
nature of things, which is more precious than anything on earth,
or at least than anything that is of the earth, might by any means
be restored to its perfect and original condition, or if that may not
be, yet reduced to a better condition than that in which it now
is." On the same page Bacon continues: "For while men are occupied in admiring and applauding *the false powers of the mind*,
they pass by and throw away those true powers, which, if it be
supplied with the proper aids and can itself be content to wait upon
nature instead of vainly affecting to overrule her, are within its
reach. There was but one course left, therefore—to try the whole
thing anew upon a better plan; and to commence a total reconstruction of sciences, arts, and all human Knowledge, raised upon
the proper foundations. *And although he was well aware how solitary
an enterprise it is, and how hard a thing to win faith*," he was resolved not to abandon it, especially "*because he knew not how long
it might be before these things would occur to anyone else*." *The Works
of Francis Bacon*, ed. Spedding, Ellis, and Heath, (London, 1857–
68), I, 7.

9. *History*, I, 157–160. But he goes on to say, "Compared with
this lithe young figure [America], Europe was actually in decrep-
itude" (*Ibid.*, p. 160).

10. *Esther*, pp. 7–9.

11. For the treatment of these see Appendix III, below.

12. *Oeuvres de Descartes*, new ed., Paris, n. d. (signature: "Henry
Adams," on second of four blank pages preceding title page.)

13. Adams's marginal note on bottom of p. lxiii. On p. 461,
Adams underlined the following: Réponse XII.—Cette méthode
pèche en ce qu'elle n'a rien de bon ou rien de nouveau, et qu'elle a
beaucoup de superflu.

14. L'Abbé P. Carbonel, *Histoire de la Philosophie*, 2d ed., p. 286.

15. The title page bears this inscription: "A Monsieur P. Janet
hommage respectueux, El. Vincent Maumus-j-".

16. The other books in the Adams Collection related to Descartes
and Scholasticism are: Xavier Rousselot, *Études sur la philosophie*

dans le Moyen-Age, 1840–42. Tertullianus Quintus Septimus Florius (Tertullien et Saint Augustin), *Oeuvres choisies,* Paris, 1845. Charles de Rémusat, *Abélard,* 1845 (Vol. II has the signature: "Henry Adams, Paris, 1901"). *Athenaeus* (Bohn), London, 1854. Charles Jourdain, *La Philosophie de Saint Thomas d'Aquin,* 1858 (Signed "Henry Adams, Paris, 1901"). Spinoza, *Oeuvres,* tr. Émile Saisset, 3 vols., 1861. Th. de Régnon, *Bañes et Molina,* 1883 (notes and scorings); *Bannésianisme et Molinisme,* Part I, 1890; *Études de théologie positive sur la Sainte Trinité* (2 vols.), 1892. *Les Confessions de Saint Augustin,* tr. Arnauld d'Andilly, Paris, n.d. (on fly leaf, "Henry Adams, Washington, D. C."). Kuno Fischer, *History of Modern Philosophy,* 1887. Alfred Fouillée, *Histoire de la philosophie,* 6th ed., 1891. V. H. Friedel, *Études Compostellanes,* Santiago de Compostela, 1897, Liverpool, 1899. B. Carra de Vaux, *Les Grands Philosophes: Avicenne,* 1900. (Signed "Henry Adams, Paris, 1901.") Joseph McCabe, *Peter Abelard,* New York, 1901.

17. The original text follows: "Voilà le grand point. L'abstraction intellectuelle ne donne pas le composé, mais la forme isolée de la matière. Or, suivant Abélard, et suivant le plus grand nombre des nominalistes, c'est la matière déterminée qui est principe d'individuation. Si donc on fait exception de la matière, l'individualité disparaît; seule, l'universalité persiste, demeure; mais, avec la matière individuelle, la réalité s'est évanouie, et avec la forme universelle, il n'est plus resté que l'opposé même de la réalité, c'est-à-dire le concept abstraît" (Hauréau, I, 283).

18. *Mont-Saint-Michel,* p. 323.

19. *Ibid.,* p. 351.

20. *Ibid.,* p. 349.

21. Maumus, I, 1.

22. *Mont-Saint-Michel,* p. 349.

23. *Ibid.,* p. 352.

24. *Education,* pp. 484, 491, 495.

25. *Op. cit.,* p. 186.

26. *Ibid.,* pp. 231, 232.

27. *Ibid.,* p. 232.

28. *Ibid.,* p. 287.

29. "Poor old nineteenth century! It is already as far off as Descartes and Newton" [*Letters 1892-1918* (to C. M. Gaskell, Paris, 14 June 1903), p. 408.] Note: this reference is not indicated in the Index.

30. *Education*, p. 42.
31. Cf. Dorothy Margaret Eastwood, *The Revival of Pascal*, *passim*; also, Ernest Renan, *Vie de Jésus*, p. 469: "Qui n'aimerait mieux être malade comme Pascal que bien portant comme le vulgaire?"
32. Prosper Faugère did not publish such a text until 1844.
33. The first American edition of Pascal's *Thoughts on Religion*, a new translation and memoir by Rev. Edward Craig, appeared in 1829 at Amherst, Massachusetts, under the imprint of J. S. and C. Adams.
34. The text is preceded by the *Vie de Blaise Pascal* by Mme Perier (Gilberte Pascal).
35. Paris, 1924.
36. Pascal, *op. cit.*, p. 186.
37. *Ibid.*, p. 303.
38. In a letter to his friend Gaskell, July 27, 1900.
39. *Pensées*, "Pari", p. 83. Quoted by W. C. Ford (*Letters, 1892-1918*, p. 295, note 3).
40. July 27, 1900.
41. *Mont-Saint-Michel*, p. 129.
42. *Ibid.*, p. 323.
43. *Ibid.*
44. See p. 195, above.
45. *Pensées*, p. 156; *Mont-Saint-Michel*, p. 324.
46. *Mont-Saint-Michel*, p. 324; *Pensées*, Section XI, in Brunschvicg.
47. *Mont-Saint-Michel*, p. 325.
48. *Ibid.*, p. 352.
49. *Ibid.*, p. 354.
50. *Ibid.*, p. 370.
51. *Ibid.*, p. 377.
52. *Education*, p. 389.
53. Italics mine. The following passage is quoted in *Mont-Saint-Michel*, p. 325; italics mine.
54. I, 153.
55. *Education*, p. 427.
56. *Ibid.*, pp. 485–487.
57. *Pensées*, p. 82. (Havet's note: "C'est-à-dire: N'ont pu trouver la vérité à l'aide des lumières de la raison.")
58. *Mont-Saint-Michel*, p. 226.

59. *Letters, 1892-1918*, pp. 265, 270.
60. *Ibid.*, p. 271, note. Italics mine.
61. *Ibid.*, p. 287.
62. *Ibid.*, p. 291; *Mont-Saint-Michel*, p. 377.
63. *Ibid.*, p. 334.
64. Ernest Renan, *Correspondance, 1846-1871*, I, 54, 55 (to E. Havet, Paris, July 6, 1852).
65. *Mont-Saint-Michel*, p. 333.
66. *Letters, 1892-1918*, p. 169, note.
67. In reference to the Pauline three planes of being—blood, brain, spirit—which parallel Pascal's orders, see Horatio Smith's essay, *Sainte-Beuve; Montaigne; Human Nature*. However, due allowance should be made for the possible use by Smith of Paul Elmore More's *The Daemon of the Absolute*. (I am indebted for this critical proviso to Professor W. M. Frohock.)

Chapter VII. THE BELATED ROMANTIC

1. From a poem of R. M. Milnes (see *The Life, Letters, and Friendships of Richard Monckton Milnes*, I, 118).
2. It was not until 1888 (Quincy, 23 Sept.) that he could write to John Hay: "I have composed the last page of my history." *Letters, 1858-91*, p. 392.
3. *Ibid.*, p. 365.
4. The copy in the Adams Collection is inscribed, "Henry Adams from John LaFarge." The Adams Collection also contains *Histoire de l'art du Japon* (Paris, 1900), and Lafcadio Hearn's *Exotics and Retrospectives*.
5. *Letters, 1858-91*, p. 366 note 1.
6. *Ibid.*, pp. 367, 369 (Yokohama, 9 July 1886).
7. *Ibid.*, p. 381 (Kioto, 19 Sept. 1886).
8. *Ibid.*, p. 463 (to Eliz. Cameron, Papeete, 6 Feb. 1891).
9. At Mass. Hist. Soc.: *Memoirs of Marau Taaroa, Last Queen of Tahiti*, Privately Printed, 1893; in Paris, 1901, he published an expanded version of that book. In it, the contents of 1893 had undergone certain transpositions, emendations as well as expansions. The difference in the total number of pages is 87. Cf. Robert Spiller's edition, Scholars Repr. and Facs. Society.

10. Cf. Gilbert Chinard, *L'Amérique et le rêve exotique dans la littérature française au XVIIe et au XVIIIe siècle*, Paris, 1913, p. 421, note 1. Vide *ibid.*, "De Jean-Jacques Rousseau à Bernardin de Saint-Pierre, 1750–1788," pp. 341 *et seq.*

11. Chinard, *op. cit.*, p. 384.

12. On the various spelling of Tahiti, see Chinard's ed. of Diderot's *Supplément au Voyage de Bougainville*, 1935, p. 9.

13. *Biographie Universelle* (Michaud) (Article on Bougainville).

14. *Biographie Universelle* (Article on Bougainville).

15. *Memoirs of Marau* (1901), p. 53; (1893), p. 6.

16. The full title of his work is: *Essai sur l'isle d'Otahiti, située dans la mer du sud; et sur l'esprit et les moeurs de ses habitants* (Avignon, 1779).

17. 1893 ed., p. 6; 1901 ed., p. 53.

18. Montessus, *Martyrologie et biographie de Commerson*, Chalon-sur-Saône, 1889. This is at the Mass. Hist. Soc. On page 58 of this book, Adams questioned the date involved in the following passage: "Commerson, dans la relation de Taïti adressée par lui à ses amis, sous forme d'une lettre insérée dans le Mercure de France, numéro de novembre *1767* [underlined by Adams], s'exprimait ainsi avec toute la naïveté d'un homme convaincu." In the left-hand, Adams wrote: "? 1769 See p. 186."

19. 1893 ed., p. 7; 1901 ed., pp. 54-55.

20. "I know that Diderot wrote a 'Supplement to Bougainville's Travels' in the form of a dialogue between the ship's chaplain and a Tahitian supposed to be named Orou, and that Orou overwhelmed the chaplain by showing the superiority of Tahiti over Paris and the immorality of constancy in marriage" (1901 ed., p. 53).

21. 1893 ed., p. 7; 1901 ed., p. 55.

22. A 2-volume work at Mass. Hist. Soc., contains scorings on pp. 449, 455, 459, 464, 465, 486. For other Tahiti items in the Adams Collection see Appendix IV.

23. 1893 ed., p. 82; 1901 ed., p. 111.

24. We do not find this at the Mass. Hist. Soc. See 1893 ed., p. 88; 1901 ed., pp. 116, 117.

25. *Letters, 1858-91*, p. 463.

26. *Letters, 1858-91*, pp. 466, 467.

27. "This eternal charm of middle-aged melancholy" (*ibid.*, p. 469).

28. Italics mine.

29. *Letters, 1858-91*, p. 469.
30. *Madame Chrysanthème*, p. 303.
31. 1893 ed., p. 44; 1901 ed., p. 27.
32. 1893 ed., p. 40; 1901 ed., p. 31.
33. 1893 ed., p. 44; 1901 ed., p. 35.
34. See *The Letters of R. L. Stevenson*, ed. Colvin, II, 197, 217 (Carré, *R. L. Stevenson et la France*, Paris, 1930, p. 6).
35. *Letters of R. L. S.*, II, 293 (Carré, p. 11).
36. *Letters, 1858-91*, p. 426.
37. *Ibid.*, p. 430 (Samoa, Oct. 21, 1890).
38. *Ibid.*, p. 447 (Nov. 27, 1890).
39. P. 3.
40. P. 110.
41. P. 194.
42. P. 211.
43. P. 219.
44. P. 232.
45. P. 236.
46. P. 241.
47. P. 238.
48. P. 269.
49. P. 289; and passage following, p. 297.
50. P. 300.
51. P. 301.
52. P. 305.
53. P. 331.
54. P. 359.
55. P. 398.
56. P. 420.
57. P. 431.
58. Samuel Foster Damon, *Amy Lowell*, p. 520.
59. Vernon L. Parrington, *Main Currents in American Thought*, III, 223.
60. *Ibid.*, pp. 214–215.
61. *Ibid.*, p. 217.
62. Carl Lotus Becker, "The Education of Henry Adams," *American Historical Review*, XXIV (1918–19), 425, 426, 434. Also, *Education*, p. 81.
63. *Op. cit.*, pp. 426–427.
64. *Ibid.*, p. 431.

65. Paul Elmer More, "Henry Adams," *Unpopular Review*, X (July-December, 1918), 272.

66. *Ibid.*, pp. 259, 260.

67. Fernand Baldensperger, "Les Scrupules d'un Américain attardé," *Le Correspondant* (1920), p. 1043.

68. *Ibid.*, p. 1047.

69. Ferner Nuhn, *The Wind Blew from the East*, p. 184.

70. *Letters, 1858-91*, p. 347 (Jan. 23, 1883).

71. *Education*, pp. 331, 360.

72. *Op. cit.*, p. 196 (Modern Library Ed.).

73. *Ibid.*, p. 197.

74. Janko Lavrin, *Romantic Types*, p. 25. The types follow: (1) The sentimental-contemplative, or "dreamy type"; (2) The fantastic-imaginative type; (3) The exotic type; (4) The mystical-philosophic type; (5) The emotional-Dionysian; (6) The analytical solipsistic type; (7) The militant rebel; the "Promethean" and Satanic type; (8) The "realistic" romanticist; (9) The romantic aesthete; (10) The social-humanitarian and Utopian type.

75. George Brandes, *Main Currents in 19th Century Literature*, II, 21.

76. Samuel Taylor Coleridge, *Biographia Literaria*, Ch. V.

77. Hoxie Fairchild, *The Romantic Quest*, p. 325.

78. St. Augustin, *Confessions* (see p. 189, above).

79. Brandes, *op. cit.*, p. 181.

80. *Ibid.*, p. 189.

81. John Cournos, *A Modern Plutarch*, p. 285.

82. *Ibid.*

83. William James, *The Will to Believe, passim*.

84. Parrington, *op. cit.*, III, 223.

85. Baldensperger, *op. cit.*, p. 1043.

86. *Letters, 1892-1918*, p. 220 (Feb. 26, 1899).

87. Van Wyck Brooks, *The Flowering of New England*, p. 165.

Chapter VIII. CONCLUSION

1. Amsterdam, 1783. Copy in Columbia University Library.

2. Published in *Harvard et La France*, Paris, 1936.

3. Adams, *Degradation of the Democratic Dogma, passim*. Space forbids here the inclusion of a treatment of Henry Adams's use

of French science. Such a study is in process and it is hoped that it will be published elsewhere.

4. Henri-Frédéric Amiel, *Fragments d'un journal intime*, 2d ed. (2 vols., Paris, 1884), II, 1. Copy in Adams Collection.

5. *Henry Adams and His Friends*, p. cvi.

6. We give here a few instances of revision:

1913 ed., bottom p. 202: "In all ages" to "Louis" (1st word), eight lines from bottom p. 204 (p. 203, genealogic table) is not to be found in 1904 ed. 1913 edition, page 216: "Holy Grail was brought in (Bartsch, 'Chrestomathie,' 183–185, 1895 ed.) Et leans . . ." (top p. 216). In 1904 edition the parenthetic reference to Bartsch is omitted; likewise is the parenthetic reference to Bartsch, 1913 ed., bottom p. 220 omitted in 1904 ed., top p. 189. 1913 ed. (pp. 222–223) contains 7 stanzas of poem, ending with "Comtesse. . . . Lowëis"; whereas the 1904 ed. quotes only five lines: "Comtesse. . . . La mere Loeis."

There are some emendations in texts quoted, as follows: 1913 ed., p. 217, last two lines: "Et li vaslet. . . . Les lis"; 1904 ed., p. 186 reads: "Les *liz*." 1913 ed., p. 220: "Quaint" etc.; 1904 ed. (p. 189) reads: "*Quant* reis Marcs" etc. In general, the 1913 edition is an expansion and amplification of the 1904 edition.

7. A. Dastre, *La Vie et la mort*, Paris, 1902 (in The Adams Collection).

Appendix I. Philological Items

THE NATURE AND EXTENT of Henry Adams's philologic erudition, in the writing of the *Mont-Saint-Michel and Chartres*, can be determined at least in part, by examining the sources he used. It is true, of course, that some of the works postdate the appearance of *Mont-Saint-Michel*. But we know that he regarded the printed form as a balloon to register the reactions of some whose opinions he respected. Since, then, he was busy with revisions and addenda, all the works listed may be regarded as sources of the book. The following books and pamphlets are in the Adams Collection; most of them contain his scorings.

Adam de la Halle. Oeuvres complètes du trouvère A. de la H., (poésies et musique) publiées sous les auspices de la Société des Sciences, des Lettres, et des Arts de Lille par E. de Coussemaker, Correspondant de l'Institut. Paris, 1872.

Adam de Saint-Victor. Oeuvres poétiques; texte critique par Léon Gautier. 3d ed. Paris, 1894. (Signed, "Henry Adams, Inverlochy Castle, 1902.")

Adgar's Marienlegenden, nach der Londoner Handschrift . . . zum ersten mal vollständig herausgegben von Carl Neuhaus. Heilbronn, 1886.

Anthologie des poëtes français, depuis le XVᵉ siècle jusqu'à nos jours. Ed. Alphonse Lemerre. Paris, n.d.

Armancourt, Comte d'. Chartres; Notes héraldiques et généalogiques. Chartres, 1908.

Aubry, Pierre. Trouvères and Troubadours. Tr. from the 2d French ed. by Claude Aveling. New York, 1914. (A sheet of music is enclosed in MS. Scoring on p. 153, with regard to rhythm of 13th century motets, reads: "This brought me to the conclusion that in documents of this time the rhythm is intrinsic, that is to say, latent; it exists, but the notation doesn't reveal it. H.A.")

Aucassin et Nicolette. Reproduced in photofacsimile and type-transliteration from the unique manuscript in the Bibliothèque Nationale at Paris . . . by the care of F. W. Bourdillon, M.A., formerly scholar of Worcester College, Oxford; Oxford, Clarendon Press, 1896. (Signed "Henry Adams, Paris, 1900.")

Aucassin und Nicolete. Neu herausgegeben nach der Handschrift mit Paridigmen und Glossar von Hermann Suchier. Paderborn, 1889.

Bartsch, Karl. Chrestomathie de l'ancien français (XIIIᵉ-XVᵉ siècles) accompagnée d'une grammaire et d'un glossaire par Karl Bartsch. 11th ed., rev. and corr. by Leo Wiese. Leipzig, 1913.

——Über Karlmeinet. Ein Beitrag zur Karlsage. Nürnberg, 1861.

Bartsch, Karl, and Eduard Koschwitz. Chrestomathie Provençale (Xᵉ-XVᵉ siècles). 6th ed., entirely rev. by Eduard Koschwitz. Marburg, 1904.

Beck, J. B. Die Melodien der Troubadours und Trouvères. Strassburg 1908.

Bédier, Joseph. Les Fabliaux; études de littérature populaire et d'histoire littéraire du moyen-âge. 2d. ed., rev. and corr. Paris, 1895.

——Les Légendes épiques; recherches sur la formation des chansons de geste. 4 vols. Paris, 1908-1913. (Scorings in Vols. I, II, IV.)

Bédier, Joseph, and Pierre Aubry. Les Chansons de croisade; publiées par J. Bédier, avec leurs mélodies publiées par Pierre Aubry. Paris, 1909.

Bertrand de Bar-Sur-Aube. Le Roman de Girard de Viane. Ed. Prosper Tarbé. Reims, 1850.

Bibliothèque de l'École de Chartres. Revue d'Érudition, consacrée spécialement à l'étude du moyen-âge. Année, 1870. Paris, 1871.

Bohn, Henry George, ed. Chronicles of the Crusades, being contemporary narratives of the Crusade of Richard Coeur de Lion, by Richard of Devizes and Geoffrey de Vinsauf; and of the Crusade of Saint Louis, by Lord John de Joinville. London, 1865.

Boudain, E. Monnaies antiques, françaises et étrangères. Vente aux enchères publiques à Paris le Mardi 4 Juillet 1899. (Price catalogue signed in H. A.'s hand.)

Bouillet, A. Le Mont Saint-Michel. Havre, 1896.

Bordier, Henri. Histoire Ecclésiastique des Francs, par Saint Grégoire . . . Suivie d'un sommaire de ses autres ouvrages et précédée de sa vie écrite au X⁰ siècle, par Odon, Abbé de Cluni. Traduction nouvelle par Henri Bordier. 2 vols. Paris, 1859, 1862.

Bourdon, Charles. Histoire et description du Mont Saint-Michel. Texte par M. Le Héricher . . . dessins de M. G. Boult, publiées par M. Ch. Bourdon, Membre de la Société des Antiquaires de Normandie. Caen, 1848.

Brutails, J. L'Archéologie du moyen-âge et ses méthodes; études critiques. Paris, 1900.

——Les Vieilles Églises de la Gironde. Publié sous les auspices de la Société Archéologique de Bordeaux. Bordeaux, 1912.

Bulteau, L'Abbé. Monographie de la Cathédrale de Chartres. 2d ed., rev. and enl. 3 vols. Chartres, 1887–1901.

Caumont. Histoire de l'architecture religieuse au moyen-âge par M. de Caumont. New ed. Caen, 1841.

Chabaneau, Camille. Les Biographies des troubadours en langue provençale. Publiées intégralement pour la première fois, avec une introduction et des notes accompagnées de textes latins, provençaux, italiens et espagnols concernant ces poètes et suivies d'un appendice. Toulouse, 1885.

Chançun de Willame, La.—"Note: The unknown 'Chanson de Geste' here transcribed belongs to the cycle of William of Orange. There has been no attempt to edit the text, or even to correct not a few very obvious minor errors. The two reproductions are of the same size as the original manuscript. Two hundred copies are printed at the Chiswick Press June 1903." Insert: *London Times* March 11, 1912, in re death of Mr. George Dunn (aetat 47) who secured the unique manuscript of the hitherto unknown "Chancun de Willame," which he transcribed himself and had 200 copies handsomely printed. This poem of 3,553 lines was hailed by scholars as a rival to the Chanson deRoland. This Mr. Dunn distributed anonymously through Sotheby, his bookseller.

Charlemagne. Kaiser Karls Leben von Einhard. Nach der Ausgabe in den Monumenta Germaniae, uebersetzt von Otto Abel. Berlin, 1850.

Christian of Troyes. Li Romans de la Charrete. Roman van Lancelot. Door Dr. W. J. A. Jonckbloet. 2 vols. in one. 'S, Gravenhage 1846, 1849.

Chronique de Turpin. Paris, 1835. (Inserts: Letters from Ward Thoron, Jan. 5 and 9, 1911, from Chartres, Eure-et-Loire; transcript of Ch. IV Book 24 of Speculum Historiale of Vincent of Beauvais and pp. 963–64 of Vol. IV of the *Speculum Majus*). ["Réimpression de l'édition de 1527 mais sans le privilège et sans la dédicace qui sont remplacés par un avis du libraire."— Brunet]

Clerval, A. Guide Chartrain: Chartres, sa cathédrale, ses monuments. Chartres, n.d.

——Petite histoire de Notre-Dame de Chartres d'après les quatorze gravures du triomphe de la Sainte Vierge dans l'Église de Chartres. Dessinées par N. de Larmessin en 1697 et reproduites pour la première fois avec l'explication de L. Mocquet. Rennes, 1908.

Coincy, Gautier de. Les Miracles de la Sainte Vierge, traduits et mis en vers par Gautier de Coincy; publiés par M. l'Abbé Poquet. Paris, 1857. (Seems to have been owned by a Spaniard who wrote marginal remarks in Spanish.)

Corroyer, Édouard. Description de l'abbaye du Mont Saint-Michel et de ses abords. Précédée d'une Notice historique. Paris, 1877.

Darcel, Alfred. Trésor de l'église de Congues, dessiné et déscrit par Alfred Darcel. Paris, 1861.

Didron, Édouard. Les Vitraux à l'Exposition Universelle de 1867. Paris, 1868.

——Vitraux du Grand-Andely. Paris, 1863.

Dupont, Étienne. Le Mont Saint-Michel inconnu d'après des documents inédits. Paris, 1912.

Durand, Paul. Monographie de Notre-Dame de Chartres. Explication des planches. Paris, 1881.

Du Sommerard, Alexandre. Les Arts au moyen-âge. 3 vols. Paris, 1838-1846.

Enlart, Camille. Manuel d'archéologie française depuis les temps mérovingiens jusqu'à la renaissance. Première partie, architecture par Camille Enlart. Paris, 1902.

——Monuments religieux de l'architecture romane et de transition dans la région picarde. Amiens, Paris, 1895.

Foerster, Wendelin. Das altfranzösische Rolandslied, text von Chateauroux und Venedig. 6th vol. Heilbronn, 1883. *Ibid.*, text von Paris, Cambridge, Lyon. Vol. VII. Heilbronn, 1886.

Francis of Assisi, Saint. La Leggenda di San Francesco, scritta da tre suoi compagni (legende triumsociorum), publicata per la prima volta nella vera sua integrità dai Padri Marcellino da Civezza e Teofilo Domenichelli dei Minori. Rome, 1899.

Gace, Brulé. Chansons. Publiées par Gédéon Huet. Paris, 1902.

Garreau, L. L'État social de la France au temps des croisades. Paris, 1899.

Gautier d'Aupais. Le Chevalier à la Corbeille. Fabliaux du XIIIe siècle, publiés pour la première fois d'après deux manuscrits, l'un de la Bibliothèque Royale à Paris, l'autre du Musée Britannique à Londres, par Francisque Michel. Paris, 1835.

Gautier, Léon. Bibliographie des chansons de geste. . . . Paris, 1897.

——La Chanson de Roland; texte critique accompagné d'une traduction nouvelle et précédé d'une introduction historique. 2 vols. Tours, 1872.

Glossarium Mediae et Infimae Latinetatis. 7 vols. Didot. Paris, 1840-1850. (Henschel, ed.)

Godefroy, Frédéric. Dictionnaire de l'ancienne langue française et de tous ses dialectes du IXe au XVe siècle. 6 vols. Paris, 1880-1892.

Gout, Paul. L'Histoire et l'architecture française au Mont Saint-Michel. Paris, 1899.

Guessard, F., and A. Montaiglon. Aliscans, chanson de geste, publiée d'après le manuscrit de la Bibliothèque de l'Arsenal et à l'aide de cinq autres manuscrits. Paris, 1870.

Guillaume de Ferrieres (dit le Vidame de Chartres). Chansons et saluts d'amour; la plupart inédite; réunis pour la première fois avec les variantes de tous les manuscrits; précédés d'une notice sur l'auteur par M. Louis Lacour. Paris, 1856.

Guillaume de Saint-Pair. Le Roman du Mont-Saint-Michel. . . . publié pour la première fois par Francisque-Michel avec une étude sur l'auteur par M. Eugène de Beaurepaire. (Extrait du XXe volume des Mémoires de la Société des Antiquaires de Normandie). Caen, 1856.

Huon de Bordeaux. Chanson de geste; publiée pour la première fois d'après les manuscrits de Tours, de Paris, de Turin, par MM. F. Guessard et C. Grandmaison. Paris, 1860.

Jacques de Voragine. La Légende dorée. Traduite du Latin d'après les plus anciens manuscrits, avec une introduction, des notes, et un index alphabétique, par Teodor de Wyzewa. Paris, 1902.

Jonckbloet, W. J. A. Guillaume d'Orange; chansons de geste des XIe et XIIe siècles. Publiées pour la première fois par le Dr. W. J. A. Jonckbloet. 2 vols. La Haye, 1854.

——Guillaume d'Orange, Le Marquis au Court Nez. Chanson de Geste du XIIe siècle. Mise en nouveau langage. Amsterdam, 1867.

——Roman van Lancelot (XIIIe Eeuw) Naar het (Eenigbekende), Handschrift der Kroninkligke Bibliotheek, op Gezag van het Gouvernment Uitgegeven door Dr. W. J. A. Jonckbloet. 2 vols. 's Gravenhage, 1846–1849.

Koschwitz, Eduard. Karls des Grossen Reise nach Jerusalem und Constantinopel; ein altfranzösisches Heldengedicht. 3d rev. ed. Leipzig, 1895.

——Sechs Bearbeitungen des altfranzösischen Gedichts von Karls des Grossen Reise nach Jerusalem und Constantinopel. Heilbronn, 1879.

Lacroix, Paul, and Ferdinand Seré. Le Moyen-Âge et la renaissance, histoire et description des moeurs et usages, du commerce et de l'industrie, des sciences, des arts, des littératures et des beaux-arts en Europe. Paris, 1848–1851.

Lasteyrie, Robert de. Archéologie du moyen-âge. Mémoires et fragments réunis. Paris, 1886.

——L'Architecture religieuse en France à l'époque Romane, ses origines, son développement. Paris, 1912.

Lenoir, Albert. Architecture monastique. Paris, 1852; IIe et IIIe partie, Paris, 1856.

Lenormant, François. La Monnaie dans l'antiquité. Leçons professées dans la chaire d'archéologie près la Bibliothèque Nationale par François Lenormant. New ed. Paris, 1897.

Leroy, Pierre. Histoire de Saint Sulpice le Pieux archevêque de Bourges et de son pèlerinage à Saint Sulpice de Favières. Paris, 1913.

Loersch, Hugo. Die Legende Karls des Grossen, im 11 und 12 Jahrhundert, herausgegeben von Gerhard Rauschen; mit einem Anhang über Urkunden Karls des Grossen und Friedrichs I für Aachen. (Publikationen der Gesellschaft für Rheinische Geschichtskunde.) Leipzig, 1890.

Lot, Fredinand. Les Derniers Carolingiens Lothaire, Louis V, Charles de Lorraine. Préface par A. Giry. Paris, 1891.

——Études sur le règne de Hugues Capet et la fin du Xe siècle. Paris. 1903.

Luquiens, Frederick Bliss. The Reconstruction of the Original Chanson de Roland. Reprinted from the *Transactions of the Connecticut Academy of Arts and Sciences*, Vol. XV, July, 1909.

Merlet, René. La Cathédrale de Chartres. Petites monographies des grands édifices de la France. Publiées sous la direction de M. C. Lefèvre-Pontalis. Paris, n.d.

Meyer, Paul. Les Derniers Troubadours de la Provence, d'après le chansonnier donné à la Bibliothèque Impériale par M. Ch. Giraud. Paris, 1871. (Insert: a bill from Librairie Alphonse Picard et Fils, dated Paris, 9/10, 1913, for $\dfrac{\text{bFr.}}{10}$)

Miracles de Nostre Dame par personnages; publiés d'après le manuscrit de la Bibliothèque Nationale par Gaston Paris et Ulysse Robert. 8 vols. Paris, 1876–1893. (Société des Anciens Textes Français.)

Misset, Eugène. Essai philologique et littéraire sur les oeuvres poétiques d'Adam de Saint-Victor. Poésie Rythmique du Moyen-Âge. Paris, 1882.

Moland, L., and C. d'Héricault. Nouvelles françoises en prose du XIIIᵉ siècle, publiées d'après les manuscrits avec une introduction et des notes. Paris, 1856.

——Nouvelles françoises en prose du XIVᵉ siècle. . . . Paris, 1858.

Molinier, Émile. Histoire générale des arts appliqués à l'industrie du Vᵉ à la fin du XVIIIᵉ siècle. 4 vols. Paris, 1896.

Monmerqué, Louis Jean Nicolas, and Francisque Xavier Michel. Théâtre français au moyen-âge, publié d'après les manuscrits de la Bibliothèque du Roi, XIᵉ-XIVᵉ siècles. Paris, 1839.

Montaiglon, Anatole de, and Gaston Raynaud. Recueil général et complet des fabliaux des XIIIᵉ et XIVᵉ siècles; imprimés ou inédits, publiés des manuscrits. 6 vols. Paris, 1872–1890. (Marginalia in I, 1–2; V, 244, 247; VI, 125, 126.)

Montreuil, Gilbert de. Roman de la violette ou de Gérard de Nevers, en vers, du XIIIᵉ siècle; publié, pour la première fois, d'après deux manuscrits de la Bibliothèque Royale par Francisque Michel. Paris, 1834. (MS notes in French—by whom?)

——Ibid. Paris, 1834. (This is No. 172 of a limited edition; it contains handwritten notes in French by an unidentified person.)

Muset, Colin. Les Chansons de Colin Muset, éditées par Joseph Bédier avec la transcription des mélodies par Jean Beck. Paris, 1912. (Les Classiques Français du Moyen-Âge publiés sous la direction de Mario Roques.)

Mussafia, A. Studien zu den mittelälterlichen Marienlegenden, I-V. Vienna, 1887–1889, 1891, 1898.

Natalis de Wailly. Récits d'un menestrel de Reims au XIIIᵉ. Publiés pour la Société de l'Histoire de France par N. de W. Paris, 1876.

Ottin, L. Le Vitrail son histoire, ses manifestations à travers les âges et les peuples. Paris, n.d.

Palustre, Léon. Adam: mystère du XIIᵉ siècle; texte critique accompagné d'une traduction. Paris, 1877.

Paris, Gaston. Histoire poétique de Charlemagne; reproduction de l'édition de 1865 augmentée de notes nouvelles par l'auteur et par M. Paul Meyer, et d'une table alphabétique des matières. Paris, 1905.

——La Littérature française au moyen-âge (XIe-XIVe siècles); manuel d'ancien français. Paris, 1888. (Scorings by H. A.)

——La Poésie du moyen-âge; leçons et lectures. 1st ser., 4th ed., Paris, 1899; 2d ser., Paris, 1895. (P. 56 turned down: "L'Esprit Normand en Angleterre.")

Partonopeus de Blois, publié pour la première fois, d'après le manuscrit de la Bibliothèque de l'Arsenal, avec trois facsimile, par G.-A. Crapelet, imprimeur. 2 vols. Paris, 1834.

Pillion, Louise. Les Sculpteurs Français du XIIIe siècle. Paris, 1912.

Racinet, M. A. L'Ornement polychrome. Cent planches en couleurs ou en argent contenant environ 2,000 motifs de tous les styles. Art ancien et antique, moyen-âge, renaissance, XVIIe et XVIIIe siècles. Recueil historique et pratique publié sous la direction de M.A.R. Paris, n.d.

Raoul de Cambrai. Chanson de geste, publiée par MM. P. Meyer et A. Longnon. Paris, 1882.

Raynouard, François Juste Marie. Choix des poésies originales des troubadours. 6 vols. Paris, 1816-1821.

Regnard, Jean François. Théâtre de Regnard suivi des poésies diverses de la Provençale des voyages en Laponie, en Suède, etc., avec une introduction par M. Louis Moland. Paris, n.d.

Rolin, Gustav. Aliscans, mit Berücksichtigung von Wolframs von Eschenbach; kritisch herausgegeben. Leipzig, 1894.

Roman de la rose, nouvelle édition revue et corrigée par Francisque Michel. Paris, 1864.

Rupin, Ernest. L'Abbaye et les cloîtres de Moissac. Publié sous les auspices de la Société Archéologique de la Corrège. Paris, 1897.

Sabatier, Paul. Vie de S. François d'Assise. 27th ed. Paris, 1894.

——ed. Floretum S. F. Francisci Assisiensis. Liber aureus qui italice dicitur I Fioretti di San Francesco. Paris, 1902.

——Speculum perfectionis, Seu S. Francisci Assisiensis Legenda antiquissima auctore fratre Leone; nunc primum edidit. [Collection de documents pour l'histoire religieuse et littéraire du moyen-âge, vol. I.] Paris, 1898.

Schindler, Kurt. Madrigals of the French Renaissance; presented by K. S. assisted by a choir . . . prologue spoken by Mme Mazarin, Grand Ballroom of the Waldorf-Astoria, March 21, 1910; programme.

Suchier, Hermann. La Chançun de Guillelme, französisches Volksepos des XI Jahrhunderts; kritisch herausgegeben. (Bibliotheca Normanica, Vol. VIII.) Halle, 1911.

Tarbé, Prosper, ed. Poètes de Champagne; antérieurs au siècle de François Ier, en proverbes champenois, avant le XVIe siècle. Reims, 1851.

——Le Roman d'Aubery le Bourgoing. Reims, 1849.

——Le Roman des quatre fils Aymon, Princes des Ardennes. Reims, 1861.

——Romancero de Champagne. (Collection des poètes de Champagne antérieurs au XVIe siècle.) 5 vols. Reims, 1863, 1864.

Thaun, Philippe de. Le Bestiaire; texte critique publié avec introduction, notes, et glossaire par Emmanuel Walberg. Paris, 1900.

Trébutien, G. S. Le Dit des trois pommes; légende en vers du XIVe siècle publiée pour la première fois d'après le manuscrit de la Bibliothèque du Roi. Paris, 1837.

Troubadours, Les Derniers. Troubadours de la Provence d'après le Chansonnier donné à la Bibliothèque Impériale par M. Ch. Giraud. Paris, 1871.

Vacaudard, L'Abbé E. Vie de Saint Bernard. Abbé de Clairvaux. 2d. ed. 2 vols. Paris, 1897.

Viollet-Leduc, Eugène Emmanuel. Ancien théâtre français au collection des ouvrages dramatiques, les plus remarquables depuis les mystères jusqu'à Corneille. Publié avec notes et éclaircissements par M. V. le D. 10 vols. Paris, 1854–1857.

——Dictionnaire raisonné de l'architecture française du XIe au XVIe siècle. 10 vols. Paris, 1854–1868.

——Dictionnaire raisonné du mobilier français de l'époque carlovingienne à la renaissance. . . . 6 vols. Paris, 1868–1875.

Wace, Robert (Master Wace). Chronicle. Tr. Edgar Taylor. London, 1837.

——Roman de Rou et des Ducs de Normandie; nach den Hand-
schriften von neuem herausgegeben von Dr. Hugo Andresen.
2 vols. Heilbronn, 1877–1879.

Wallensköld, Axel. Chansons de Conon de Bethune; trouveur
artésien de la fin de XIIᵉ siècle; édition critique précédée de la
biographie du poète. Helsingfors, 1891.

Appendix II. Historical Items

A. AT WESTERN RESERVE

Bacourt, de. Souvenirs d'un diplomate—lettres intimes sur l'Amérique. Paris, Calmann Lévy, 1882. Many scorings.

Bastiat, Frédéric. Oeuvres complètes. 2d ed. Paris, Guillaumin, 1862-64. Vols. II, III, V, VI, VII. Scorings in Vol. I (1862).

Conway, Moncure Daniel. Omitted Chapters of History Disclosed in the Life and Papers of Edmund Randolph. New York and London, 1888. See the French material herein.

——Life of Thomas Paine. 2 vols. Vol. I, London, Putnam's, 1892. Scorings in Vol. II.

Coulanges, Fustel de. La Cité antique. 3d ed. Paris, Hachette, 1870.

Godoy, Don Manuel. Mémoires du prince de la paix. Traduits en français d'après le manuscrit espagnol, par J. G. D'Esménard. Paris, London, and Madrid, 1836. Vols. I, II, IV. Scorings in Vol. III.

Grandmaison, Geoffroy de (Charles Alcan). L'Ambassade française en Espagne pendant la révolution (1789-1804). Paris, Plon, 1892.

Locke, John. Conduct of the Understanding. John Sharpe, 1820. With it is bound Occasional Reflections by Robert Boyle.

Michaux, F. A. Travels to the Westward of the Alleghany Mountains. Tr. from the French by B. Lambert. London, 1805. Scorings.

Michelet, J. Histoire du XIX siècle. New ed., revised and annotated. Paris, Marpon and Flammarion, 1880. Vols. I, II, III.

Moniteur. Réimpression de l'ancien *Moniteur,* Mai 1789–Nov. 1799. Introduction historique. Paris, Bureau Central, 1843. Vols. XI, XIII–XV, XVII–XXIX. Scorings in Vols. XII and XVI.

Récamier, Madame. Souvenirs et correspondance tirés des papiers de Madame Récamier. 3d ed. Paris, Lévy frères, 1860. No notes in Vol. I; Vol. II, p. 379, at the third line from the bottom, "les rapprots o/r/."

Staël-Holstein, Baron de. Correspondance diplomatique du baron . . . et de son successeur . . . le baron Brinkman. Ed. L. Leouzon Le Duc. Paris, Hachette, 1881. On the false title page above the title of the book "An enthusiastic account of Baron de Stael in 1785 is given in a letter of Abigail Adams, May 10. (*Letters of Mrs. Adams,* p. 249. Fourth edition, 1848.)"

Taine, H. Les Origines de la France contemporaine. Vol. I, La Révolution. 11th ed. Paris, Hachette, 1882. Vol. II has scorings at the top of page 179 (see p. 99 above).

Vergennes, Charles Gravier, comte de. Mémoire historique et politique sur la Louisiane. Paris, Lepetit jeune, an X, 1802. Contains scorings.

Witt, Cornélis de. Jefferson and the American Democracy. Tr. Church. London, Longman, 1862. Scorings.

B: AT THE MASSACHUSETTS HISTORICAL SOCIETY

Adams, Henry. "Napoléon Ier et Saint-Domingue," *Revue historique,* XXIV (January-April, 1884), 92–130.

——. "Count Edward de Crillon," *American Historical Review,* I, No. 1 (October, 1895), 51–69.

Babeau, Albert. Le Village sous l'ancien régime. Paris, Didier et Cie, 1879, 2 ed.

Bouillet, Marie Nicolas. Altas universel d'histoire et de géographie. Paris, L. Hachette et Cie, 1865.

Brissot de Warville, Jacques P. Nouveau voyage dans les États-Unis de l'Amérique septentrionale, fait en 1788. 3 vols. Paris, Buisson, 1791.

Charras, Jean Baptiste. Histoire de la campagne de 1815, Waterloo. 3d ed. Leipzig, A. Durr, 1858.

——. Histoire de la guerre de 1813 en Allemagne. . . . 2d ed. Paris, A. Le Chevalier, 1870.

Choisy, François Timoléon, Abbé de. Mémoires pour servir à l'histoire de Louis XIV. 2 vols. Utrecht, Van-de-Water, 1727.

De Nervo, Jean B., Baron. Les Finances françaises, 1814–1830. Paris, Michel Lévy frères, 1865, 2 vols.

Drumont, Edouard A. La France juive devant l'opinion. Paris, C. Marpon and Flammarion, 1866.

Goncourt, Edmond de. Histoire de la société française pendant le Directoire. Paris, Didier et Cie, 1864.

Gourgaud, Gaspard, Baron. Sainte-Hélène, Journal inédit de 1815 à 1818, 2 vols. Avec préface et notes de MM. le Vicomte de Grouchy et A. Guillois. Paris, E. Flammarion. 1903?.

Guizot, François. Histoire de France. 5 vols. Paris, Hachette, 1875–76.

——. Mémoires pour servir à l'histoire de mon temps. 8 vols. Paris, 1858–67.

Hanotaux, Gabriel. Histoire du Cardinal de Richelieu. 2 vols. Paris, Firmin-Didot, 1893-99.

Hanoteau, Jean. Lettres du Prince de Metternich à la Comtesse de Lieven 1818-1819, publiées, avec une introduction . . . par J. H.; préface de A. Chuquet. Paris; Plon-Nourrit et Cie, 1909.

Houssaye, Henry. Histoire financière de la France, 1814. Paris, 1895.

Jubainville, Henry d'Arbois de. Deux Manières d'écrire l'histoire: Critique de Bossuet, d'Augustin Thierry et de Fustel de Coulanges. Paris, E. Bouillon, 1896. (Bill January 7, 1896, to Henry B. Adams $1.15 On Approval. Lineations.)

La Gorce, Pierre de. Histoire du Second Empire. 7 vols. Paris, 1896–1905.

Lalanne, Ludovic. Dictionnaire historique de la France. Paris, Hachette, 1872.

Le Beau, Charles. Histoire du Bas Empire. 19 vols. Paris, 1819.

Michelet, Jules. History of France from the Earliest Period to the Present Time. Vol. I., tr. by G. H. Smith. New York, D. Appleton and Co., 1847.

I found in this volume a penciled note, in a very clear hand, inserted between pp. 216 and 217, as follows: "The Virgin's hair, a piece of the cross (both worn by him in his grave); the leather girdle of Christ with Constantine's seal still visible; a nail of the cross; the sponge that was filled with vinegar; some manna from the wilderness, and some bits of Aaron's rod. The robe worn by the Virgin at the nativity; the swaddling clothes in which Jesus was wrapped; the cloth in which John the Baptist's head was laid; the scarf worn by the Savior at the Crucification, still marked with stains of blood."

Moreau de Saint-Méry. Voyage aux États-Unis, 1793, 1798. New Haven, Conn., Yale University Press 1913. (Signed "Henry Adams 1914.")

Parquin, Charles. De la paix de Vienne à Fontainebleau. Paris, Michaud, 1911.

Revue Historique. Volumes XXIV, XXV, XXVI (1884).

Sainte-Beuve. Monsieur de Talleyrand. Paris, 1870.

Sorel, Albert. L'Europe et la révolution française. 8 vols. Paris, E. Plon, Nourrit et Cie, 1895–1910.

Sybel, Heinrich Karl L. von. Histoire de l'Europe pendant la révolution française. Traduit en français par Marie Basquet. 6 vols. Paris, 1869-1838.

Tatischev, Sergei. Alexandre Ier et Napoléon, d'après leur correspondance, inédite, 1801–1812, par Serge Tatistcheff. Paris, Perrin et Cie, 1891. (Notes by Henry Adams.)

Ternaux, Mortimer. Histoire de la terreur (1792–94) (Signed "A ma soeur Adolphine Hommage de l'Auteur M. Ternaux"). 8 vols. Paris, Michel Lévy frères, 1868–81.

Thierry, Augustin. Histoire de la conquête de l'Angleterre par les Normands. Bruxelles, L.. Hauman et Cie, 1835.

Thiers, Adolphe. Histoire du Consulat et de l'empire, faisant suite à L'Histoire de la révolution française. 20 vols. Paris, Paulin, 1845–62.

——. Histoire de la révolution française. 10 vols. Paris, Lecointe et Pougin, 1832.

Vandal, A. Napoléon et Alexandre Ier: l'alliance russe sous le Premier Empire. 3 vols. Paris, E. Plon, Nourrit et Cie, 1893–96.

Viel Castel, Horace de. Mémoires du Comte Horace de V. C. sur le règne de Napoléon III, 1851–64. 6 vols. Paris, Leduc, 1883–84.

Witt, Cornélis de. Thomas Jefferson: étude historique sur la démocratie américaine. Paris, Didier et Cie, 1861.

Appendix III. Descartes (Marginalia)

ADAMS'S COPY of Jules Simon's edition of Descartes is full of lineations and marginal remarks. These scorings and marginalia appear also in the long introduction by Simon. We give here both the passages underlined and Adams's comments on them: "La pensée de Dieu implique l'existence de Dieu, parceque *si j'existe, moi imparfait, je ne puis supposer un seul instant, si j'applique ma pensée au parfait, qu'il n'existe point.*"[1]

I exist, an Energy, and at once admit that I am an infinitesimal portion of a greater energy but is that greater necessarily perfect? Is it necessarily infinite except in time and space? Is it not necessarily weaker in some parts of space than others? What is perfection in it?[2]

In a footnote Jules Simon speaks of the dilemma of the *One* and the *Many*:

. . . la difficulté d'expliquer que l'un crée le multiple; grande difficulté en effet, car créer est une opération dont notre esprit ne connaît point l'analogue, de plus un ne voit pas le motif, ni comment il y a du rapport entre l'éternité et l'esprit d'une part; l'étendue et la durée de l'autre. Enfin, *il semble que* ce soit une imperfection en Dieu de créer.[3]

To this Adams adds: "and is not self-consciousness a defect, since it implies a non ego? And is not knowledge a defect since it implies ignorance?"[4]

"*L'acte de Dieu est créateur, conservateur; providentiel tout à la fois, et n'est pas pour cela successif.*"[5] "The Athanasian Creed is a

joke to this. Why not say at once, as he has hinted multiplicity
is unity? XXXVIII, LXI."⁶ Adams refers us to pages 38 and 61
because there the interlocking question of the one and many are
touched upon. Accordingly, we shall give these passages now:

La conception même du multiple par Dieu sans la création est déjà un problème
insoluble; et grand Dieu ne ferait que concevoir le monde sans le produire, il y aurait
là quelque chose d'impénétrable à la raison humaine. C'est à cette conception, en
effet que le langage humain commence à balbutier et à affirmer l'être du non-être
par une fiction *sans laquelle il ne peut sortir de la proposition indentique qui est tout
l'éléatisme, savoir: Dieu est celui qui est.*⁷

La *Métaphysique toute entière est attachée à la détermination de l'idée d'infini; il n'est
point de difficulté métaphysique qui ne naisse de l'opposition entre le fini et l'infini;*
mais en même temps, quoique cette opposition soit radicale, et qu'e le creu e entre
la nature de Dieu et le monde un abîme que la science ne saurait combler, plus on
fera voir la dépendance mutuelle des divers problèmes, plus on enfermera la science
dans un nombre restreint d'hypothèses, jusqu'à ce qu'enfin on la réduise à cette
heureuse nécessité: ou d'accepter la création libre et volontaire, la providence de
Dieu, les causes secondaires libres et morales, *malgré une suite de difficultés enchaînées
l'une à l'autre et dont la première est insoluble;* ou de se jeter, non pas dans la confusion
de l'un et du multiple, ce qui n'est pas la solution, mais l'ignorance du problème;
ni dans la coëxistence éternelle de Dieu et du monde, car alors la raison du multiple
n'est pas donnée; ni dans l'unité de Dieu qui conçoit éternellement un monde intelligible, puisque la difficulté qu'on veut fuire est déjà toute entière dans la mul-
tiplicité nécessaire de ce monde; mais dans *la négation absolue du multiple dans le
système rigoureux et extravagant des éléates.*⁸

The next passage that elicits a comment from Adams is this:
"Dieu n'agit pas constamment, il n'agit pas suivant des lois, il
agit, si je l'ose dire, *uniquement, éternellement. La loi est ce qui
reste dans l'effet, de l'unité qui est dans la cause.*"⁹ Adams's comment
this time is in French: "Alors nécessairement puisque l'acte et la
volonté sont une seule chose,— un acte."¹⁰

Following Simon's Introduction, we learn that the laws of nature
exist only in phenomena but that these laws are there only through
the will of God. As for their essence, they are in the world and form
part of it: ". . . et quant à leur origine, *elles viennent de l'acte
même créateur, organisateur et conservateur, qui est un et simple
comme l'être dont il émane.*"¹¹ Adams queries at this point: "Was
it not because he saw that this view might require a necessitarian
universe?"¹²

Jules Simon concludes, in the course of his exposition,

C'est donc un rationalisme complet que constitue l'école de Descartes; c'est la conscience percevant le je suis dans le je pense. . . . C'est à dire qu'il est un esprit des idées positives, complètes, nécessaires, et *prouvant par le fait seul de leur existence la réalité de leur objet.*[13]

Again Adams makes his remark in French: "Réaliste alors! Et pourtant Descartes le nie!"[14]

Towards the end of his Introduction, Simon asserts: "*Le car-tésianisme, comme système, a péri, et pour jamais;* l'esprit du car-tésianisme est immortel."[15] Adams seems to second this in a summary note he indites on the bottom margin of the page following Simon's statement.

The Spirit of Cartesianism seems to be essentially realistic and scholastic. There was nothing new in his method or his conclusions that warrants the name of orig-inality. His only conclusion was that of a mechanical universe and he did not under-stand that, without Energy—p. 461.[16]

We come to the Discours de la Méthode proper, the Quatrième Partie, where Adams makes a marginal comment.

. . . je me résolus de feindre que toutes les choses qui m'étaient jamais entrées en l'esprit n'étaient non plus vraies que les illusions de mes songes. Mais aussitôt après je pris garde que, pendant que *je voulais ainsi penser que tout était faux,* il fallait nécessairement que moi qui le pensais fusse quelque chose; et remarquant que cette vérité: *je pense, donc je suis* (italics), était si ferme et si assurée que toutes les plus extravagantes suppositions des sceptiques n'étaient pas capables de l'ébran-ler, je jugeai que je pouvais la recevoir sans scrupule pour le premier principe de la philosophie que je cherchais.[17]

Adams's remark here is this: "penser is cogito, and means reason. Does Pascal (*sic!*—he means Descartes)[18] mean it as reason or only consciousness."[19] It is convenient, at this point, to gather up the other instances where Adams persists in his distinction between reason and consciousness.

Passons donc aux attributs de l'âme, et voyons s'il y en a quelqu'un qui soit en moi. Les premiers sont de me nourir et de marcher; mais s'il est vrai que je n'ai point de corps, il est vrai aussi que je ne puis marcher ni me nourir. *Un autre est de sentir; mais on ne peut aussi sentir sans le corps.* . . . Un autre est de *penser, et je trouve que la pensée est un attribut qui m'appartient: elle seule ne peut être détachée de moi.*[20]

As before, Adams questions: "penser means here reason or con-sciousness? surely reason 'peut-être détachée' and leaves only con-sciousness."[21]

Mais qu'est-ce donc que je suis? Une chose qui pense. *Qu'est-ce qu'une chose qui pense? C'est une chose qui doute, qui entend, qui conçoit, qui affirme, qui nie, qui veut,*

qui ne veut pas, qui imagine aussi et qui sent . . . toutefois . . . il est certain
qu'il me semble que je vois de la lumière, que j'entends du bruit et que je sens de la
chaleur; cela ne peut être faux, et *c'est proprement ce qui en moi s'appelle sentir, et
cela précisément n'est rien autre chose que penser.*[22]

Henry reiterates: "penser then is sentir, or consciousness, not
reason."[23]

"Mais enfin que dirai-je de cet esprit, c'est-à-dire de moi-même?
car jusqu'ici je n'admets en moi rien autre chose que l'esprit."[24]
—"Properly," says Adams, "one has admitted only consciousness
of oneself as a thought. All the rest is assumption of the non-
ego."[25]

What am I?—Descartes answers this question as follows:

Je suis *une chose qui pense, c'est-à-dire qui doute, qui affirme, qui nie, qui connaît peu
de choses, qui en ignore beaucoup, qui aime, qui hait, qui veut, qui ne veut pas, qui
imagine aussi, et qui sent. . . .*[26]

Rather captiously, Adams snaps at Descartes (in French): "mais
qui ne raisonne pas! le chien fait tout ça! Est-ce qu'il pense?"[27]
—So much then for the problem of consciousness and reason.

When Descartes applies his scepticism in the field of mathematics
—as in the instance where, supposing a triangle, it follows that the
sum of its angles equal two right angles, and yet he sees nothing to
assure him of the existence of a triangle—he opens the door for an
extension of that scepticism on the part of Adams, who underlines

mais je ne voyais rien pour cela qui m'assurât qu'il y eût au monde aucun triangle;
au lieu que, revenant à examiner l'idée que j'avais d'un Être parfait je trouvais que
l'existence y était comprise en même façon qu'il est compris en celle d'un triangle
que ses trois angles sont égaux à deux droits, ou en celle d'un sphère que toutes ses
parties sont également distantes de son centre. . . .[28]

On this Adams comments in French: "C'est à dire, supposant
un Dieu, ce serait la même chose comme supposant un triangle."[29]

In the Méditations Métaphysiques Adams underlines first the
following passage:

Or dans la suite de ce traité je ferai voir plus amplement comment, de cela seulement
que j'ai en moi l'idée d'une chose plus parfaite que moi, il s'ensuit que cette chose
existe véritablement.[30]

Comment: "The same law holds of all truths, then, as of mathematical figures—a circle for instance."[31]

On the question of ideas per se, Descartes declares (and Adams
underlines as follows):

Maintenant, pour ce qui concerne les idées, si on les considère seulement en elles-mêmes et qu'on ne les rapporte point à quelque autre chose, *elles ne peuvent, à propre-ment parler, être fausses; car soit que j'imagine une chèvre ou une chimère, il n'est pas moins vrai que j'imagine l'une que l'autre.*[32]

Adams comments: "As concepts which have no reality 'hors de ma pensée'—all this is as old as Plato and was thrashed out by Abe-lard."[33] Descartes continues:

Quand je dis qu'il me semble que cela m'est enseigné par la nature, *j'entends seule-ment par ce mot de nature une certaine inclination qui me porte à le croire, et non pas une lumière* naturelle qui me fasse connaître que cela est véritable.[34]

This *distinguo*, on the part of Descartes, raises a wrinkle on Adams's forehead; for besides underlining that statement, he puts a ques-tion-mark in the left-hand margin.

Adams's objection grows when Descartes says:

De plus, celle [i.e. l'idée] par laquelle je conçois un Dieu souverain, éternel, infini, immuable, tout connaissant, tout-puissant, et créateur universel de toutes les choses qui sont hors de lui; celle-là, dis-je, *a certainement en soi plus de réalité ob-ective* que celles par qui les substances finies me sont représentées.[35]

Adams: "Comment donc?—ai-je déjà conçu tout ça avec plus de réalité objective etc?"[36]

Remembering his Milton too well, Adams carps at the following passage which he underlines:

Mais, pour imparfaite que soit cette façon d'être par laquelle une chose est objectivement ou par représentation dans l'entendement par son idée, certes on ne peut pas néanmoins dire que cette façon et manière d'être ne soit rien, ni par conséquent que cette idée tire son origine du néant.[37]—The idea of Satan has been and is still as clear as that of God. The argument proves too much. p. 244.[38]

The continuation of the last passage belongs to a series of state-ments by Descartes and remarks on them by Adams, which might be gathered under the rubric of some such title as, "The Gyrations of the Circle."

. . . mais il faut à la fin parvenir à *une première idée dont la cause soit comme un patron ou un original dans lequel toute la réalité ou perfection soit contenue formellement et en effet, qui se rencontre seulement objectivement ou par représentation dans ces idées.*[39]

Comment: "The idea of a circle, therefore, represents a pattern or original circle, objectively existing as a perfect circle."[40] In the right-hand margin of the lines just quoted, Adams writes "188, 321," thus referring us to those pages where he marked certain passages. Accordingly, we proceed to quote these in a footnote below.[41]

. . . Car, encore que j'aie remarqué ci-devant qu'il n'y a que dans les jugements que se puisse rencontrer la vraie et formelle faussetté, *il se peut néanmoins trouver dans les idées une certaine faussetté matérielle*, à savoir, lorsqu'elles représentent ce qui n'est rien comme si c'était quelque chose.[42]

Adams: "A circle, for example? or a triangle? or God? in short objectively altogether?"[43]

Car lorsque je pense que la pierre est une substance ou bien une chose qui de soi est capable d'exister, et que je suis aussi moi-même une substance, quoique *je conçoive bien que je suis une chose qui pense et non étendue.*

(Next to the preceding statement Adams puts a question-mark in the right-hand margin)

et que la pierre au contraire est une chose étendue et qui ne pense point, et qu'ainsi entre ces deux conceptions il se rencontre une notable différence; toutefois elles semblent convenir en ce point qu'elles représentent toutes deux des substances. . . . Pour ce qui est des autres qualités dont les idées des choses corporelles sont composées, à savoir, l'étendue, la figure, la situation, et le mouvement, il est vrai qu'elles ne sont point formellement en moi, puisque je ne suis qu'une chose qui pense; mais parce que *ce sont seulement de certains modes de substance*, et que je suis moi-même une substance, il semble qu'elles puissent être contenues en moi éminemment.[44]

Questions Adams: "Is a circle a mode of substance?"[45]

. . . Et, par conséquent, il faut nécessairement conclure de tout ce que j'ai dit auparavant que Dieu existe; car encore que l'idée de la substance soit en moi de cela même que je suis une *substance, je n'aurais pas néanmoins l'idée d'une substance infinie, moi qui suis un être fini, si elle n'avait été mise en moi par quelque substance qui fût véritablement infinie* . . . comment serait-il possible que je pusse connaître que je doute que je désire, c'est-à-dire qu'il me manque quelque chose et que je ne suis pas tout parfait, *si je n'avais en moi aucune idée d'un être plus parfait que le mien, par la comparaison duquel je connaîtrais les défauts de ma nature?* . . . Et l'on ne peut pas dire que peut-être cette idée de Dieu est matériellement fausse, et par conséquent que je la puis tenir du néant, c'est-à-dire qu'elle peut être en moi pour ce que j'ai du défaut, comme j'ai tantôt dit des idées de la chaleur et d'autres choses semblables; car, au contraire, cette idée étant fort claire et fort distincte et contenant en soi *plus de réalité objective qu'aucune autre* il n'y en a point qui de soi plus vraie, ni qui puisse être moins soupçonnée d'erreur et de faussetté.[46]

Adams's question here is: "Can I not have the idea of a perfect circle without its being put into me by some substance perfectly circular?"[47]

. . . l'être objectif d'une idée ne peut être produit par un être qui existe seulement en puissance, leguel à proprement parler n'est rien, mais seulement par un être formel ou actuel.[48]

Adams: "Then the concept of a circle is due to a formal or actual objective perfect circle?"[49]

Mais peut-être la duquel je dépends n'est pas Dieu, et que je suis produit ou par mes parents, ou par quelques autres causes, moins parfaites que lui? Tant s'en faut, cela ne peut être: car, comme j'ai déjà dit auparavant, *c'est une chose très évidente qu'il doit y avoir pour le moins autant de réalité dans la cause que dans son effet. . . .*[50]

In comment on this, Adams writes: "And the objective perfect circle must have at least as much reality as my mental circle."[51]

Mais il faut nécessairement conclure que *de cela que j'existe et que l'idée d'un Être souverainement parfait, c'est-à-dire de Dieu, est en moi, l'existence de Dieu est très-évidemment démontrée.*[52]

Comment: "The idea of a perfect circle exists in me and therefore proves the existence of the perfect objective circle."[53]

The next comment in this series on the circle is found in the section devoted to the *Premières objections faites par M. Catérus* (pp. 129–137).

Que maintenant Saint Thomas réponde à soi-même et à M. Descartes. Posé, dit-il, que chacun entende que par ce nom Dieu il est signifié ce qui a été dit, à savoir, ce qui est tel que rien de plus grand ne peut être conçu, il ne s'ensuit pas pour cela qu'on entende que la chose qui est signifiée par ce nom soit dans la nature, mais seulement dans l'appréhension de l'entendement. Et on ne peut pas dire qu'elle soit en effet, si on ne demeure d'accord qu'il y a en effet quelque chose tel que rien de plus grand ne peut être conçu; ce que ceux-là nient ouvertement qui disent qu'il n'y a point de Dieu.[54] D'où je réponds aussi en peu de paroles: Encore que l'on demeure d'accord que l'Être souverainement parfait par son propre nom emporte l'existence, néanmoins il ne s'ensuit pas que cette même existence soit dans la nature actuellement quelque chose, mais *seulement qu'avec le concept ou la notion de l'être souverainement parfait, celle de l'existence est inséparablement conjoints.* D'où vous ne pouvez pas inférer que l'existence de Dieu soit actuellement quelque chose, si vous ne supposez que cet Être souverainement parfait existe actuellement; *car pour lors, il contiendra actuellement toutes les perfections,* et celle aussi d'une existence réelle. . . . Trouvez bon maintenant qu'après tant de fatigue je délasse un peu mon esprit. *Ce composé, un Lion existant, enferme essentiellement ces deux parties, à savoir, un lion et l'existence;* car si vous ôtez l'une ou l'autre, ce ne sera plus le même composé. Maintenant Dieu n'a-t-il *pas de toute éternité* connu clairement et distinctement ce composé? Et l'idée de ce composé, en tant que tel, n'enferme-t-elle pas essentiellement l'une et l'autre de ces parties? c'est-à-dire l'existence n'est-elle pas de l'essence de ce composé: Un Lion Existant? *Et néanmoins la distincte connaissance que Dieu en a eue de toute éternité ne fait pas nécessairement que l'une ou l'autre partie de ce corps soit,* si on ne suppose que tout ce composé est actuellement; car alors il enfermera et contiendra en soi toutes ses perfections essentielles, et partant aussi l'existence actuelle.[55]

In comment of all this, Adams remarks:

A perfect idea of a perfect circle includes the objective existence of that circle, otherwise it wants perfection. But its objective existence, in matter, would be imperfection. Hence. . . .[56]

The antiphonal comments of Adams continue through the *Réponses de l'auteur aux premières objections* (pp. 138–153)—i.e. Descartes' answers to Catérus.

". . . en qui est-ce que toute cette réalité ou perfection se pourra ainsi rencontrer, sinon en Dieu réellement existant?"[57] Adams echoes: "Where can the reality or perfection of the idea of the circle be found except in the circle existing in objective reality?"[58]

The following selection underlined by Adams and then followed by his comment is among the *Réponses de l'auteur aux deuxièmes objections* (pp. 160–192).

. . . toute la réalité, ou toute la perfection, qui n'est qu'objectivement dans les idées, doit être formellement ou éminemment dans leurs causes. . . . Et toutefois, en faveur de ceux dont la lumière naturelle est si faible qu'ils ne voient pas que c'est une première notion que "toute la perfection qui est objectivement dans une idée doit être réellement dans quelqu'une de ces causes," je l'ai encore démontré d'une façon plus aisée à concevoir, en montrant que l'esprit qui a cette idée ne peut pas exister par soi-même; et partant je ne vois pas ce que vous pourriez désirer de plus pour donner les mains, ainsi que vous avez promis.[59]

"The whole reality of a perfect circle, which exists only objectively in the idea," says Adams, "exists formally in its cause."[60]—Thus we have come to the end of the "circular" (*sic*!) argument.

We go on to the question of the reality of objective concepts. Says Descartes:

. . . je trouve en moi une infinité d'idées de certaines choses qui ni peuvent pas être estimées un pur néant, quoique peut-être elles n'aient aucune existence hors de ma pensée, et qui ne sont pas feintes par moi, bien qu'il soit en ma liberté de les penser ou de ne les penser pas, mais qui ont leurs vrais et immuables natures. Comme par example, lorsque j'imagine un triangle, *encore qu'il n'y ait peut-être en aucun lieu du monde hors de ma pensée une telle figure, et qu'il n'y en ait jamais eu, il ne laisse pas néanmoins d'y avoir une certaine nature, ou forme, ou essence déterminée de cette figure, laquelle est immuable et éternelle, que je n'ai point inventée et qui ne dépend en aucune façon de mon esprit* . . . je puis former en mon esprit une infinité d'autres figures dont on ne peut avoir le moindre soupçon que jamais elles ne soient tombées sous les sens, et je ne laisse pas toutefois de pouvoir démontrer diverses propriétés touchant leur nature, aussi bien que touchant celle du triangle; *lesquelles, certes, doivent être toutes vraies, puisque je les conçois clairement: et partant, elles sont quelque chose, et non pas un pur néant; car il est très-evident que tout ce qui est vrai est quelque chose, la vérité étant la même chose que l'être*. . . .[61]

Here Adams insists: "But he has repeatedly said the objective conception *must* have reality."[62]

Dieu devrait passer en mon esprit *au moins pour aussi certaine que j'ai estimé jusqu'ici toutes les vérités mathématiques* . . . ayant accoutumé dans toutes les autres choses de faire distinction entre l'existence et l'essence, je me persuade aisément que l'existence peut être séparée de l'essence de Dieu, et qu'ainsi on peut concevoir Dieu comme n'étant pas actuellement. Mais néanmoins, lorsque j'y pense avec plus d'attention, je trouve manifestment que *l'existence ne peut non plus être séparée de l'essence de Dieu que de l'essence d'un triangle rectiligne* la grandeur de ses trois angles égaux à deux droits. . . .[63]

—Adams's observation simply consists of repeating the above-quoted words of Descartes, viz: "encore qu'il n'y ait peut-être en aucun lieu du monde *hors de ma pensée*, une telle figure."[64] The text continues: ". . . la nécessité de l'existence de Dieu, me détermine à avoir cette pensée: car il n'est pas en ma liberté de concevoir un Dieu *sans existence*";[65] Adams echoes: " 'hors de ma pensée'?"[66]

". . . je reconnais en plusieurs façons que cette idée[67] n'est point quelque chose de feint ou d'inventé, dépendant seulement de ma pensée, mais que *c'est l'image d'une vraie et immuable nature*."[68] This raises a question which Adams expresses in French: "comme le triangle? Alors tous les deux existent nécessairement hors de ma pensée et objectivement?"[69] Descartes continues:

. . . car y a-t-il rien de soi plus clair et plus manifeste que de penser qu'il y a un Dieu, *c'est-à-dire un Être souverain et parfait, en l'idée duquel seul l'existence nécessaire* ou éternelle est comprise, et par conséquent qui existe?[70]

Again Adams had a query in French: "La Nature alors? L'énergie? Le Cosmos? Puisque le triangle n'existe pas 'hors de ma pensée'—peut-être."[71]

To Descartes's assertion, *"la certitude et la vérité de toute science dépend de la seule connaissance du vrai Dieu,"* Adams exclaims, "Voilà un cercle! en effet!"[72] This time Adams is really accusing Descartes of circular argument.

Et parce que les idées que je recevais par les sens étaient beaucoup plus vives, plus expresses, et même à leur façon plus distinctes qu'aucunes de celles que je pouvais feindre de moi-même en méditant, ou bien que je trouvais imprimés en ma mémoire

il semblait qu'elles ne pouvaient procéder de mon esprit; de façon qu'il était nécessaire *qu'elles fussent causées en moi par quelques autres choses.* Desquelles choses
n'ayant aucune connaissance, sinon celle que me donnaient ces mêmes idées, il ne
me pouvait venir autre chose en l'esprit sinon que *ces choses-là étaient semblables
aux idées qu'elles causaient.*[73]

Again, using mostly Descartes's own words, Adams asks: "Comment? une odeur, une couleur 'semblables à l'idée qu'elles cau-
sent.' "[74]

To the declaration, *"j'ai une claire et distincte idée de moi-même
en tant que je suis seulement une chose qui pense et non étendu"*[75]
Adams retorts with the question: "Comment sais-je que mon âme
n'est pas 'étendue'? Et 'Pense' doit dire 'raisonner' ou seulement
'être conscient'?"[76] Adams seems to side here with Gassendi.

Descartes's proof of the existence of God may be found briefly
stated in the following words underlined by Adams: ". . . Cette
faculté d'avoir en soi l'idée de Dieu ne pourrait être en nous si
notre esprit était seulement une chose finie. . . ."[77] Comment:
"The faculty of conceiving an infinite straight line could not be in
us if our mind were finite."[78]

Answering the objections of M. Catérus further, Descartes says:
"Voire même j'ajouterai ici de plus, ce que néanmoins je n'ai point
écrit ailleurs, *qu'on ne peut pas seulement aller* jusqu'à une seconde
cause . . ."[79] "Downwards too?" asks Adams. "Then all is God
and there are no secondary causes?"[80]

". . . l'existence nécessaire n'est contenue que dans l'idée seule de
Dieu."[81] Comment: "Then necessary truths which are necessarily
in God have only a possible existence, not a necessary existence."[82]

Et je prétends maintenir que *de cela seul que quelque perfection qui est au-dessus de
moi devient l'objet de mon entendement, en quelque façon que ce soit qu'elle se présente
à lui . . . je puis conclure nécessairement . . . que cette puissance que j'ai de comprendre . . . ne me vient pas de moi-même, et que je l'ai reçue de quelque autre* être
qui est plus parfait que je ne suis.[83]

Adams adds: "The conception of a perfect man must come from a
man who is perfect."[84]

When Descartes undertakes to state flatly, *"toute connaissance
qui peut être rendu douteuse ne doit pas être appelée du nom de
science,"*[85] Adams lashes out in syllogistic style: "All hypothesis
is unscientific. Every generalisation is hypothesis. God is unscientific."[86]

Mais la majeure de mon argument a été telle: 'Ce que clairement et distinctement nous concevons appartenir à la nature de quelque chose, cela peut être dit ou affirmé avec vérité de cette chose! C'est-a-dire, si être animal appartient à l'essence ou à la nature de l'homme, on peut assurer que l'homme est animal; si avoir les trois angles égaux à deux droits appartient à la nature du triangle recti igne, on peut assurer que *le triangle rectiligne* a ses trois angles égaux à deux droits; si exister appartient à la nature de Dieu, on peut assurer que Dieu existe, etc.[87]

To this our commentator adds: "or, that man exists as a species apart from the individual, and the triangle apart from our concept. . . ."[88]

Sooner or later Descartes is confronted with the necessity of defining a *thought* (pensée—italicized in the text). His definition seems to stress the integral and the intuitive aspects of thought.

Par le nom de *pensée*, je comprends tout ce qui est tellement en nous que nous l'apercevons immédiatement par nous-mêmes et en avons une connaissance intérieure: Ainsi *toutes les opérations* de la volonté, de l'entendement, de l'imagination et des sens sont des pensées.[89]

Adams wonders, "or is it not rather, first my consciousness of the operation."[90]

Among the *Axiomes ou notions communes*, Adams underlines the following: ". . . l'immensité même de sa nature [i.e. de Dieu] est la cause ou la raison pour laquelle il n'a besoin d'aucune cause pour exister. . . .[91]

IV. *Toute la réalité* ou perfection qui est *dans une chose se rencontre formellement ou éminemment dans sa cause première et totale.*"[92] Question: "How can mere immensity be anything but a petitio principii?"[93]

Descartes's *Proposition troisième* is stated thus: "L'existence de Dieu est encore démontrée de ce que nous-mêmes qui avons son idée, nous existons.—Démonstration." Then he states: ". . . celui par qui je suis conservé a en soi formellement ou éminemment *tout ce qui est en moi* (par l'axiome quatre)."[94] Skeptically, Adams inquires: "Including animal properties, mental processes? reason? doubts? liberty to do wrong?"[95] Then follows a *Corollaire*[96]— Démonstration:

. . . nous y [i.e. in the third proposition] avons prouvé l'existence de Dieu, parce qu'il est nécessaire qu'il y ait un être qui existe dans lequel *toutes les perfections* dont il y a en nous quelque idée soient contenues formellement ou éminemment. . . . Or, est-il que nous avons en nous l'idée d'une puissance si grande que, par celui-là seul en qui elle réside, non-seulement le ciel et la terre, etc., doivent avoir été créés, mais aussi *toutes les autres choses que nous concevons comme possible* peuvent être produites. . . .[97]

Here Adams reminds us that "The axiom IV speaks of realities *or* perfections, and here also *things*" and he asks, "Is unlimited power to do ill a reality?"[98]

The next question touched upon is one which we recognize today as belonging to the domain of *Semantics*. ". . . l'assemblage qui se fait dans *le raisonnement n'est pas celui des noms, mais bien celui des choses signifiées par les noms*."[99] "Give a man an algebraic formula to work out: does he reason by the symbols or by the things; and what does he know of the 'things'?"[100] asks Adams.

An objection raised to his Third Meditation ran as follows: "Mais l'autre idée du soleil est prise des raisons de l'astronomie, c'est-à-dire de certaines notions qui sont naturellement en moi." To this Descartes replied: "Je réponds derechef que ce qui est dit ici n'être point l'idée du soleil, et qui néanmoins est décrit, *c'est cela même que j'appelle du nom d'idée*."[101] Adams inquires: "Is this the case? Hobbes objects that the idea is not double but single; reason, not concept."[102]

J'ai déjà plusieurs fois remarqué ci-devant que nous n'avons aucune idée de Dieu ni de l'âme; j'ajoute maintenant ni de la substance; car j'avoue bien que la substance, en tant qu'elle est une matière capable de recevoir divers accidents, et qui est sujette à leurs changements, est aperçue et prouvée par le raisonnement; mais *néanmoins elle n'est point conçue, ou nous n'en avons aucune idée*. . . . *Et j'ai suffisamment expliqué* comment la réalité reçoit le plus et le moins, en disant que la substance est quelque chose de plus que le mode et que s'il y a des qualités réelles ou des substances incomplètes, elles sont aussi quelque chose de plus que les modes, mais quelque chose de moins que les substances complètes; et enfin que s'il y a une substance infinie et indépendante, cette substance a plus d'être ou plus de réalité que la substance finie et dépendante.[103]

Adams's comment: "Encore! is it sufficiently explained? Is substance more real than form or energy?"[104]

". . . *il ne suffit pas, pour prouver la création du monde, que nous puissions imaginer le monde créé . . . par le mot d'idée j'entends la forme de toute perception. . . .*"[105] At this point Adams takes logic by the neck and twists it: "Syllogism is a form of reason and a source of ideas—God syllogises?"[106]

. . . dans l'idée d'un être infini, l'infinité de sa durée y est contenue, c'est-à-dire qu'elle n'est renfermée d'aucunes limites, et partant qu'elle est indivisible, permanente et subsistante toute à la fois, et dans laquelle on ne peut sans erreur et qu'improprement, à cause de l'imperfection de notre esprit, concevoir de passé ni d'avenir.[107]

To this Adams remarks: "Admirably reasoned! but what becomes of Descartes's dear and unanimous idea of God? 168."[108]

Among the *Réponses de l'auteur* (i.e., Descartes) *aux cinquièmes objections* (pp. 346–379), Adams underlined as follows:

Ce que vous alléguez ensuite contre les universaux des dialecticiens ne me touche point, puisque je les conçois tout d'une *autre façon qu'eux. Mais pour ce que regarde les essences que nous connaissons clairement et distinctement telles qu'est celle du triangle ou de quelque autre figure de géométrie,* je vous ferai aisément avouer que les idées de celles qui sont en nous n'ont point été tirées des idées des choses singulières; car ce qui vous meut ici à dire qu'elles sont fausses n'est que parce qu'elles ne s'accordent pas avec l'opinion que vous avez conçue de la nature des choses.[109]

Adams's question here is: "What is the difference between a universal and the essence of a universal qua reality?"[110]—It is anent this question that he underlines the text that follows and puts a question-mark beside it in the right-hand margin:—"les figures géométriques ne sont pas considérées comme des substances, *mais seulement comme des termes sous lesquels la substance est contenue.*"[111]

To the allegation, "C'est l'erreur la plus absurde et la plus exorbitante qu'un philosophe puisse admettre, que de vouloir faire des jugements *qui ne se rapportent pas aux perceptions* qu'il a des choses,"[112] Adams poses four questions: "1. What is a perception? 2. Is it a conception? 3. Do I perceive a concept? 4. Do I conceive a percept?"[113] These succinct psychologic questions recall the type of marginalia we find in his copy of William James's *Principles of Psychology.*[114]

. . . Ceux qui admettent des accidents réels, comme *la chaleur, la pesanteur, et semblables, ne doutent point que ces accidents ne puissent agir contre le corps; et toutefois il y a plus de différence entre eux et lui, c'est-à-dire entre des accidents et une substance qu'il n'y a entre deux substances.*[115]

Adams: "These so-called accidents act materially.—Is this meant as an admission that the soul acts in the same way?"[116]

On the positive or negative value of skepticism, the following underlined text and its accompanying marginalium are interesting:

. . . tout le monde sait que celui qui se défie, pendant qu'il se défie et que par conséquent il n'affirme ni ne nie aucune chose, ne peut être induit en erreur par aucun génie, pour rusé qu'il soit. . . .[117]

—"but on the contrary, he *must* be in error, since he, at least, is sure of reaching no truth."[118]

On the fundamental problem of the critical approach to the nature of things (including oneself), Descartes finally resorts to a simile in which he compares thought to a basket of apples.

Si d'aventure [he says] *il avait une corbeille pleine de pommes, et qu'il appréhendât quelques-unes* ne fussent pourries, et qu'il voulût les ôter, de peur qu'elles ne corrompissent le reste, comment s'y prendrait-il pour le faire? Ne commencerait-il pas tout d'abord à vider sa corbeille; et après cela, regardant toutes ces pommes les unes après les autres, ne choisirait-il pas celles-là seules qu'il verrait n'être point gâtées, et, laissant là les autres, ne les remettrait-il pas dans son panier? Tout de même aussi, ceux qui n'ont jamais bien philosophé ont diverses opinions en leur esprit qu'ils ont commencé à y amasser dès leur bas âge; et appréhendant avec raison que la plupart ne soient pas vraies, ils tâchent de les séparer d'avec les autres, de peur que leur mélange ne les rende toutes incertaine.[119]

It is apropos the apple apologue that Adams delivers himself of a quizzical and almost cynical observation: "Assuming first that he does not set out to prove that apples are apples."[120]

In answering the *auteur des Septièmes Objections*, Descartes continues:

Je suis donc un esprit? Il n'est pas vrai non plus que j'aie examiné si j'étais un esprit; car pour lors *je n'avais pas encore expliqué ce que j'entendais par le nom d'esprit* [italicized in text]. Mais j'ai examiné si j'avais en moi quelqu'une des choses que j'attribuais à l'âme dont je venais de faire la description; et, ne trouvant pas en moi toutes les choses que je lui avais attribuées, mais n'y remarquant que la pensée, pour cela je n'ai pas dit que j'étais une âme, mais seulement j'ai dit que j'étais une chose qui pense, *et j'ai donné à cette chose qui pense le nom d'esprit, ou celui d'entendement et de raison*, n'entendant rien de plus par *le nom d'esprit que par celui d'une chose qui pense.* . . .[121]

As if he were trying to unravel a puzzle, by breaking it down into its individual elements, Adams wrote: "Esprit = intelligence = reason = me = something that thinks? Surely there is more or less in these."[122] Descartes resumes: "*Mais s'il feint que j'aie voulu dire par le nom d'esprit quelque chose de plus que par celui d'une chose qui pense, c'est à moi à le nier.*"[123] Adams formulates the whole issue thus: "Alors: Cogito, ergo sum spiritus. Je pense: donc je suis esprit. I think, therefore I am reason."[124]

Apparently weary of answering endlessly his Jesuit opponents, Descartes reflects his weariness in the following:

Mais je suis las de le reprendre de ne pas dire la vérité, que dorénavant je ne ferai pas semblant de le voir, et écouterai seulement sans rien dire le reste de ses railleries jusques à la fin. Quoique pourtant, si c'était un autre que lui, je croirais qu'il se serait voulu déguiser pour satisfaire à l'envie déréglée qu'il aurait eue de railler, et qu'en contrefaisant tantôt le craintif, tantôt le paresseux, et tantôt l'homme de peu de sens, il aurait voulu imiter, non les Epidiques ou les Parménons de l'ancienne Comédie, *mais le plus vil personnage de la nôtre*, qui par ses niaiseries et bouffonneries prend plaisir d'apprêter à rire aux autres.[125]

Adams grins a bit: "The Jesuit father seems to have hit him very hard."[126]

. . . Mais de peur que ceux qui ne font que commencer ne se persuadent que rien ne peut être certain et évident à celui qui doute s'il dort ou s'il veille, mais peut seulement lui sembler et lui paraître, je les prie de se ressouvenir de ce que j'ai ci-devant remarqué sous la cote F; c'est à savoir que ce que l'on conçoit clairement et distinctement, par qui que ce puisse être qu'il *soit ainsi conçu est vrai*. . . .[127]

Adams comments: "That is, the conception is, or exists; but only true as existence. p. 106, 107. Dream is true in that sense."[128]
   Descartes returns to his *apple* analogy:

. . . pour prendre garde que dans un panier *plein de pommes* il n'y en ait quelques-unes qui soient gâtées, il les faut toutes vider du commencement, et n'y en laisser pas une, et puis n'y remettre que celles qu'on aurait reconnues être tout à fait saines.[129]

Adams's final marginalium follows: "plein d'idées de pommes que je veux prouver être pommes réelles."[130]

NOTES

1. *Oeures de Descartes*, new ed. with introduction by Jules Simon, Introduction p. xxiv.
2. Bottom margin, pp. xxx, xxxi.
3. Pp. xxx, xxxi, (note).
4. P. xxxi, bottom margin.
5. P. xxxiv.
6. Pp. xxxiv, xxxv, bottom margin.
7. P. xxxviii.
8. P. lxi.
9. P. xli.
10. *Ibid.*, bottom margin.
11. P. xliii.
12. *Ibid.*, bottom margin.
13. P. lv.
14. *Ibid.*, bottom margin.

15. P. lxii.

16. Sometime between 1899 and 1900 Adams read with great attention *La Conservation de l'énergie* par Balfour Stewart, de la Société royale de Londres. Professeur de philosophie naturelle au collège de Manchester, suivie d'une étude sur la nature de la force par P. De Saint-Robert sixième Ed., Paris. Ancienne Librarie Germer Baillière Et Cie. Félix Alcan, Editeur. 108 Boulevard Saint-Germain 108. 1899. This copy in Adams's collection is full of lineations and marginal notes.

17. P. 22.

18. Apparently Adams had Pascal as well as Descartes in his mind at this time.

19. P. 22, bottom margin.

20. P. 73.

21. *Ibid.*, bottom margin.

22. *Ibid.*, Pp. 75, 76.

23. *Ibid.*, P. 76, bottom margin.

24. P. 79.

25. *Ibid.*, bottom margin.

26. P. 80.

27. *Ibid.*, bottom margin.

28. P. 24.

29. *Ibid.*, bottom margin.

30. P. 59.

31. *Ibid.*, bottom margin.

32. P. 83.

33. *Ibid.*, bottom margin. The Adams Collection has Henry Cary's *The Works of Plato:* A new and literal version, chiefly from the text of Stallbaum. Vol. I containing the Apology of Socrates, Crito, Phaedo, Gorgias, Protagoras, Phaedrus, Thaetetus, Euthyphron, and Lysis. London, 1848; John Llewelyn Davies and David James Vaughan's *The Republic of Plato* translated into English with an analysis and notes by J.L.D. and D.J.V. London, 1898 (Golden Treasury Series). For Abelard items see p. 283, note 16.

34. P. 84.

35. P. 85.

36. *Ibid.*, bottom margin.

37. P. 86.

38. *Ibid.*, bottom margin.

39. P. 87.

40. *Ibid.*, bottom margin.

41. The passage underlined by Adams on p. 188 is section X of the *Axiomes ou notions communes: "Dans l'idée ou le concept de chaque chose, l'existence y est contenue,* parce que nous ne pouvons rien concevoir que sous la forme d'une chose qui existe; mais avec cette différence que, *dans le concept d'une chose limitée, l'existence possible ou contingente est seulement contenue:* et dans le concept d'un Être souverainement parfait, la parfaite et nécessaire y est comprise." After putting an interrogation mark in the left-hand margin, Adams wrote at the bottom of the page this question: "Does or does not this axiom contain the extreme realist doctrine of Univerals?"

The passage on p. 321 is found in the section devoted to the *Objections faites par M. Gassendi contre les six méditations* (pp. 263–346).—"Je remarque seulement que cela semble dur de voir établir quelque nature immuable et éternelle autre que celle d'un Dieu souverain. Vous direz peut-être que vous ne dites rien que ce que l'on

Descartes (Marginalia)

enseigne tous les jours dans les écoles, à savoir, que les natures ou les essences des choses sont éternelles, et que les propositions que l'on en forme sont éternelles, et que les propositions que l'on en forme sont aussi d'une éternelle vérité. Mais cela même est aussi fort dur, et fort difficile à se persuader; et d'aillerus le moyen de comprendre qu'il y ait une nature humaine lorsqu'il n'y a aucun homme, ou que la rose soit une fleur lors même qui n'y a encore point de rose? . . .

Toutefois comment soutiendront-ils que l'essence de l'homme qui est, par exemple, dans Platon, soit éternelle et indépendante de Dieu? En tant qu'elle est universelle diront-ils? Mais il n'y a rien dans Platon que de singulier; et de fait l'entendement a bien de coutume, de toutes les natures semblables qu'il a vu dans Platon, dans Socrate, et dans tous les autres hommes, d'en former *un certain concept commun en quoi ils conviennent tous, et qui peut bien par conséquent être appelé une nature universelle ou l'essence de l'homme.*

42. P. 88.
43. *Ibid.*, bottom margin.
44. P. 89.
45. *Ibid.*, bottom margin.
46. P. 90.
47. *Ibid.*, bottom margin.
48. P. 92.
49. *Ibid.*, bottom margin.
50. P. 93.
51. *Ibid.*, bottom margin. On bottom margin of p. 94, he adds: "And the objective perfect circle must have power to possess all the perfections I conceive for it."
52. P. 95.
53. *Ibid.*, bottom margin.
54. "Posé . . . Dieu" is italicized.
55. Pp. 136, 137.
56. P. 137, bottom margin.
57. P. 140.
58. *Ibid.*, bottom margin.
59. P. 166.
60. *Ibid.*, bottom margin.
61. P. 106.
62. *Ibid.*, bottom margin; Adams italicises the word "must".
63. P. 107.
64. *Ibid.*, bottom margin.
65. P. 108.
66. *Ibid.*, bottom margin.
67. That is, "l'idée de Dieu."
68. P. 109.
69. *Ibid.*, bottom margin.
70. P. 110.
71. *Ibid.*, bottom margin.
72. P. 111, bottom margin.
73. P. 115.
74. *Ibid.*, bottom margin.
75. P. 117. Adams writes the number 337 in the right-hand margin of this text.

The reference is to a passage underlined by Adams which is included in the *Cin-quièmes Objections Faites par M. Cassendi Contre les Six Méditations.* ". . . supposé, comme vous dites, que vous soyez une chose qui n'est point étendue, je nie absolu-ment que vous en puissiez avoir l'idée."

76. P. 117, bottom margin.
77. P. 117.
78. *Ibid.*, bottom margin.
79. P. 141.
80. *Ibid.*, bottom margin.
81. P. 145.
82. *Ibid.*, bottom margin.
83. P. 169.
84. *Ibid.*, bottom margin.
85. P. 170.
86. *Ibid.*, bottom margin.
87. P. 177.
88. *Ibid.*, bottom margin.
89. P. 183.
90. *Ibid.*, bottom margin.
91. P. 187.
92. *Ibid.*
93. *Ibid.*, bottom margin.
94. P. 190.
95. *Ibid.*, bottom margin.
96. P. 191. "Corollaire: Dieu a créé le ciel et la terre, et tout ce qui y est contenu; et outre cela il peut faire toutes les choses que nous concevons clairement, en la manière que nous les concevons."
97. P. 191.
98. *Ibid.*, bottom margin.
99. P. 199.
100. *Ibid.*, bottom margin.
101. P. 204.
102. *Ibid.*, bottom margin.
103. P. 205.
104. *Ibid.*, bottom margin.
105. P. 207.
106. *Ibid.*, bottom margin.
107. P. 227.
108. *Ibid.*, bottom margin. No. 168 refers us back to a passage underlined by Adams, to be found among D's answers to the second set of Objections: ". . . *tous les métaphysiciens s'accordent unanimement dans la description qu'ils font des attributs de Dieu,* au moins de ceux qui peuvent être connus par la seule raison humaine, en telle sorte *qu'il n'y a aucune chose physique ni sensible, aucune chose dont nous ayons une idée si expresse et si palpable, touchant la nature de laquelle il ne* se rencontre chez les philosophes une plus grande diversité *d'opinions qu'il ne s'en rencontre touchant* celle de Dieu." (In the left-hand margin Adams has two cross-references, one to page xxviii the other to page 227. Following is the passage Adams under-lined on page xxvii: "L'idée de Dieu, c'est-à-dire d'un être parfait existant, laisse donc, quoique nécessaire, place à toutes les démonstrations et à toutes les spécula-tions de la métaphysique, depuis le fétichisme indien et la mythologie grecque, jus-

qu'au panthéisme des alexandrins et de Spinoza." This is in the *Introduction* by
Jules Simon).

109. P. 372.
110. *Ibid.*, bottom margin.
111. P. 373.
112. P. 383.
113. *Ibid.*, bottom margin.
114. Cf. Max I. Baym, "William James and Henry Adams," *The New England
Quarterly*, X (December 1937), 717–742; see especially pp. 737–739. James credited
Descartes with having been first to conceive of a completely self-sufficient nervous
mechanism capable of performing complicated and intelligent acts. But he pointed
out that Descartes stopped short of this view in dealing with animals. They were
mere mechanisms; while the higher acts of man were the result of the agency of his
rational soul. (*Principles*, I, 130). On the matter of the continuity of consciousness,
James says that "Cartesians, who hold that the *essence* of the soul is to think, can of
course solve it *a priori*, and explain the appearance of thoughtless intervals either by
lapses in our ordinary memory, or by the sinking of consciousness to a minimal
state, in which perhaps all that it feels is a bare existence which leaves no particulars
behind to be recalled. . . . Locke was the first prominent champion of [the Cartesian view], and the pages in which he attacks the Cartesian belief are as spirited as
any in his Essay. 'Every drowsy nod shakes their doctrine who teach that their soul
is always thinking.' " (*Ibid.*, p. 200). On *The Seat of the Soul* problem, James points
out that Descartes thought that the inextended soul was immediately present to the
pineal gland. (*Ibid.*, p. 214). The last reference to Descartes is found in James's discussion of *Substantialism*. "If we ask what a Substance is, the only answer is that it
is a self-existent being, or one which needs no other subject in which to inhere. At
bottom its only positive determination is Being, and this is something whose
meaning we all realize even though we find it hard to explain. The Soul is moreover an *individual* being. What that is we learn by intuition, by looking in upon
our Self.—The Substantialist view of the Soul was essentially the view of Plato and
Aristotle. It received its completely formal elaboration in the middle ages. It was
believed in by Hobbes, Descartes, Locke, Leibniz, Wolf, Berkeley, and is now de-
fended by the entire modern dualistic or spiritualistic or common-sense school."
(*Ibid.*, p. 344).
115. P. 386.
116. *Ibid.*, bottom margin.
117. P. 473.
118. *Ibid.*, bottom margin.
119. Pp. 475, 476.
120. P. 475, bottom margin.
121. Pp. 477, 478.
122. P. 478, top margin.
123. P. 478.
124. *Ibid.*, bottom margin.
125. Pp. 478, 479.
126. P. 479, bottom margin.
127. P. 480.
128. *Ibid.*, bottom margin. For reference to pp. 106, 107, see earlier comments.
129. P. 481.
130. *Ibid.*, bottom margin.

Appendix IV. Tahiti Items in the Adams Collection

An Account of the Discoveries Made in the South Pacifick Ocean Previous to 1764. Part I. London, 1767.

Annuaire des éstablissements français de l'Océanie, pour 1890. Papeete, April, 1890.

Bougainville, Louis Anotine de. Voyage autour du monde, par la frégate du roi La Boudeuse, et La Flûte l'Étoile; en 1766, 1767, 1768 et 1769. 2d ed., enlarged. 2 vols. Paris, 1772. Maps.

——Voyage de M. Bougainville; contenant le journal d'un voyage autour du monde, fait par MM Banks et Solander, Anglois, en 1768, 1769, 1770, 1771. Traduit de l'anglois par M. de Fréville. Vol. III. Paris, 1793.

Brissot de Warville, Jean Pierre. Nouveau voyage dans les États-Unis de l'Amérique Septentrionale, fait en 1788, par J. P. Brissot (Warville), citoyen françois. 3 vols. Paris, 1791. Autograph signature, "Thomas Dodd."

Brunet, Léon. La Race polynésienne, son origine, sa disparition. Thèse pour le doctorat en médicine. Paris, 1876.

[Cook]. Centenaire de la mort de Cook célébré le 14 février 1879 à l'Hotel de la Société de Géographie. Extrait du bulletin de la Société de Géographie, Mai, 1879. Paris, 1879.

Cuzent, G. L'Archipel des Iles de la Société (l'Annexion de Taïti à la France.) Brest, 1885.

——Tahiti. Recherches sur les principales productions végétales de l'ile. n.p., n.d.

Delessert, Eugène. Voyages dans les deux océans, Atlantique et Pacifique, 1844 à 1848. Brésil, États-Unis, Cap de Bonne-Espérance, Nouvelle-Zélande, Taïti, Philippines, Chine, Java, Indes Orientales, Égypte. Paris, 1848.

Dulaurier, E. Des langues océaniennes considérées sous le rapport ethnographique et philologique. Discours prononcé le 17 décembre, 1849, à l'École Spéciale des Langues Orientales Vivantes. Paris, 1850.

Foley, Antoine-Edouard. Quatre années en Océanie. Paris, 1866.

——Quatre années en Océanie. Histoire naturelle de l'homme et des sociétés qu'il organise. Moeurs et coutumes de certains Papous australiens, anatomie et physiologie du plus arriéré des noirs. Paris, 1876.

Garnier, Jules. La Nouvelle-Calédonie (Côte Orientale). Voyage autour du monde. Paris, 1871.

——Voyage autour du monde. Océanie, les Iles des Pins, Loyalty et Tahiti. Paris, 1871.

Garnot. Notice sur l'Ile de Taïti. Académie Ébroïcienne. Louviers, 1836.

Gaussin, P. L. J. B. Du dialecte de Tahiti, de celui des Iles Marquises, et, en général, de la langue polynésienne. Paris, 1853.

Gerstäcker, Friedrich. Tahiti. Roman aus der Südsee. Gesammelte Schriften, Vol. XIX: Volks-und-Familien-Ausgabe. 4th ed. Jena, n.d.

Jacolliot, Louis. La Vérité sur Taïti (Affaire de la Roncière). Paris, 1869.

Jaussen, Tepano, Mgr. L'Ile de Paques: historique-écriture et répertoire des signes des tablettes ou bois d'hibiscus intelligents. Ouvrage posthume rédigé par le R.—P. Idelfonse Alazard. Paris, 1893.

Lang, John Dunmore, D.D., A.M. Origin and Migrations of the Polynesian Nation. 2d ed. greatly extended and improved. Sydney, Melbourne, and Adelaide, 1877.

Lutteroth, Henri. O—Taïti. Histoire et enquête. Paris, 1845.

Monchoisy. La Nouvelle Cythère. Paris, 1888.

Moerenhout, J. A. Voyage aux îles du grand océan contenant des documents nouveaux sur la géographie physique et politique, la langue, la littérature, la religion, les moeurs, les usages et les coutumes de leurs habitants. Paris, 1837.

Prat, E. Topographie médicale de l'ile de Taïti (Océanie). Considérations générales sur les affections dominantes, principalement envisagées au double point de vue itéologique et théropeutique. Relations sommaires sur quelques cas chirurgicaux avec déductions pathologiques. Toulon, 1869.

Rienzi, G. L. Domeny. Océanie au cinquième partie du monde. Revue géographique et ethnographique de la Malaisie de la Muronésie, de la Polynésie, et de la Malanésie. Paris, 1836, 1837.

Taïti. Combat de Mahabéna (17 Avril 1844). In *Revue Coloniale*, October, 1844.

Taufapulotu, Grégoire. La Langue de l'Archipel Toga. Textes inédits du chef Grégoire Taufapulotu, avec traduction par un missionnaire mariste (P. Roulliaux). Paris, 1887.

Thomson, William J. The Pito Te Henua, or Easter Island. Washington, 1891. (Smithsonian Institution, National Museum.)

[Vason, George]. An Authentic Narrative of Four Years' Residence at Tongataboo, One of the Friendly Islands in the South Sea by——Who Went Thither in the Duff, under Captain Wilson, in 1796. With an Appendix. London, 1810. [The name of the author is written in by Henry Adams after the word "by."]

Bibliography

THE FOLLOWING LIST does not repeat items in the Appendices, but gives the books most frequently cited or quoted.

MANUSCRIPT MATERIAL

Adams, Brooks. ALS, to Henry Vignaud, Jan. 30, 1898. Ann Arbor, Michigan: Clements Library.

Adams, Henry. Holograph catalogue of his books, dated 1858. Boston: Massachusetts Historical Society.

——Charge books at Harvard College Archives, 1854–58; 1870–76. Henry Adams's charges.

——Black notebook full of notes and citations in French for a Study of Toussaint l'Ouverture. Boston: Massachusetts Historical Society.

——Black notebook of expense-account in Yokohama, containing part of Sonnet by Alfred de Musset. Boston: Massachusetts Historical Society.

——Unpublished letters to Henry Vignaud. Ann Arbor, Michigan: Clements Library.

——Transcripts of *Affaires étrangères*. Washington: Library of Congress.

——Marginalia in his books (*passim*). Boston: Massachusetts Historical Society.

Bishop, William Wallace. Unpublished letter to the late President Leroy Burton of the University of Michigan, Ann Arbor, December 29, 1922. Details of purchase of Vignaud Collection.

Hitt, R. R. Unpublished letter to the Minister of the Marine. National Archives: Records of the Department of State, Diplomatic Posts, France, Press Copies of Miscellaneous Correspondence sent, August 9, 1879, to May 21, 1880, pp. 120-121.

Vignaud, Henry. Unpublished letter to Henry Adams. National Archives: Records of the Dept. of State, Diplomatic Posts, France, Press Copies of Miscellaneous Correspondence sent, May 21, 1880, to March 17, 1881, pp. 119, 120.

GENERAL BIBLIOGRAPHY

Adams, Brooks. The Law of Civilization and Decay; an Essay in History. London, S. Sonnenchein and Co., Ltd.; New York, The Macmillan Co., 1895.

Adams, Charles Francis, Jr. An Autobiography. Boston, Massachusetts Historical Society, 1916.

——Charles Francis Adams. Boston and New York, Houghton Mifflin Co., 1900.

Adams, Charles Francis, Jr., and Henry Adams. Chapters of Erie and Other Essays. Boston, James R. Osgood and Co., 1871.

Adams, Henry. "Coulanges' Ancient City." *North American Review*, CXVIII (April, 1874), 390–397.

——"Count Edward de Crillon." *American Historical Review*, I (October, 1895), 51–69.

——A Cycle of Adams Letters, 1861–65. Ed. Worthington Chauncey Ford. 2 vols. Boston and New York, Houghton Mifflin Co., 1920.

——The Degradation of the Democratic Dogma. With an Introduction by Brooks Adams. New York, The Macmillan Co., 1919.

——Democracy; an American Novel. New York, Henry Holt

and Co., 1880. (Published in French as *Démocratie; roman américain*, Paris, Plon, 1883.)

——The Education of Henry Adams. Privately printed, Washington, 1907. (Reprinted with Introduction by James Truslow Adams, Modern Library, 1931. Published in French as *Mon éducation*, tr. by R. Michaud and F. Schoell; Paris, Boivin et Cie. The copy at the Mass. Hist. Soc. is inscribed, "For the Henry Adams Library in the Massachusetts Historical Society from Worthington C. Ford, Paris, December, 1938.")

——Esther: a Novel. By Frances Snow Compton, pseud. New York, Henry Holt and Co., 1884. (Reprinted with an Introduction by Robert E. Spiller, New York, Scholars' Facsimiles and Reprints, 1938.)

——"Freeman's Historical Essays." *North American Review*, CXIV (January, 1872), 193–196.

——"Freeman's History of the Norman Conquest." *North American Review*, CXVIII (January, 1874), 176–181.

——"Harvard College." *North American Review*, CXIV (January, 1872), 110–147.

——Henry Adams and His Friends: a Collection of His Unpublished Letters. Comp., with biographical introduction, by Harold Dean Cater. Boston, Houghton Mifflin Co., 1947.

——Historical Essays. New York, Scribner's Sons, 1891.

——History of the United States of America during the First Administration of James Madison. 2 vols. New York, Scribner's Sons, 1890.

——History of the United States of America during the Second Administration of James Madison. 3 vols. New York, Scribner's Sons, 1891.

——History of the United States of America during the First Administration of Thomas Jefferson. 2 vols. New York, Scribner's Sons, 1889.

——History of the United States of America during the Second Administration of Thomas Jefferson. 2 vols. New York, Scribner's Sons, 1890.

——John Randolph. Boston, Houghton Mifflin Co., 1882.

——"ΚΑΤΟΙΗΣΙΣ ΚΕΙΛΕΙΑ." *Harvard Magazine*, III (December, 1857), 397–405.

——"Kitchen's History of France." *North American Review*, CXIX (October, 1874), 442–447.

——A Letter to American Teachers of History. Privately printed, Baltimore, J. H. Furst and Co., 1910.

——Letters, 1858–1891. Ed. Worthington Chauncey Ford. Boston and New York, Houghton Mifflin Co., 1930.

——Letters, 1892–1918. Ed. Worthington Chauncey Ford. Boston and New York, Houghton Mifflin Co., 1938.

——Letters to a Niece and Prayer to the Virgin of Chartres. With a Niece's Memories, by Mabel La Farge. Boston and New York, Houghton Mifflin Co., 1920.

——The Life of Albert Gallatin. Philadelphia, J. P. Lippincott, 1879.

——The Life of George Cabot Lodge. Boston, Houghton Mifflin Co., 1911.

——Memoirs of Marau Taaroa, Last Queen of Tahiti. Privately printed, n.p., 1893.

——Mont-Saint-Michel and Chartres. Privately printed, Washington, 1904. (Reprinted with Introduction by Ralph Adams Cram, Boston and New York, Houghton Mifflin Co.. 1913.)

——"Napoléon Ier à Saint Domingue." *La Revue Historique* (Paris), XXIV (April, 1884), 92–130.

——"Reading in College." *The Harvard Magazine*, III (October, 1857), 307–317.

——Syllabus, History II: Political History of Europe from the 10th to the 15th Century. Archives, Harvard College Library, 1874.

——"The Tendency of History." *American Historical Association Report for 1894* (Washington, 1895), pp. 17–23.

——Travels in Tahiti. Paris, 1901. (Reprinted, with Introduction by Robert E. Spiller, New York, Scholars' Facsimiles and Reprints, 1947.)

——ed. Documents Relating to New England Federalism, 1800–1815. Boston, Little, Brown and Co., 1877.

——ed. and tr. Memoirs of Arii Taimai E, Marama of Eimeo, Teriirere of Tooarai, Terrinui of Tahiti, Tauraatua I Amo. Paris, 1901.

Adams, James Truslow. Henry Adams. New York, A. and C. Boni, Inc., 1933. (Bibliography, pp. 211–229.)

Adams, John. John Adams's Book, Being Notes on a Record of Births, Marriages and Deaths of Three Generations of the Adams Family, 1734–1807. Comp. Henry Adams II. Privately printed, Boston Athenaeum, 1934.

——Correspondence with Benjamin Waterhouse, 1784–1822. Ed. Worthington Chauncey Ford. Boston, Little, Brown and Co., 1927.

——Correspondence with Thomas Jefferson, 1812–1826. Selected with Comment by Paul Wilstach. Indianapolis, the Bobbs-Merrill Co., 1925.

——Works. With a Life of the Author, and Notes and Illustrations, by His Grandson Charles Francis Adams. 10 vols. Boston, Little, Brown and Co., 1851–1866.

Adams, John Quincy. A Catalogue of the Books of J.Q.A. deposited in the Boston Athenaeum. With notes on books, Adams seals and book plates by Henry Adams, and an introduction by Worthington Chauncey Ford. Boston Athenaeum, 1938.

——Life in a New England Town: 1787, 1788, Diary of John Quincy Adams while a student in the offices of Theophilus Parson at Newburyport, Preface by Charles Francis Adams. Boston, Little, Brown and Co., 1903.

——Memoirs of John Quincy Adams, comprising portions of his Diary from 1795 to 1848. Edited by Charles Francis Adams. Philadelphia, J. B. Lippincott and Co., 1874–1877, 12 vols.

——Report of the Secretary of State upon Weights and Measures, Printed by order of the Senate of the United States. Washington, Gales and Seaton, 1821.

——Writings. 7 vols. Ed. Worthington Chauncey Ford. New York, Macmillan Co., 1913–17.

Adams, Marian. The Letters of Mrs. Henry Adams, 1865–1883. Ed. Ward Thoron. Boston, Little, Brown and Co., 1936.

Adams, Randolph Greenfield. Three Americanists. Philadelphia, University of Pennsylvania Press, 1939.

Arnold, Matthew. Essays in Criticism. London, Macmillan, 1883.

——Notebooks. With a Preface by the Honorable Mrs. Wodehouse and a portrait. New York, Macmillan Co., 1902.

Arnoult, Émile. Pinney [Norman] and Arnoult's French Grammar, with the pronunciation of all the words. New York, Mason Bros., 1861.

Atlantic Monthly. Boston, 1857–1900.

Augustin, Saint. Les Confessions de Saint Augustin. Traduction française d'Arnauld d'Andilly très soigneusement revue et adaptée pour la première fois au texte latin. Avec une Introduction par M. Charpentier, Inspecteur honoraire de l'Académie de Paris. Agrégé à la Faculté des Lettres, Paris, Garnier Frères, n.d.

Aulard, François Alphonse. Taine, historien de la révolution française. Paris, A. Colin, 1907.

Bacon, Francis. The Works of Francis Bacon. Collected and edited by James Spedding, M.A. of Trinity College, Cambridge. Cambridge, London, Boston, Brown and Taggard, 1858–1868.

Baldensperger, Fernand. "Les sources d'un Américain attardé." *Le Correspondant* (Paris, 1920), pp. 1040–1062.

Baym, Max I. "Baudelaire and Shakespeare." *Shakespeare Association Bulletin*, XV, No. 3 (July, 1940), 131–148; No. 4 (October, 1940), 195–205.

——"The 1858 Catalogue of Henry Adams's Library." *Colophon*, III, n.s., No. 4 (Autumn, 1938), 483–489.

——"Emma Lazarus and Renan." *Publications of the American Jewish Historical Society* XXXVII (New York, 1948), 17–29.

——"Henry Adams and Henry Vignaud." *The New England Quarterly*, XVII, No. 3 (September, 1944), 442–449.

——"Henry Adams and the Critics." *The American Scholar*, XV, No. 1 (Winter 1945–46), 79–89.

——"Recurrent Poetic Theme." *The Shakespeare Association Bulletin*, XII, No. 3 (July 1937), 155–158.

——"William James and Henry Adams." *The New England Quarterly*, Norwood, X, No. 4 (December, 1937), 717–742.

Becker, Carl Lotus. "The Education of Henry Adams." *American Historical Review*, Lancaster, XXIV (1918-19), 422–434.

Bouillier, Francisque Cyrille. Histoire de la philosophie cartésienne. 2 vols. Paris, Ch. Delagrave et Cie., 1868.

Bourget, Paul. Essais de psychologie contemporaine. Paris, 1885.

——In Studies in European Literature. Oxford, 1900.

Bowen, Francis. The Principles of Metaphysical and Ethical Science Applied to the Evidences of Religion. Boston, Brewer and Tileston, 1855.

——Modern Philosophy, from Descartes to Schopenhauer and Hartmann. 4th ed. New York, C. Scribner's Sons, 1877.

Brandes, Georg. Main Currents in 19th Century Literature. 6 vols. New York, Macmillan, 1901–1905.

Brooks, Van Wyck. The Flowering of New England, 1815–1865. New York, Dutton and Co., 1936.

Brown, Horatio F. John Addington Symonds, a Biography Compiled from His Papers and Correspondence, with Portraits and Other Illustrations. 2 vols. London, John C. Nimmo, 1895.

Brown, Ralph H. "American Opinion on Ernest Renan, 1863–1892." M.A. thesis, Columbia University, May, 1938.

Buckle, Henry Thomas. History of Civilization in England. 2 vols. New York, D. Appleton and Co., 1901. (From the 2d London ed.)

Byron, Lord. "Childe Harold." In his Poetical Works. Oxford University Press, 1914.

Cameron, Kenneth Walter. Ralph Waldo Emerson's Reading. Raleigh, N. C., The Thistle Press, 1941.

Canat, René. Une forme du mal du siècle: du sentiment de la solitude morale chez les romantiques et les parnassiens. Paris, 1904.

Carbonel, Abbé P. Histoire de la philosophie depuis les temps les plus reculés jusqu'à nos jours, ouvrage destiné à compléter les Excerpta Philosophica D. Thomae. 2d ed., rev. and enld. Avignon, 1886; 2d ed. Paris, 1882.

Cargill, Oscar. "The Mediaevalism of Henry Adams." In *Essays and Studies in Honor of Carleton Brown*, pp. 296–329. New York, New York University Press, 1940.

Carré, Jean-Marie. Michelet et son temps, avec de nombreux documents inédits. Paris, 1926.

——R. L. Stevenson et la France. Extrait des Mélanges Baldensperger. Paris, H. Champion, 1930.

Carrère, Jean. Les Mauvais Maîtres. Paris, 1904.

Chateaubriand, François René. Voyages en Amérique, en Italie, au Mont Blanc. New ed. Paris, 1873.

[Chavannes de la Giraudière, L. de]. L'Amérique délivrée, esquisse d'un poème sur l'indépendance de l'Amérique, avec Epître dédicatoire à M. John Adams. Amsterdam, J. A. Crajenschot, 1783.

Chevrillon, André. Taine, formation de sa pensée. Paris, Plon, 1932.

Chinard, Gilbert. L'Amérique et le rêve exotique dans la littérature française au XVIIᵉ et au XVIIIᵉ siècle. Paris, Hachette et Cie., 1913.

——Honest John Adams. Boston, Little, Brown, and Co., 1933.

Coleridge, Samuel Taylor. Biographia Literaria. Ed., with his Aesthetical Essays, by J. Shawcross. Oxford, The Clarendon Press, 1907.

Coolidge, Thomas Jefferson. Thomas Jefferson Coolidge, 1831–1920: an Autobiography. Boston, Massachusetts Historical Society, 1923.

Cournos, John. A Modern Plutarch. New York, Bobbs-Merrill Co., 1928.

Damon, Samuel Foster. Amy Lowell. New York, Houghton Mifflin Co., 1935.

Descartes, René. Oeuvres de Descartes. Nouvelle édition, collationée sur les meilleurs textes et précédée d'une introduction par M. Jules Simon de l'Académie Française. Discours sur la méthode, Méditations, Traité des passions. Paris, Bibliothèque Charpentier, Eugène Fasquelle Editeur, n.d. (Identical with editions of 1850 and 1868.)

Diderot, Denis. Jacques le fataliste et son maître, avec une préface et des notes par Louis Asseline et André Lefèvre. Paris, G. Charpentier et Cie., 1885.

——Supplément au Voyage de Bougainville, publié d'après le manuscrit de Léningrad avec une Introduction et des notes par Gilbert Chinard. Baltimore, Johns Hopkins; London, Oxford University Press, 1935.

Eastwood, Dorothy Margaret. The Revival of Pascal. London, Oxford University Press, 1936.

Eliot, George. George Eliot's Life as Related in Her Letters and Journals. Arranged and edited by her husband, J. W. Cross. 3 vols. Edinburgh and London, 1885.

Emerson, Ralph Waldo. Journals. Ed. E. W. Emerson. 10 vols. Boston, Houghton Co., 1909.

——Works. In one volume. New York, Walter J. Black, Inc., n.d.

Espinasse, Francis. Life of Renan. London, Scott Co., 1895.

Faguet, Émile. Dix-neuvième siècle. Paris, B. Grasset, 1887.

Fairchild, Hoxie. The Romantic Quest. New York, Columbia University Press, 1931.

Fischer, Kuno. History of Modern Philosophy (Descartes and His School). Tr. J. P. Gordy; Ed. Noah Porter. New York, C. Scribner's Sons, 1887.

Fiske, John. Classroom Taine. New York, Holt and Williams, 1872.

——Letters of John Fiske. Ed. Ethel F. Fisk. New York, The Macmillan Co., 1940.

——Outlines of Cosmic Philosophy. Boston, J. R. Osgood and Co., 1875. (Vol. I.)

——The Unseen World, and Other Essays. Boston, Houghton, 1876.

Flaubert, Gustave. Correspondance, 1830–1880. 4 vols. Paris, 1889–1893.

——Madame Bovary. Moeurs de province. Ed. déf. suivies des réquisitoire, plaidoirie et jugement du procès intenté à l'auteur devant le Tribunal Correctionnel de Paris. Audiences des 31 janvier et 7 février, 1857. Paris, 1891.

Foster, John Watson. Diplomatic Memoirs. 2 vols. Boston, Houghton, 1909.

Fouillée, Alfred. Histoire de la philosophie. 6th ed. Paris, 1891.

——Le Mouvement idéaliste et la réaction contre la science positive. Paris, 1896.

Freeman, Edward Augustus. History of the Norman Conquest. 3d ed. 6 vols. London, Oxford University Press, 1877.

Friedman, Lee M. Zola and the Dreyfus Case: His Defense of Liberty and Its Enduring Significance. Boston, The Beacon Press, Inc., 1937.

Fromentin, Eugène. Les Maîtres d'autrefois. Paris, E. Plon et Cie., 1876.

The Galaxy. New York, January-June, 1867.

Gastinel, Pierre. Romantisme d'Alfred de Musset. Paris, n.d.

Gibbon, Edward. Autobiography. As originally edited by Lord Sheffield, with an introduction by J. B. Bury. London, Oxford University Press, n.d.

Gide, André. Prétextes. Paris, Mercure de France, 1923.

Giraud, Victor. Essai sur Taine: son oeuvre et son influence, d'après des documents inédits, avec des extraits de quarante articles de Taine, non recueillis dans ses oeuvres. 2d ed. Paris, Hachette, 1901.

Gooch, George Peabody. History and Historians in the Nineteenth Century. London, Longmans, Green and Co., 1928.

Gosse, Edmund William. Life of Algernon C. Swinburne. London, W. Heinemann, 1917.

Guérin, Maurice de. Journal, lettres et poèmes publiés avec l'assentiment de sa famille par G. S. Trébutien, et précédés d'une étude biographique et littéraire par M. Sainte-Beuve. 12th ed. Paris, 1868.

Halphen, Louis. L'Histoire en France depuis cent ans. Paris, 1914.

Harrisse, Henry. "M. Ernest Renan: a Biographical Essay." Introduction to Renan's *Studies of Religious History and Criticism*, tr. O. B. Frothingham. New York, Carleton, 1864. (The Introduction is signed H.H.)

Harvard College Catalogues, 1854–1858, 1870–1878.

Harvard Magazine, Vol. III, 1855–1858.

The Harvard University Catalogue of Officers and Students, 1871–1872.

Hauréau, Barthélémmy. De la philosophie scolastique. 2 vols. Paris, 1850.

Hawkins, Richmond Laurin. Auguste Comte and the United States, 1816-1853. Cambridge, Mass., Harvard University Press, 1936.

Hearn, Lafcadio. Exotics and Retrospectives. Boston, Little, Brown, and Co., 1898.

——Literary Essays. Ed. Ichiro Nishizaki. Tokyo, The Hoku sei do Press, 1939.

Holmes-Pollock Letters. See Howe, Mark De Wolfe.

Hooker, Kenneth Ward. The Fortunes of Victor Hugo in England. New York, Columbia University Press, 1938.

Housatonic [William Henry Smith]. A Case of Hereditary Bias: Henry Adams as an Historian . . . New York, 1891.

Howe, Mark De Wolfe, ed. Holmes-Pollock Letters: the Correspondence of Mr. Justice Holmes and Sir Frederick Pollock, 1874–1932. With an Introduction by John Gorham Palfrey. 2 vols. Cambridge, Mass., Harvard University Press, 1941.

Hugo, Victor. La Légende des siècles. Édition ne varietur. Paris, L. Hachette et Cie., 1865.

——Les Châtiments. Paris, 1882.

——William Shakespeare. Paris, 1864.

Huysmans, Joris-Karl. The Cathedral. Tr. Clare Bell, and ed. with a prefatory note by Kegan Paul. London, K. Paul, Trench, Trübner and Co., 1898. (French translation, *La Cathédrale*, Paris, A. Blaizot, 1909.)

James, William. A Pluralistic Universe. New York, Longmans, Green and Co., 1909.

——The Principles of Psychology. 2 vols. New York, Henry Holt and Co., 1902.

——The Will to Believe, and Other Essays in Popular Philosophy. New York, Longmans, Green and Co., 1917.

[Jervis, William Henley P.] Student's History of France. New York, Harper and Bros., c. 1872. (Author's name does not appear on the title page.)

Jones, Howard Mumford. America and French Culture, 1750–1848. Chapel Hill, N. C., University of North Carolina Press, 1927.

Jourdain, Charles. La Philosophie de Saint Thomas d'Aquin. 2 vols. Paris, 1858.

Jusserand, J. J. Histoire littéraire du peuple anglais, . . . 2d ed. 2 vols. Paris, 1896.

Kelso, Alexander P. Matthew Arnold on Continental Life and

Literature. London, Oxford University Press, 1914. (The Matthew Arnold Memorial Prize Essay, 1913.)

Lanson, G., and Paul Tuffran. Manuel d'histoire de la littérature française. Paris and Boston, 1938.

La Rochefoucauld, Duc de. Maximes du Duc de la Rochefoucauld, précédées d'une notice sur sa vie par Suard. (Also contains "Pensées diverses de Montesquieu" and "Oeuvres choisies de Vauvenargues".) Paris, n.d.

Lavrin, Janko. Romantic Types. New York, Dutton, 1927.

Le Breton, Maurice. "Henry Adams et la France." In *Harvard et la France*, pp. 74–96. Paris, 1936.

Leconte de Lisle. Poèmes antiques. Paris, 1852.

Leland, Waldo. "Henry Vignaud." In *Dictionary of American Biography*.

Lemaître, Jules. Les Contemporains . . . 4th ed. Paris, 1896.

Lewes, George Henry. A Biographical History of Philosophy. 2 vols. London, 1852.

Lewisohn, Ludwig. The Story of American Literature. New York, Modern Library, 1939.

Long, O. W. Frederic Henry Hedge, a Cosmopolitan Scholar. Portland, Me., The Southworth-Anthoensen Press, 1940.

Loti, Pierre. Madame Chrysanthème. Dessins et aquarelles de Rossi et Myrbach. Paris, Gravure de Guillaume Frères, 1888.

Lowell, Amy. John Keats. 2 vols. Boston and New York, Houghton Mifflin Co., 1925.

Mallarmé, Stéphane. Vers et prose; morceaux choisis. 2d ed. Paris, 1893.

——"La Musique et les lettres." In *Studies in European Literature*, Oxford, 1900.

Mandelbaum, Maurice. Problem of Historical Knowledge. New York, Liveright, 1938.

Mann, Klaus. André Gide and the Crisis of Modern Thought. New York, Creative Age Press, 1943.

Maudsley, Henry. Body and Will. New York, D. Appleton and Co., 1884.

Maumus, Le R. P. (Elisée-Vincent des Frères-Prêcheurs). Thomas

D'Aquin et la philosophie cartésienne; études de doctrines comparées. 2 vols. Paris, 1890.

McCabe, Joseph. Peter Abelard. New York, G. P. Putnam's Sons, 1901.

Mead, George H. Movements of Thought in the Nineteenth Century. Ed. Merritt H. Moore. Chicago, University of Chicago Press, 1936.

Mémorial diplomatique. Paris, 1863 *et seq.*

Meredith, George. Letters of George Meredith. Collected and edited by his son. 2 vols.: Vol. I, 1844–1881; Vol. II, 1882–1909. New York, Scribner's Sons, 1912.

Mérimée, Prosper. Lettres à une inconnue; précédées d'une étude sur Mérimée par H. Taine. 3d ed. 2 vols. Paris, 1889.

Merz, John Theodore. A History of European Thought in the Nineteenth Century. 4 vols. Edinburgh and London, W. Blackwood and Sons, 1903–1914.

Michaud, Régis. "Un amateur de décadence: Henry Adams." In *Autour d'Emerson.* Paris, Bossard, 1924.

Mill, John Stuart. Autobiography. With an appendix of hitherto unpublished speeches and a preface by Harold J. Laski. London, Oxford University Press, 1924.

——Dissertations and Discussions. 3 vols. New York, H. Holt and Co., 1874.

Moerenhout, Jacques Antoine. Voyages aux îles du grand océan. 2 vols. Paris, 1837.

Monod, Gabriel. "Du progrès des études historiques en France depuis le XVIᵉ siècle." *Revue Historique,* Vol. II, 1876.

——Renan, Taine, Michelet. 3d ed. Paris, 1895.

——La Vie et la pensée de Jules Michelet, 1798–1852. Cours professée au Collège de France. 2 vols. Paris, 1923.

Montaigne, Michel de. Essais Suivis de sa *Correspondance* et de la *Servitude volontaire* de la Boëtie. Édition variorum, accompagnée d'une notice bibliographique, de notes historiques, philologiques, etc. et d'un index analytique, par Charles Louandre. 4 vols. Paris, Charpentier, n.d.

——Textes choisis et commentés par Pierre Villey. Paris, 1912.

Montessus, F.-B. de. Martyrologie et biographie de Commerson:

Médicin, botaniste et naturaliste du Roi, médecin de Toulon-sur-Arroux (Saône-Loire) au XVIIIe siècle. Châlon-sur-Saône, 1889.

More, Paul Elmer. "Henry Adams." *Unpopular Review* (New York), X (July-December, 1918), 255–272.

Morison, Samuel Eliot. Admiral of the Ocean Sea. Boston, Little, Brown and Co., 1942.

——ed. The Development of Harvard University since the Inauguration of President Eliot, 1869–1929. Cambridge, Mass., Harvard University Press, 1930.

Morley, John. Diderot and the Encyclopaedists. 2 vols. London, Macmillan and Co., 1886.

——Life of William Ewart Gladstone. 3 vols. New York, The Macmillan Co., 1903.

Mumford, Lewis. The Golden Day. New York, W. W. Norton and Co., 1933.

Musset, Alfred de. Comédies et proverbes. Seule édition complète revue et corrigée par l'auteur. 2 vols. Paris, Charpentier, 1859. Vol. I.

——Confession d'un Enfant du siècle. Paris, G. Charpentier, 1887.

——Oeuvres complètes. Éd. ornée de 28 gravures d'après les dessins de M. Bida d'un portrait gravé par M. Flameng d'après l'original de M. Landelle et accompagnée d'une notice sur Alfred de Musset par son frère. 6 vols. Paris, 1866.

——Oeuvres completes. 6 vols. Paris, 1877.

Nordau, Max. Degeneration. New York, D. Appleton and Co., 1895.

——The Interpretation of History. New York, Willey Book Co., 1910.

North American Review. 1815–1878.

Norton, Charles Eliot. Letters of Charles Eliot Norton; with biographical comment by his daughter Sara Norton and M. A. De Wolfe Howe. 2 vols. Boston and New York, Houghton Mifflin Co., 1913.

Nuhn, Ferner. The Wind Blew from the East. New York, Harper and Bros., 1942.

Paris, Gaston. Histoire poétique de Charlemagne. Reproduction de l'édition de 1865 augmentée de notes nouvelles par l'auteur et par M. Paul Meyer et d'une table alphabétique des matières. Paris, 1905.

——La Littérature française au moyen-âge (XIᵉ-XIVᵉ siècles). Paris, 1888.

——La Poésie du moyen-âge. Paris, 1905.

Parrington, Vernon Louis. Main Currents in American Thought. 2 vols. New York, Harcourt, Brace and Co., 1927, 1930.

Pascal, Blaise. Pensées de Pascal sur la religion et sur quelques autres sujets. Nouvelle édition conforme au véritable texte de l'auteur et contenant les additions de Port-Royal, indiquées par des crochets. Paris, Garnier Frères, [1866].

Pater, Walter. Marius the Epicurean. New York, The Macmillan Co., 1898; new ed., London, 1924.

——"Prosper Mérimée." In *Studies in European Literature*, Oxford, 1900.

——The Renaissance. New York, Modern Library, 1924.

Perry, Ralph Barton. The Thought and Character of William James. 2 vols. Boston, Little, Brown and Co., 1935.

Plato. The Republic. Tr. into English with an analysis and notes by John Llewelyn Davies and David James Vaughan. London, 1898. (The Golden Treasury Series.)

——Works: a New and Literal Version, chiefly from the Text of Stallbaum. London, 1848.

Pollock, Frederick. "Some Recollections of Ernest Renan." *The Nineteenth Century*, Vol. XXXII, 1892.

Prescott, William Hickling. The Correspondence of William Hickling Prescott, 1833-1847. Transcribed and edited by Roger Wolcott. Boston and New York, Houghton Mifflin Co., 1925.

Rand, Benjamin. "Philosophical Instruction in Harvard University from 1636 to 1900." *The Harvard Graduate Magazine*, September, 1928.

Reid, T. Wemyss. The Life, Letters and Friendships of Richard Monckton Milnes, First Lord Houghton. 2 vols. London, Cassell and Co., 1890.

Rémusat, Charles de. Abélard. 2 vols. Paris, 1845.

Renaissance Louisianaise, La. 1861, 1862.

Renan, Ernest. L'Antéchrist. 2d ed. Paris, 1873.

——Les Apôtres. Paris, Michel Lévy Frères, 1866.

——Avenir de la science. 8th ed. Paris, 1894.

——Averroès et l'averroïsme. Paris, 1882.

——Caliban. Paris, 1878.

——Catalogue de la bibliothèque de M. Ernest Renan. Paris, Calmann-Lévy, 1895.

——Conférences d'Angleterre. Paris, 1897.

——Correspondance. 2 vols. Vol. I, 1846–1871; Vol. II, 1872–1892. Paris, Calmann-Lévy, 1898.

——Correspondance (E. Renan et M. Berthelot), 1847–1892. 2d ed. Paris, Calmann-Lévy, 1898.

——Dialogues et fragments philosophiques. Paris, Calmann-Lévy, 1876.

——Feuilles détachées. Faisant suite aux *Souvenirs d'enfance et de jeunesse*. Paris, Calmann-Lévy, 1892.

——Leaders of Christian and Anti-Christian Thought. Tr. W. M. Thomson. London, Methuen and Co., 1891.

——Patrice. Paris, Calmann-Lévy, 1909. (Reprint.)

——Recollections of My Youth. With Introduction by G. G. Colton. Boston and New York, Houghton Mifflin Co., 1929.

——Saint Paul. Paris, Michel Lévy Frères, 1869.

——Souvenirs d'enfance et de jeunesse. Paris, Calmann-Lévy, 1883.

——Vie de Jésus. Paris, Calmann-Lévy, 1863.

Riley, Isaac Woodbridge. American Philosophy: the Early Schools. New York, Dodd, Mead and Co., 1907.

——"La Philosophie française en Amérique." *Revue philosophique de la France et de l'étranger*, XLIV, Nos. 5–6 (May-June, 1919), pp. 369–423.

Rostand, Edmond. Academy Speech on Henri de Bornier. Paris, June 4, 1903.

Rousseau, Jean-Jacques. Confessions. Paris, Plon, n.d.

——Confessions. Nouvelle éd. revue . . . d'après les meilleurs textes. Paris, Garnier Frères, 1886.

Rousselot, Xavier. Études sur la philosophie dans le moyen-âge. 3 vols. Paris, 1840–42.

Rusk, Ralph L., ed. Letters of Ralph Waldo Emerson. 6 vols. New York, Columbia University Press, 1939.

Sainte-Beuve, Charles-Augustin. Causeries du lundi. 15 vols. Paris, 1853–1862.

——Nouveaux lundis. 13 vols. Paris, 1864–1870.

Saint-Victor, Paul de. Les Deux Masques: Tragédie, Comédie. 3 vols. Vol. I, Les Antiques, Paris, 1881; Vol. II, Les Antiques, Paris, 1882; Vol. III, Les Modernes, Paris, 1884.

Schapiro, Jacob Salwyn. Condorcet and the Rise of Liberalism. New York, Harcourt, Brace and Co., 1934.

Sells, Esther. Matthew Arnold and France: the Poet. Cambridge, England, Cambridge University Press, 1935.

Senancour, Étienne. Obermann. Préface par George Sand. Paris, 1852, 1872.

Sewanee [Tenn.] *Review*, Vol. XXXVI (January-December, 1928).

Shakespeare, William. The Tempest. Cambridge ed.

Simon, Jules. See Descartes, *Oeuvres.*

Smith, Horatio. Sainte-Beuve, Montaigne: Human Nature. New York, American Society of the French Legion of Honor (Franco-American Pamphlets 3d ser., No. 6), 1946.

Smith, William Henry. See Housatonic.

Spiller, Robert E. "A Case for W. E. Channing." *New England Quarterly*, III, No. 1 (January, 1930), 55 f.

Spinoza, Benedict. Oeuvres. Tr. par Émile Saisset, avec une introduction critique. 3 vols. Paris, 1861.

Stevenson, Robert Louis. The Letters of R. L. S. Ed. Sidney Colvin. 2 vols. London, Methuen and Co., 1901.

Stewart, Balfour. La Conservation de l'énergie, suivie d'une étude sur la nature de la force par P. de Saint-Robert. 16th ed., Paris, Félix Alcan, 1899.

Studies in European Literature, Being the Taylorian Lectures, 1889–1899, Delivered by S. Mallarmé, W. Pater, E. Dowden, W. M. Rossetti, I. W. Rolleston, A. Morel-Fatio, H. Brown, P. Bourget, C. H. Herford, H. Butler-Clarke, W. P. Ker. Oxford, 1900.

Sully-Prudhomme, René. Oeuvres de poésies. 6 vols. Paris, 1865–1866.

Swinburne, Algernon Charles. Letters. Ed. Edmund Gosse, C.B., and Thomas James Wise. New York, John Lane Co., 1919.

——A Study of Shakespeare. London, Chatto and Windus, 1880.

——Victor Hugo. London, Chatto and Windus, 1886.

——William Blake. London, J. C. Hotten, 1868.

——Works. Bonchurch ed. 20 vols.

Taine, Hippolyte. De l'intelligence. Paris, 1870.

——Histoire de la littérature anglaise. 5 vols. Paris, Librairie Hachette et Cie., 1866–73.

——Introduction à l'histoire de la littérature anglaise (L'Histoire, son présent et son avenir). Ed. from the original text with a Preface by H. B. Charlton. Manchester, England, Manchester University Press, 1936.

——La Fontaine et ses fables. Paris, L. Hachette et Cie., 1861.

——On Intelligence. Tr. T. D. Haye and rev. with additions by the author. New York, Holt and Williams, 1872.

——Les Origines de la France contemporaine. Vol. I: La Révolution. 11th ed. Paris, Hachette, 1882.

——Les Philosophes français du dix-neuvième siècle. Paris, L. Hachette et Cie., 1857.

Taitbout, (?). Essai sur l'isle d'Otahiti, située dans la mer du sud; et sur l'esprit et les moeurs de ses habitants. Avignon, Froulle, 1779.

Taupin, René. L'Influence du symbolisme français sur la poésie américaine de 1910 à 1920. Paris, Librairie ancienne Honoré Champion, 1929.

Tinker, Chauncey B., and H. F. Lowry. The Poetry of Matthew Arnold: a Commentary. New York, Oxford University Press, 1940.

Townsend, Harvey Gates. Philosophical Ideas in the United States. New York, American Book Co., 1934.

Trent, W. P. "Review of Giraud's Book on Taine." American Historical Review, VII, No. 4 (July 1902), xxi, 311.

Trilling, Lionel. Matthew Arnold. New York, W. W. Norton and Co., 1939; Columbia University Press, 1949.

Vignaud, Henry. Études sur la vie de Colomb. Paris, 1911.

——Histoire critique de la grande entreprise de C. Colomb. Paris, 1911.

Villemain, Abel François. Choix d'études sur la littérature contemporaine. Paris, 1857.

Vinaver, Eugène and T. B. L. Webster, eds. Prière sur l'Acropole by Ernest Renan. With readings from the original manuscript. Manchester, England, Manchester University Press, 1934.

Voltaire, François Arouet. Romans de Voltaire. Paris, 1844.

Welby, T. Earle. A Study of Swinburne. New York, George H. Doran Co., c. 1926.

Williams, Blanche Colton. George Eliot: a Biography. New York, The Macmillan Co., 1936.

Wilson, Edmund. To the Finland Station. New York, Harcourt Brace, 1940.

Zola, Émile. See Friedman, Lee M.

Index